OIL WARS

DATE DUE

DEC 1 4 2011	

Oil Wars

Edited by Mary Kaldor, Terry Lynn Karl
and Yahia Said

Pluto Press
London • Ann Arbor, MI

First published 2007 by Pluto Press
345 Archway Road, London N6 5AA
and 839 Greene Street, Ann Arbor, MI 48106

www.plutobooks.com

British Library Cataloguing in Publication Data
A catalogue record for this book is available from the British Library

Hardback
ISBN-13   978 0 7453 2479 1
ISBN-10   0 7453 2479 7

Paperback
ISBN-13   978 0 7453 2478 4
ISBN-10   0 7453 2478 9

Library of Congress Cataloging in Publication Data applied for

10 9 8 7 6 5 4 3 2 1

Designed and produced for Pluto Press by
Curran Publishing Services, Norwich, England
Printed and bound in the European Union by
Antony Rowe Ltd, Chippenham and Eastbourne, England

Contents

Figures, Boxes, Tables and Maps

Abbreviations

AAP	Academic Associates Peaceworks
ACDAINSO	Community Association for the Agro-industrial Development of El Morro
ACP	Colombian Petroleum Association
AIOC	Azerbaijan International Operating Consortium
ANC	African National Congress
ANUC	Peasant Association for Unity and Reconstruction
ASNLF	Aceh Sumatra National Liberation Front
AUC	United Self-Defence Forces of Colombia
AVS	Anambra State Vigilante Service
bbl/d	barrels per day
BPMIGAS	Indonesian regulatory agency for oil and gas
BPS	Central Statistics Bureau, Indonesia
BPXC	British Petroleum Exploration Colombia
CAFOD	Catholic Agency for Overseas Development
CBM	confidence-building measure
CIIR	Catholic Institute for International Relations
CIS	Commonwealth of Independent States
CMI	Crisis Management Initiative
COHA	Cessation of Hostilities Agreement
CPF	Central Production Facility
DAS-Rural	rural arm of the Colombian intelligence service
DOM	daerah operasi militer (military operations area)
DP	displaced person
DSC	Defence Systems Colombia
EBRD	European Bank of Reconstruction and Development
EITI	Extractive Industries Transparency Initiative
ELN	National Liberation Army (Colombia)
EMOI	ExxonMobil Oil Indonesia
FAA	Forças Armadas Angolanas
FARC	Revolutionary Armed Forces of Colombia
FCO	Foreign and Commonwealth Office
FESA	Eduardo dos Santos Foundation
FLEC	Front for the Liberation of the Enclave of Cabinda
FLN	National Liberation Front (Algeria)
FNLA	National Liberation Front of Angola
FOM	Public Opinion Foundation
FOWA	Federation of Ogoni Women's Association
GAM	Free Aceh Movement
hCa	Helsinki Citizens Assembly

IEA	International Energy Agency
IFIs	International financial institutions
ILRF	International Labour Rights Fund
IMF	International Monetary Fund
INC	Ijaw National Council
INCORA	Agrarian Reform Institute (Colombia)
JILCO	Japanese Indonesia LNG Co.
JSC	Joint Security Committee
LNG	liquefied natural gas
MOI	Mobil Oil Indonesia
MOSIEN	Movement for the Survival of Ijaw Ethnic Nationality
MOSOP	Movement for the Survival of the Ogoni People
MOU	Memorandum of understanding
MPLA	Popular Movement for the Liberation of Angola
MPRI	Military Professional Resources Incorporated
NAD	Nanggroe Aceh Darussalam (Aceh, as renamed under Law 18/2001)
NDDC	Niger Delta Development Commission
NDVF	Niger Delta Volunteer Force
NGO	non-governmental organisation
NNPC	Nigerian National Petroleum Corporation
NYCOP	National Youth Council of the Ogoni People
OCENSA	Oleoducto Central S.A. (Colombian crude oil pipeline)
OPEC	Organization of the Petroleum Exporting Countries
OKPH	Operasi Pemulihan Keamanan dan Penegakan Hukum (Operation for the Restoration of Security and Upholding the Law)
OSCE	Organization for Security and Co-Operation in Europe
PDP	People's Democratic Party
PfP	Partnership for Peace
PNR	National Rehabilitation Programme
PSC	production-sharing contract
SIRA	Sentral Informasi Referendum Aceh (Aceh Referendum Information Centre)
SOCAR	Azerbaijan State Oil Company
SOFAR	Azerbaijan State Oil Fund
SPDC	Shell Petroleum Development Company of Nigeria
SWAPO	South West Africa's People's Organisation
TACIS	Technical Assistance for the Commonwealth of Independent States
TNI	Indonesian armed forces
UNDP	United Nations Development Program
UNICEF	United Nations Children's Fund
UNITA	National Union for the Total Independence of Angola

Preface

In 1998, I was invited to the BP Christmas party. It was held in the British Museum in the room where the Elgin Marbles are displayed. Champagne flowed and delicious canapés were served. I didn't know anyone so I plucked up courage and went up to a man with a BP sign on his lapel. I introduced myself and explained that I didn't know why I had been invited. He turned out to be the Managing Director, Chris Gibson-Smith, and he explained that I had been invited because BP had decided to become a human rights company.

That was the origin of this book. It was a time when BP was coming under public criticism for its behaviour in Colombia, as were Shell in the Niger Delta and Exxon in Aceh. As one of the oil executives we interviewed explained, oil companies are increasingly exploring oilfields in unstable parts of the world; they are facing what he described as the 'social equivalent of deep sea drilling'. I and my colleague Yahia Said decided that, as social scientists, it is our task to investigate and analyse the 'social equivalent of deep sea drilling' and to work out what it might mean to be genuinely a 'human rights company'.

Our idea was to combine my work on 'new wars' with the work of those scholars who had developed the concept of a petro-state, and therefore we approached Terry Karl and asked her to join our team. To ensure objectivity, we sought independent funding. The Ford Foundation provided an initial grant for the research. We also received a grant from the Rockefeller Foundation, which enabled us to hold a meeting at Bellagio, the Italian villa owned by the Foundation, where we presented our case studies to oil industry executives. Many of the policy recommendations in the conclusion result from that meeting.[1]

We would like to thank the Ford Foundation and the Rockefeller Foundation for their support for this project; David Rice of BP who agreed to co-host the Bellagio meeting and invite the oil executives; the many people from NGOs and oil companies who participated in our meetings and discussed our ideas with us but are too numerous to mention by name; Jonas Moberg from the Prince of Wales International Business Leaders Forum, who acted as a rapporteur and helped to draft the recommendations; Liz Phillipson, who began the Indonesia study; Joanne Hay, Rita Field, and Jen Otoadese for administrative assistance; and Lord Meghnad Desai, our former Director, for intellectual advice.

We are particularly grateful to Peter Harrington for the thankless task of putting together all the final corrections and managing the book in its last stages

Mary Kaldor, November 2005

1. See http://www.lse.ac.uk/Depts/global/Publications/ oilandconflictbellagioreport.pdf.

Introduction

Mary Kaldor, Terry Lynn Karl and Yahia Said

> The Iraq war has nothing to do with oil, literally nothing to do
> with oil.
>
> (Donald Rumsfeld, Secretary of Defense, 2002)

> The most important difference between North Korea and Iraq
> is that economically we just had no choice in Iraq. The country
> swims on a sea of oil.
>
> (Paul Wolfowitz, Deputy Defense Secretary, 2003)

> Oil has literally made foreign and security policy for decades.
>
> (Bill Richardson, Secretary of Energy, 1999)

Iraq is sitting on top of the second-largest proven oil reserves in the
world. It may possess up to a quarter of total world reserves, and it has
the potential in the future to become the world's largest oil exporter.[1]
Supporters of the war, while denying that military action in Iraq was
initiated to control its oil, do assert that these massive reserves are of
vital strategic interest to the West, and thus the installation of a friendly
regime in Iraq is essential for national security. Overthrowing Saddam
Hussein, creating a stable state in Iraq and opening up its oil for
exploitation, they argue, are central to a broader effort to secure access
to global oil resources, especially in the energy heart of the world – the
Middle East/Central Asian region. Most opponents of the war cite
Iraq's immense resources as a significant factor in the onset of war, and
criticise the willingness of some Western governments to kill Iraqis and
risk the lives of their own citizens to secure access to these resources.
Whatever role security of oil supplies played in the thinking of policy
makers, three years after the invasion it is evident that the global
energy supply is neither more stable nor more secure. Iraq's oil output
and exports have barely reached their low pre-war levels, while the war
itself and the associated instability it has generated in the region has
sent oil prices soaring to new heights. Despite promises to the contrary,
they have stayed high over an extended period of time. As Iraq threat-
ens to descend into chaos and become like another ungovernable
Afghanistan, Al Qaeda and other terrorist groups are now in a better
position to disrupt oil supplies from the entire region.

The relationship between oil and governability in Iraq is nothing new. As the country's main source of income, oil has shaped the state and the successive authoritarian regimes that ruled it, including the regime of Saddam Hussein. For decades since Iraq became a major exporter, the rent from petroleum shaped the state as the chief distributor of wealth and oppression in equal measure and this, in turn, affected the behaviour of all Iraqis.[2] Could it be that this relationship, rather than geopolitical competition for the country's vast resources, explains Iraq's conflict-prone modern history?

The debate over the role of petroleum in the invasion of Iraq raises a more general question. What is the relationship between oil and war? The aim of our study, which was begun well before the Iraq war, is to examine this relationship. As we shall see, there is widespread agreement in both qualitative and quantitative social science research (as well as in the minds of mass publics) that oil and war are linked. But this association is complex and often difficult to untangle, especially through quantitative work alone. Thus we undertook six case studies in different regions across the globe – Angola, Azerbaijan, Colombia, Indonesia, Nigeria and Russia/Chechnya – in order to shed light on the following questions:

- To what extent does oil cause, exacerbate or mitigate conflict, and what are the specific mechanisms through which this occurs?
- Does the possession of petroleum in conflict-ridden countries change the nature of conflict, and if so, how?

By illuminating the various ways in which oil affects the prospects, propensity and types of violence, our hope is to identify measures that can be taken by all stakeholders in the oil sector – governments of producing and consuming countries, corporations, international organisations and civil society groups – to mitigate or even prevent bloodshed in the future.

Oil and war have been linked since the beginning of the twentieth century, but the nature of this relationship has changed over time. Arguments over the war in Iraq are generally posed in terms of a concept of military power based on the 'old wars' of the twentieth century – in particular, the two world wars and the Cold War. In these wars, oil was considered a key strategic commodity and security of oil supplies could be achieved only through the direct military control of territory or the exercise of influence over the generally authoritarian rulers of exporting countries. What we shall call 'new oil wars' are different. Although petroleum is still considered a vital strategic commodity for the West, in these wars the ability to secure supply through control over the government and territory has been sharply eroded. New wars are associated with weak and sometimes ungovernable states where non-oil tax revenue is falling, political legitimacy is declining and the monopoly of organised violence is being eroded. In such wars, the massive rents from petroleum are used in myriad ways to finance violence and to foster a predatory political economy. In the worst instances, like Chechnya or Iraq, major actors' sources of income actually depend on the perpetuation of violence and vice versa, and war zones become havens for terrorism. Even in the best cases, where oil rents appear to be successful in propping up some form of centralised authority, rents tend over time to exacerbate state weakness, risking the creation of state failure and the threat of further 'new oil wars'.

Oil wars are *rentier* wars. Whatever the motivations of fighters, and whatever religious, ethnic or other differences also drive conflict, where oil is present these wars tend to involve struggles for control over the exceptional gains generated by this valuable resource. While historically this has always been the case, what has changed in the latter part of the twentieth century is the combination of actors involved in rent-seeking behaviour. 'Old wars' were geopolitical wars; they involved competition between states, especially the Great Powers, for control over territory and the forging of strong alliances with domestic actors to construct and influence strong centralised authority – if only for the purpose of awarding oil contracts and concessions.

Nowadays, this geopolitical competition is supplemented by struggles among various domestic actors that effectively parcel out or even dismantle the state itself (for example secessionist wars), and by violent predatory behaviour on the part of non-state foreign and local actors for direct access to oil rents in legal and illegal ways. In other words, rent seeking in oil-exporting countries has gradually filtered downwards throughout society – from the level of international competition to domestic competition at the state level and, finally, to competition among non-state actors at a local level.[3] When this occurs in the context of failing states, instead of providing arms and monies to centralised oil governments to govern their people, rents become linked with violence at every level, making it especially difficult to re-establish authority through the control of territory. This linkage between rent-seeking behaviour and violence is explained in terms of what we shall call an 'oil rent-seeking cycle' – a perverse development that has the capacity to unravel what appear to be rich oil states.

There are competing explanations of the exact causal linkages between oil and war, as we shall see. Some emphasize geo-strategic concerns while others stress the greed of insurgents or the grievances of the general population. A major theme of this book is that policies to end conflict that derive only from one single set of explanations are bound to fail. In particular, policies stemming from strategic visions shaped by geopolitical competition are counterproductive in new oil wars. Paradoxically, the consequence of the belief that territory can be militarily controlled and governments forcibly re-established in conflict-ridden oil-exporting countries is not greater control over oil supplies or prices but greater political and economic instability. Indeed, the more the Great Powers or nation states attempt to control access to oil militarily by building fortresses around oil enclaves or placing soldiers along pipelines, the greater the insecurity of supply. As the Iraq war poignantly demonstrates, new oil wars threaten to produce 'rogue' or failed states that vastly increase global insecurity.

However, oil can also have a mitigating influence on conflict. With the exception of some offshore deposits, oil, by its very nature, cannot be developed and extracted under conditions of total state collapse. All potential beneficiaries of oil rents are ultimately interested in safe-guarding the large investments and modicum of rule of law required to keep oil flowing. The risk of state failure and the interruption of supply eventually creates incentives for the actors who once conspired in state weakness to cooperate in the construction of some form of legitimate authority – if for no other reason than to keep the rents flowing. Oil's strategic importance also means that conflicts rarely escape high-profile international scrutiny. Oil conflicts remain at the centre of attention of governments, multilateral international actors and civil society actors, and attract external interventions.

We illustrate this argument by first using the case of Iraq as a metaphor to examine the changing nature of war. We then present a summary of some of the explanations for the relationship between oil and war. Next we examine key properties of the exploitation of oil that help to illustrate why oil-exporting countries are especially susceptible to war and how, over time, elements of the relationship between oil and war can interact to produce a cycle of descent into new oil wars. While this is not always the case and is not inevitable, as some of the cases that follow demon-strate, the risk of war in oil-exporting countries is greater than in other countries and the need to address this danger is more urgent.

IRAQ AS METAPHOR OF OLD AND NEW WARS

'In the images of falling statues', said President Bush on 1 May 2003, as he announced the end of hostilities in Iraq, dressed in fatigues, on the deck of USS *Abraham Lincoln*, 'we have witnessed the arrival of a new era.'[4] President Bush claimed to have discovered a new form of warfare, making use of information technology to make war rapid, precise and low in casualties. The ongoing war in Iraq is indeed a new type of war, in which all kinds of new technologies ranging from sophisticated satellite-based systems to mobile phones and the Internet are used. But if we are to understand the war in ways that are useful to policy makers, then its novel character should not be defined in terms of technology. Instead, what defines this war is the embeddedness of violence in different social relations and the gradual disintegration of the state under the impact of globalisation. Under these conditions, when authoritarian states collapse, the state itself loses the monopoly of force and law ceases to exist, to be replaced by privatised violence, private profit, growing linkages between the two, and the spread of crime and disorder aimed at ordinary civilians. Where a high-stakes commodity like oil is present, this danger is even greater.

This is the meaning of Kaldor's distinction between 'old' and 'new' wars.[5] 'Old wars' are wars between states or actors aspiring to state power, where the aim is the military capture of territory and the decisive encounter is battle between armed forces. As evidenced by the First and Second World Wars, these wars require states to mobilise their societies as never before, and they result in the construction of different states and regimes in the defeated territory. 'New wars', in contrast, take place in the context of failing states, where borders become increasingly irrelevant. They are fought by networks of state and non-state actors, where out-and-out battles are rare and violence is directed mainly against civilians or symbols of order, and they are characterised by a new type of political economy involving a combination of extremist politics and criminality. Examples include Somalia, Afghanistan, Sudan and now Iraq. In 'new wars', it remains to be seen whether occupying states can retain the support of their mass publics over the period necessary to construct new state authority, and whether failing states can be reconstructed largely by external rather than domestic forces.

US government officials planned the war in Iraq as an updated version of 'old war' – using new technology to overwhelm an enemy, re-establish centralised authority and gain immediate control over the country's chief resource. Their idea of the war drew on a narrative originating in the Second World War, in which the United States uses its superior military technology to capture territory and bring democracy to a tyrannised and defeated people. The geopolitical competition for oil has always been a part of this narrative, but it has become a constant and growing preoccupation for all Great Powers (and even some smaller ones), and especially the United States. The emphasis on petroleum as a vital interest received a huge boost as talk of 'the peak of oil' gained currency in US and British government circles, and government leaders worried that they could run out of secure hydrocarbon energy supplies or that the present availability of easy, cheap oil could decline dramatically at a time when global demand was exploding.[6] Vice President Cheney's Energy Task Force, created just ten days after the Bush administration took office, explicitly argued that it was in the vital interests of the United States to protect its sources of oil in the Middle East at a time of increasingly tight and volatile markets. The Task Force studied detailed maps of Iraqi oilfields that were out of reach of US and

British multinational energy companies under Saddam Hussein, and called upon the countries of the Persian Gulf to open their energy sectors to foreign investment (Klare 2006).

This oil narrative facilitated the decision to go to war. The fact that Iraq possessed oil removed from the debate the projected costs of the war, thus lowering potential congressional opposition that might have stiffened if the real financial burden of the conflict (almost $290 billion to date) had been at issue.[7] Iraq's petroleum helped to create the impression that there would be no choice between guns and butter. Instead, not only would American troops be welcomed in the streets as liberators, the United States would not have to foot the bill for its actions. The new Iraqi administration and the Coalition forces could initially use funds made available under the oil-for-food programme and through seized assets from the former regime. With Iraqi oil, the war would pay for itself, and even the reconstruction would be self-financing. Repeated assurances that Iraq was a 'wealthy country' with 'tremendous resources', and that it could 'shoulder much of the responsibilities' created the impression that the war would be nearly cost free – as long as Iraq's oil could rapidly come on stream.[8] The fact that specific plans to mortgage future oil revenues to pay for reconstruction contracts had already been put in place seemed to provide further assurances that the war would be cost free – until those plans proved to be either illegal or politically unacceptable to Iraqis as an 'oil grab'.[9]

Given the role that petroleum was supposed to play in the immediate aftermath of the war, not to mention the enormous profits it was projected to generate, it is not surprising that the first military objective of the invasion of Iraq, known as Operation Iraqi Freedom, was to secure control over the oilfields and refineries of southern Iraq. Once in Baghdad, US forces seized and occupied the Oil Ministry while permitting looters to overrun all other government buildings, libraries, museums and cultural centres, thus sending a powerful signal to already suspicious Iraqis that petroleum was the reason for the war.

But even though the American-led forces initially met little resistance and the Iraqi people seemed ready (at least temporarily) to give them the benefit of the doubt, oil revenues were never going to be able to play their intended role. This became apparent as the impression of an easy victory was quickly dispelled. The occupation of Iraq took place in the context of a failing state – a reality that invasion planners did not seem to grasp, perhaps because, as Said (2004) points out, both President Bush and Saddam Hussein had a common interest in portraying the Iraqi regime as a classic totalitarian system, controlling every aspect of society and only removable by force. At the time of Operation Iraqi Freedom, the regime exhibited characteristics that are typical of the last phases of authoritarian rule: a system breaking up under the impact of globalisation, constant warfare and economic sanctions, and thus unable to sustain its closed, autarchic and tightly controlled character. Attempting to fix this situation was going to be a very costly, long-term project requiring significantly more resources than Iraq's oil revenues.

The signs of state failure were everywhere. Oil revenues were insufficient to cover the costs of the devastating war with Iran (1980–88), and both the 1991 Gulf War and the imposition of UN sanctions had ruined the economy. This resulted in dramatic falls in GDP, increased infant mortality, declines in literacy, and de-urbanisation as the proportion of those engaged in agriculture doubled (Hiro 2003). In this context, there were important indicators of loss of government control, even before Saddam Hussein's removal, including underground movements and parties,[10] efforts to create new public space,[11] and especially the growing resistance of both Sunni and Shi'ite mosques, which began to develop a strategy of 'quiet strangulation' of the regime reminiscent of the Catholic Church in Poland and Chile. A parallel dollar economy was another sign of decline, based increasingly on UN agencies, remittances, income from Iranian pilgrims, smuggling and contraband petrol sales, and this in turn multiplied the opportunities for various types of criminal activities, as Duelfer's 2004 'Comprehensive Report of the Special Advisor to the DCI on Iraq's WMD' vividly illustrates. State institutions were decaying and fragmenting. Indeed, the state was literally divided with the establishment of Kurdish autonomy in the north after 1991. Saddam Hussein's effort to mobilise tribal, ethnic and religious politics in order to generate more political support and to divide the opposition compounded the fragmentary tendencies in society. On the eve of the invasion, Iraq showed all the signs of irreversible state failure – lack of legal revenue sources, decline of state services, loss of legitimacy, the simultaneous erosion and proliferation of military and security agencies, sectarian identity politics and a rise in criminality. The invasion simply condensed state failure into a short three-week period.

In this respect, American-led forces sought to fight an 'old war' even as a 'new war' was in the making. US information technology was grafted on to traditional institutional defence structures and old war assumptions about the ways in which military force should be used, involving a combination of aerial bombardment at long distance, and rapid offensive manoeuvres.[12] But however showy and impressive the immediate results, this obscured what was actually happening in Iraq. As Coalition forces proclaimed that they had toppled the Iraqi regime 'with a combination of precision, speed, and boldness the enemy did not expect and the world had not seen before',[13] loose networks of former state and non-state actors, appearing more like social movements than the typically vertically organised guerrilla insurgencies of the past, began to form a new opposition among Iraqi nationalists, Sunni Islamists and some Shi'ite groups. These were given a huge boost in both numbers and know-how when Saddam's army was disbanded, effectively encouraging former military personnel from Fallujah, Mosul, Tikrit and Baghdad to return home to form the backbone of the insurgency. Often opposed to Saddam Hussein as well as the occupation,[14] they should be set apart from former Ba'athists, who reportedly often constitute a quite separate group (see Cordesman 2004), and Al-Qaeda-type Islamist groups for whom Iraq is a battleground in a cosmic conflict.[15] Finally, various organised crime groups operate under the cover of the insurgency, and include many criminals released from prison just before the invasion. All have access to weaponry, varying from simple improvised explosive devices to more sophisticated equipment, and all use highly decentralised cell structures which means that members often do not know who their leaders are or where their funding comes from. What all the groups share is the narrative of resistance to foreign occupation.

Like the movements that have emerged in other 'new wars', their effect is to spread insecurity and disorder, with civilians bearing the brunt of the conflict. While the vast majority of insurgent attacks are directed against Coalition forces, foreigners, Iraqi security forces and others who are considered collaborators, the main casualties are ordinary Iraqis. As the number of attacks has increased and extremist groups, especially those affiliated with Al Qaeda, appear to increasingly specialise in grisly, spectacular incidents designed to gain maximum media attention, their effect has been to create a generalised sense of pervasive insecurity and fear, in which people feel forced to seek protection from sectarian militias. American tactics aimed at defeating the insurgency exacerbate civilian deaths because insurgents cannot easily be distinguished from the civilian population. Attacks by all sides have resulted in very high civilian casualties, estimated at 600,000 by the British medical journal *The Lancet*,[16] as well as large numbers of displaced persons as civilians flee the fighting or are made homeless by the destruction of their houses.

'New wars' involve large numbers of non-state actors, whose activities increase civilian casualties and the general sense of disorder. The Iraq war is no exception. In the context of the disbanding of the Iraqi army and police and the slow formation of replacement units, and the huge gap between actual forces and the desired end strength,[17] a range of private security groups have compounded the absence of any monopoly of legitimate violence. Dozens of armed groups attached to the political parties involved in the government are still in existence. There are also various militias attached to religious organisations that were already in existence during the former regime, tribal armed militias, and newly formed and trained groups. At the same time, the United States has made widespread use of 'non-state actors'. There are an estimated 25,000 foreign security contractors in Iraq, of which 6000 are engaged in 'armed tactical roles' (Special Inspector General for Iraq

Reconstruction Report to Congress 2005). Indeed, this combination of regular troops and private contractors is reminiscent of the networks of regular troops and paramilitary groups in other 'new wars', where the latter are often used to carry out tasks that fall outside the laws of war.[18] The lack of centralised control over private forces contributes to the pervasive sense of insecurity.

What sets Iraq apart from many other 'new wars', however, is the role of oil, not only acting, as we discussed, as a motivation or a mechanism for lowering opposition to war but also as the source of rents to support this vast and growing informal violent network. Oil fuels the conflict in a variety of ways. American officials claim that the insurgents have 'unlimited money' supplied by members of the former regime, Saudi and other religious charities, or criminal activity – most of it derived from Middle Eastern oil rents.[19] This means that families of suicide bombers can receive 'martyrdom bonuses' and ordinary criminals (or even the huge reservoir of unemployed) can be well paid to conduct attacks.[20] Oil money does not only flow in from outside. Criminal networks, previously honed on the huge infrastructure for illicit oil sales that Saddam Hussein created to breach UN sanctions, loot Iraqi oil through a smuggling chain that stretches all the way down the Persian Gulf on the one side and through Turkey on the other. The trade is so big, so blatant, and so intertwined with other activities that it has proved too deeply rooted to stop.[21] Just as in Saddam's time, the sums of money that disappear are huge (illegal oil trading was the largest source of illicit revenue for the former regime, estimated at $9.2 billion during the Oil for Food programme from sales to Jordan, Syria and Turkey).[22] But what is different now is that the oil money, estimated at billions of dollars every year, no longer flows into the central government and thus cannot serve as a unifying force; instead, it flows into private networks, and religious, tribal and partisan interests.[23] Oil rents are certainly not the only source of funding for criminality and violence in a country characterised by widespread looting, hostage taking and convoy hijacking for money, but they are the principal source. And the fight over their allocation is especially divisive, weakening allegiances to any central state authority.

Oil is also deeply intertwined with the threat of secession and the problem of constructing a new polity in Iraq; in this respect as well, therefore, oil rents help to exacerbate the conflict. While concerns like the rights of women and the role of Islam are certainly volatile, there is only one issue that appears to have the potential to spark much greater violence and even the disintegration of Iraq: whether political power and oil revenues will be controlled by a centralised national government or by regional authorities. Kurdish leaders in the north, already accustomed to US-protected autonomy, know that their sought-after capital, the oil city of Kirkuk, produces 50 per cent of Iraq's oil output and sits on anywhere between 10 and 20 per cent of Iraq's vast oil reserves. Thus they demanded and succeeded in negotiating a 'federal system' which could devolve the management of oil wealth to the regions, especially when it comes to new discoveries. This also suits religious Shia politicians in the south who argue that the impoverished region near Basra, where almost 60 per cent of Iraq's proven reserves lie, has never received its fair share of oil money. But Sunni Arabs in the centre (whose land consists of sand and scrub rather than petroleum) and nationalist Shia parties would like more power to remain in the capital and oil rents to be distributed by the central government, where both groups hope to exercise more control over the country's economic resources.[24] Thus the constitution passed in October 2005 had an almost unanimous Sunni 'no' vote, and it is subject to amendments in the next parliament because no durable compromise has been reached. (In September 2006, at Sunni insistence, Iraq's feuding ethnic and sectarian groups formed a committee to consider amending the constitution, but only after their leaders agreed to delay any division of the country into autonomous regions until 2008.) Neighbouring countries add to the volatility of the federalism debate. Turkey, Iran and Syria, concerned about the impact an independent Kurdistan would have on their own Kurdish populations, oppose the Iraqi Kurds having control over oil resources, while Saudi Arabia balks at the idea of an autonomous south since it fears independence movements among its own Shia minority and growing Iranian influence. Thus oil, mingled as it is with identity, lies at the heart of the debate over the design of a new polity – a debate that is linked to escalating sectarian violence.

The war has developed its own logic. The massive presence of largely unwanted foreigners, loose networks based on violent resistance, a proliferation of private actors (who appear to be making huge profits), rival demands over the degree of regional autonomy and the control of oil revenues, and especially high civilian casualties mean that the combined effect of attacks and counter-attacks is to increase the sense of insecurity and injustice. This, in turn, appears to substantiate competing claims that this is a war of the West against Islam and for oil, on the one hand, or a war against terror, on the other. Part of the logic, from the side of the insurgency, is to ensure that oil revenues cannot be turned into street-level improvements, thereby undermining the Iraqi people's faith in the country's new government. Since petroleum is the lifeblood of the Iraqi economy, this means insurgents target not only export-oriented installations like pipelines but also refineries, power plants and other facilities for domestic energy production. Driving oil prices higher appears to be another objective of the insurgency, and attacks on facilities are praised as a way of hurting the United States and other Western economies.[25]

As a result of insurgent attacks, oil output from the northern fields of Kirkuk almost never reaches international markets. Attacks on oil storage, transportation networks, engineering workers, executives and civil servants are relentless. Local tribes recruited by the multinational forces and the Iraqi government to help protect the network are suspected of involvement in some of these attacks as a way of sustaining a significant source of income. The result is that Iraq, almost three years after the war, has not managed to produce above 2 million bbl/d (barrels per day) or export above 1.5 million bbl/d – well below the pre-war average of 2.5 million bbl/d (Special Inspector General for Iraq Reconstruction Report to Congress 2005). Insecurity on the roads has also hampered maintenance efforts at Iraq's ageing refineries, leading to extensive environmental damage and forcing the government to import $2.6 billion worth of oil products last year to satisfy demand (IMF 2005). Power stations and transmission lines have also suffered from insurgent activities, looting and government incompetence, and power supply remains below pre-war levels. The lack of electricity, which dipped in the scorching summer of 2005 to below two hours a day in Baghdad, is one of the main complaints of Iraqis. Thus, despite the efforts to create a new institutional order, each stage of the conflict accelerates the process of unravelling state institutions and shared norms and rules inside Iraq, while creating an ever more insecure global oil market. Most significant, it is the prospect of Iraqi democracy that may be defeated in this new oil war.

NATURAL RESOURCES AND CONFLICT: OIL IS DIFFERENT

The strong link between oil and war – so evident in the conflict in Iraq – is a pattern we shall find in differing forms in all of the cases we explore in this book. While there are many oil states not present in this study that do not face these kinds of conflicts, there is a growing scholarly consensus based on both qualitative and quantitative studies about the strong association between oil and war. Though some scholars contend that the linkages between any natural resource and war are unusually strong (hence Klare's coining of the term 'resource wars'), there is no question that oil plays a very special role in conflict. As Klare later concluded: 'Petroleum is unique among the world's resources. ... [I]t has more potential than any of the others to provoke major crises and conflicts in the years ahead' (2006:xiii).

Quantitative work concurs with this assessment. Collier and Hoeffler's works 'On Economic Causes of Civil War' (1998) and *Greed and Grievance in Civil War* (2004) produced an intellectual evolution strikingly parallel to that found in qualitative work. Thus, while the existence of a pattern linking primary commodities in general (meaning oil, non-fuel minerals and agricultural goods) to either the onset or duration of war is still disputed, the evidence about the association between oil and war is not ambiguous: *dependence on oil for export is associated with conflict.* In this respect, the violently lived experiences of oil-rich countries like Angola, Colombia, the Republic of Congo, Indonesia, Iraq, Nigeria and Russia/Chechnya are captured in the shared conclusions of various scholars (for example Collier and Hoeffler 2002; de Soysa 2002; Fearon and Laitin 2003; Fearon 2004) – all of whom demonstrate the robust linkages between petroleum and conflict. As Fearon so succinctly puts it, 'oil predicts civil war risk' (2005:483).

Why should the possession of oil be particularly associated with war? Why is oil different from other natural resources? Oil, in itself, is neither a blessing nor a curse, but simply a black viscous material. Yet it is a commodity which, when exploited for export, has a bundle of characteristics that are unique and that ultimately help to explain conflict. With the exception of its depletability, these are not 'natural' features but instead are socially constructed. While other mineral commodities may share some of them, none are like petroleum (Karl 1997).[26]

Economic rents

In a diversified economy which relies on material production and service delivery, most income in economic terms is generated by labour. In the United States in 2002 wages accounted for 72 per cent of national income.[27] In such an economy, roughly speaking, every dollar earned is a dollar produced and every consumer is also a producer. A country can exchange its output with the outside world on the basis of its relative competitiveness and needs. It can at times consume more than it produces, as the United States has been doing since the late 1970s. This is then reflected in a negative trade balance which has to be financed through 'dissaving' (the drawing down of previously accumulated assets) and eventually foreign debts and investments.

This is not true for countries which derive a significant portion of their income from the export of oil or other natural resources. In these economies, income is composed mostly of economic rents – profits which exceed reasonable levels of return on labour and capital. Rents traditionally accrue to government by virtue of its jurisdiction over natural resources. The government passes these rents on to citizens either through transfers or via spending and investments. Unlike labour income, economic rent generally is not matched by products and services produced within the economy. The demand it creates has to be satisfied through import. In other words a dollar earned in an oil-dependent country is not a dollar produced, and most consumers are not producers. Compared to a diversified economy, an oil-dependent one almost always consumes more than it produces, and finances this consumption through the sale of oil. This process could be viewed as the drawing down of existing assets – oil reserves. But it is different from the dissavings which occur in more diversified economies, where existing assets have been accumulated from previous earnings through savings and capital formation. Oil assets in contrast are like manna from heaven. The rents in this instance constitute a transfer of wealth from oil consumers to oil producers.

The amount of rent may differ widely in oil-exporting countries. On the one hand, rents depend on where oil is located and the technological difficulties in removing, transporting and refining it. For example, complex geopolitical manoeuvring as well as a modicum of domestic stability in half a dozen countries is necessary to get Azeri oil onto international markets, and its extraction costs are high. Angolan offshore oil, by contrast, was able to keep flowing while the country was in the grips of civil war, while Saudi oil has remarkably low extraction costs. On the other hand, rents also depend on the international price of oil and the capacity of different actors to capture them. Oil prices have risen by $40 per barrel since the run-up to the war in Iraq, the equivalent of a transfer of rents of $700 billion a year from oil importing nations to oil exporting ones.[28]

However welcome such transfers may be, rents are a double-edged sword. In a diversified economy, labour is the main way to generate wealth, but where there are huge economic rents, these actually create a disincentive to work. This applies both for individuals and for the economy as a whole. Because national wealth is generated externally and independently of labour, all individuals need to do to access wealth is to tap government which controls economic rents – a structural incentive that fosters widespread rent-seeking behaviour in oil-exporting countries.

Capital intensive enclaves

Before oil's extraordinary rewards can be reaped, significant investments are required. Oil is capital intensive in all stages of its production cycle; it requires large and long-term financial outlays and very little labour, and this perpetuates the de-linking between wealth and work. This is quite different from, say, diamonds or timber, which can be labour intensive, require significantly less capital outlays and have a relatively quick turnaround.

Capital intensity has two contradictory outcomes. On the one hand, the major investments that are needed to explore, extract, transport and process oil, and the agreements required with various parties to carry out and safeguard these investments, mean that a modicum of rule of law and legitimate authority is necessary to ensure uninterrupted flow. On the other, only a small workforce is needed to produce and export oil, which means that it is not necessary to secure the consent of large domestic constituencies to maintain production.

Furthermore, oil is an enclave activity with little positive spill-over effect on the rest of the economy. Not only is it de-linked from labour, but it is also not connected to most other industrial and agricultural activities. As a result oil compounds stand out from the surrounding country as enclaves with high concentrations of wealth, jobs and foreigners. This contrast turns them into flashpoints of social and political tensions as they attract the attention of various groups seeking to stake a claim to oil wealth.

Price volatility

Oil prices are not only high enough to generate extraordinary rents, they are also extremely volatile. Unlike most other commodities, whose prices have tended to stabilise over the long term, oil prices have exhibited increasing volatility, especially since the 1990s. Oil prices are twice as variable as those of other commodities. In 1998 they dropped to as low as $12 per barrel, then they rose to $30 in 2000 and fell again to $20 in 2002. In 2005 they exceeded $60. In July 2006, they reached a record level of $78.40. For an oil-exporting country where oil represents 50 per cent of GDP, the fall in the oil price between 2000 and 2002 of 30 per cent would have resulted in a huge economic contraction of 15 per cent. However, the impact of price volatility is asymmetric. A 50 per cent increase in the price of oil today is estimated to cut US GDP by one quarter of a per cent in the first year and by half a point in the second (EIA 2005).[29] A poor consuming nation which uses more energy per unit of output will suffer more.

These violent fluctuations in price over relatively short periods of time represent an extreme example of trade volatility, estimated by some to be as much as three times greater than that experienced by the industrial counties, and they have serious consequences for economic development. Extreme price volatility means that oil economies are likely to face more frequent economic shocks and boom–bust cycles. This exerts a strong negative influence on budgetary discipline and the control of public finances as well as state planning; it also aggravates investor uncertainty and encourages 'stop–go' spending patterns as well as unsustainable consumption, with negative consequences for growth, distribution and poverty alleviation (Karl 2004). These economic outcomes in turn often generate political instability, which also affects price volatility and creates a type of vicious cycle.

The world's most strategic commodity

Oil rents are a function of the world's insatiable demand for energy. Oil continues to be the motor of global industrialisation and transportation networks, and the main source of the world's energy. It accounts for 40 per cent of total energy consumption in the United States, rising to 63 per cent when combined with natural gas.[30] Although greater use is being made of non-oil energy sources,[31] dramatic economic growth in China, India and elsewhere, and the failure of the United States to adopt strict conservation measures mean that the absolute consumption of energy continues to grow. World oil use is expected to reach 103 million barrels per day in 2015, up from 78 million barrels per day in 2002.[32] As demand soars, worries that oil exploration has reached a peak contribute to the strategic importance of previously discovered resources. The role played by oil in the world economy is largely responsible for the welcome and unwelcome attention oil conflicts receive from the international community.

Depletability

Oil is non-renewable and finite, meaning that once it is 'spent', it is gone forever. This raises the question not just of geographical equity between producer and consumer nations but of internal and intergenerational equity. Current oil producers are in effect using the wealth of future generations as well as that of their own populations. The intergenerational equity problem of oil becomes more evident when oil resources are thought of as a stock of assets rather than a flow of revenue. Should the current generation safeguard these assets for their offspring? Should they transform oil into more sustainable revenue-generating assets?

During boom times this dilemma creates an incentive for spending on large investment projects aimed at 'sowing the petroleum'. In the 1970s most oil-producing countries embarked on ambitious industrialisation projects aimed at creating an alternative economic base that was independent of oil. Most failed. The push for industrialisation is in part determined by the differences between oil countries themselves. The size of oil resources in relation to the population, which determines both the relative wealth of the country and the potential share of oil revenues in its income, is especially significant. Thus Qatar, with a tiny population of 300,000 and huge oil reserves, has options that are not available to Ecuador, with a large population and a smaller amount of oil. But this calculation can vary over time. While Saudi Arabia remains one of the wealthiest oil producers, its growing population is changing the dynamic through which oil affects its politics and economics in ways that differ from its more sparsely populated neighbours in the Gulf Cooperation Council. Russia and Norway continue to be among the largest oil producers but have a much closer depletion point than Iraq and Saudi Arabia, and this creates more pressure for diversification.

Finally, oil depletion does not only refer to the fact that oil reserves may run out. It also refers to the possibility of oil becoming obsolete as a source of energy, thus significantly reducing its value and the rents it can generate. Indeed, some argue that the latter is likely to be the main avenue of 'depletion'. As former Saudi Oil Minister Yamani put it: 'The Stone Age did not come to an end because we had a lack of stones, and the oil age will not come to an end because we have a lack of oil.'[33]

OIL AND CONFLICT: COMPETING EXPLANATIONS OF GEOPOLITICS, GREED AND THE PETRO-STATE

Consensus exists over the strong association between oil and war, but there are competing claims about whether oil increases the incidence, duration or intensity of war and whether it makes conflict more diffi-cult to settle. Furthermore, very different explanations about the causal mechanisms that elucidate the oil–war relationship are advanced. Why should oil lead to a greater likelihood of war, perpetuate war, or perhaps make wars more difficult to settle? Broadly speaking, there are three types of arguments, derived from studies of the causes of war, which attempt to answer at least some of these questions. We shall refer to these three strands as the 'geopolitical', 'greed' and 'petro-state' explanations. Each aims at explaining somewhat different types of conflict and draws on a specific (and usually different) type of evidence to support its claims. Nonetheless, many of the special features of petroleum delineated above figure prominently in each approach, most especially its strategic character and its generation of extraordinary economic rents.

Geopolitics: oil as 'vital interest'

This argument, most commonly used in political discourse, rests on the recognition that states pursue their national interest by controlling oil for either strategic or economic reasons. In international relations theory, this is the calculus of interests described by Machiavelli and Clausewitz. Sectors that make up the heart of the economies of the West and the core of US military strength rest on access to petroleum and simply cannot survive without it. Thus, it is of vital interest to the West that no single country be permitted to dominate oil supplies, and the ultimate guaran-tor of the security of supply is force. As the advanced industrialised coun-tries (and increasingly emerging economies like China's) become more heavily dependent on imported fuel and shortages of supply appear more frequently, oil has come to be viewed not only as a foreign policy issue but a national security matter – and one of growing importance. Proponents of geopolitical arguments point to the fact that the American military is being used more and more as a 'global oil protection service'

(Klare 2006:7), for the protection of overseas fields and the supply routes that are also needed to keep oil flowing.

Those who put forward geopolitical explanations of the strong relationship between oil and war rely heavily on the examples of 'old wars', particularly the two world wars, where petroleum played an essential strategic role and thus was quickly established as a 'vital interest'. Oil was critical for the conduct of these wars due to a revolution in military strategy that for the first time relied upon motor vehicles, tanks and aircraft and swifter naval warships. 'The Allies floated to victory on a flood of oil,' Lord Curzon said after the First World War (quoted in Yergin 1992). The geo-strategists argue that key to that victory was the destruction of the rich Romanian oilfields and the denial of German access to the oilfields of Baku, then the second largest producer in the world. Indeed, given the way modern wars were being fought, by 1919 oil had proved itself to be the strategic raw material of the future – a reality all major powers recognised. Thus Britain, as the dominant colonial power, used the conflict to lay the basis for the long-term control of Middle Eastern oil, seeking to make the Persian Gulf into a 'British lake'.

The First World War marked the first time oil was recognised as a strategic commodity whose control was essential for imperial designs. Security of supply depended either on the direct control of territory or indirect control through the establishment of clients, usually friendly authoritarian governments. Oil meant power; thus conflict and rivalry were inevitable inside Europe, between Europe and the United States, among the large oil companies, and between the companies and the governments of oil states. As massive finds were announced in the Middle East and Latin America, the threat of violence and coercion hung over each new proven reserve. Nowhere was this rivalry greater than in Mexico, where the United States landed troops in 1912, shortly after the discovery of huge new fields, and Standard Oil ran guns and money to a newly installed government so that the United States could replace British oil domination. Subsequent confrontations over petroleum brought Mexico and the United States close to war several more times, while British and American petroleum interests continued to battle ferociously over the country's oil until late 1938, when President Cardenas' nationalisation of all foreign oil holdings led both countries to boycott Mexico for the next 40 years (Meyer 1977).

In the Second World War, just as the Mexican conflict presaged, the role of oil supplies was considered even more important, not only for the conduct of war but as motivation for it. As Rommel put it: 'The bravest men are nothing without guns, the guns nothing without plenty of ammunition, and nether guns nor ammunition are much use in mobile warfare unless there are vehicles with sufficient petrol to haul them around' (Yergin 1992:343). Both Germany and Japan were dependent on imported oil, and worries about a cut-off of petroleum is said to have guided their actions, since access to fuel ultimately meant victory or defeat (Goralski and Freeburg 1987; Yergin 1992).

As the Japanese drove deeper into China and Asia, they could not withstand the oil embargo imposed by the Roosevelt administration and the freezing in the United States of funds which were used to purchase their fuel. Escaping this stranglehold was said to be the main motivation for the Japanese attack on Pearl Harbor. By incapacitating the US fleet, they believed they could protect their tanker routes from Sumatra and Borneo, thus permitting access to the oilfields of the East Indies. In Germany, access to oil was a main motive for the invasion of the Soviet Union; in fact, German forces ran out of oil before they reached the Caucasus, which was their ultimate strategic goal, and the Nazis desperately used slave labour to manufacture synthetic oil. Petroleum even defined Germany's war strategy against a Britain desperate for fuel, especially the use of U-boats to try (unsuccessfully) to cut off abundant oil supplies from the United States. Eventually, US control over oil is thought to have been a decisive factor shaping the course and the outcome of the war – a fact that was not lost on post-war policy planners.

Oil came to be regarded as the new centre of gravity in the post-war order, especially as the United States began to rely on foreign oil to supply its growing energy demand. Oil became a key part of the narrative of an imagined 'old war' drawn from the experience of two world wars. The energy policies of the United States and Britain, based on setting up client states, or 'local surrogates', in the Middle East to ensure long-term supply, became the lynchpin of the Truman, Eisenhower and Nixon doctrines. This was challenged in Iran by its leader, Mohammed Mossadegh, who eventually sought to nationalise the Anglo-Iranian Oil Company in 1953. This led to his ousting by the CIA and British intelligence, who overthrew his government and reinstalled their preferred ruler, Reza Shah Pahlevi – a loyal client until his misuse of oil rents led to his own downfall in 1979 (Zabih 1982; Bill and Louis 1988).

Similar dynamics shaped the crisis over the Suez Canal when Egypt's Nasser nationalised the waterway through which over two-thirds of European oil flowed, but this time the military response was far more blatant. Because the Suez Canal was considered the key oil transportation route, the British and French, working with Israel, carried out airborne assaults on the canal zone in 1956 until forced to withdraw by a Saudi Arabian embargo against both countries, acts of sabotage against their oil facilities, and the insistence of Eisenhower, who did not want to 'get the Arabs sore at all of us' (Yergin 1992:491). Although military activity lasted a very short time, the Suez conflict starkly exposed the issue of the security of Middle Eastern oil, or what Harold Macmillan called 'the biggest prize in the world'.

The Arab oil embargo after the 1973 Yom Kippur war linked oil and war in a qualitatively different way, signalling a whole new era for viewing oil as a strategic resource. As a way of protesting against the policy tilt of the West towards Israel, Arab nations cut production, thus definitively linking war in the Middle East to spectacular oil price shocks, consumer panics, the search for new supplies, and the first consciousness of an impending energy crisis. This, together with the fall of the Shah of Iran, provided the rationale for the Carter Doctrine, which assumed that the United States, and not local surrogates, would assume primary responsibility for the defence of the Gulf 'by any means necessary, including military force' (Klare 2006:46). It also specifically directed US military planning to this goal, placing oil under the purview of the Department of Defense and other government bodies responsible for national security and establishing a Rapid Deployment Joint Task Force that could immediately deploy US troops in the region – policies continued by the Reagan and Bush administrations.

The first post-Cold War crisis, the 1991 Gulf War, helped to reinforce the narrative of 'old oil wars'. When Saddam Hussein launched a surprise invasion of his neighbour, Kuwaiti and Iraqi oil together represented at least 20 per cent of OPEC production and 20 per cent of world reserves (Yergin 1992:773). Had Hussein been permitted to keep the territory he conquered, he would have become the world's dominant oil power with a decisive say over the global economy. When 4 million barrels of oil were abruptly removed from the world market and prices skyrocketed, the United States immediately deployed troops (supposedly temporarily) to protect the nearby fields of Saudi Arabia. Mounting Operation Desert Storm to drive Iraq back into its borders and to protect Saudi Arabia was justified, President Bush said, because 'our country now imports nearly half the oil it consumes and could face a major threat to its economic independence' (Klare 2006:50). As Saddam's forces withdrew, burning Kuwait's oilfields and causing the largest oil spill in history, American forces remained, establishing a permanent military presence in Kuwait and Saudi Arabia in order to guard the oilfields, maintain 'no-fly' zones over Iraq, and contain Hussein.

But while the 1991 Gulf War appears to fit an 'old war' vision, the reality is more complicated. While it is true that from the point of view of the West, the main threat to oil was a hostile power, explanations based on 'vital interests' and 'national security' do not fully explain why Saddam would invade Kuwait in the first place – an issue we shall revisit below. Nor does it explain why his regime would shift, in the eyes of the US government, from being an authoritarian ally who could guarantee stability and thus was worthy of support to one who seemed to contribute to insecurity. The problem, as we shall see, is no longer who is in power but what form power (or its absence) takes.

Greed: fuelling conflict

The political economy school of conflict (Keen, Duffield and others) argues that economic motivations are the driving force of contemporary conflicts. In conflicts where the rule of law and taxation systems have collapsed, sources of income consist of war-related activities – loot, pillage, 'taxation' of humanitarian aid, unfair terms of trade, or illegal trading in valuable commodities like oil or drugs. In contrast to the geopolitical theorists, who are primarily concerned with international war and the motivations of the so-called Great Powers, the political economy school is primarily concerned with civil wars and the private greed of both state and non-state actors. Thus, whereas the geopolitical theorists see oil as a strategic commodity necessary for the nation as a whole, the greed theorists are more concerned with private profit and with sources of finance for the belligerents in civil war, with a special focus on insurgents.

The greed argument applies both to motivation and to opportunity. Access to oil revenues may be a motive for initiating or continuing conflicts as well as an opportunity to finance military activities. As Paul Collier and Anke Hoeffler (2001) put the argument, rebel organisations with genuine grievances can raise funds through the extortion of commodity exports as a way of financing their struggles (grievance), but the extortion of primary commodity exports will also occur where it is profitable (greed) 'and the organisations which perpetuate this extortion will need to take the form of a rebellion' (2001:3). In other words:

> We propose that the endowment of unskilled labour and guns which characterises rebel organizations is particularly suited to raise funds through the extortion of commodity exports. Our proposition can be interpreted in two ways. On the universal grievance interpretation, rebellions need to finance themselves and the extortion of primary commodity exports offers the best opportunity for financial viability. In the limit, only where there are such opportunities, can rebel organizations escalate to the scale needed for civil war. On the literal greed interpretation, the extortion of primary commodity exports will occur where it is profitable, and the organizations which perpetuate this extortion, will need to take the form of a rebellion.
>
> (Collier and Hoeffler 2001:3)

Collier and Hoeffler's statistics suggest that insurgencies are most likely when primary commodities comprise approximately one-third of a state's GDP. Above that level, governments can use their economic rents to suppress rebellions. Below that level, primary commodity revenues are insufficient to finance the belligerents.

This greed argument applies to all types of primary commodities. But some theorists do distinguish between types of primary commodities, and argue that the specific characteristics of particular commodities have a profound influence on the shape of conflict as well as the character of the belligerents. Le Billon, for example, argues that primary commodities can be characterised as 'point' or 'diffuse', and as 'proximate' or 'distant'. The point–diffuse distinction refers to spatial spread and mode of exploitation, while the proximate–distant distinction refers to distance from the government. Oil is a point resource. It involves concentrated capital-intensive exploitation with few linkages to the rest of the economy. Where oilfields are close to government, or easily controlled by governments as is the case with offshore fields like Angola's, the typical form of conflict is the coup d'état to gain control of the government. Where oilfields are distant, the typical form of conflict is secessionist. Thus Le Billon concludes that:

> Resources can serve to shape the conflict taking place, the territorial control objectives, the duration and intensity of the conflict, and relations between belligerents and populations. Resources can also affect the internal cohesion of armed movements and motivate collusion between adversaries, especially when exploitation or trading requires such partnership.
>
> (Le Billon 2005:48)

There is abundant evidence in the case studies in this book to support this greed argument. In Chechnya, for example, bootlegged oil is a key source of income, along with loot, pillage and hostage taking. Chechen fighters sell oil extracted from backyard oil wells to Russian forces, who sell it on the Russian market (see Chapter 3). In Chapter 6, Jenny Pearce shows how the different groups of combatants have made use of oil in Colombia. The FLN bombed pipelines and forced the oil companies to introduce social programmes, thereby gaining a 'Robin Hood' image, while the FARC gained access to oil through controlling municipalities. Right-wing paramilitaries were paid by BP to offer protection. A similar pattern took shape in Aceh, Indonesia (see Chapter 5) and in the Niger Delta (see Chapter 1).

But while the greed argument explains how conflicts are financed and why well-financed conflicts are especially difficult to end, it is less satisfactory as an explanation of the complex causation of contemporary conflicts in the first place. What is lacking in both the geopolitical and greed arguments is an analysis of the changing character of the state in the context of oil dependence and how this creates extensive grievances that feed into explanations based both on greed and geopolitics.

The petro-state argument: financing patronage, repression and corruption

This argument is based on the notion that oil dependence has political effects akin to the economic effects known as the 'Dutch disease' or the 'resource curse'.[34] Indeed, these political effects are primarily responsible for generating subsequent economic problems. In effect, oil rents eventually weaken state institutions, and this hollowing out of the state occurs in the context of growing grievance. This makes it less likely that conflicts can be handled without violence and more likely that they will be addressed primarily through the distribution of oil rents – a strategy that only works when rents are plentiful. Since oil prices are highly volatile, this is not always the case.

The theory of the petro-state starts from the Weberian premise that the economic foundations of the state matter and that the sources of income shape the structure and dynamics of state power. As Karl puts it:

> It matters whether a state relies on taxes from extractive activities, agricultural production, foreign aid, remittances or international production because these different sources of revenue, whatever their relative economic merits or social import, have a powerful (and quite different) impact on the state's institutional development and its abilities to employ personnel, subsidise social and economic programmes and direct the activities of private interests.
>
> (Karl 1997:13)

To illustrate this point, it is possible to distinguish between two types of states in capitalist countries. The first type consists of states largely financed by taxation, where the taxpayers' income is independent from the state. These are societies where the government does not control the economy and has to bargain with its citizens. A 'tax and spend' state eventually tends to be democratic; the state gains the consent to tax its citizens in exchange for the provision of services and the guarantee of order, and governments acquiesce to being changed through the holding of elections. The second type also consists of states financed by revenue from domestic production, but in this case the state also controls the economy. This is typical of the former communist countries. These states use a combination of ideology and coercion to spur on the domestic economy so as to ensure that they can continue to finance themselves.

The 'rentier' state is very different and can be conceived of as a 'no tax and spend' model. These are states whose revenue base is generated from the possession of a natural resource or from some form of rent generated from abroad, and their governments largely control the economy. Oil-dependent states are one variant of rentier states. Rent, which as we have seen is one of the chief features of oil production, differs from profits and wages in that it arises from the quality of the land rather than from productive efficiency. This has important implications for how rentier states are governed. Oil revenue, for example, accrues from the fact that the state controls territory where reserves are located, not because of the labour invested by the state in oil production. Classical theorists associated rentiers and landlords with militarism because territory was controlled by military means; thus the shift in the composition of income from rent to profits and wages was viewed as a shift to more 'civilised' forms of politics (Smith 1776; Schumpeter 1943). But contemporary rentier states do not rely solely on coercion to control their territory. Their governments use political means, especially patronage and forms of ideological mobilisation, to ensure the consent of their subjects. Favours are distributed through networks based on families, clans or ethnic and religious identity, and extensive patronage is difficult to disentangle from outright corruption. Thus corruption is not a private phenomenon but part of the way the political system operates. As Beblawi explains in relation to Arab states:

> The whole economy is arranged as a hierarchy of layers of rentiers with the state or the government at the top of the pyramid, acting as the ultimate support of all rentiers in the economy. It is important to add here that the rentier nature of the new state is magnified by the tribal origin of these states. A long tribal tradition of buying loyalty and allegiance is now confirmed by an *état providence*, distributing favours and benefits to its population.
>
> (Beblawi 1990:89)

In these types of economies, allocating resources to different interests is a way of 'buying' a type of skewed development to secure loyalty (Luciani 1990), but this is also risky because new interests may be created that can escape government control. Especially after the first oil price increase in 1973, petro-states embarked on ambitious programmes of state-led industrialisation, with Venezuela providing the classic example (Karl 1997). But even though favours are distributed unevenly in oil-led industrialisation, it is very difficult to mobilise a broad-based political opposition when petrodollars flow, and not only because of repression. 'To the individual who feels his benefits are not enough, the solution of manoeuvring for personal advantage within the existing set-up is always superior to seeking an alliance with others in similar conditions' (Luciani 1990:76). Thus, even though petro-states are prone to conflict and instability when prices are especially volatile, they are paradoxically quite stable most of the time. It is only when the oil price falls that the capacity for patronage correspondingly declines. This intensifies competition and repression and can produce popular insurrections, wars of secession and foreign adventures.

The type of rent also influences the character of the state. Theorists of the petro-state have emphasised the importance of a lead sector in dominating the distribution of revenue and hence the institutional structure and trajectory of the state. Because oil is a fixed asset – one that cannot be moved to the most easily governable parts of a country – and because its internal benefits depend on the manner in which petrodollars are allocated, certain institutions tend to come to the fore, especially a dominant executive branch, the state oil company, and the ministries of energy and finance (Karl 1997). But where oil is located in dangerous neighbourhoods or unstable regions, the lead sector also buffers the ministries of defence and the interior, and society is likely to be more militarised. These lead sectors constitute a bureaucratic vested interest in oil dependence, and an obstacle to structural change away from such dependence.

Nowadays, the classic authoritarian model of the rentier state is harder to sustain, but this may not be the case for petro-states. While the sources of income for many non-oil rentier states may have declined over time as a result of the end of the Cold War and fluctuations in commodity prices, oil prices are at record highs. However, it is much more difficult to control territory militarily because of the availability of weapons and equipment to non-state actors and, most importantly, it is much harder to insulate territory from external pressures under the impact of globalisation. Even in Saddam Hussein's Iraq, dissident bloggers were able to maintain their websites in opposition to the regime.

Combining explanations: the oil/rent-seeking/conflict cycle

We argue that all three explanations – geo-strategic, greed, and the petro-state – can be portrayed as rent-seeking arguments at different levels and at different times. Thus the geopolitical argument is actually about rent seeking among oil-consuming countries, which underpins the idea of direct or indirect conflicts among the Great Powers based on classic military force. The greed argument is about rent seeking at a local level, involving non-state actors, and it draws on the burgeoning literature about what are called civil wars and the economic motivations for conflict. The petro-state argument is about rent seeking in the oil-producing state and society; it represents the intersection of greed and geopolitics and can help to explain different types of conflict, internal, external and mixed. All of these levels are relevant in our case studies.

This is what is meant by 'new oil wars'. In 'old oil wars' only the first or 'strategic level' was relevant. This is because Great Powers were able to control directly or indirectly the territories where the revenues from oil accrued. In the 'new oil wars', all three levels are combined. 'New oil wars' are both global and local, and thus the distinction between civil war and cross-border or internationalised conflicts is less relevant. In reality, this distinction is breaking down, and this becomes ever more the case as prices grow increasingly volatile, discoveries become more infrequent, and known reserves are depleted. 'New oil wars' involve state and non-state actors who both seek rents and are sustained by them. Under these circumstances, it is much harder to control territory either directly through military means or indirectly through support for authoritarian regimes. Each of these different levels of rent seeking becomes salient at different times, and this explains the tendency for an oil/rent-seeking/conflict cycle to develop, in which efforts to introduce appropriate policies to manage oil revenues are undermined by ever intensifying rent-seeking behaviour and ever intensifying grievances. At an early stage of the cycle, something akin to the assumptions underlying an 'old war' model applies, when efforts to monopolise oil revenues presume a monopoly of legitimate organised violence through the state and the control over territory. But as the cycle progresses, the state itself is eroded – a process that may not be visible since it is being hollowed out by rentier behaviour. What does become visible, and often very suddenly, is the loss of the monopoly of organised violence, the difficulty of protecting oilfields either militarily or politically, and, in the worst cases, the collapse of the oil state itself.

Rent seeking by both public officials and private interests, domestic and international, weakens state institutions and makes it less likely that these institutions can counter the perverse effects of oil dependence. Although it is possible to devise appropriate policies to counter the economic problems faced by oil-dependent countries by, for example, 'sterilising' oil revenues through investment abroad, this is especially difficult to do effectively when all politically important sectors are trying to 'get a piece of the oil pie'.[35] Oil price volatility requires especially prudent budgetary planning, hedging on international financial markets, and policies aimed at promoting savings and investment – all of which are unlikely in a rentier setting. Not only do most oil producers consistently fail to follow such policies, they often exacerbate their problems by excessive borrowing, protection of domestic markets and profligate spending.

Rent seeking at all levels of state and society explains this systematic policy failure. By rent seeking, we mean an intense political competition aimed at gaining short-term access to oil revenues, as opposed to political competition over what policies might be in the long-term public interest. The finite and concentrated nature of oil and the exceptionally huge sums generated from this resource explain why rent-seeking behaviour is so importunate and why it is often territorially focused. Several scholars have noted a cycle in the behaviour of oil-dependent states, which they explain largely in terms of price volatility. Our argument is that, although the cycle is influenced by price volatility, it is the historical combination of rent seeking by different state and non-state actors, both within oil-dependent states and abroad at different times, that largely explains the cycle. Table I.1 provides a schematic version of the oil rent-seeking cycle.

The initial phase of the cycle could be described as the state-building phase, which may occur when oil is being discovered and initial

Table I.1 The oil rent-seeking cycle

Phase	Actors	Type of state revenue	Policies	Form of politics	Type of conflict
State building	Great Powers	Non-oil taxation	Oil funds construction of state infrastructure	Nationalist and ideological (left/right)	'Old oil wars'
Stabilisation	Oil-producing state	Oil and non-oil taxation	Development and public goods, repressive apparatus	Nationalist and ideological	Frozen or offshore conflicts
Predation	Oil-producing state and non-state actors	Mainly oil revenues and 'forced donations'	Oil extraction and repression	Identity politics (ethnic, religious, tribal)	'New oil wars'
State failure	Mainly non-state actors	Very low	Terrorism and corruption	As above	As above

investments are being made. This is associated with the introduction of
appropriate policies to manage the oil revenues in the case of developed states like Norway, and the construction of state infrastructure
necessary for the successful functioning of the oil industry and the
distribution of oil rents. This initial phase characterised the oldest oil
exporters like Indonesia, Venezuela, Saudi Arabia and Iraq, which
eventually built sophisticated industries and development ministries.
In an earlier period, when the Great Powers dominated the scramble
for petroleum, oil-producing states were 'manufactured', especially in
the Middle East, or existing states were strengthened, especially in
Latin America, in order to provide a legitimate vehicle for the extraction and delivery of oil and its rents. This was the stage of 'old wars'
when the Great Powers competed for direct or indirect control of the
territories to which oil rents accrued. In so far as control was indirect,
stable, compliant authoritarian regimes were established and strengthened. In Iraq, for example, in the period after the First World War, more
than 50 per cent of the revenues were passed on to the Iraqi Petroleum
Corporation – a consortium of British, French and American companies
that had full control over Iraqi oil even before Iraq was created. Of the
remainder, two-thirds were set aside for the Iraqi Development Board,
whose main goal was to insulate the economy from the impact of
economic rents and invest to increase the 'fertility of the land'. Agriculture was deemed a more sustainable base for the Iraqi economy. This
strategy had the convenient by-product of shoring up the landed aris-
tocracy – the main political powerbase of the ruling monarchy. In its
early years the Board showed admirable restraint in the spending of oil
resources. Its projects, which included most of Iraq's industrial and
architectural landmarks, were of consistently high quality.

Where only a weak state was in existence to 'receive' oil revenues
(every case but Norway), this state-building process in the oil-producing countries faced formidable challenges from the outset as more and
more groups and individuals came forward to claim a piece of the rent.
When Iraq began to experience its first oil boom in the mid 1950s, pressure began to mount to loosen the purse strings.[36] Urban nationalists
demanded investments in industries, agricultural interests called for
protection, political groups demanded the nationalisation of oil, oil
workers sought special favours and the poor sought a more equitable
distribution of wealth. In some places, like Biafra and the Niger Delta
in Nigeria or Aceh in Indonesia, claims to oil rents were couched in
ethnic and regional terms.

This expanded rent-seeking behaviour eventually gives rise to the
second phase of the cycle, the stabilisation phase. The petro-state retains
the capacity for autonomous actions and is able to deliver public goods,
but it survives through a combination of patronage and repression based
primarily on the distribution of petrodollars.

The Iraqi monarchy, like the succession of military rulers which followed it until 2003, showed typical characteristics of the stabilisation phase. The monarchy responded to the mounting clamour for oil rents with a combination of repression and patronage. From that point onward the Iraqi state came to resemble an oil company compound – a place with a high concentration of power, jobs and money, surrounded by barbed wire. Its interaction with the rest of society was either through handouts or repression. The new Iraqi state being built behind the walls of the Green Zone is not dissimilar from this model. The blend of repression and patronage is replicated in oil compounds and oil-dependent states throughout the developing world. Exxon used to run community outreach and development programmes while hiring the Indonesian military to protect it from the very community it was reaching out to. Nigerian dictators were executing Niger Delta rebels while increasing the region's share of the oil revenues.

In Iraq, however, the spending binge and stepped-up repressions came too late to save the Iraqi monarchy, which was toppled in 1958. Its successors helped themselves to more resources, ultimately nationalising oil in 1972 and unlocking tens of billions of dollars worth of rents. While the scale was changed, the nature of the relation between state and society remained the same. A middle class was created, sustained and terrorised with oil rents.

During the stabilisation phase, the state is able to contain domestic rent seeking to some extent and to produce a modicum of political stability and development (albeit at an exorbitant price). Whether democratic (very seldom) or authoritarian (almost always), it is propped up by an international regime based on a series of Faustian pacts that promise developed, oil-consuming nations a steady supply of oil in exchange for a seal of legitimacy and the freedom to carry out its own policies at home – even repression, as the governments of consuming countries look the other way. Most important, its stability rests on its growing capacity to wrest greater shares of petroleum rents from the international system, which petro-states have done most successfully through the price hikes and spate of nationalisations in the 1970s.

The stabilisation phase is unsustainable, not only because of price volatility but also because patronage and oppression exacerbate both greed and grievance. Petro-states are characterised eventually by parasitic private sector and political groups, communities and entire societies which feel entitled to ever greater handouts while expecting the worst from their governments. As expectations rise beyond the financial and administrative capacity of governments to meet them, underlying conflicts may flare into the open, offering new opportunities for domestic competitors and further degrading institutional capacities. This is especially true in the places where oil is actually located and exploited. Here the systematic degradation of the environment, the inability to provide jobs to populations untrained in oil technology, the spread of disease associated with prostitution accompanying the influx of foreign workers, and the often dramatic rise in inflation around oil enclaves create powerful local grievances while providing specific targets for extortion (for example, oil facilities and oil workers) that can be used to fund opposition groups and, eventually, criminal gangs. The chapters by Ibeanu and Luckham and by Jenny Pearce vividly illustrate this process in Nigeria and Colombia, showing how rentier behaviour becomes slowly transformed into conflict.

Conflict is not always internal, however. Key indicators of the gradual shift from a stabilisation phase to a more conflict-ridden predatory phase are the rise of militarism and military forces, on the one hand, and the increasing reliance by governments on nationalism and external enemies, on the other. Since petro-states have such difficulty delivering development to their constituencies, it often suits their rulers to promote an ideology directed against an enemy that seems to explain why domestic problems cannot be solved. Hence, for the Arab states, the perpetuation of the Israeli–Palestinian conflict has proved a convenient method of rallying domestic support when necessary. The Nagorno Karabakh conflict plays a similar role for Azerbaijan.

Nowhere has this been more apparent than in Saddam Hussein's Iraq, where war became a way of sustaining the nationalist ideology that supported his power. The unexpected and dramatic increase in oil prices in 1973–74 expanded the aspirations of the rulers of all oil-exporting countries, permitting Saddam to promulgate a grand vision of a Greater Iraq with hegemony over the oil of the Persian Gulf. Having used his new petrodollar bonanza to turn Iraq into the world's largest purchaser of arms, Saddam suddenly attacked a weakened Iran, still reeling from the fall of the Shah.[37] While the hostility between the two countries was longstanding, and the reasons for war a complex mix of ethnic, religious and ideological issues, the seizure of oilfields located where a border dispute had long simmered was viewed as the central strategic goal for both Iraq and Iran.[38] Both countries also sought the support of ethnic minorities within each other's territory – minorities who were sitting atop considerable reserves of crude and thus might be encouraged to secede – encouraging conflicts that smoulder to this day.[39] This eight-year war had all the trappings of an 'old war', with armies facing each other in a form of trench warfare reminiscent of the First World War, but it ended up contributing to the conditions for a 'new war'. The battle to draw new borders resulted in one of the deadliest conflicts since the Second World War, with at least 1.5 million dead in Iran alone, the use of chemical weapons by Iraq, and the employment of human waves of child soldiers by Iran. In 1988, it was settled on the basis of a return to the status-quo boundaries prior to conflict. The war had drained state coffers even before the fall in the oil price, imposed intolerable pressures on state infrastructure and killed hundreds of thousands of young men, with devastating social implications.

Oil-dependent states were further weakened by the end of the Cold War and the international regime that provided them with legitimacy. The wave of liberalisation and democratisation has empowered new groups, domestic and foreign, to question existing arrangements and raise new claims. Previously oppressed communities, multinational oil companies and large consumer nations feel emboldened to make their bid for a larger share in the oil rents. If one of the manifestations of globalisation is to challenge the state monopoly on legitimate use of force, than another is to challenge the oil-producing state's monopoly on rents.

The tension of deadly wars and localised but seemingly perpetual conflict can give rise to the third phase of the cycle – the predatory phase. This is where violence and repression become more important tools than patronage and where the name of the political game is rent seeking without limits: that is, seeking to capture petrodollars as quickly as possible, regardless of the legality of the methods used. The likelihood of this phase occurring has been exacerbated by the loss of former Cold War patrons who once might have helped buffer shaky regimes, as well as the rise of neo-liberal ideologies that challenge the desirability of state control over oil resources. In this phase, the state retains its monopoly of violence and monopoly of oil rents but regimes abandon any long-term developmental pretensions and simply try to hang on as long as possible while enriching themselves. In Saddam Hussein's Iraq, state institutions were so badly hollowed out that, by the time of his downfall, all that was left of the state was a system for the extraction and distribution of oil rents and mechanisms of repression. Whatever ideological glue had previously held together the regime was supplanted by more divisive identity politics, in which oil rents are claimed in the name of ethnicity or religion or tribe.

This final stage of the cycle is a twilight period, when predatory oil states begin to fail and can no longer sustain either the monopoly of legitimate violence or the monopoly on oil rents. This challenge to the state monopoly on rents has been on display in Iraq since the fall of Saddam. Houses still bear signs from the days of looting which immediately followed the war stating that 'This house is private property' – the implication being that it is acceptable to loot state property. A significant portion of political and civic activism since the fall of the regime has been geared towards capturing oil rents. Public debate is less about the long-term future of Iraq and more a competition for access to oil rents.[40] This rent seeking cannot be explained only by the removal of an oppressive ruler. It is in part a result of the disappearance of any unifying idea – a commitment to a shared commons –

combined with the belief that Iraqis can get rich both from oil and from the influx of billions of dollars of donor monies. Most importantly, it is a manifestation of the primary effect of living in a petro-state: a deep-seated feeling of entitlement to a slice of the oil rent. Iraq is not alone in this respect. In Chapter 1 on the Niger Delta, Ibeanu and Luckham describe how this culture of rent seeking even infects civil society, with NGOs competing for their share of oil rents so that, despite the successful campaign against Shell, the situation in the Delta region has not stabilised.

Not all states go through the cycle we have described. Especially in the contemporary period, when Cold War dynamics no longer require the construction of more permanent loyalties, states may directly enter a particular stage. For example, where states are especially weak before oil is discovered or exploited, as in much of West Africa, these states may directly enter the predatory phase. Thus Le Billon (Chapter 2) shows how Angola, with its late decolonisation followed by a devastating civil war financed in part by oil, does not follow a cyclical pattern and instead entered this predatory phase without passing through phases of state-building or stabilisation linked to petrodollar rents.

Both the predatory state and the failing state are associated with the 'new oil wars' we have depicted above as well as with growing instability in the oil sector itself. In these phases, conflicts involve a combination of state and non-state actors – remnants of the regular army, paramilitary groups, warlords, criminals and insurgents – and a political economy of predation becomes the pervasive form of economic exchange. A failing state is not quite the same as a collapsed state, although some of the regions we describe have come perilously close to that point. In the case studies that follow, probably only Chechnya came near the verge of state collapse. As long as oil extraction requires a state infrastructure, all the parties that have so far partaken in weakening the state have an incentive to shore it up. As a result one can see oil-dependent states hovering precariously on the brink of collapse in Iraq, Algeria, Azerbaijan, Angola, Sudan and elsewhere.

It is at this stage of the cycle that new possibilities arise for returning to the state-building phase. Outside actors – Great Powers, international institutions, and multinational corporations – as well as local groups have an interest in promoting peace processes and new reconstruction efforts aimed at restarting the flow of oil, rebuilding infrastructure and introducing relevant policies aimed at countering the rent-seeking cycle. These possibilities should not of course be over estimated. 'New wars' have devastating consequences for society and institutions from which it is extremely difficult to recover. This twilight phase may turn out to be the enduring one, so that the cycle can be treated as a transition rather than a recurring phenomenon.

CONCLUSION

What can be done to avoid a perverse oil/conflict cycle? While the greatest possibilities for intervention come when states fail and disaster is abundantly obvious, these are not the only moments when successful policy making may prevent a political resource curse. In the conclusion of this book, we contend that it is possible to introduce relevant policies aimed at countering the rent seeking at every phase of this cycle. But first the specific linkages between oil and war need to be examined. Our six case studies offer special insights into these different phases. Nigeria, Indonesia and Russia have all at different times exhibited classic characteristics of the state-building and stabilisation phase. Angola and Azerbaijan are closer to the predatory state stage. Colombia is a somewhat different case since rent seeking, linked to drugs, pre-dated the dynamics linked to oil. Though it historically possessed a relatively high degree of statehood, the combination of oil, drugs and conflict are hollowing out its bureaucratic capacities and its governability. In all cases, regardless of their place in our cycle, actual conflicts involve the spread of predatory behaviour linked to rent seeking. Thus our different phases are differences in degree, not in kind.

In all six cases the oil factor directly contributed to the causes of war, although it was by no means the only factor. In the case of Nagorno Karabakh and Chechnya, Russian geopolitical concerns about control over the Caucasian oilfields contributed to the outbreak of war. These concerns were part of the narrative of traditional Russian strategists that dates back to the discovery of oil in the region in the late nineteenth century. In Nigeria, Indonesia and Angola, the oil factor was central to efforts to achieve secession or autonomy of particular oil-rich provinces, and in all of these cases, including Colombia, oil rents have been central to debates over the distribution of income and wealth. Only in the case of Colombia can it be argued that oil was not a factor because the conflict pre-dated the production and export of oil.

Oil has also been significant in sustaining and even fuelling conflict in many of the ways pointed out by scholars who focus on greed and grievance. Oil has financed conflict through the contribution of petrodollars to government revenues – of key importance in Angola, Azerbaijan, Russia, Nigeria, Colombia and Indonesia. But more interestingly, oil revenues financed non-governmental actors in all sorts of indirect ways, from backyard oil wells in Chechnya to techniques of extortion such as kidnapping, hostage taking, drilling holes in pipelines and controlling municipalities, which are vividly described in the cases of Casanare (Colombia), Aceh (Indonesia) and the Delta region (Nigeria).

Finally, and most important, the six case studies also illustrate the double-sided nature of the oil factor. At all stages of the cycle, there were what Jenny Pearce calls 'contingent moments' when alternative strategies might have avoided or mitigated conflict. This is where it is essential to understand how some of the key features of oil – its strategic value, capital intensity, depletability and price volatility – can be turned into potential benefits. Because oil is such an important commodity, because it involves very significant sunken assets, and because it is becoming both scarcer and more expensive, conflicts involving oil will increasingly be the focus of international attention. This attention has generally taken the form of geopolitical behaviour (predatory competition by outside powers), but this does not have to be the case. As the biggest consuming countries and the largest energy companies learn that it is in their long-term interests to stabilise the energy sector, these very features can also lead to more cooperative international approaches aimed at restricting rent seeking and, hence, preventing and stabilising conflicts. Both of these contradictory approaches can be observed in the Nagorno Karabakh conflict, for example, or in Angola and Nigeria. As it becomes harder to defend oil installations through traditional military means, and harder to explain the instability of energy to citizens of consuming countries, it becomes evident that the acceptance of the rule of law, greater democracy, and especially greater transparency in the use of oil revenues are crucial to the solution to the oil-conflict cycle. Without such measures, conflicts will continue, even if they are partially frozen, as in the Nagorno Karabakh conflict, Russia's peace-making efforts after the first Chechnya war, the current peace processes in Angola and Aceh, and the prolonged transition to democracy in Nigeria.

Because of the stakes involved in oil at all levels, the behaviour of states, companies and outside powers is provoking a civil society reaction in oil-exporting countries, pushing these actors towards more cooperative and responsible policies. This is one of the main conclusions of the Nigeria case study. In Casanare, the Delta region and Aceh, local protests have shamed BP, Shell and ExxonMobil respectively and led to changes of strategy. This same civil society dynamic can be seen in consuming countries, where movements concerned with climate change, high energy prices, human rights and indigenous rights, and the oil-related debt of extremely poor countries are uniting to demand better policies in the energy sector. The extent to which these movements, both domestic and transnational, can take advantage of these 'contingent moments' depends on whether they and other stakeholders can act in a combined and coherent way to offset systematic rent seeking.

These case studies offer clues about whether it is possible to avoid the oil rent-seeking cycle. In our final chapter, we set out possible policies to counter the rent-seeking cycle. But two initial conclusions can be drawn. The first has to do with the negative consequences of Great Power competition – of imposing geopolitical rivalries on oil-producing states according to the assumptions of 'old war'. This no longer leads to greater control over territory where oil is located; rather it precipitates the cyclical process that results in 'new oil wars'. The role of international institutions and multilateral action offers a better model for outside involvement since this has a greater chance of operating in the global public interest. The second conclusion has to do with the importance of transparency and accountability, and the need to stimulate a broad public discussion about the use of energy based on fossil fuels. Only this sort of debate can offer an alternative to the divisive and exclusivist politics used to legitimate rent-seeking behaviour.

NOTES

1. Estimating oil reserves is a tricky business, but by all accounts Iraq's are enormous. The US Energy Information Agency estimates that in addition to its 112 billion barrels in proven reserves – which are more than five times as much as US reserves – it has anywhere from 100 to 220 billion barrels in unexplored territory. See 'Country Analysis Briefs: Iraq': www.eia.doe.gov/cabs/iraq.html.
2. In Adam Smith's (1776) classic definition, rent is unearned income or profits 'reaped by those who did not sow'. According to economists, rents are earnings in excess of all relevant costs, including the market rate of return on invested assets. They are the equivalent of what most non-economists consider to be monopoly profits.
3. For a more complete discussion of oil rents at the global and state level, especially the concept of oil states as rentier states, see Karl (1997). For a discussion of how these rents affect the local and societal level as well, see Karl (1999 and 2004).
4. President George W. Bush, 'President Bush Announces Major Combat Operations in Iraq Have Ended' – Remarks by President Bush from the USS *Abraham Lincoln*, 1 May 2003.
5. For a more complete discussion of this concept, see Mary Kaldor (1999). For its application to Iraq, see Kaldor (2006), upon which this section is based.
6. A spate of books made the same point as government memos. See, for example, Richard Heinberg (2003) and David Goodstein (2004).
7. All $ figures = US dollars. For more on war costs see: http://nationalpriorities.org/index.php?option=com_wrapper& Itemid=182, last accessed 19 June 2006.
8. See, for example (in order): Ari Fleischer, White House Press Briefing, 18 February 2003; Deputy Secretary of State Richard Armitage, House Committee on Appropriations Hearing on a Supplemental War Regulation, 27 March 2003; and comments by Secretary of Defense Donald Rumsfeld and Deputy Defense Secretary Paul Wolfowitz at the same hearings:

(www.house.gov/schakowsky/iraqquotes_web.htm,
last accessed 7 November 2006).

9. There were all sorts of grandiose plans to restart Iraqi exports quickly, and secret contracts were awarded well before the war was officially launched. For example, Vice President Cheney's former company, Halliburton, received a no-bid contract to rebuild oil facilities (reportedly up to $7 billion) through its subsidiary, Kellogg Brown and Root. But it soon became clear that, if oil were produced, it might be impossible to find buyers due to the problem of legal title. Members of the coalition were prohibited by international law from selling the oil and there was no recognised Iraqi government. Later, a plan hatched in a US Export-Import Bank memo, which was leaked, made provisions for mortgaging Iraqi oil to pay for reconstruction, but this too hit legal snafus.

10. These included the Al Da'wa Party (Shi'ite Islamist), the Communist Party, the General Union of Students (GUSIA) and the League of Iraqi Women who did a lot to support the widows of the victims of Saddam's regime.

11. For example, the Hewar (dialogue) gallery was established by a well-known artist who left the Ba'ath Party at the time of the invasion of Kuwait. It became a place where artists could exhibit their work and find foreign buyers, with a café where they could meet and talk. It included artists like the Najeen (survivors) group who openly opposed the regime. Likewise, a group known as the Wednesday group composed of current and ex-Ba'athists met every Wednesday to discuss political and intellectual issues even after one of their members was arrested and executed.

12. These haven't changed significantly despite the new headings every decade – 'Airland Battle', 'Revolution in Military Affairs' and now 'Defence Transformation'. Kersti Hakansson has demonstrated this point in a comparison of tactics in Vietnam and Afghanistan. See 'New Wars, Old Warfare? Comparing US Tactics in Afghanistan and Vietnam', in Jan Angstrom and Isabelle Duyvesteyn (2003) *The Nature of Modern War: Clausewitz and his Critics Revisited*.

13. President George W. Bush, Remarks by President Bush from the USS *Abraham Lincoln*, 1 May 2003.

14. For example, a Fallujah-based group called 'Awakening and Holy War' sent a tape to Iranian television in July 2003 saying that Saddam and the United States were two sides of the same coin. For more details see Samir Haddad and Mazin Ghazi's 'An Inventory of Iraqi Resistance Groups: Who Kills Hostages in Iraq?' (*Al Zawra*, Baghdad, 19 September 2004). This translation by the CIA's Foreign Broadcast Information Service was originally posted on the FAS website, but is no longer there; it is available on the Global Policy Forum site. See also an earlier Jihad Unspun, 'An Insider's Look at the Iraqi Resistance'.

15. Some of these groups are linked to Al Qaeda, such as the Jama'at al-Tawi led by Abu Musab al-Zarqawi, responsible for the deaths of Nicholas Berg and Ken Bigley, or the groups based in Northern Kurdistan before the invasion such as Ansar al-Sunna or Ansar al-Islam. Some of these include foreign fighters, though the numbers may have been exaggerated.

16. See G. Burnham, R. Latta and L. Roberts, 'Mortality after the 2003 invasion of Iraq: a cross-sectional cluster sample study', *The Lancet*, Vol. 368, Issue 9545, 21 October 2006.

17. See the official US Defense Department website www.defendamerica.mil.

18. Hence when the scandals about torture in the Abu Ghreib prison became

public, it was evident that private contractors had carried out some of the most dubious practices.

19. *New York Times*, 22 October 2004.

20. According to Major General Raymond T. Odierno, Commander of the Army's Fourth Infantry Division, 'when we first got here, we believed it was about $100 to conduct an attack and $500 if you are successful. We now believe that it's somewhere between $1000 and $2000 if you conduct an attack and between $3000 and $5000 if you are successful.' According to him, 70–80 per cent of captured insurgents were ordinary criminals (quoted in Hoffman 2004).

21. In the south, pipelines are directly tapped into by smugglers, which allows tankers to top up their loads at will. Since this can generally happen only with the cooperation of oil ministry employees, it is evident that corruption in the industry is rampant. In April, the Iraqi oil ministry sacked more than 450 employees suspected of selling fuel on the black market and one oil ministry official discovered more than 20 illegal taps on one pipeline alone. (Interview with representative of Iraq Oil Workers Union from Basra, London, June 2005.)

22. Like the current smuggling, this was well-known by US administrations, which looked the other way. Senator Carl Levin (Democrat, Michigan) during a 15 February 2005 Hearing of the Permanent Subcommittee on Investigations into Oil-for-Food Program allegations, explained in his opening statement: 'It is clear that the whole world, including the United States, knew about Iraq's oil sales to Turkey, Jordan and Syria. In the case of the United States, we not only knew about the oil sales, we actively stopped the United Nations Iraq Sanctions Committee, known as the 661 Committee, from acting to stop those sales. ... Hundreds of millions of dollars went into the pockets of Saddam Hussein as a result.'

23. In 2003, officials estimated a loss of $250,000 per day from the south alone. This estimate is based on an average of 2000 tons of gasoline, diesel and crude oil, enough to fill about 65 tanker trucks, or about 10 per cent of local output. See Robert Collier, 'Black Market Drains Iraq Oil', *San Francisco Chronicle*, 22 October 2003.

24. See Alissa J. Rubin, 'Oil Wealth Divides Iraqis', *Los Angeles Times*, 1 August 2005, and Edward Wong, 'Secular Shi'ites in Iraq Seek Autonomy in Oil-Rich South', *New York Times*, 30 June 2005.

25. 'Coupled with the goal of raising the Iraqi public's frustration,' comments Gal Luft of Global Security, 'they see these attacks as a ways to kill two birds with one stone.' See Howard La Franchi, 'Why Iraqi Oil Money Hasn't Fuelled Rebuilding', *Christian Science Monitor*, 4 July 2005.

26. The discussion in this section is based on Karl (1997, Chapter 2, especially pp 46–9) unless otherwise indicated.

27. Chairman of the Council of Economic Advisors, 'Economic Report to the President', 2002, GPO, Washington, D.C., 2002.

28. Maring Wolf, 'How Rising Oil Prices Add to the World Economy's Fragility', *Financial Times*, 7 September 2005.

29. US EIA, Rules-of-Thumb for Oil Supply Disruptions, see: www.eia.doe.gov/emeu/security/rule.html. Viewed 13 June 2005.

30. See www.eia.doe.gov/emeu/cabs/usa.html, last accessed February 2006.

31. US energy intensity (energy costs per unit of output) has been steadily declining and today it stands at half the level it was in 1970. Energy intensity

in Europe is even lower. In 2002, Germany consumed 45 per cent less energy per dollar of output and almost 50 percent less energy per person than the United States (US Energy Information Administration, 'Germany Country Analysis Brief', www.eia.doe.gov/emeu/cabs/germany.html. Viewed 13 June 2005) China today consumes one-third the amount of energy per dollar of output that it did in 1980.

32. China's oil use alone is projected to increase by a huge annual average of 7.5 per cent from 2002 to 2010. See International Energy Outlook 2005: www.eia.doe.gov/oiaf/aeo/, last accessed 7 November 2006.

33. Andrew Callus, 'Yamani Says OPEC Accelerating End of the Oil Era', Reuters, London, 5 September 2000.

34. The Dutch disease argument is based on what happened to Holland after the discovery of North Sea oil in the 1970s, and identifies a similar pattern in economies adapting to new discoveries of oil. In this argument, resource booms cause real exchange rates to rise and labour and capital to migrate to the booming sector. Oil exports lead to an appreciation of currency and a fall in other tradable sectors, especially manufacturing. This results in higher costs and reduced competitiveness for domestically produced goods and services, effectively crowding out previously productive sectors. Even when the oil price falls, and the currency depreciates, the manufacturing sector does not recover, either because of economies of scale or the rigidities of financial markets. The phenomenon has been observed in almost all oil-dependent states, though there are measures to counteract this, most notably creating an oil fund to manage oil revenues and insulate them from the rest of the economy. The fact that states do not take these measures is explained by the character of the petro-state.

35. Indonesia was able to do so, but only under the strictest international conditionality (see Usui 1996).

36. Government oil income rose from ID6 million in 1950 to ID76 million in 1956 (Fenelon 1970).

37. Indications are that Saddam Hussein believed that Iran would present an easy victory in the disarray that followed the overthrow of the Shah. Washington, eager for payback after the hostage crisis, also encouraged the attack on Iran, feeding intelligence to Iraq that indicated a speedy triumph (Engdahl 1992:213). Although formally neutral, the United States later 'tilted' towards Iraq with covert arms transfers, intelligence support and loans.

38. The contested Shatt-al-Arab River forming the boundary between the two countries was a critical route to the Gulf. Iran's Abadan oil refinery was built in its delta, Iraq's principal port city of Basra lay on the river, and both countries had a considerable part of their oil infrastructure, including fields, refineries, pipelines and storage tanks, located along the waterway.

39. In the years prior to the war, the Shah provided aid to the Kurds in a region where much of Iraq's oil lay, while during the war Hussein appealed to ethnic Arabs in Iran's Khuzistan, where 90 per cent of Iran's oil reserves were located, and targeted his attacks on the heart of the Iranian oil industry. The belief that the Kurds were 'pro-Iranian' was one of the justifications used by Hussein for his genocide against them.

40. For example, the various associations of regime victims are seeking state pensions, land plots and government jobs for their constituents. The exiled political parties are obsessed with getting Ba'athists out and their own members into every public sector job, from school teacher to prime minister.

Kurds in the north and Shias in the south are proposing federal arrangements which include the distribution of oil assets and revenues as a central
component.

BIBLIOGRAPHY

Bastian, S. and Luckham, R. (eds) (2003) *Can Democracy Be Designed? The Politics of Institutional Choice in Conflict-torn Societies* (London: Zed Books).
Beblawi, H. (1990) 'The Rentier State in the Arab World', in Luciani, G. (ed.) *The Arab State* (London: Routledge).
Berdal, M.R. and Malone, D.M. (eds) (2000) *Greed and Grievance: Economic Agendas in Civil Wars* (Boulder, Colo.: Lynne Rienner).
Bill, J.A. and Louis, W.R. (eds) (1988) *Musaddiq, Iranian Nationalism and Oil* (London: Tauris).
Collier, P. and Hoeffler, A. (1998) 'On Economic Causes of Civil War', *Oxford Economic Papers*, Vol. 50.
—— (2001) *Greed and Grievance in Civil War* (Washington, D.C.: World Bank).
—— (2002) 'Aid, Policy and Peace', *Defence and Peace Economics*, Vol. 13, No. 6.
—— (2004) 'Greed and Grievance in Civil War', *Oxford Economic Papers*, Vol. 56.
Cordesman, A.H. (2004) 'The Developing Iraqi Insurgency: Status at End 2004' (Washington, D.C.: Centre for International and Strategic Studies, working draft updated December 2004).
de Soysa, I. (2002) 'Greed, Creed and Governance in Civil War, 1989–99', *Journal of Peace Research*, Vol. 39, No. 4.
Duelfer, C. (2004) 'Comprehensive Report of the Special Advisor to the DCI on Iraq's WMD, 30 September 2004' (Central Intelligence Agency).
Duffield, M. (2001) *Global Governance and the New Wars: The Merging of Development and Security* (London: Zed Books).
EIA (Energy Information Administration) (2005) Annual Outlook, 2005. http://www.eia.doe.gov/oiaf/archive.html, last accessed 7 November 2006.
Eifert, B., Gelb, A. and Tallroth, N.B. (2002) *The Political Economy of Fiscal Policy and Economic Management in Oil-exporting Countries* (Washington, D.C.: World Bank, Africa Regional Office, Office of the Chief Economist, policy research working paper 2899).
Engdahl, F.W. (1992) *A Century of War: Anglo-American Oil Politics and the New World Order* (London: Pluto).
Fearon, J.D. and Laitin, D. (2003) 'Ethnicity, Insurgency, and Civil War', *American Political Science Review*, Vol. 97, No. 1.
Fearon, J.D. (2004) 'Why do Some Civil Wars Last So Much Longer than Others?', *Journal of Peace Research*, Vol. 41, No.3.
—— (2005) 'Primary Commodity Exports and Civil War', *Journal of Conflict Resolution*, Vol. 49, No. 4.
Fenelon, K.G. (1970) *Iraq: National Income and Expenditure 1950–6* (Baghdad: Shafik Press).
Goodstein, D. (2004) *Out of Gas: The End of the Age of Oil* (New York: W.W. Norton).
Goralski, R. and Freeburg, R. (1987) *Oil and War: How the Deadly Struggle for Fuel in WWII Meant Victory or Defeat* (London: William Morrow).
Hakansson, K. (2003) 'New Wars, Old Warfare? Comparing US Tactics in Afghanistan and Vietnam', in Angstrom, J. and Duyvesteyn, I. The *Nature of*

Modern War: Clausewitz and his Critics Revisited (Stockholm: Swedish National Defence College, Department of War Studies).

Heinberg, R. (2003) *The Party's Over: Oil, War and the Fate of Industrial Societies* (Gabriola, B.C.: New Society).

Hiro, D. (2003) *Iraq: A Report from the Inside* (London: Granta).

Hoffman, B. (2004) 'Insurgency and Counterinsurgency in Iraq' (Santa Monica, Calif.: Rand Corporation).

IMF Iraq Statistical Appendix (August 2005) 'IMF Country Report No. 05/295'.

International Energy Agency (2005) *Saving Oil in a Hurry* (Paris: OECD/IEA).

Kaldor, M. (1999) *New and Old Wars: Organised Violence in a Global Era* (Cambridge: Polity Press/Stanford University Press).

—— (2006) *New and Old Wars: Organised Violence in a Global Era,* 2nd edn (Cambridge: Polity Press).

Karl, T.L. (1997) *The Paradox of Plenty: Oil Booms and Petro-states* (Berkeley: University of California Press).

—— (1999) 'The Perils of Petroleum: Reflections on The Paradox of Plenty', *Fueling the 21st Century: The New Political Economy of Energy,* special edition of *The Journal of International Affairs,* Vol. 53, No. 1.

—— (2003) *Bottom of the Barrel: Africa's Oil Boom and the Poor* (Catholic Relief Services).
http://www.crs.org/get_involved/advocacy/
policy_and_strategic_issue/oil_report_one.cfm, last accessed 7 November 2006.

—— (2004) 'Oil and Development: The Global Record', in *Oil Change: Petro-Politics Briefing Book* (Foreign Policy In Focus).
http://www.fpif.org/papers/03petropol/index.html, last accessed 7 November 2006.

Keen, D. (2005) *The Economic Functions of Violence in Civil Wars* (Oxford: Oxford University Press).

Klare, M.T. (2006) *Blood and Oil* (New York: Henry Holt).

Le Billon, P. (2005) 'Fuelling War: Natural Resources and Armed Conflicts', *Adelphi Paper 373* (London: IISS).

Luciani, G. (ed.) (1990) *The Arab State* (London: Routledge).

Luckham, R., Goetz, A. and Kaldor, M. (2000) 'Democratic Institutions and Politics in Contexts of Inequality, Poverty and Conflict', *International Development Studies* (IDS Working Paper 104).

Meyer, L. (1977) *Mexico and the United States in the Oil Controversy,* 1917–1942, translated by Muriel Vasconcellos (Austin: University of Texas Press).

Roberts, L., Lafta, R., Garfield, R., Khudhairi, J. and Burnham, G. (2004) 'Mortality Before and After the 2003 Invasion of Iraq: Cluster Sample Survey', *The Lancet,* Vol. 364, No. 9448.

Said, Y. (2004) 'Civil Society in Iraq', in Anheier, H., Glasius, M. and Kaldor, M. (2004) *Global Civil Society 2004/5* (London: Sage).

Schumpeter, J.A. (1943) *Capitalism, Socialism and Democracy* (London: G. Allen & Unwin Ltd).

Smith, A. (1776) *An Inquiry into the Nature and Causes of the Wealth of Nations* (Wealth of Nations) (London).

'Special Inspector General for Iraq Reconstruction Report to Congress', October 2005.
http://www.sigir.mil/pdf/Oct_05_Congress/October_2005_report.pdf, last accessed 7 November 2005.

Usui, N. (1996) 'Policy Adjustments to the Oil Boom and their Evaluation: The Dutch Disease in Indonesia', *World Development*, Vol. 24, No. 5.

Yergin, D. (1992) *The Prize: The Quest for Oil, Money and Power* (New York: Free Press; reissue edition, 1 January 1993).

Zabih, S. (1982) *Iran Since the Revolution* (Baltimore, MD: Johns Hopkins University Press).

1 Nigeria: political violence, governance and corporate responsibility in a petro-state

Okey Ibeanu and Robin Luckham

OIL, THE STATE AND CONFLICT IN NIGERIA

On Independence Day, 1 October 2004, President Obasanjo held talks with Alhaji Mujahid Dokubo Asari, the leader of the so-called Niger Delta Volunteer Force, to persuade him to call off Operation Locust Feast, a militia offensive against oil firms. Asari and his associates demanded greater local control of the region's oil and gas resources, together with a national conference to renegotiate Nigeria's Federal Constitution and devolve powers to states, local authorities and local communities.

Political activists and pro-democracy groups in the Niger Delta have pressed the same demands for many years. Asari and his cohorts differ, however, in that they are linked to organised crime and are armed with relatively sophisticated weapons, including machine guns and rocket-propelled grenades. Thus, behind the reformist rhetoric, the violence in the delta is becoming privatised, interlocking with corruption and electoral politics, including the deployment of militias by state governors to intimidate opponents.

Indeed a recent World Bank study claims that protests in the Niger Delta are being 'transformed into something more akin to American gangland fights for control of the drug trade' (Collier et al 2003:77). The threats to oil facilities are serious enough for the Nigerian federal government and oil companies to hold discussions with emergent warlords like Asari and his rival Ateke Tom, despite the charge that this rewards the use of violence.[1] These are some of the most recent twists in Nigeria's evolution during the past 40 years into a prototypical petro-state. Its economy is heavily dependent upon petroleum, which contributes about 50 per cent of the country's GDP, 95 per cent of foreign exchange earnings and 80 per cent of budgetary revenues.[2]

Oil has been a burning political issue since the Nigerian civil war of 1967–70, which almost ripped the country apart, causing up to a million war-related deaths and displacing some 6 million people. Since the war, Nigeria has remained in a state of suppressed, 'silent' or 'structural' or 'repressive' violence,[3] punctured by periodic outbreaks of actual violence, some causing significant casualties and making thousands refugees in their own country. Shell and other oil majors have forged close alliances with Nigeria's ruling classes, including its military dictatorships. Little of the oil revenue has been invested in the communities in the Niger Delta, where most oil is produced. These communities have born the brunt of the extensive environmental damage from oil extraction, and have become increasingly alienated from the oil companies and from the government. During the 1990s, originally peaceful protests by the Movement for the Survival of the Ogoni People (MOSOP) in the Niger Delta were brutally suppressed, culminating in the trial and execution of MOSOP leaders, including Ken Saro-Wiwa. Although the Ogoni are one of the smaller Delta communities, their protests resonated throughout the delta and in the rest of Nigeria. They also acquired an iconic status in international debates about the environment and about the power and corporate responsibilities of multinational oil corporations.

By 1998, when 'the hand of God' removed the military dictator, General Abacha,[4] and the military started a hurried retreat from power, the erosion of state authority and political violence had become so severe that many feared the country might be on the brink of another civil war. New outbursts of inter-communal, criminal and citizen–state violence accompanied the transition to constitutional governance. President Obasanjo's government was caught unprepared and all too often responded repressively. At the same time it canvassed policies to provide security and public order, and to manage violent conflict in a series of presidential retreats, commissions and conflict assessments. Yet it appears the security crisis is too fundamental to be resolved through policy adjustments alone, being embedded in a state crippled by its lack of legitimacy, endemic corruption and inability to deliver development or security, even under a supposedly democratic regime.

The Nigerian state appears increasingly powerless to counter the powerful market forces and economic incentive systems driving violence in an oil-dominated economy. Yet in contrast to some other analyses of 'resource wars', we argue that in Nigeria the relationships between mineral rents and violent conflicts have been complex and mediated through the relationships between the state and the oil multinationals.[5] Oil differs from some other resources, in that its exploration and production entail substantial capital requirements, with large sunk costs in exploration and production, and hence intimate long-term relationships with the state. It contrasts with 'lootable' resources like alluvial diamonds, which lend themselves more readily to the financing of insurgents. At the same time the dispersed and 'obstructable' infrastructure of wells, pipelines and storage facilities has remained vulnerable to disruption by protesters and insurgents, as in the Niger Delta. Indeed criminal mafias have recently devoted considerable ingenuity to turning even oil into a lootable commodity, through the process known as 'bunkering', fuelling the growth of an informal economy of violence.[6]

However, we are sceptical of determinist accounts of the nexus between oil and political violence. The Nigerian civil war did not reignite, and was indeed followed by a period of state and national reconstruction. Political violence, though still endemic, remained less severe than in other resource-dependent African countries, like Angola or the Democratic Republic of Congo. By the end of the military era in 1999, many of the conditions which generated civil wars elsewhere in Africa seemed also to threaten Nigeria – but they did not precipitate large-scale armed conflict.

Hence in this chapter we focus on two central analytical concerns. First, we seek to understand how both violent conflict and its absence have been determined by the shifting and troubled relationships between the Nigerian post-colonial state and the oil sector. Second, we consider how both oil and violence have seeped into and transformed Nigeria's complex and varied social formations, slowly embedding a political economy and a culture of violence, especially (but not only) in the Niger Delta. We will show how Nigeria became a near-prototypical rentier or petro-state. Initially Nigeria's military rulers used swelling oil revenues to finance state building and state-managed development. But oil-financed state building soon acquired a more perverse and regressive face, typifying Karl's 'paradox of plenty' (1997). Oil revenues insulated the state from accountability to citizens in general and to communities in oil-producing regions in particular. An abundance of oil fostered a deficit of democracy, as well as a surplus of corruption and violence. The corruption and ultimately hollowing-out of the state was reinforced by a flawed 'cohabitation' between state (especially military) élites and international oil firms. This enabled Nigeria's military rulers and their acolytes to accumulate wealth and power. And it allowed oil multinationals to extract oil with little effective government regulation or community voice in their operations or in the distribution of oil surpluses.

What is less frequently considered, however, is how oil penetrated and reconfigured the country's social formations, including the complex web of relationships among different nationalities and local communities. This too has proved to be a contradictory and contested process. On the one hand it spawned active grassroots movements, which arose in the Niger Delta to protest against environmental degradation and the mal-distribution of oil revenues. Their protests articulated a strong sense of the rights and entitlements of Niger Delta communities to control their own resources. They also seemed to herald new forms of democratic politics, demanding renegotiation of Nigeria's federal structure to bring government closer to the people, a demand which also resonated outside the Niger Delta. But in the train of the protest movements, there emerged a new political economy of privatised violence, fuelled by oil. Its protagonists played on the grievances of Niger Delta communities to foster a different kind of entitlement politics more in tune with the rentier nature of the Nigerian state. There emerged a new and dangerous version of the 'politics of the belly', featuring seizures of oil installations, hostage taking, bunkering, intimidation and violence. Privatised violence began to eat into the social fabric of Niger Delta communities, corrupted grassroots protests and resonated with the intimidation and corruption marring democratic governance in the state and federal political arenas.

Petroleum dependence, state corruption and privatised violence indeed pose serious threats to Nigeria's unconsolidated democratic transition. But in our view it is not helpful simply to lament them. Instead we stress the double-sided nature of Nigeria's petro-state and of grassroots contestation of it. At critical junctures, *different* policy decisions and political choices might have been made about Nigeria's oil assets, so as to break the vicious cycle of oil dependence and economic and political decline. Moreover, transition to democracy, whatever its flaws, could still create spaces for better governance of the petroleum sector and to tackle the growth of violence. To focus solely on the malign legacies of oil-funded authoritarianism and corruption would be to write off Nigeria's new democracy from the start, and to condemn the country to a future of escalating conflict. Similarly we see the vibrant tradition of grassroots protest in the Niger Delta and elsewhere as a potential foundation for democratic politics. Protest movements posed an alternative vision of the state in the dying years of the military era. Although that vision has been badly compromised by the social divisions, rent seeking and conflicts now tearing Niger Delta communities apart, it has not been entirely extinguished, and could still pose a credible alternative to violence.

MILITARY RULE AND NIGERIA'S PETRO-STATE, 1966–99

Nigeria's experience of violence has intertwined with its history of authoritarian, and more specifically military, governance. The country was under military rule for 30 years, most of its post-independence history. The militarised state was authoritarian and rapacious, but at the same time increasingly fragile, corrupt and unable to deliver development.

The historical turning point in the formation of a petro-state was the civil war. War broke out in 1967 because of the political and economic contradictions of the post-colonial state, including the legacy of uneven development under colonial rule, vicious oligopolistic competition amongst members of Nigeria's political class for power and patronage in a three (later four) region federation, and two military coups whose impact reverberated outside the armed forces themselves and came close to breaking up the federation.[7] There remains some dispute about how far the start of oil exports caused the civil war. What is beyond doubt is that it had a decisive impact on its course and outcome, including the creation of the de facto alliance between the government of Nigeria, foreign powers (notably Britain) and international oil companies (especially Shell-BP) which defeated Biafra's secession.

After the war, the politics of rent extraction both consolidated and subverted the emergent petro-state through struggles to appropriate oil revenues. The federal military government appropriated the bulk of these revenues to expand state investment, to build a large federal bureaucracy, to sustain a well-armed coercive apparatus and to construct an extensive patronage system, redistributing jobs and rents at every level of the political system and entrenching systemic corruption. Rival élites contested control of the state and its oil revenues, making the politics of revenue allocation (between the government, the states and local governments) a central focus of Nigerian federalism. As long as oil production, prices and revenues increased, factional struggles were mostly contained within the military and political élite – although even then they could be deadly, spawning several coups and coup attempts. But as Nigeria drifted deeper into debt and fiscal crisis from the 1980s, the struggles over oil revenues became more intense. Economic and fiscal recession turned into political recession, generating deep crises of political authority. There occurred a hollowing-out of the state, including diminished capacity to deliver security and other public goods. This extended to the military establishment itself and even more to the underfunded, inefficient and corrupt national police force, whose inability to ensure public order and cope with rising criminality became a major security problem in its own right.

We distinguish a number of phases in the petro-state's creation and subsequent crisis, as outlined below. These are linked both to political transitions and to the transformations in the petroleum economy shown in the graph of Figure1.1 (which relates to the period discussed here, and is of interest, since it was made by the Presidential Advisor on Petroleum and Energy (Daukoru 2004). They may be summarised as:

- The initially disastrous phase of military governance from 1966 to 1970, when both the federation and military establishment came close to falling apart but were eventually restructured to fight the civil war, fortified by their alliance with the oil multinationals.[8]
- The 1970–79 post-war period of soaring oil production and revenues,

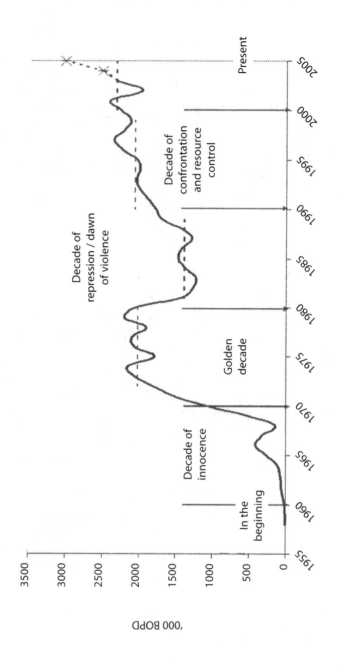

Figure 1.1 Nigerian crude oil production performance 1958–2003

Source: Daukoru 2004

and the establishment of the essential structures of the petro-state under the military governments of Generals Gowon, Mohammed and Obasanjo, culminating in the first return to civilian rule in 1979.

- Oil-linked economic and political recession during the 1980s, marked by stagnant oil production and revenues, fiscal crisis and the growth of external indebtedness, a coup overthrowing President Shagari's government in 1983 and the emergence of new generations of political soldiers with the power to 'chop' Nigeria's resources under the Buhari and Babangida military regimes. This phase witnessed the open emergence of the contradictions of the petro-state, the imposition of de facto structural adjustment, and a further highly orchestrated but abortive return to civilian rule.

- The reconsolidation (after the annulled 1993 elections) of a new and especially vicious military regime under General Abacha, notable for the scale of its corruption and plunder of oil resources, as well as its intensification of state repression. This was when minority protests in the Niger Delta also came to a head, placing the spotlight on the unhealthy cohabitation between the military regime and the oil companies. Worse political violence was only averted by General Abacha's death in 1998, and the 1999 retreat from power by a demoralised military establishment.

Below we summarise the central structural contradictions of the petro-state, which crystallised under military governance, and the ways they fostered political violence. The key political events, petroleum sector development and episodes of violence are chronicled in Table 1.1.

Oil dependence and the paradox of plenty

The economic mainstay of government before the civil war had been agricultural commodity production, notably of cocoa, oil palm, groundnuts and cotton. This anchored the accumulation of wealth and power in exploitation of the peasantry. It also fostered strong regional political élites, with core support in Nigeria's three largest ethnic nationalities, the Yoruba in the west, the Igbo in the east and the Hausa-Fulani in the north. At the start of the civil war, oil revenues, though growing, contributed no more than 30 per cent of the government budget.

The civil war was the catalyst for the emergence of Nigeria as a petroleum economy and petro-state. There were massive rises in oil production, peaking at over 2 million bbl/d by the late 1970s. The country's traditional agricultural exports were wiped out in less than a decade and its economy became heavily oil dependent.

Fast growth of the oil economy was initially seen as an opportunity to construct a strong developmental state which would lift the country out of poverty and underdevelopment. The federal military government was

Table 1.1 Oil, politics and conflict in Nigeria: a chronology 1953–2005

Main political watersheds	Major protests/ violent conflicts	Oil industry developments
• 1954: establishment of federation.	• 1953: killing of southerners in northern cities.	• 1956: first commercial oil find.
• 1958: Willink Commission on Minorities.		• 1958: start of oil production and exports.
• 1960: Nigeria gains independence.		• 1961: Niger Delta Development Act.
• 1963: declaration of republic.	• 1965–66: Western Region political violence.	• 1965: completion of Port Harcourt refinery and Trans-Niger pipeline.
• 1966: January and July military coups.	• 1966: May and September massacres of Igbos and other southerners in northern cities.	
• 1967: military government replaces four regions with twelve-state system; Eastern Region secedes as Biafra.		

Nigerian Civil War, May 1967 to January 1970

		• 1969: Petroleum Decree vests petroleum ownership in Nigerian state, and creates regulatory framework.

Table 1.1 continued

Main political watersheds	Major protests/ violent conflicts	Oil industry developments
• 1970–74: Second National Development Plan.		• 1971: establishment of Nigerian National Oil Corporation (NNOC), reorganised (1977) with enhanced powers as Nigerian National Petroleum. Corporation
		• 1971: Nigeria joins OPEC.
		• 1971–73: partial nationalisation of oil industry begins; Nigeria acquires equity status in all oil company operations.
• 1975 and 1976: military coups; Obasanjo military government initiates programme for return to civilian rule.		• 1977: formation of NUPENG oil workers union.
• 1979: hand-over to elected government under Second Republic constitution which replaces parliamentary with presidential system and brings in 'federal character' principle.		• 1979: constitution entrenches state ownership of petroleum, minerals and natural gas.
		• 1979: oil production peaks at 2.3 million bbl/d.
• 1983: Buhari military coup brings down Second Republic.	• 1980: paramilitary police crush peasant protests against Bakalori irrigation scheme in Sokoto.	

Table 1.1 continued

Main political watersheds	Major protests/ violent conflicts	Oil industry developments
• 1985: Babangida coup.	• 1980-85: religious insurrections by Maitatsine sect in northern cities.	
• 1986: Babangida regime launches Structural Adjustment Plan and proposals for eventual return to civilian rule.	• 1987: Muslim-Christian violence in Kaduna and Kano states. • 1988: riots against structural adjustment.	
• 1990: proclamation of Ogoni Bill of Rights. • 1986–93: elaborate orchestration of democratic transition programme by military regime.	• **1990: Mobile Police (paramilitary) violence against protestors in Umuechem (Niger Delta).**	• 1990-91: oil price recovery. • 1991: new MOUs offered to companies to attract investment.
• 1993: annulment of presidential election; installation of interim (Shonekan) administration • 1993: Abacha military coup. • 1995: hanging of Saro-Wiwa and eight other Ogoni activists; Nigeria suspended from Commonwealth.	• **1992-95: MOSOP protests and occupations of oil installations escalate; systematic campaign of state violence waged against Ogoni.** • **1994: oil workers strike, protesting election annulment and Abacha coup.**	• 1992: OMPADEC established to promote use of oil funds for development in Niger Delta. • 1992: Environmental Impact Assessment Decree. • 1993: Shell forced to close production in Ogoni. • 1994: Okigbo Commission estimates $12bn oil earnings 'disappeared' 1990-94. • 1995: revival of plans to construct LNG facility in Bonny.

Table 1.1 continued

Main political watersheds	Major protests/ violent conflicts	Oil industry developments
		• 1995: Petroleum Special Trust Fund initiated. • 1995: governments of Nigeria, Benin, Togo and Ghana endorse an agreement to develop the West Africa Gas Pipeline to convey gas from the Niger Delta, through 800 km of dedicated onshore and offshore pipelines.
• 1998: Kaiama Declaration by All-Ijaw Youth Conference. • 1998: death of Abacha and initiation of transition to democracy.	• **1997: Ijaw-Itsekiri conflict in Warri.** • 1997-98: Ife-Modakeke (intra-Yoruba) violence. • **1998-99: first and second Egbesu youth 'wars' in Ijaw areas of Niger Delta.** • **1999: Aguleri-Umuleri (intra-Igbo) violence.**	• 1998: explosion of ruptured pipeline kills 1000 people at Jesse near Warri. • 1999: constitution increases proportion of oil revenues distributed to states on basis of derivation to 13 per cent. • Federal Environmental Protection Agency scrapped and a new Federal Ministry of Environment created.
1999: enactment of new constitution; election of General Obasanjo as President and of new federal and state legislatures. Only three political parties are legally recognised to contest the elections.	• **1999: Ijaw-Ilaje conflict flares and spreads to Lagos.** • 2000: introduction of Sharia criminal law in Northern States triggers reciprocal religious/ethnic violence in Kaduna and in Lagos and Aba.	• Large oil spill from Mobil facilities in Akwa Ibom State pollutes Nigerian coastline. • 2001: Construction of West African Gas Pipeline begins.

Table 1.1 continued

Main political watersheds	Major protests/ violent conflicts	Oil industry developments
	• 2000: armed vigilantes known as the Bakassi boys funded by some state governments in the southeast kill many people believed to be criminals, but there are strong suggestions that victims were opponents of state governments.	• 2001: Niger Delta Development Commission (NDDC) established to replace OMPADEC.
• 2002: postponement of local elections. • 2002: recognition of more political parties brings the total to 30, following protracted legal cases against the government and the Independent National Electoral Commission (INEC).	• 2001: military reprisals against Tiv communities during Tiv-Jukun violence. • 2001: Jos religious killings • 2002: Bakassi boys outlawed by the Federal Government.	• 2002: Supreme Court ruling giving control of offshore petroleum deposits to Nigerian Federal Government.
• 2003: national elections return Obasanjo as President and his party, the Peoples Democratic Party (PDP), amid accusations of widespread vote rigging organized by the PDP, notably in the Niger Delta, where eight of the nine serving governors were returned to office.	**• 2003: oil company workers taken hostage and military personnel killed by persons believed to be oil bandits ('bunkerers') in creeks around Warri.**	• 2003: Managing Director of NDDC is replaced amid accusations of fraud or attempted fraud in the Commission. • 2003: two consecutive national strikes by the Nigeria Labour Congress to protest against increases in the prices of petroleum products.

Table 1.1 continued

Main political watersheds	Major protests/ violent conflicts	Oil industry developments
	• **2003: renewed conflict between the Ijaw, and Itsekiri over the delineation of wards triggers major electoral violence around Warri, threatening oil installations and leading to production losses.** • **2003: Deputy National Chairman of the main opposition party, the All Nigeria Peoples' Party, Chief Dikibo, murdered.**	• Presidential advisor on petroleum matters and former OPEC Secretary-General resigns from government, presumably over disagreement with President Obasanjo on reform of the NNPC. • 2003: appointment of a new group Managing Director for the NNPC, an ethnic Yoruba (his predecessor came from a minority ethnic group), is trailed by claims that the appointment is part of a domination agenda by the Yoruba. • 2003: Niger Delta activists attempt to block the renewal of passage rights for Shell pipelines in the Delta.
• 2004: Federal Government in conjunction with the Amnesty International and the World Bank launch the Extractive Industries Transparency Initiative (EITI) focusing mainly on the petroleum industry.	• **2004: two American and five Nigerian employees of Chevron murdered by oil 'bunkerers' in creek near Warri; further kidnappings of expatriate staff follow.**	• 2004: Engineer Omene, Managing Director of NDDC, removed after allegations of unauthorised expenditure; his supporters claim he was set up due to his insistence on transparency.

Table 1.1 continued

Main political watersheds	Major protests/ violent conflicts	Oil industry developments
• 2004: Federal Government establishes a committee to prepare for a national political conference following repeated public demands.	• **2004: assassinations in Rivers and Bayelsa States master-minded by different cult groups, principally those led by Asari Dokubo, leader of the so-called Niger Delta Volunteer Force, and Ateke Tom of the Niger Delta Vigilantes.** • **2004: Rivers State government proclaims law against cult members. Offers amnesty and arms-for-cash to those surrendering weapons.** • **2004: Ateke Tom surrenders some weapons, although many believe only a small fraction given up.** • **2004: President Obasanjo meets with Asari Dokubo to discuss ways of ending the violence and disruptions of oil operations; mass rally in Port Harcourt in Asari Dokubo's honour on his return.**	• 2004: long awaited NDDC master plan for the Niger Delta published. • Federal Government launches Extractive Industries Transparency Initiative (EITI) in collaboration with oil firms, World Bank and Amnesty International. EITI expected to collaborate with Soros Foundation's 'Publish What You Pay' campaign.

Table 1.1 continued

Main political watersheds	Major protests/ violent conflicts	Oil industry developments
• 2005: President of Senate and Ministers of Education and Housing removed after a series of housing scandals.	• **2005: struggles between political factions in Odioma, Bayelsa State lead to death of twelve local councillors. Odioma invaded and destroyed by detachment of soldiers from 'Operation Restore Hope', the military task force established to quell the Warri crisis.**	• 2005: new Chairman of NDDC, Ambassador Sam Edem, appointed to replace Chief Ugochukwu. Both considered Obasanjo loyalists. • 2005: Federal Government initiates National Political Reform Conference in Abuja, though its remit falls short of earlier demands for such a conference. It invites MOSOP to attend, after the latter warned Ogonis would not respect the outcome if they were excluded.

Note: Conflicts in oil-producing regions in bold.
Source: compiled by the authors.

highly conscious of the dangers of state and military disunity, and had a keen appreciation of the strategic role of petroleum. It was essentially a coalition between military and bureaucratic élites, but also included certain business interests and members of the former political class.

Nigerian soldiers and bureaucrats were ideologically disposed toward a centralising state, with development propelled by public spending and financed by swelling oil revenues. The 1970–74 and 1975–80 Development Plans proposed massive increases in public investment, some 2300 per cent more under the 1975–80 plan than in 1962–68.

The achievements of this state-building era should not be underestimated. The federation held together. Nigeria's civil war did not follow the course of other civil wars, where hostilities have ended only to re-ignite. Biafra was reintegrated with surprisingly little mutual recrimination – although deep traumas from the war still festered (see Harnet-Sievers et al 1997). During the 1970s, the economy expanded, albeit entirely because of the oil boom. The armed forces, bloated by the war, were retrenched and restructured, and military spending was restrained, despite a process of military modernisation.

However, a major opportunity was missed to invest the proceeds of oil in sustainable development, and to establish the Nigerian state on democratic foundations. Oil instead became the lubricant for protracted military governance and 'prebendal' politics.[9] The state became larger, more intrusive and more repressive; but also more volatile, corrupt, inefficient and vulnerable. Nigeria's economic problems were exacerbated by gross neglect of the agricultural sector, ill-conceived structural adjustment policies and failure to regulate the oil industry properly. These were not simply policy errors. They were also the outcome of money politics, cut-throat competition for power and resources, and systemic corruption, all intensified by massive injections of oil money into a political and administrative system that lacked the capacity to absorb them. Moreover a state funded by revenues extracted from oil multinationals could all too easily resist accountability for its failings to its taxpaying citizens.

State regulation of the petroleum sector: a problematic 'cohabitation' between the military regime and the oil multinationals

State building also involved the assertion of national control over the petroleum sector in an international climate in which OPEC (which Nigeria joined in 1971) had put oil multinationals on the defensive. Nigeria never established full state control over petroleum exploration and production. Instead it forged a fraught cohabitation between the state and the multinationals, which was later to drag Shell and other firms into the conflicts in the Niger Delta

The 1969 Petroleum Decree vested petroleum ownership in the

Nigerian state, and sketched out a regulatory framework for the industry. From 1971 the government began partial nationalisation of upstream operations through joint venture agreements with the oil companies, eventually raising its equity stake to a typical 60 per cent. The Nigerian National Oil Corporation (later the Nigerian National Petroleum Corporation) was established in 1971 and took over the government's equity stake in the joint ventures. It marketed and distributed oil on its own account and for some time also exercised government's regulatory functions. These commercial arrangements established a de facto political alliance between successive Nigerian regimes and oil multinationals. The problems of corporate governance and of Nigerian national governance became mutually and disastrously entangled. State regulation of the oil sector neither produced responsible corporate governance, nor ensured that the proceeds of oil were invested productively, least of all in the Niger Delta where local communities bore the brunt of large-scale environmental damage.

Regulation was supposed to maximise the government's revenue intake and to maintain a modicum of state control over the industry through joint venture and production by means of contracts administered by the NNPC and other regulatory bodies.[10] But there was creeping de facto deregulation during the 1980s and 1990s due to the corruption and inefficiency of the petroleum ministry and of NNPC, aggravated by the absence of accountability mechanisms. The government's bargaining power was undermined by its fiscal difficulties, in particular its failure to come up with the funds for NNPC to cover its share of joint venture exploration and production costs.

The regulatory framework for environmental impact, including oil spills and large-scale flaring, was rudimentary and inadequately enforced.[11] Government and NNPC complicity reinforced the oil companies' disregard of local communities and negligence concerning pollution. When members of local communities protested and began to occupy or damage oil installations, the oil firms were complicit in the military government's heavy-handed repression of protestors. The problem, however, was not just the weakness of the regulatory framework. Oil rents fostered *comprador* relations between state officials, their protégés and oil firms.[12] The oil multinationals found themselves in a de facto political alliance with the military government in confrontations with protesting Niger Delta communities.

How, if at all, did the oil companies benefit from this 'marriage made in hell' (Okonta and Douglas 2001)? The oil firms, especially Shell, which bore the brunt of the protests, have portrayed themselves as reluctant partners. Their relationships with the military governments were indeed fraught with tensions. But this does not seem to have prevented them from cooperating with the government during the troubles in the delta. Critics have claimed that oil firms profited from and indeed fostered Nigeria's political instability and corruption, which weakened the government's capacity to regulate the industry (see Frynas 1998; Detheridge and Pepple 1998, 2000). Yet it is clear that by the late 1990s Shell's global image, consumer relations and profits were seriously dented by the globalisation of the Niger Delta protests and the furore over the executions of Ken Saro-Wiwa and the 'Ogoni Nine'. This forced it to re-examine its corporate responsibilities, not only in Nigeria, but in all its global operations.

The vampire state: military kleptocracy and the oil sector

Oil reinforced contradictions that were already present in the Nigerian post-colonial state. Even under Nigeria's First Republic in the 1960s, political competition was never about alternative policy programmes or visions of development. Rather, the state was a vehicle for prebendal politics organised around the division of the national 'cake' among competing claimants, with little serious conception of the public good, or of the state's responsibility to generate growth or promote social equity. In other words it was refashioned as an instrument for private accumulation and money politics, where wealth, patronage and ethnic mobilisation determined access to political power.

This was undoubtedly intensified by the availability of oil surpluses, and took an extreme form under military rule. The military's centralising, state-building enterprise soon became the vehicle for a narrow class project of personal accumulation by political soldiers, federal and state bureaucrats and their business associates. Already endemic under previous administrations, corruption and money politics were systematised under the Babangida military regime and became outright plunder under General Abacha. Corruption also seeped into the oil firms, weakened their efforts at corporate governance and poisoned their relationships with Niger Delta communities.

Mechanisms for the misappropriation of oil rents included their diversion into 'special funds' controlled by the president (which also funded the less salubrious activities of state security agencies); bribes or 'taxation' paid on oil contracts, especially but not solely in downstream activities; extensive smuggling of refined petroleum across Nigeria's borders (facilitated by artificially depressed domestic prices); and illegal lifting of crude oil (bunkering); as well as secret accounts held by the NNPC (six such accounts in London were uncovered as early as 1997). Some indication of the scale of the diversion can be gleaned from estimates of funds put away by members of the Abacha family in foreign bank accounts.[13] Another indicator is the highly visible presence of retired officers, especially those who held government posts under military regimes, in Nigeria's business and political élite (Adekanye 1999).[14]

Failed development and the politics of socio-economic exclusion

Nigeria's conflicts have been sharpened by the alienation of groups and individuals excluded from the benefits of oil and of development. Oil dependence not only destroyed the agrarian export economy, it generated economic distortions, including large international debts, rampant inflation, stagnating per capita incomes, structural unemployment, inequality and widespread poverty.[15] During the 1980s, governments could argue that Nigeria's economic difficulties arose from falling oil prices, production and revenues after these had peaked in the boom years of the late 1970s. But when the economy failed to respond to improved oil earnings from the 1990s, it became evident that the problems were structural – in seeming contrast to oil producers like Indonesia, which had invested oil revenues in diversifying a more rapidly growing economy.

Nigeria's military governments also pursued contradictory and inconsistent policies of economic liberalisation. On the one hand they rejected IMF and World Bank economic stabilisation and adjustment packages, spurning the facilities offered to them. On the other hand they effected half-hearted public expenditure cuts, froze public sector employment, reduced state subsidies on mass consumption goods, including petrol, and sold public enterprises, despite public outcry. Poverty increased, most notably in oil-producing communities. In 2000, average per capita incomes were less in constant dollar terms (by some 7 per cent) than in 1970. Studies have reached varying conclusions about increases in poverty, some suggesting it was mainly the extremely poor who became even poorer, and others that impoverishment became more widespread (Ross 2003). One study suggested that while 17 million people lived below the poverty line of less than one dollar per day in 1980, that number almost quadrupled by 1996. In relative terms, 27 per cent of Nigerians lived in poverty in 1980, but in 1996, two-thirds of the population were below the poverty line, rising to almost 70 per cent in rural areas.

Rural impoverishment was also associated with an apparent shift from the politics of manipulating the peasantry to the politics of suppressing them. An early instance was the elected Shagari government's uncaring and violent response in 1980 to peasant protests against the Bakalori irrigation scheme in Sokoto State. The government response to protests by rural communities in the Niger Delta, when their interests conflicted with those of the petroleum industry, was even more brutal.

The national question and the betrayal of minorities: state creation,
ethnic tinkering and revenue allocation[16]

Identity politics and ethnic conflict preceded military rule, the civil war
and the oil boom. But they were reshaped and intensified by all three.
Even before independence in 1960, state and nation building involved
the articulation and reconciliation of many shifting layers of national,
regional, ethnic, local and religious identity.[17] The undiminished salience
of ethnicity and religion has reflected a search for a moral compass in a
society in permanent upheaval, where 'development' and oil have
wreaked havoc on values as well as livelihoods.[18] At the same time identities have been mobilised in competition for political power, patronage,
commercial advantage and access to land, oil and other assets.

Under military rule, federalism was a somewhat fictitious concept,
with military power conflicting with the underlying realities of a
multinational, multi-religious and multi-ethnic society. Nigeria's
regimes were constantly manipulating the structure and rules of the
federal system. On the eve of the civil war, the Gowon military government changed the federal structure of the country from four regions to
twelve states. Two of these, the Rivers and South-East States, catered
for minorities in the Niger Delta, which until then had formed part of
the Eastern Region. The latter, which had declared itself the State of
Biafra in May 1967, had been composed of the Igbo as the dominant
ethnic group, with two-thirds of the population, and several ethnic
minorities. Most of these minorities, including the Ijaw, Efik, Ibibio and
Ogoni, cast their lot with the federal government during the war.[19]
Their leaders included the Ogoni militant Ken Saro-Wiwa. The creation
of new states not only detached minorities from the Biafran cause but
also placed the bulk of Niger Delta petroleum resources outside Igbo-
controlled areas, undermining the secessionist claim that petroleum
could assure Biafra's viability as a state.

After the civil war the military government moved to secure a firm
grip over crude oil reserves and to reverse the centrifugal tendencies
the war had brought to a head. The proportion of oil revenues allocated
to states on the basis of derivation was reduced step by step, from
around 50 per cent at the time of the civil war, to 30 per cent in 1970, 25
per cent in 1977, 5 per cent in 1981 and a mere 1.5 per cent by 1984. The
bulk of the revenues were appropriated by the federal government
itself, reaching 57 per cent by 1977, with the rest being distributed
among the states according to complex calculations based on equality
among states, population and need.

State creation also focused ethnic politics squarely around petroleum and the sharing of oil revenues. There was a groundswell of
demands for new states to be created and for boundary controversies
arising from state creation to be settled. Starting with the creation of

seven more states in 1976, successive adjustments increased the number of states to the current 36, plus the Federal Capital Territory. Yet none of this benefited the peoples and communities of the Niger Delta, who felt they were short-changed by state creation and the revenue allocation system. Indeed they came to see themselves as the real losers from the civil war, all the more so as they bore the brunt of the environmental damage and social disruption caused by petroleum exploitation. Nor were they assuaged by later adjustments to increase the share of petroleum revenues allocated to development in the Niger Delta – to 3 per cent in 1992 and 13 per cent under the 1999 Constitution – since much of the money went to specially created agencies for the development of the delta, which were mired in the corruption and inefficiency of the military regime. Far from destroying the power blocs of Nigeria's dominant majorities, the restructured federal system reconsolidated their ascendancy at the centre. Subdivision into different states only increased their share of government patronage, funded (through the revenue allocation system) by oil revenues. The North's grip on the federal state was indeed tightened under the Buhari, Babangida and Abacha military administrations.

In sum, state creation and revenue allocation reinforced perceived regional disparities in the distribution of government spending, jobs, welfare and influence. This accelerated the political mobilisation of Nigeria's ethnic nationalities, including the minorities in oil-producing areas, and the rise of ethnic politics. As the new states often bisected ethnic communities, this laid the basis for future conflicts across and within state boundaries. States controlled by ex-minorities often contained their own minorities, such as the Ogoni, who were to play such a pivotal role in the Niger Delta protest movement.

The Nigerian state as agent of security or agent of insecurity?

Not only did Nigeria's military governments have a poor record in controlling the country's simmering conflicts, but part of the violence was state-induced. Ake et al have argued that many conflicts could be more accurately characterised as violent aggression by a privatised state, because:

> those who are aggressed, communities, ethnic groups, minorities, religious groups, peasants, the poor, counter élites, are often not in any dispute or even systematic interaction with the people who aggress them. The aggression often occurs in the routine business of projecting power, carrying out policies without consultation or negotiation with other parties, or spreading terror to sustain domination.
>
> (Ake et al not dated).

Yet the military could not and did not rule by the gun alone. Nigeria's military rulers sometimes proved adept at managing dissent and conflict through a mixture of persuasion, co-optation, patronage and ideological manipulation. Such tactics were especially evident during the protracted but ultimately abortive 'transition to democracy' under President Babangida before 1991. Potential ethnic, regional or religious opposition was headed off through redistributive mechanisms, including the 'federal principle' of proportional representation in central government posts. The rules of the political game that banned ethnically and regionally based parties were strengthened in successive constitutions.

When political manipulation failed to deter protests, however, these were suppressed by the use of military force, as in the Niger Delta. By the end of the military era it was clear that the state's legitimacy and its authority to govern were questioned as never before. There was not only a profound crisis of state legitimacy, but also one of state capacity. There was a hollowing-out of the entire government machine due to corruption, mismanagement and the under-resourcing of key state functions like policing or regulation of the oil sector. The armed forces, police and security agencies were not exempt, being in deep professional and institutional crisis when the military regime disbanded itself in 1998–99 (see Fayemi 2003:57–66). As we shall see, these legacies of state violence have been difficult to shake off even following transition to constitutional governance in 1999, continuing the violence and undermining any potential democratic dividend (Human Rights Watch 2002a, 2002b).

The pattern and escalation of violent conflicts

Nigeria's conflicts have been played out within a vertical array of interlocking political arenas. Nigeria's ramshackle government has remained the prime beneficiary of oil rents, the apex of decision making and the centre of patronage cascading down to other levels of governance. It has also controlled the country's interface with the oil companies, donors and international institutions. State governments and élites have been increasingly vocal, especially since the end of military rule, for instance demanding larger shares of oil revenues in Niger Delta States; or insisting on the introduction of extreme versions of Sharia criminal law in northern states.

Below the states are further layers of local government authorities and local communities, with varying structures. All are permeated by struggles for oil rents, patronage and the control of land and resources, nowhere more so than in the Niger Delta. Increasingly it has been these lower levels of the system which have asserted themselves by disengaging from state authority, seeking their own ways of extracting rents, engaging in vigilantism to provide their own security and turning to violence in conflicts with their neighbours and with the state.

One cannot be precise concerning the extent of political and criminal violence in Nigeria, all the more so as it is less internationally visible than in other African conflicts that have escalated into outright civil war. However it has been widespread, affecting many parts of the country, not just oil-producing regions. It resulted in an estimated 10,000 deaths from violence during the first four years following transition to constitutional rule in 1999, and shows few signs of abating.[20] In the Niger Delta alone annual deaths have continued to exceed the 1000 threshold used by the Stockholm Peace Research Institute to define 'armed conflict'. It has also caused widespread destruction of property and livelihoods, and large-scale population displacements. Estimates made by one of the authors in 1999 suggest that as many as a million and a quarter people were driven from their homes by political violence during the preceding decade (Ibeanu 1999a).

The sheer diversity of Nigeria's conflicts also makes it hard to fit them into a single conceptual or causal framework,[21] let alone spell out their relationships to oil. In Table 1.1 we distinguish the conflicts in oil-bearing regions from those elsewhere. Whilst it is only in the delta that oil exploration and production have been directly linked to political violence, the distorting impacts of oil on the state and political economy have contributed indirectly to violence everywhere in Nigeria. Violence, like oil, has permeated both the centre of the political system and its multiple peripheries. Parochial struggles within local communities on the basis of class, generation, clan or locality have triggered or interacted with wider conflicts, as we shall see in the case of factional struggles among the Ogoni in the Niger Delta. Communities have also clashed against each other, notably when land and resources have risen in value, as in oil-producing areas, or when inter-communal boundaries have been contested, as during the process of state creation.

Conflicts between 'indigenes' and 'settlers' – like the urban riots and massacres which have scarred northern cities, or the Itsekiri–Ijaw–Urhobo clashes in the Niger Delta – have originated from internal migrations in search of economic opportunities. So-called settlers may have been resident for generations and even share common ethnic origins with the indigenous communities, as with the Ife–Modakeke violence in Ife. Yet they still tend to be perceived as outsiders, competing for land, government amenities and political power.

Conflicts with ostensibly religious or ethnic dimensions also have a long history. They include the recent disturbances triggered by the adoption of Sharia criminal law by northern states. Violence has also arisen from subaltern class-based or generational discontents, as when rural development programmes, oil operations or economic adjust-ment programmes have destroyed livelihoods; such conflicts have often been redefined – as in northern cities or in the Niger Delta – in terms of the discourses of community, tribe or religion. Recent years have seen a dangerous escalation of privatised criminal and vigilante violence, reflecting and reinforcing state failure to ensure law and public order. At the same time vigilante and criminal groups have also been manipulated by state and federal politicians. The Bakassi Boys in Nigeria's south-east, the Niger Delta Volunteer Force and the Niger Delta Vigilantes are prominent examples (Human Rights Watch and Centre for Law Enforcement Education 2002), all of them at one point or another sponsored by state governors, who deployed them against political opponents.

Far from diminishing the violence, it seems that democratisation has been linked to its spread. Under military rule numerous local conflicts arose from struggles to control elected local authorities (Ibeanu 1999a:172–4). The opening of political space for the expression of pent-up grievances during the transition to constitutional government in 1998–99 brought a further spate of conflicts. Federal, state and local elections in 2003 and 2004 saw another wave of violence, especially but not solely in the Niger Delta, compromising many election results though not triggering the wider escalation some had feared (see Proceedings of the Retreat on the Electoral Process and Violence 2002).

OIL AND CRISIS IN THE NIGER DELTA

Nigeria has been unique in its vigorous grassroots protests against the petro-state and oil multinationals. Protest movements developed new forms of popular mobilisation, based on a political discourse of self-determination. They not only sought compensation for lost oil revenues and environmental damage. They also demanded local control of petroleum resources, corporate responsibility of oil firms and the renegotiation of the political contract between the state and its citizens ('true federalism').

For far from bringing prosperity to the Niger Delta, oil exploration and production caused large-scale environmental degradation, destroyed rural livelihoods and aggravated poverty. It was all the more destructive because it occurred in densely settled forest, agricultural and creek areas. State neglect of the concerns of Delta communities was compounded by the skewed distribution of oil revenues, diverted into 'development' (in practice élite accumulation) elsewhere in Nigeria. But even the elected post-military regime has failed to satisfy the protest movements' demands. At the same time the movements themselves have become corrupted by the political economy of oil. Demonstrations, takeovers of oil installations, attacks on pumping stations and pipelines, and kidnappings of foreign and

Nigerian oil workers have increasingly been used by 'youths', community 'big men', political entrepreneurs and armed criminal gangs to extract their own shares of resource rents. They have also become increasingly violent, pitting communities against each other, as well as opening deep rifts within them.

Impoverishment and environmental degradation

Nigeria's emergence as a major petroleum producer has done little for the welfare of the people of the Niger Delta. There has been glaring immiseration according to all social indicators. Only about 27 per cent of households in the delta have access to safe drinking water and 30 per cent to electricity, both below the national average. There are 82,000 people per doctor, rising to 132,000 in some areas, more than three times the national average of 40,000 (Ibeanu 2002:163). While 76 per cent of Nigerian children attend primary school, only 30–40 per cent attend in some parts of the delta.

Deprivation is aggravated by the environmental damage caused by crude oil exploration and production. Pollution from oil spills has destroyed marine life and crops, made water unsuitable for fishing and rendered large areas of farmland unusable. Oil pipelines form a mesh across farmlands and are conducive to acid rain, deforestation and destruction of wildlife. Gas flaring is said to release 35 million tonnes of carbon dioxide and 12 million tonnes of methane into the atmosphere annually (Mittee 1997:6–9). Although oil companies have attempted to reduce flaring, it remains worse than in most other oil-producing countries.[22]

Popular resistance and state violence: the Ogoni case

The Ogoni (one of the Niger Delta's smaller minorities) and their popular organisation, Movement for the Survival of Ogoni People (MOSOP) formed in 1990, became the flagship for a wider popular mobilisation, which spread to other delta communities during the following decade.

MOSOP's distinctive approach was to mobilize the Ogoni and peacefully confront both the oil companies and the military regime. Its founders were accomplished and well-respected members of the élite. Ken Saro-Wiwa had been the administrator of Bonny during the civil war and Education Commissioner of Rivers State. Dr G.B. Leton, the founding president, had served as a federal commissioner under the military government.

MOSOP published an Ogoni Bill of Rights on 26 August 1990, claiming that Ogoniland had provided Nigeria with $30 billion in oil money since 1958, for which the Ogoni people had received almost nothing in return. It complained that:

the Ogoni languages of Gokana and Khana are underdeveloped and are about to disappear, whereas other Nigerian languages are being forced on us. ... That the Shell Petroleum Development Company of Nigerian Limited does not employ Ogoni people at a meaningful or any level at all. ... That the search for oil has caused severe land and food shortages in Ogoni, one of the most densely populated areas of Africa. ... That Ogoni people lack education, health and other social facilities. That it is intolerable that one of the richest areas of Nigeria should wallow in abject poverty and destitution.

(MOSOP 1992:11).

MOSOP committed itself to the peaceful pursuit of its objectives by mobilising support and raising awareness about the plight of the Ogoni across Nigeria and in the international community. With Saro-Wiwa as its public relations officer, it mounted a brilliant media campaign. Saro-Wiwa used his local and international contacts as a writer and journalist to publicise the struggle and embarrass the military government and the oil companies, especially Shell. As he put it, 'by the time I finish, Nigeria is going to be ashamed standing before the council of the world' (cited in Ibeanu 1999a:21) – a prophesy which was tragically fulfilled by the international outrage aroused by his trial and execution in 1995.

Yet MOSOP's plan for a peaceful campaign underestimated the military regime's anxiety about dissent in oil-producing areas, as well as the violence of its response, which took four main forms. First, there was the surveillance, arrest and detention of Ogoni leaders, notably Saro-Wiwa, Dr Leton and Ledum Mittee. Second, divide and rule tactics were used to foster disagreements within the MOSOP leadership and among the Ogoni people. These became so bitter that they culminated in the killing of four prominent Ogoni leaders in May 1994. The military seized upon this killing as a perfect opportunity to solve the Ogoni problem, by trying Saro-Wiwa and other MOSOP leaders for murder. Third, the government intervened to suppress the ethnic clashes it had itself stirred up between the Ogoni and their neighbours. In 1993–94 alone there were at least three such clashes,[23] involving loss of life, destruction of villages and forced population displacement. Finally, there was direct military and police repression; extra-judicial killings, flogging, torture, rape, looting and extortion by security forces were widely reported. The Rivers State government established an Internal Security Task Force, with a de facto mandate to employ systematic violence against the Ogoni. Its commander Major (later Lt Colonel) Okuntimo was to brag on primetime national television that the army taught him 204 ways of killing people, but he had only used three against the Ogoni.

The rise and implosion of MOSOP

MOSOP evolved through a number of phases. Initially Ogoni intellectuals and professionals articulated the disaffection of the mass of their people, epitomised in the Ogoni Bill of Rights. During a second phase the movement was consolidated into six zones (based on the six Ogoni kingdoms), two special zones and ten federating organisations such as those for women (FOWA), youths (NYCOP) and chiefs. Roles and offices were parcelled out among militants, though this subsequently gave rise to cliques and struggles among loyalists to control the organisation. Implosion characterised the third phase, when simmering power struggles and personality clashes came to a head.

The involution and implosion of MOSOP, fostered by the military regime, climaxed on 21 May 1994, when an irate crowd of Ogoni youths attacked and killed four prominent chiefs. The seeds of these incidents had been sown in a series of events in 1993. When MOSOP had controversially called for an Ogoni boycott of the June 1993 presidential elections, supposed to usher in a democratic regime, the Movement's leadership had split into two. Dr Leton and Chief Kobani resigned their positions as president and vice-president of the movement, accusing Saro-Wiwa of being brash, confrontational and authoritarian. They also claimed that he was turning the National Youth Council of the Ogoni People (NYCOP) into a private army to intimidate his opponents and that there was a plot by the Saro-Wiwa faction to kill 13 Ogoni leaders, among them some of those who were later killed on 21 May 1994.

In early 1995, Ken Saro-Wiwa, who by then had become MOSOP's leader, Ledum Mittee, its vice-president and eleven other Ogoni activists were charged before a tribunal with involvement in murder. The accused were held in army custody despite being civilians; they were denied bail; their lawyers were harassed by security men and the tribunal refused the tendering of vital evidence. At one point, the leading defence counsel, Chief Gani Fawehinmi, a prominent human rights lawyer, abandoned the case citing the infringement of due process. The show trial ended with Saro-Wiwa and eight others being convicted and condemned to death. Before the accused could lodge an appeal, they were executed on 10 November 1995. This stunned Nigerians, as well as appalling the international community. It was widely believed there had been an a priori decision to kill the MOSOP leaders, whether or not the evidence stood up in court.

The implosion of MOSOP and the executions shattered the Ogoni struggle. In the trial, the principal prosecution witnesses included some of their own people (Civil Liberties Organisation 1996:194). The execution of the Ogoni Nine shocked a majority of Ogoni people and spread fear among activists. Many were detained for long periods; others fled into exile.

The spread of community militancy in the Niger Delta

Despite MOSOP's implosion, the movement inspired other ethnic nationalities to articulate their own demands. The nightmare scenario for the military was the entire Niger Delta exploding in an anti-state, anti-oil company confrontation. As early as 1990 the village of Umuechem had become the first practical example of a policy of violent suppression of community dissent. Villagers had decided on a protest march to Shell facilities, demanding the same things that have become a refrain in the Niger Delta: schools, water, electricity and jobs. Shell requested security backup from the state government, provided in the form of the dreaded paramilitary Mobile Police. Over 80 villagers, including the traditional ruler, were killed and over 400 houses were razed. This became the pattern for many other clashes between state and oil company security services and local communities in the Niger Delta (Human Rights Watch 1999).

Saro-Wiwa and other MOSOP leaders were active in forging broad alliances with other Niger Delta communities. Groups like the Ijaw, Urhobo, Ogbia and Ogba formulated their own bills of rights. Even after MOSOP's brutal suppression, pan-Niger Delta alliances continued to expand. Especially prominent was the struggle of the Ijaw, the largest group in the Niger Delta (and the fourth largest in Nigeria). What became known as the first *Egbesu* war began toward the end of the Abacha military dictatorship when an Ijaw youth leader was detained without trial on the orders of the military governor of Bayelsa State for distributing 'seditious' documents questioning the governor's financial probity. A group of youths, said to be members of an Ijaw cult, the *Egbesu*,[24] stormed Government House, where their leader was held, and set him free. Policemen and soldiers believed that members of the cult were able to break in because they wore charms that made them impervious to bullets. This enhanced the profile of the youth cult, and encouraged more young people in Bayelsa, where youth unemployment was high, to join the protests. The success of the *Egbesu* youth tapped into wider demands by the Ijaw for more petroleum revenues, articulated by other groups like the Ijaw National Council (INC) and the Movement for the Survival of Ijaw Ethnic Nationality (MOSIEN), whose formation had been influenced by MOSOP and Ken Saro-Wiwa. The latter continues to be regarded as an icon of the Ijaw as well as the Ogoni struggle.

General Abacha's death in June 1998 opened the political space for Ijaw and other demands to become more openly articulated and vigorously pursued. The first *Egbesu* war had guaranteed a central role for the youth, confirmed in a spate of hijacks of oil installations by Ijaw youths. Indeed in some cases armed youths who were employed by oil companies to defend oil installations carried out some of the hijacks, these ragtag armies turning their weapons against their employers for ransom.

ate, which marginalised the communities in the first place
of this alliance remain a potent source of insecurity and
e Niger Delta.

military regimes misappropriated oil revenues on a truly
e, repressed dissent and fanned the flames of community
ded to this were their multiple acts of omission. These
ir dismal failure to regulate the oil operators, to invest in
Delta's development, and to provide public goods, like
es, clean water, education and security. As one oil execu
d it, years of state neglect meant that in many parts of th
he idea of government hardly exists. ... [T]here is hardl
ent presence of any kind, whether you are talking abou
government, the states, or even local authorities.' The o
pts to distance themselves from the excesses of the mil
by playing the non-political card – claiming that they ha
of politics and could not oppose the regime without jeop
iness operations – do not convince. The reality on th
that they were entangled with the state at many levels.
, oil funded a large and corrupt state apparatus, and lubr
tionship between oil multinationals and the state. So clo
tionship that it was sometimes 'difficult to distinguis
from the oil companies, since theirs was more than just a
il firms tended to become surrogates for an absent
vernment. At the same time they became over-relia
mobile police, army and naval detachments to prote
tions and to suppress community protests.
rface with government must also be understood in t
regulatory system introduced during the oil boom yea
and this secured partial nationalisation of the oil and g
endowed federal government agencies, notably
a range of regulatory powers – also enabling military a
cream off oil revenues to feed a corrupt and bloat
apparatus. On the other hand, the actual business of
extraction and marketing abroad largely remained in
government's joint venture technical partners, the larg
Shell Petroleum Development Company, Mobil Produc
mited, Elf Petroleum Nigeria Limited, Chevron Nige
Nigerian Agip Oil Company Limited. These compar
contractors carried out the great bulk of oil explorat
ion and thus interacted directly with local communi
perated. Niger Delta communities held them responsi
ment's as well as their own neglect and human rig
lling them that 'we don't see the government, but we
ed 'the logic of community protests was that by puttir
ction, they could get the federal government to sit up

This phase of resistance, as the youths called it, culminated in a Grand
Convention of Ijaw youths in Kaiama town in December 1998. The meeting issued the Kaiama Declaration addressed to the Nigerian government and oil companies, raising issues of control of oil resources and
environmental protection. The declaration gave oil companies until the
end of the month to withdraw from Ijawland (Ijaw Youth Council 1999).
In his 1999 New Year broadcast, General Abubakar, Abacha's successor,
warned of military action against the youths. There was a massive military build-up in Bayelsa State, including the positioning of frigates in the
Gulf of Guinea. The second *Egbesu* war followed, when military units in
Yenagoa, the capital, confronted Ijaw youths participating in a cultural
festival. The ensuing violence lasted over a week, many youths and
others lost their lives, property worth millions of naira was destroyed
and large numbers of people were displaced.

Protest movements and conflict entrepreneurs

In principle, the transition to democracy in 1999 should have opened
the political arena to Niger Delta protest movements, facilitated negotiations with federal and state governments and with oil firms and
reversed the spread of violence. The reality has been much more
complex and problematic.

On the one hand protest movements and youths have been brought
into stakeholder meetings and consultations by the oil operators and
the government. A Niger Delta Youth Stakeholders Workshop organised by the Nigerian National Petroleum Corporation in Port Harcourt
in March 2004 (AAP and NNPC 2004) was addressed by President
Obasanjo himself, as well as the governor of Rivers State, the Presidential Advisor on Petroleum and Energy and NNPC's Managing Director,
and by Oronto Douglas, the leading activist and co-author of the
scathing critique of Shell, *Where Vultures Feast* (Okonta and Douglas
2001). Oil activists have been forging relationships with federal and
state legislators, especially the Senate and House committees covering
petroleum, energy and the environment. And there has been some
progress in meeting their demands, at least at a declaratory level.

At the same time there have been disturbing signs of violence and
corruption being entrenched in the Niger Delta as never before. Factional
disputes have wracked the main umbrella protest and youth movements, linked to power struggles at the state and federal levels – for
instance when leading activists opposed the re-nomination of Bayelsa
State's governor at the 2003 elections on the grounds of his corruption.
The 2003 campaign was marred by large-scale poll rigging, inter-ethnic
violence and attacks on oil installations. Violence around Warri, linked to
disputes over electoral boundaries, brought operations in Delta State to
a halt, resulting in shutdowns at two oil refineries. Estimated losses from

deferred production in 2003 were over $2 billion, not far short of those sustained during the 1999 protests.

Many Niger Delta communities remain torn by disputes between competing groups of chiefs, youths and cult leaders, in the great majority of cases linked to struggles for access to oil sector community development funding, jobs and contracts. Factional and inter-ethnic disputes have always plagued Niger Delta communities and protest movements, not least those which tore MOSOP apart during the 1990s.[25] But struggles over oil rents and the attendant corruption and violence are being carried to new levels and embedded in the fabric of Niger Delta societies. These struggles are amplified by the contest for political power, whose stakes are magnified by the increased revenues available to state governments under the new allocation arrangements. Ballot rigging, intimidation and 'unacknowledged' violence were more widespread in the Niger Delta during the 2003 elections than in any other part of Nigeria (Human Rights Watch 2004).[26] State governors and state branches of the ruling PDP have been accused of distributing weapons and of deploying armed militias, vigilante groups and criminal elements linked to oil bunkering to terrorise opponents. The federal government itself has responded to community crises with arbitrary force – as when army units razed the community of Odioma to the ground in early 2005, following the deaths of twelve councillors in community clashes.

Most ominous of all has been the rise of increasingly well-armed groups like the Niger Delta Volunteer Force referred to at the outset of this chapter. Their leaders, like Alhaji Mujahid Dokubo Asari and Ateke Tom, talk the same talk of resource control and self determination as the leaders of the protest movements. They are being taken seriously by the political authorities. Dokubo Asari was even welcomed back from his late 2004 talks with President Obasanjo by a mass rally in the streets of Port Harcourt. Yet they are involved in oil bunkering and other criminal endeavours, have links to cult activities, are relatively well armed and compete with rival conflict entrepreneurs to control extortion opportunities. In all these respects they are reminiscent of conflict entrepreneurs like Liberia's Charles Taylor, or Sierra Leone's Foday Sankoh – in contrast to the earlier and more idealistic generation of Niger Delta activists, like Saro-Wiwa.

CORPORATE RESPONSIBILITY AND THE GOVERNANCE OF OIL

Multinationals and the Nigerian state: reforming the 'alliance made in hell'?

The initial response of oil multinationals to Niger Delta militancy during the military era was to support state repression. It is common

knowledge that they made payments
financial and other backing to the s
communities in check. But these pol
able, especially during the dying y
Ogoni crisis, the execution of the Ogo
nity resistance elsewhere in the Nig
giants, as well as the military regime,
for degrading the environment, ex
supporting the repression of protest.

The case against the major oil cor
damning (see in particular Human F
and Douglas 2001). It had a tangible
cially for Shell, which bore the brunt c
a worldwide review of its policies, in
communities.[27] In 1997 it published
Principles'. Its Nigerian subsidiary,
'People and the Environment' report:
expanded community developmen
environmental monitoring. Other oil
varying enthusiasm and impact on t

According to the oil corporations,
has been partnership between all sta
try, including the oil communities, t
and the corporations themselves. N
(MOUs) have been negotiated to def
benefits of the various stakeholders.
situation in which the companies
Nigerian federal government and n
state authorities. MOUs have typi
contribute to the development of hos
in return to protect installations
dialogue, with the government as
have criticised MOUs on a number
have tended to regard them as atter
the wider demands advanced by d
rights. Fundamental issues, such as
oil, and community involvement i
have not been addressed by the N
remains that good community relatic
lifting oil unmolested. According t
company 'does more than it would r
... because if we didn't, we wouldn'
In our view, concentrating solely
the oil firms is not enough. For this d
between arrogant and irresponsible c

take notice.' So when community protests erupted, it was, as another executive put it, 'our offices, our installations, our staff, who have been held to ransom.'[30]

The normal contractual arrangement in longer established onshore fields has been the joint venture contract. MOUs between the joint venture partners have split revenues into three parts.[31] First, 'cost oil', the funds set aside for the joint ventures' operating costs and investment. Second, 'profit oil', the margin shared among the private shareholders. Third, 'government oil', the government take in taxes, royalties and equity share. The companies have typically received fixed margins for their costs and profits within defined oil price ranges, and the government has taken the rest.

In negotiations with government concerning investments in the fast-expanding offshore sector, oil firms have tended to prefer production-sharing contracts. Under these they undertake all the investment in exploration and development, and assume the risks – but are guaranteed a larger share of the oil upfront until investment costs are recouped. The advantage of production sharing for government is that it does not have to fund investments upfront, and is less exposed to risks. Its disadvantage is that the flow of royalty and profit payments is deferred, potentially aggravating budget deficits and cutting into spending programmes. Government revenues, especially those from the joint ventures, have remained highly exposed to fluctuations in global oil prices. In good times the state has benefited from substantial windfalls – though these have tended to feed government corruption (including 'presidential oil'[32] creamed off under Presidents Babangida and Abacha) rather than being invested in development. In bad times, fluctuations have exposed government to intense financial pressures, reinforced economic decline and made the economy hostage to the stabilisation and structural adjustment policies insisted on by IFIs and donors.

The regulatory framework established in the 1970s has proved defective. It has not prevented abuses by the oil firms, nor has it been effective against the government's own abuses. Enforcement has been made harder by the endemic corruption surrounding government and the oil sector. When the peoples and communities of the Niger Delta have protested, the government has tended to back the oil companies.[33] Critics of oil multinationals go further, arguing that, at least in the military era, they actually stood to benefit from political instability and conflicts in the Niger Delta. A corrupt, unaccountable and unstable military government, the critics contend, was not really interested in subjecting the companies to stringent regulation. Nor did it assert itself in negotiations over the terms for joint venture and production-sharing contracts, thus allowing oil companies to enjoy profits from their Nigerian operations in excess of those they could obtain elsewhere.[34] A rather more credible charge is that oil firms became complacent and risk-averse because of their massive sunk costs, reinforced by a poorly enforced regulatory regime and revenue-sharing arrangements that shielded them from the full impact of global oil price fluctuations. They were encouraged in their complacency by the weakness of the NNPC, its closeness to government and its mixture of regulatory and commercial functions, which made it neither a reliable joint venture partner nor an effective overseer of the industry (Khan 1994).

The oil companies are now willing to own up to past errors.[35] But they reject the accusation of actually profiting from military governance or from the Niger Delta conflicts.[36] They argue that Nigeria is a high-cost production environment (Khan 1994:85–6), and that government misappropriation of oil revenues in the military period tended to starve the industry of investment due to NNPC's failure to finance its joint venture obligations. At the same time they assert that 'community problems' disrupted their exploration and production, which reached a peak in 1999, when Shell had to defer production of almost 90 million barrels of crude oil, or roughly 30 per cent of its normal annual production.[37] But over the longer run, the principal constraint on the oil companies' output has remained Nigeria's OPEC quota, rather than such conflict-related output losses.

Oil firms do not deny their reluctance to confront the military regime, for instance over the hanging of the Ogoni Nine. But they hold that as business enterprises they would have incurred substantial risks in challenging a sovereign government. According to industry sources, senior oil executives worked behind closed doors to contain the Abacha government's excesses and to nudge it toward reform. Shell's Managing Director and other oil industry notables, like the former interim president Chief Shonekan, played key roles in the Vision 2010 fora that discussed the country's political and economic future.[38] They also lobbied for the increase in oil revenues allocated to states on the basis of derivation to 13 per cent, which was introduced in 1999. They also claim they had little leverage over the military government. As a senior executive put it:

> We said to government, if you don't solve these problems [in the Niger Delta] your revenues will not be materialising. We argued it was not just an industrial problem and the government shared responsibility for resolving it. ... You might think that [our] Managing Director was always on the hotline to Abacha. But it wasn't so. The number of times the Managing Director tried to contact the President about our concerns, but got no response was countless.[39]

By the late 1990s, however, the damage to the oil firms' corporate reputations was so extensive that they had little alternative but to reassess their relationship with the Nigerian state. By the time of President Abacha's death in 1998, the commercial losses arising from cooperation with the military regime may have exceeded the gains of cooperating with it. Transition to an elected government in 1999 got the oil companies off the hook.

Nigerian oil company executives seem, however, to have had few illusions that democracy alone could undo all the legacies of government neglect and corporate irresponsibility. The oil economy hastened 'the collapse of the local economies. All the traditional institutions came down like ninepins. The nub of the problem was and still is the lack of any positive impact of the oil economy on the local economy.' Before the Niger Delta erupted in the 1990s, oil companies had 'no proper understanding of the environment in which they worked. ... They knew little about the problems of fishing communities and did not trouble to ask.' The company was 'inward-looking, with a strong organisational culture. It concentrated on its core business. Its mindset was to be deaf, dumb and even a bully in pursuit of its commercial interests. So it has been necessary [for its public affairs division] to persuade it of the need for change, and that it was part of the problem itself.' Indeed some managers felt MOUs signed with chiefs and elders may have deepened the fissures between oil operators and communities. They reinforced the tendency for oil companies to become a 'surrogate government, replacing a state, which has abdicated its development responsibilities. A community assistance approach based upon pay-offs to communities, tended if anything to reinforce community grievances and create an "appropriations syndrome"':

> Frankly, many of those involved in our community development programmes didn't know what they were doing. Money was put into projects or payments were made to chiefs, without consulting people on the ground or thinking about sustainable development. [The tendency was to] respond to grievances by asking, 'what can we do for you, what can we pay you?' But the peoples and communities of the delta found this insulting. ... Easy money breeds a culture of compensation and encourages the social fragmentation of communities. In Nembe, for example, where the youths were once together in a single youth organisation, there are now no less than twenty-six youth groups, so that even if one paid off one or two, the others would demand a share and this is a recipe for conflict.[40]

Oil firms and insecurity in the Niger Delta

Not only have the oil companies found themselves replacing a neglectful government, they have been dragged into the security maelstrom created by the inept and repressive handling of protest and conflict. 'Many of the company's security problems', it was put to us by one executive, 'have arisen from the dilemmas and difficulties of getting the government to function properly.' Table 1.2, derived from an oil company security assessment framework, provides a graphic picture of the threats oil firms perceive themselves facing, and spells out the implications for company operations. However only during the *Egbesu* wars of 1999 and during the 2003 electoral violence around Warri did they believe 'lawlessness and anarchy' seriously compromised their operations.[41]

Oil firms claim that they became more and more involved in security questions because 'under a military head of state, the government itself was not interested in providing a sustainable civilian police force; in fact it starved the police of resources.' At the same time the heavy-handed methods of the Nigerian armed forces and the Mobile Police reflected upon the oil firms too, for 'when government security agencies over-reacted, it was us [oil companies], who were blamed.'

Oil operators and contractors still provide back-up – transport, logistics and funding – to state security agencies, though trying to avoid the kind of high-profile cooperation that became so controversial during the Ogoni crisis. They employ security consultants, maintain their own security departments, and employ supposedly unarmed Supernumerary Police, normally on secondment from the Nigerian Police Force.[42] This raises important issues about the arming and rules of engagement of what are widely regarded as paramilitary forces (see Human Rights Watch 1999).[43] Perceptions by delta communities are coloured by the vast disparity between the handful of police, who supposedly assure their safety, and the far more lavish police and security presence surrounding oil installations.[44]

In sum, oil firms have willy-nilly participated in the governance of the Niger Delta, its development and its security. Despite claiming that 'politically [we] are a toothless bulldog,' a former senior executive admitted that 'we can't operate in this environment, without influencing what is being done in government.' Thus the companies have continued to ventilate their security concerns at all levels of government, from the presidency down, including ministers, state governors, oil industry regulatory bodies and the police and security agencies.

During the military era, this could not but involve some collusion with the military regime. When asked what lessons they had learned from the mistakes of the military era, managers echoed that:

> we must slowly extricate ourselves from being '*in loco governmentalis*'. For industry reasons and for constitutional reasons this is untenable. Oil firms must concentrate their resources on

Table 1.2 Oil operating company security scenarios

Indicator level	Security state	Typical incidents	Protection measures	Business impact
1	**Law and order**	Petty crime	Security awareness	'Business as usual'
		Some violent crime	Physical security	
------------		Protests/ demos (non-violent)	Guarding	
			Contingency plans	
		Industrial actions	Standard operating procedures (SOPs)	
2			Community relations	
			Liaison (intra/inter)	
			Communica-tions	
3			Law enforcement	
	Low risk level			
2000-02	**Isolated lawlessness**	Blockades/ lock outs	Briefings	Skeleton manning of exposed sites
4		Inter-communal conflict	Information gathering and sharing	Some shut downs
	(AREA 'T')	Armed robbery		Review of logistics
	Area B / General	Piracy Intimidation	Dialogue with communities	Morale

Table 1.2 continued

Indicator level	Security state	Typical incidents	Protection measures	Business impact
5 **Early 2003**	(AREA 'A') **Medium** risk level Area C	Vandalism Site invasions Illegal detention Extortion	Minimise exposure Escorts Selective use of government forces	Some production loss
6		Bunkering		
7	**Lawlessness & Anarchy**	Hostage taking Kidnapping Hijacking Sabotage	Deployment of government forces Repatriation of non-essentials (nationals and expatriates) Restrict business visits	International reputation issue Downsizing Review business investment
8 **Late 1999**		Proliferation of armed groups Riots Killings/ assassinations Inter-commu-nal fighting Attacks on government forces	State of emergency declared	Major production loss ('force majeure')
9	**High** risk level	Terrorism Loss of law enforcement control		

Table 1.2 continued

Indicator level	Security state	Typical incidents	Protection measures	Business impact
10	**Civil War**	Guerrilla operations	Staff evacuation	Minimal business operations
		Widespread armed attacks	Military control	National management only
		Fighting government forces		
	Critical risk level			

Source: Unpublished internal oil company document of 2003. The dates in the left-hand column are the company's assessments of when security threats reached particular levels, e.g. isolated lawlessness in 2000/2 or lawlessness and anarchy in 1999. Bold type as in original document.

what they do most effectively, by concentrating on business development, rather than being providers of services. ... The onus should not be on us to resolve conflicts; it should be on the elected representatives at each level of government.

Is democratic governance encouraging better corporate governance?

Both oil executives and some of their civil society critics believe democracy has 'opened spaces for dialogue and discussion',[45] even if these spaces have not always been used to best advantage. Put at its most optimistic, 'if democracy thrives, there will be no more Ogoni conflicts.' Liberalisation has 'created a more enabling environment in which it is easier to work with federal and state governments':

> The Obasanjo government is open compared to the military regime, and also spreads the stakes of oil more widely in oil-producing areas. Larger revenues for state and local governments have helped to keep agitation to the minimum. It also means ... aggression against [oil companies] may shift to state and local governments.

Democratic governance should in principle assure a more transparent regulatory environment. But transparency and accountability have until recently been resisted both by the operators and by government agencies, each tending to blame the other. According to one executive:

> both at the centre and in the states the executive is too powerful and the legislature, especially in the states, is a rubber stamp. Governors can easily influence legislatures by handing out contracts, or withholding funds from recalcitrant representatives. ... All this affects law and order. Sometimes you'll find the executive is behind people stirring up trouble, and a phone call to Government House may be needed to call them off.

One major difference from the military era is increased oversight by the federal parliament, which has used it to influence the oil industry's community and environmental programmes. As a senator put it, because 'we have to scrutinise the NNPC budget, it is our responsibility to ensure it is properly used.' Federal legislators also facilitate the resolution of community disputes 'to save the costs and problems of potential litigations and violent disturbances'.[46] For example, when an occupation closed a flow station in Nembe, three senators negotiated with community representatives and oil operators to agree on a new MOU, allowing its reopening. Nevertheless what legislators can achieve has been severely constrained, in part by the limited facilities of Senate and House of Representative committees, but also by the manifold contradictions of Nigerian politics. Legislators have scarcely been impartial in the many factional and political disputes dividing oil-producing states and local communities. Most were involved in the political infighting, electoral disputes and efforts to unseat state governors, which created a heated political atmosphere during the 2003 elections.

When the 'Publish What You Pay' campaign (backed by the Soros Foundation) visited Nigeria in 2003 it argued that the major oil companies have a responsibility to take an open stand on the use of oil funds for development, and to use their leverage to ensure a fair return for Niger Delta communities. But the companies have remained wary of the implications of greater transparency. When asked whether the 'Publish What You Pay' proposals might be tried out in Nigeria, the response was far from enthusiastic: 'You forget we are a private company' was a typical comment in our own interviews. Since then Nigeria has signed up to the Extractive Industries Transparency Initiative (EITI), though it remains to be seen in practice how much this will change government and corporate behaviour.

Meanwhile oil firms continue to downplay their room for manoeuvre and capacity to influence government:

The idea that just because the country is 95 per cent dependent on oil, this gives the oil firms leverage and they should use it is very simplified. On the ground it isn't so easy. It is also a very political thing. ... Nevertheless companies can legitimately make their views heard, and say to government that it must address the needs of the communities, to keep oil revenues flowing.

That of course is something the companies were either unable or unwilling to do under military governance. Moreover, reforms would not necessarily stem the tide of violence, which is also rooted in the tensions of governance in a multicultural society and is by no means confined to oil-producing areas. As an oil executive complained, 'in Kaduna they see it as sectarian violence, but in Warri they pin it on the oil companies.' Even so, neither the oil firms nor the Nigerian state can escape responsibility for the prevailing insecurity in oil-producing areas.

OIL AND VIOLENT CONFLICT IN THE POST-MILITARY ERA

Where are the dividends of democracy?

President Abacha's death in 1998 rescued Nigeria from a looming political crisis, which might have engulfed the Niger Delta and the country in violence. It cleared the path for a rapid transition toward multi-party democracy. A new constitution was cobbled together under the interim military administration of President (General) Abdulsalam Abubakar with no public debate, paving the way for flawed, but hotly contested, elections and the installation in 1999 of an elected civilian government headed by President (formerly General) Obasanjo.[47] President Obasanjo argued that the second elections, in 2003, would constitute 'the supreme test of our commitment to a democratic system' and that if they went badly, Nigeria could break 'limits beyond which anarchy, unending and pervasive violence and even national disintegration would be the only outcome' (cited in Economist Intelligence Unit 2002:13). In the event, the elections were flawed by large-scale fraud and intimidation (Human Rights Watch 2004). President Obasanjo was confirmed in office, and the political dominance of the ruling PDP was reinforced. However, the violence associated with the elections, though considerable, especially in the Niger Delta, was not severe enough to vitiate the elections or tip the country into a major crisis.

Constitutional government had been expected to deliver a number of potential 'democratic dividends', including:

- more legitimate, inclusive and effective governance
- management of conflict through the political process, rather than

by violence and repression, helping to resolve Nigeria's crisis of public order
- greater government accountability and reduced corruption, allowing the investment of oil revenues in development
- better regulation of the oil industry and improved corporate governance.

Regarding the first of these dividends, we argue that a major opportunity was lost to rethink the nature and goals of Nigeria's multinational, multi-ethnic and multi-religious system of government – despite efforts of pro-democracy groups and social movements to put this on the transition agenda, not least in the Niger Delta. By focusing almost exclusively on the need for a stable transition, the government failed to address major issues of social justice and inclusion, which are essential for a truly democratic system. Not only was there no public debate of the Constitution in 1999, widespread calls for a National Conference prior to the 2003 elections were ignored – although the government recently (in 2005) inaugurated a national consultative conference with limited terms of reference.

Secondly the expectation that democracy would stem the tide of political and criminal violence has proved unrealistic at best and dangerously complacent at worst. As already noted, deaths resulting from conflicts under constitutional governance may well have matched or exceeded those under the dictatorship of General Abacha. Indeed it has been suggested that democratisation may have brought conflicts into the open, which were previously held in check by military repression (Strategic Conflict Assessment 2003:17–25).

Nor, thirdly, has democratic governance reduced corruption, assured more equitable distribution of oil revenues or ensured their reallocation to poverty reduction. The country remains as oil dependent as ever. And oil continues to feed a political system constructed around patronage and money politics, and structurally resistant to any kind of reform.

Regarding the fourth goal, however, there seems to have been limited progress in the oil sector itself, both in regard to corporate governance, and in government and legislative oversight over oil firms. Yet the clean-up of corporate governance is still in its early stages, and may not be sustainable in a context of deepening corruption at all levels of government. Recent revelations suggest that improper payments by TSJK, the construction consortium formed by Halliburton and others to construct Nigeria's gas export plant, continued after the transition to constitutional government.[48]

In the Niger Delta, the nexus between oil and violence is far from broken. Violence peaked in late 1999, soon after the change to elected government, though reflecting oil community militancy initiated before the transition. Large-scale unrest broke out again before and during federal and state elections in 2003, especially around the oil town of Warri. Arguments over electoral boundaries and candidate selection tapped into longer-term inter-communal land disputes. Once more oil companies found themselves under attack. Community militants seized flow stations and threatened to blow up pipelines and installations, unless oil operators ceased collaborating with the armed forces.[49]

One crucial difference from the military era, however, is that the linkages between oil, conflict and stalled development have been openly acknowledged in official circles and debated in the public arena. Official and semi-official reports offer important insights into these debates, including the 'Report of the First Presidential Retreat on National Security' (2001); the 'Proceedings of the Presidential Retreat on the Electoral Process and Violence' (2002); the 'Report of the Special Security Committee on Oil-Producing Areas' (2002); and the 'Strategic Conflict Assessment' (2003), prepared for the federal government by the Institute for Peace and Conflict Resolution. Some of these documents remain confidential and others have entered the public domain, though none have been widely circulated outside government. These reports situate Niger Delta violence within a wider picture of lawlessness in the whole country. As the Director General of the State Security Service cautioned at the Presidential Retreat on National Security:

> the pattern of political behaviour in Nigeria has been both positive and worrisome. On a positive note, the culture of democracy is beginning to gain ground. ... On the negative side we are beginning to see the resurgence of political conduct which in the past contributed to the collapse of democracy. These include indecent struggle for political power, abuse of office, thuggery, factionalisation, fragmentation of party institutions and apprehensions of electoral rigging.[50]

Participants at the Presidential Retreat, including the president,[51] identified the main structural determinants of insecurity as poverty, inequality, money politics, corruption and politicisation of ethnic and religious disputes. They asserted that Nigeria's crises are volatile, with conflicts swiftly 'provoking retaliation and duplication in other places'; and becoming 'highly militarised over the years. Nigerians now prosecute communal feuds, inter-ethnic conflicts, boundary and other similar disputes with the use of military-type weapons.'[52] Brutally frank views were expressed about the law and order system, notably the 'police's dwindling performance and pathetic state' (Report of the First Presidential Retreat on National Security 2001:12).

Violence and the public security gap

Neither the federal nor the state governments have yet taken the hard political decisions required to address the lack of public security. The promised refurbishments of the police and law and order system have not materialised. The government itself has aggravated conflicts through its needlessly violent responses, as in Odi in the Niger Delta in 1999, in Zaki Biam in Benue State during the 2001 Tiv–Jukun disturbances, and in Odioma in 2005. In all three cases army detachments killed large numbers of civilians and razed entire villages in retaliation for armed attacks on soldiers, police and local councillors.

The public security gap may even have widened under civilian governance. To fill it, there has been a proliferation of vigilante organisations, ethnic militias, paramilitaries, private security companies and other privatised forms of security provision – paralleling the growth in political, criminal and communal violence. State governments themselves have sponsored vigilante groups, as in Anambra, where the former Bakassi Boys were reorganised as an officially recognised Anambra State Vigilante Service (AVS). But vigilante organisations have tended to become a source of public disorder in their own right, as was the case with the AVS, which was ultimately disbanded under federal government pressure, being discredited by its freelance criminal activities and human rights violations (Human Rights Watch and Centre for Law Enforcement Education 2002). They have become linked to cult as well as criminal activities, and are increasingly well armed, like the Niger Delta Volunteer Force (NDVF), whose leader, Alhaji Mujahid Dokubo Asari, is a former Rivers State security officer.[53] Added to these has been a proliferation of criminal gangs and political syndicates responsible for large numbers of killings, kidnappings of oil workers, protection rackets and bunkering, which have often benefited from de facto political impunity.[54]

The 'Special Security Committee on Oil-Producing Areas' spelled out the implications of public disorder for the oil sector. The committee appeared to recreate the old alliance between the military and the oil firms, as it included the Chiefs of Staff of all three armed forces, the Inspector General of Police, the Director General of the State Security Service, a representative of the National Security Adviser, the secretaries to the governments of the oil-producing states, the Director of the Department of Petroleum Resources, the Managing Director of NNPC and the managing directors of all the main oil operating companies. The committee's terms of reference confined it to reporting:

> on the ways and means of instituting effective security of oil operations and installations. [But] it became quite obvious during its deliberations that the root causes of insecurity in the

areas had to do with the neglect, frustration and the sense of abandonment shared by the people.

(Report of the Special Security Committee on Oil-Producing Areas 2002:1–2)

Thus it concluded that security problems could not be resolved 'by militarization or the security approach' (2002:2) but required action on many levels. These included a more holistic security management system; more adequate resourcing of the police; changes in the regulatory framework governing oil to protect the environment and the rights of oil-producing communities; major changes in revenue allocation to assure states and local authorities at least 50 per cent of revenues on the basis of derivation (rather than the 13 per cent minimum in the 1999 constitution); and making state governments primarily responsible for development under 'an identifiable and transparent system that embraces the oil-producing communities in the utilisation of funds so that their needs can be properly reflected in the projects being executed' (2002:65).

The committee's report was, however, quietly shelved, largely because its revenue proposals proved too sweeping for the federal government and for some oil companies.[55] As an industry source we interviewed put it:

oil is at the centre of political differences between north and south. The committee touched on the basic conflict between the interests of the south-south governors and the north, and in the end the President was unable to come down on one side or the other.

Oil revenues, constitutional change and Niger Delta communities: where is there political space for reform?

The tussle for oil revenues is certainly not over, and how they are distributed remains at the heart of debates about Nigeria's Federal Constitution. Indeed if there is a single issue which unites all the contending state governments, ethnic communities and political factions in the Niger Delta, it is the demand that the revenues allocated to oil-producing states and communities should be substantially increased. If the Special Security Committee's proposal that 50 per cent of revenues should be allocated to states on the basis of derivation were to be seriously pressed by state governments, it would prove overwhelmingly popular in the Niger Delta.

Oil-producing states have also confronted the federal government over whether revenues from Nigeria's fast-expanding offshore fields should be covered by the derivation formula applying to onshore fields, or be considered a purely federal resource. A 2002 Supreme Court ruling declared that the oil-producing states had no entitlement to offshore oil resources. When the states protested, President Obasanjo tabled a bill to grant them revenues from oilfields in a 'contiguous' zone of 24 nautical miles. When the National Assembly tabled an amendment extending their derivation rights to the entire 200 miles continental shelf, however, the president controversially withheld his consent. Above all, the government remains reluctant to agree changes in the basis of revenue allocation which might seriously threaten its revenue base. It has been supported by non-oil states in the north, whose governors urged the president not to sign the amended offshore oil Bill. Yet non-oil states in the south have supported the oil producers as part of a general push against federal power, including proposals to increase the states' overall share of the fiscal cake. The issue remains potentially explosive, especially in the Niger Delta, where the Ijaw Youth Council and other community organisations, as well as the NDVF, have periodically threatened to occupy or destroy oil installations if the government does not give way on the onshore/offshore dispute and other revenue allocation issues.

Yet there is not an open and shut case that social equity and poverty reduction criteria would be best served by massive changes in the basis of revenue allocation. It is true that the development of oil-producing states in the delta has been scandalously neglected and that the damage to the environment and livelihoods caused by oil exploration and production needs to be redressed. Some revenue redistribution from the federation to the states might help cut federal waste and bring government closer to the people. Yet drastic cuts in the development budgets of the federation and of the poorer non-oil states would potentially deepen poverty and popular discontent in a political situation already enflamed by the Sharia dispute in the north. Moreover, redistribution is entangled with other issues about a chaotic budgetary process and the use of oil revenues to fund investment and stabilise the economy. The Supreme Court judgment, which ruled on offshore resources, also determined that the government could not make cash call payments to joint-venture oil companies a prior charge on revenues before their division among the federation, the states and local authorities. This could make it harder to use revenues to cover debt payments, or to stabilise the economy during oil price fluctuations.

During the military era, Niger Delta activists posed a simple choice between the use of oil revenues to improve conditions of life in their communities and corruption and waste by the federal military government. But since 1999 oil-producing states have received substantial injections of additional revenues under the 13 per cent derivation formula. Further large transfers of oil revenues from the federation to the states, as under the mooted 50 per cent formula, might indeed simply shift the Dutch disease, money politics and corruption to the oil-producing states. The current state governments in the delta are hardly shining examples of probity, or of wise and accountable development spending.

Yet in the Niger Delta itself such objections are dismissed. As a community leader with links to the Bayelsa State government expressed it, if oil revenue 'doesn't come to Bayelsa, that means someone else is taking it. Local corruption is better than national corruption, because some of it will reach our own people.'[56] Other Delta activists and politicians were less brutally cynical. They contended that democratic governance can ensure that oil revenues reach Delta communities. According to one, 'the struggle with the oil companies sitting on our very sources of survival will continue side by side with the struggle with government.' Neither a larger slice of the revenue cake, nor better oil company community programmes will satisfy them, for 'we don't need Shell to build schools and clinics, we want to do this ourselves.'[57]

The communities' central demand remains that the government and oil firms should 'allow us space in our own land',[58] and 'legally identify us as the legitimate owners of these resources. ... The essential need is for a legal regime, which recognises communal rights, and finds a formula that gives revenues back to oil-producing communities.' Oil operators would still have 'the right to negotiate with us as stakeholders, just as they do now with the government under joint venture agreements',[59] pay taxes to government and take a reasonable profit. Local communities would regulate them through MOUs and Environmental Impact Assessments agreed directly with the oil firms.

When they were agitating against military rule, as we saw earlier, Niger Delta activists had linked their demands for community control of oilfields to proposed renegotiation of Nigeria's entire constitutional and legal structure. But they have found themselves marginalised by the political parties formed to contest for power in the 1999 and 2003 elections. These parties are ramshackle coalitions of national and state-level interests. They lack policies and political programmes, being cemented together by money, patronage and the prospect of power. Ex-military élites are prominent in politics and government. The three most widely supported presidential candidates at the 2003 elections (Obasanjo, Buhari and Ojukwu) were ex-soldiers. None of the current parties (except a small party formed to fight the 2003 election on a radical platform) have much interest in fundamental constitutional and political reform. The best that can be said is that a handful of progressive-minded politicians have formed 'platforms' inside the main parties, including the ruling PDP – and have used the legislature's committee system to pressure oil firms on their corporate responsibilities, community programmes and environmental monitoring. This de facto closure of democratic space by Nigeria's élites makes it all the harder to generate political will for reforms to address the roots of conflict. The NGOs and civil society groups which mobilised against military and corporate abuses are overstretched and lack clout at high levels of federal and state government. The national movements, community groups and youth associations of the Niger Delta are divided by factional and inter-ethnic disputes.

Disputes were common even at the height of the agitation against the military and the oil firms – which was why the 1999 Kaiyama Declaration made better inter-community and inter-ethnic relations one of its central planks. The Chikoko Movement, a loose federation of different national and community movements, remains active in trying to resolve inter-ethnic crises, since 'there is realisation among our people that where we are fighting, our enemies will continue to enjoy.'[60] Yet such bodies have not secured sustainable reductions in inter-communal conflicts. The 2003 pre-electoral violence among the Isekiri, Ijaw and Urhobo communities in Warri was a case in point, undoing earlier efforts to build cooperative relations among the three groups.[61]

Niger Delta activists and politicians hold the oil firms responsible for fomenting intra and inter-communal disputes under alleged policies of divide and rule. It is not easy to verify these charges, and not surprisingly the companies deny them. In our view, however, the structural links between oil and conflict are more critical. Oil revenues have magnified the stakes in long-running community disputes over land and resources. They have bred the 'appropriations syndrome' or 'rentier' mentality referred to earlier. Money politics and corruption, fed by oil, pervade Nigeria's entire system of governance. They have been deeply corrosive of oil communities themselves, opening fissures within and between them of the kind that ripped apart MOSOP and the Ogoni nation during the 1990s, and fed the electoral violence in Warri in 2003. Arguably, rent seeking, more than community or environmental or political concerns, lies behind many recent occupations of oil installations, kidnappings and community conflicts. The Niger Delta and Nigeria as a whole are in danger of slipping into the vicious cycle of violence for profit found in conflicts elsewhere in Africa (see Strategic Conflict Assessment 2003:26–31; Collier et al 2003). The traditional leadership of delta communities has been undermined 'and new instruments of power have been created under the instruments of violence', including increasingly sophisticated weapons now proliferating.[62] The line between community protest and criminal extortion is being blurred. Bunkering, threats against oil installations and ransom demands for kidnapped oil company employees have become endemic. The mafias and criminal groups engaged in these activities have used the profits of bunkering and protection payments from oil contractors to buy political and military protection as well as weapons (two rear admirals were recently convicted for complicity in bunkering).[63]

Democratic governance acts as a two-edged sword. It has opened channels through which Niger Delta states and oil-producing communities can press demands for accountability and more equitable distribution of oil revenues. Yet democracy has by no means erased the 'legacies of the military period. All it has done, has been to bring in some sharing of "Ghana must go" [corruption] to a wider group of people, including politicians in the Niger Delta.'[64] It has also created new forms of political and social exclusion, with state governors and political appointees diverting oil revenues and using the advantages of incumbency to accumulate wealth, buy political support and intimidate opponents. During the 2003 elections, all the Niger Delta governors survived efforts to unseat them from within their own political parties and by the opposition. Their deployment of money, patronage and violence to resist accountability for misuse of public funds has in turn encouraged direct action by their opponents, including violence.

Nevertheless civil society activists remain hopeful that democracy will slowly, if sometimes painfully, make a difference to the conduct of politics, development priorities and how conflict is managed. They believe that if a larger share of oil revenues is retained in the Niger Delta, democracy too will benefit. It will be easier to hold state governments and local authorities accountable for their failure to use these revenues for the development and welfare of their own communities – and harder for them to shift responsibility onto the federal government or the oil firms. For in order to sustain democracy:

> being elected by itself is not enough, they have to earn the respect of their people. Even now some parliamentarians cannot go home to their towns and villages. People are telling them that if they continue looting and do not bring resources to the community, 'we will tell the whole world.'[65]

Activists have stepped up their pressure on state and local administrations, as well as on the oil firms. In the run up to the 2003 election, the Ijaw Youth Council and other community organisations sought to dislodge notoriously corrupt state governors, notably in Bayelsa State. In the event they failed, mainly because the incumbents blackmailed President Obasanjo into supporting their candidacies in exchange for endorsing him at the ruling PDP presidential primaries, as well as rigging their way to victory in the elections themselves.

Meanwhile Niger Delta communities still face the utmost difficulty bringing their concerns to the attention of government authorities and the oil operators. The corruption and inefficiency of the authorities reinforces the deficiencies of the oil firms. To be sure, the latter have tried to clean up their act. In 2004 SPDC introduced a new Sustainable Community Development Programme, including 13 'Big Rules' to

reduce inefficiency and corruption in its own ranks and improve relationships with oil communities. But oil executives have few illusions
about the ability of their community development initiatives to achieve
such goals:

> We are becoming a development company, not an oil company.
> Some of us feel that the sooner we leave the development busi-
> ness the better. There has been the perception that the more we
> did, the less government did, and in the long run this is not
> healthy for the company, or for government.[66]

During his second term, President Obasanjo has at last been addressing
the roots of the crisis gripping Nigeria's petro-state: by proceeding with
the Extractive Industries Transparency Initiative in collaboration with
the oil firms, the World Bank, Amnesty International and the Soros
Foundation's 'Publish What You Pay' campaign; by starting to address
the issue of revenue allocation; by taking albeit timid steps in the direction of constitutional reform through the convening in 2005 of the
National Political Reform Conference; by well-publicised sackings of
corrupt ministers and of the Inspector General of Police; and by
dialogues with Niger Delta youths and activists. The problem,
however, is that he is a lame duck president who confronts enormously
powerful vested interests, not least inside the ruling PDP. All too often
he seems to be operating from a position of weakness, not strength, as
in his dealings with Dokubo Asari, which reinforce the perception that
the ability to create violent mayhem is the best way of gaining the
attention of Nigeria's political authorities and of Western donors (it was
allegedly pressure from the latter, which persuaded the president to
talk with Asari).

Fortunately the military still remains aloof from politics, despite
well-publicised disagreements with the government, for example, over
the role of MPRI (a US-based military contractor) in reorganising the
armed forces. Its more professional elements are concerned about its
continuing deployment for internal policing and to contain political
and sectarian violence.[67] A major political crisis in which the protagonists resorted to force to maintain or secure power at the centre would
be potentially fatal. Nigeria could not afford the risks of escalating
violence, which would be inherent in further coups or a return to
authoritarian governance.

CONCLUSION: RESOLVING NIGERIA'S CRISIS OF GONERNANCE

Nigeria's ongoing crisis of governance is allowing more divisive and
violent local, regional and religious particularisms to emerge – like the

disputes concerning the application of Sharia law in northern States and the continuing conflicts in the Niger Delta, along with the emergence of armed conflict entrepreneurs exploiting such disputes. So far most of the violence has been localised and episodic. It has not seriously challenged the survival of the Nigerian state itself. But were it to do so, it might trigger a cataclysm which would be potentially more anarchic and destructive than the 1967–70 civil war.

The risks come from two main directions. First, from violence that sparks flames across community, state or zonal boundaries. Religious and settler–indigene disputes both have the potential to initiate widening cycles of tit-for-tat violence. The festering insecurities in the Niger Delta could also set off wider national struggles. Protestors and the new generation of conflict entrepreneurs have both questioned the nature and viability of Nigerian federalism. Their demands for local control of petroleum resources could become explosive if they were to threaten large cuts in government revenues and development funding in the federation and in non-oil states, especially in the north, where poverty-alleviation is just as pressing as in the Niger Delta.[68]

Second, the present loss of public confidence in Nigeria's democratic institutions could fatally undermine their ability to manage conflicts and control any escalation of violence. This loss of confidence is aggravated by the failure of politicians to let these institutions mature – exemplified by debilitating squabbles between the presidency and the National Assembly, between state governors and legislatures, between federal and state élites, and within the political parties, including the ruling PDP. Added to this is the continuing blight of corruption, the misuse of oil revenues and government failure to address poverty, the plight of rural communities and the needs and demands of ordinary Nigerians. Hence fundamental reform is needed of the élite pact which secured the exit of the military from politics, to ensure more inclusive and effective governance. This is why it is vital that the current National Political Reform Conference should be fully representative and be endowed with sufficiently comprehensive terms of reference.

Democracy in general and improved democratic governance in the oil sector, however, can only be assured if there is pressure from grassroots. This is one of the central lessons of the protest movements in the Niger Delta. Thus it is essential to reinforce the established tradition of democratic politics in the Delta, and not allow it to be subverted by conflict entrepreneurs and the political economy of violence. Oil firms do not act in a political vacuum, and must engage with Niger Delta communities in ways that reinforce democratic politics, rather than corruption and violence.

NOTES

1. Attacks by federal helicopter gunships helped bring Ateke to the negotiating table. See *Africa Confidential*, Vol. 45, Nos 18 and 20, 10 September and 8 October 2004.
2. Petroleum exploration dates back to the early twentieth century. In 1956, the Anglo-Dutch group, Shell D'Archy, discovered oil in commercial quantities at Oloibiri, a small community in the Niger Delta, and in 1958 Nigeria became an oil exporter. Yet it was not until after the 1967–70 civil war that it became a major global producer. Nigeria is the fifth largest producer of crude oil in OPEC. Its oil, so-called Bonny Light, is said to be environmentally friendly because of its low sulphur content.

   State ownership of all mineral deposits in Nigeria, including crude oil and natural gas, is established under the constitution and through the statutes governing the industry, some dating back to colonial days. The federal government controls oil revenues, and through legislation determines the formula for distributing them to the states and local governments. Shell Petroleum Development Corporation (SPDC), a joint venture between Shell, the state-owned Nigerian National Petroleum Corporation (NNPC) and two other oil companies, remains the largest producer, producing historically between 50 and (currently) 35 per cent of total production, and controlling about 53 per cent of the total hydrocarbon reserve base. The latter is mainly located in the Niger Delta, although production from shallow and deep offshore deposits has become increasingly important.

   Apart from Shell, other multinational oil companies, including ExxonMobil, Elf Aquitane, Chevron-Texaco, Eni-Agip, TotalFinaElf and Phillips, are engaged in upstream and downstream operations. Operations have been for the most part organised as joint ventures with NNPC, although production-sharing contracts, principally for offshore oil exploration and production, are increasingly common.
3. On the concept of 'structural violence' see Galtung (1976). Watts (1983) used the concept of 'silent violence' to analyse agrarian protest in Nigeria. Some Nigerian scholars talk of 'repressive violence' to capture the idea that structural violence has often been linked to state repression too.
4. The Argentine footballer Maradona's attribution of his World Cup goal against England to the 'hand of God' resonated in Nigeria. The former head of state, General Babangida, was nicknamed Maradona because of his talents as a political manipulator. The 'hand of God' was used to refer to Abacha's death, both because it was so opportune and as an ironic comment on the official view that it was due to natural causes.
5. The World Bank's influential analysis of the role of natural resources and other economic incentives in civil wars is summarised in *Breaking the Conflict Trap: Civil War and Development Policy* (Collier et al 2003). An excellent analysis and critique of arguments concerning resource conflicts can be found in Ross (2004). In short, mineral rents create powerful incentives (a) for ruling classes to use state power, including military force, to control and appropriate their proceeds; and (b) for armed rebels and secessionist groups to 'capture' rents by using military force against the state
6. 'Bunkering' is the practice of siphoning oil from pipelines and pumping stations, sometimes with the collusion and corruption of state and oil company employees.

7. The coups and their impact upon Nigerian politics, including the drift to civil war, are analysed in Luckham (1971).
8. Hence this was hardly an 'age of innocence' as characterised in Figure 1.1.
9. Richard Joseph, uses the adjective 'prebendal' to 'refer to patterns of political behaviour which rest upon the justifying principle that such [political] offices should be competed for and then utilised for the personal benefit of office holders as well as of their reference or support group' (1987:8). Prebendal politics has characterised all three of Nigeria's Republics, as well as all its military administrations.
10. The most thorough study of the oil industry and its regulatory framework to date remains Sarah Ahmad Khan (1994), though this focuses primarily on the economics of the industry.
11. The charges against the companies are documented in Human Rights Watch (1999), Okonta and Douglas (2001) and Frynas (1998).
12. Terisa Turner (1976) documented the emergence of these comprador relationships as early as 1976. See also Okonta and Douglas (2001).
13. There are various estimates of the famed Abacha loot, some running into hundreds of billions of dollars in bank accounts in Europe, the Americas and even North Korea. The best 'official' figures come from a 'deal' struck between the Abacha family and the Obasanjo government as a basis for dropping charges against Mohammed Abacha in his trial for the death of Kudirat Abiola, wife of the winner of the (aborted) 12 June 1993 presidential election. The deal is for the Abacha family to return $1.2 billion to government and keep a handsome sum of at least $100 million.
14. Not all cases involved outright corruption. Military élites could also profit from the eagerness of businesses to bring them on board as partners or directors.
15. See Forrest (1993) and the contrast with Indonesia in Bevan et al (1999).
16. Nigerian scholars and activists refer to the 'national question', since the country's larger ethnic groups have potential claims to nationhood at least comparable to those of ethnic nations elsewhere – like Serbs, Croatians, Slovenes, Latvians or Basques in Europe.
17. Peter P. Ekeh (1975; 1990) argues that citizens of African states inhabit two contrasting public spheres: the distant, amoral and corrupt state sphere; and the moral communities of indigenous communities. In our view this contrast is over-drawn, since indigenous communities can also be manipulated by the powerful, experience corruption and be riven by disputes and conflicts, as increasingly in the Niger Delta.
18. Toyin Falola's excellent (1998) book *Violence in Nigeria: The Crisis of Religious Politics and Secular Ideologies*, persuasively analyses the spiritual and ideological dimensions of the country's conflicts.
19. Their longstanding feelings of marginalisation had already been forcefully expressed before independence to the 1958 Willink Commission, when their representatives had complained about autocratic rule by the Igbo-dominated ruling party in the region, the NCNC, skewed appointments to the public service and economic and social discrimination.
20. The widely quoted estimate of 10,000 conflict-related deaths since transition originates from the Centre for Law Enforcement Education (2002).
21. Recent attempts to analyse Nigeria's conflicts include the official 'Strategic Conflict Assessment' (2003); Otite and Albert (1999: Chapters 1, 2, 12); and Bassey (2002: Chapter 1).
22. For instance, Shell set itself the target of ending 'routine' gas flaring by 2008,

despite earlier government targets. See Shell Petroleum Development Company of Nigeria 'Challenges of Gas Flare-out in Nigeria', SPDC Briefing Notes No. 4, 2001.

23. Including clashes with the Andoni in July, 1993, the Okrika in December, 1993 and the Ndoki in April, 1994. In each case, the security forces blamed the Ogoni.

24. *Egbesu* is the Ijaw god of war. The 1998 *Egbesu* wars were reminiscent of events a century earlier when King Koko mobilised 1000 Nembe warriors in 1895 to attack Goldie's headquarters at Ashaka, bolstered by their belief in *Egbesu* .

25. See the insightful analysis of Niger Delta politics by Watts (2003), as well as Ibeanu (1996) and Human Rights Watch (2002a).

26. According to Human Rights Watch, intimidation, rigging and violence were also rife during the 2004 local elections.

27. For an overview of Shell's dialogue with human rights organisations and of its Statement of General Business Principles see Anne T. Lawrence (2002:71–85). Shortcomings in Nigeria are discussed in Human Rights Watch (2002:29–33).

28. The quotations in this section and the next are from interviews and discussions with executives (most of them Nigerian) from Shell Petroleum Development Company, Mobil Nigeria Production Unlimited and Chevron (Nigeria) Limited, as well as from the Nigerian National Petroleum Corporation (NNPC) and a small independent operator, in London, Lagos, Port Harcourt, Warri and Abuja during January and early February, 2003. Names and company identifications are not disclosed, to ensure confidentiality. Members of federal legislative committees dealing with the oil industry and of Niger Delta civil society groups were also interviewed and (where quoted) are cited by name.

29. Interview with Professor Kimsi Okoko, President of the Ijaw National Council, January 2003.

30. Further quotes from interviews with oil executives.

31. Details from SPDC (2001:8–11).

32. Oil industry figures close to NNPC in the military era claim there was no 'presidential oil' as such, nor could presidents direct NNPC to allocate contracts to particular people. But military regimes could cream off oil funds in a variety of different ways including (a) exchange rate manipulation, selling government oil at the parallel rate, but passing on the proceeds at the official rate; (b) corruption in contract allocation, especially in the downstream sector, and (c) direct presidential calls on funds from the Central Bank.

33. Interviews with Professor Kimsi Okoko, Oronto Douglas and Ledum Mittee, January 2001.

34. This case is made both by Okonta and Douglas (1998) and by Frynas (1998) who indeed argues that oil companies fostered political instability in Nigeria because they stood to benefit from it. Similar views were expressed in our January 2003 interviews with delta activists. See Detheridge and Pepple (1998 and 2000) for Shell's response.

35. These paragraphs are based on interviews with two former Deputy Managing Directors of SPDC and a former Managing Director of NNPC during January 2003.

36. See for example the exchanges between Frynas and Shell spokesmen referred to earlier (Frynas 1998; Detheridge and Pepple 1998 and 2000).

37. The percentages are rough estimates, calculated from the data presented in SPDC (2001a:8–11).
38. Chief Shonekan, the former interim President, was the driving force behind Vision 2010. Brian Anderson, SPDC's then Managing Director was Chair of Vision 2010's sub-committee on the economy.
39. See note 28.
40. See note 28
41. The scenario only covered events up to January 2003. The 2003 violence near Warri in the western Delta may have had a similar impact on oil company operations to the 1999 protests.
42. Unarmed (in theory) except in dire emergencies. Nevertheless oil activists consider the arming of oil company security employees very much a live issue. Purchases of weapons for the police and their own security personnel have been documented by Human Rights Watch (1999).
43. The companies themselves point out that their supernumerary police are not armed – although this was previously not the case.
44. In one community we visited there was one poorly resourced police constable serving a group of villages, comprising 30,000 or 40,000 people, in contrast to the half a dozen armed police guarding a nearby exploration platform.
45. The phrase used by a well-known activist, Oronto Douglas in our interview with him.
46. Interviews with Senator David Brigide, the Chair of the Senate Petroleum Committee.
47. The non-transparency of the constitution-making exercise was epitomised by the fact that the constitution's contents were not divulged until after the election, just before President Obasanjo's inauguration.
48. It was not until 2004 that Halliburton finally terminated its relationship with those in its subsidiary companies accused of involvement in corruption.
49. *Guardian*, 24 March 2003, referring to threats by the Ijaw Youth Council and the Ijaw National Congress to widen the conflict.
50. L.K.K. Are, Director General of the SSS, 'Politics and Public Security', in the Report of the First Presidential Retreat on National Security (2001:110).
51. 'Address by His Excellency President Olusegun Obasanjo' at the Retreat. See Report (2001:75–78).
52. Joint presentation on 'Domestic Crisis Management' by the Chief of Defence Staff, Vice Admiral Ibrahim Ogohi, and the Inspector General of Police, Mr Musiliu Smith, at the Retreat. See Report (2001:99).
53. The NDVF, however, seems to be a highly unstable mixture of vigilante group, cult group, rebel force and mercenary/criminal gang.
54. Both Asari and his rival, Ateke Tom, claim that Peter Odili, the state governor, used them to help rig the 2003 elections; though Odili rejects these claims. The murky politics of the NDVF and other Delta gangs, and their political links, are highlighted by *Africa Confidential*, Vol. 45, Nos 18 and 20, 10 September and 8 October 2004, as is their involvement in cult and fetish activities, including the alleged supply of supernatural services to politicians during the elections.
55. The oil companies were not unanimous either, and the Managing Director of ExxonMobil withheld his signature from the document, as did the National Security Advisor.
56. Interview with Professor Kimsi Okoko, President of the Ijaw National Council, January 2003.

57. Interview with Oronto Douglas, January 2003.
58. Similar views were expressed by Niger Delta activists interviewed, even those otherwise bitterly opposed to each other, as well as by some oil executives originating from Delta communities.
59. Interview with Senator David Brigide, Chair of the Senate Petroleum Committee, January 2003.
60. Interview with Oronto Douglas, January 2003.
61. The sources of conflict in Warri, and the efforts over the years to resolve it are examined in some detail in Imobighe et al (2003).
62. Interview with Senator Brigide, January 2003
63. *Africa Confidential*, Vol. 46, No. 7, 1 April 2005.
64. Interview with Oronto Douglas, January 2003.
65. Interview with Oronto Douglas, January 2003.
66. Interview with oil executive, January 2003.
67. According to the former Army Chief of Staff General Victor Malu's evidence to the constitutional review conference (see *Africa Confidential*, Vol. 46, No. 7, 1 April 2001), which almost certainly reflects the view of many serving officers. General Malu also warned that Nigeria was 'sitting on a powder keg' of discontented former officers and soldiers who had not received retirement benefits. When he was still army commander, General Malu was the most outspoken critic of MPRI involvement in the restructuring of the armed forces – and his uncle was among the people killed by the army when it was deployed in the 2001 Tiv–Jukun dispute.
68. For a sympathetic assessment of the Ogoni struggle, which nevertheless spells out the potentially negative impact on the rest of the country if the demands of Niger Delta communities for control of petroleum resources were to be satisfied, see Eghosa E. Osaghae (1995).

BIBLIOGRAPHY

Academic Associates Peaceworks and Nigerian National Petroleum Corporation (2004) 'Report of the Niger Delta Youths Stakeholders Workshop, Port Harcourt April 15–17 2004' (Abuja: Academic Associated Peaceworks).

Adekanye, J. (1999) *The Retired Military Phenomenon* (Ibadan: Heinemann).

Ake, C., Nnoli, O. and Nwokedi, E. (not dated) 'The Causes of Conflict in Africa' (Research proposal for the Centre for Advanced Social Science, Port Harcourt).

Bassey, C.O. (2003) 'Framework for the Conflict Transformation Project in Warri', in Imobighe, T.A., Bassey, C.O. and Asuni, J.B. (eds) *Conflict and Instability in the Niger Delta: The Warri Case* (Ibadan: Spectrum Books for Academic Associates PeaceWorks).

Bevan, D.L., Collier, P. and Gunning, J.W. (1999) *Nigeria and Indonesia* (Oxford: Oxford University Press).

Centre for Law Enforcement Education (2002) *Education, Hope Betrayed? A Report on Impunity and State Violence in Nigeria* (Lagos: Centre for Law Enforcement Education).

Civil Liberties Organisation (1996) 'Civil Liberties Organisation Annual Report 1995: A CLO Report on the State of Human Rights in Nigeria' (Lagos: Civil Liberties Organisation).

Collier, P., Elliott, L., Hegre, H., Hoeffler, A., Reynal-Querol, M. and Sambanis, N. (2003) *Breaking the Conflict Trap: Civil War and Development Policy* (Washington, D.C.: the World Bank and Oxford University Press).

Daukoru, Dr E., Presidential Adviser on Petroleum and Energy (2004) 'Niger Delta Community Crisis: Agenda for Sustainable Peace', in *Report of the Niger Delta Youths Stakeholders Workshop* (Abuja: Nigeria National Petroleum Corporation and Academic Associates).

Detheridge, A. and Pepple, N. (1998) 'A Response to Frynas', *Third World Quarterly*, Vol. 19, No. 3.

—— (2000) 'Shell in Nigeria: A Further Contribution', *Third World Quarterly*, Vol. 21, No. 1.

Economist Intelligence Unit (2002) *Country Report, Nigeria* (London: Economist Intelligence Unit).

Ekeh, P.P. (1975) 'Colonialism and the Two Publics in Africa: A Theoretical Statement', *Comparative Studies in Society and History*, Vol. 17, No. 1.

—— (1990) 'Social Anthropology and Two Contrasting Uses of Tribalism', *Comparative Studies in Society and History*, Vol. 32.

Falola, T. (1998) *Violence in Nigeria: The Crisis of Religious Politics and Secular Ideologies* (Rochester: Rochester University Press).

Fayemi, K. (2003) 'Governing the Security Sector in a Democratising Polity, Nigeria', in Cawthra, G. and Luckham, R. (eds) *Governing Insecurity: Democratic Control of Military and Security Establishment in Transitional Democracies* (London: Zed Press).

Forrest, T. (1993) *Politics and Economic Development in Nigeria* (Oxford: Oxford University Press).

Frynas, J.G. (1998) 'Political Instability and Business: Focus on Shell in Nigeria', *Third World Quarterly*, Vol. 19, No. 3.

Galtung, J. (1976) *Essays on Peace Research* (Oslo: Peace Research Institute of Oslo).

Harnet-Sievers, A., Ahazuem, J.O. and Emezue, S. (1997) *A Social History of the Nigerian Civil War: Perspectives from Below* (Enugu and Hamburg: Jemezie Associates and LIT Verlag).

Human Rights Watch (1999) *The Price of Oil: Corporate Responsibility and Human Rights Violations in Nigeria's Oil Producing Communities* (New York: Human Rights Watch).

—— (2002a) *The Niger Delta: No Democratic Dividend* (New York: Human Rights Watch).

—— (2002b) *Nigeria: Military Revenge in Benue – A Population Under Attack* (New York: Human Rights Watch).

—— (2004) *Nigeria's 2003 Elections: The Unacknowledged Violence* (New York: Human Rights Watch).

Human Rights Watch and Centre for Law Enforcement Education (2002) *The Bakassi Boys: the Legitimization of Murder and Torture* (New York: Human Rights Watch).

Ibeanu, O. (1999a) 'Exiles in Their Own Home: Conflicts and Internal Population Displacement in Nigeria', *Journal of Refugee Studies*, Vol. 12, No. 1.

—— (1999b) 'Ogoni: Oil, Resource Flow and Conflict', in Granfelt, T. (ed.) *Managing the Globalized Environment* (London: Intermediate Technology Publications).

—— (2002) 'Janus Unbound: Petro-business and Petropolitics in the Niger Delta', *Review of African Political Economy*, Vol. 29, No. 91.

Ijaw Youth Council (1999) *The Kaiama Declaration: Resolutions of the 11December 1998 All Ijaw Youths Conference held in the Niger Delta, Nigeria* (Port Harcourt: Ijaw Youth Council).

Imobighe, T.A., Bassey, C.O. and Asuni, J.B. (2003) *Conflict and Instability in the Niger Delta: The Warri Case* (Abuja: Academic Associate PeaceWorks).

Joseph, R. (1987) *Democracy and Prebendal Politics in Nigeria: The Rise and Fall of the Second Republic* (Cambridge: Cambridge University Press).

Karl, T.L. (1997) *The Paradox of Plenty: Oil Booms and Petro-states* (Berkeley: University of California Press).

Khan, S.A. (1994) *Nigeria: The Political Economy of Oil* (Oxford: Oxford University Press).

Lawrence, A.T. (2002) 'The Drivers of Stakeholder Engagement: Reflections on the Case of Royal Dutch/Shell', *Journal of Corporate Citizenship*, Vol. 6, summer.

League for Human Rights (1958) *Sir Henry Willink's Report of the Commission Appointed to Enquire into the Fears of Minorities and Means of Allaying Them* (Jos, Nigeria: League for Human Rights).

Luckham, R. (1971) *The Nigerian Military: A Case Study of Authority and Revolt* (Cambridge: Cambridge University Press).

Mittee, B. (1997) 'The Social-cultural Impact of Oil Exploration on an Indigenous People: the Ogoni Case' (paper presented at international symposium on Economic, Social and Cultural Rights among the Sami, the Maasai and the Ogoni, University of Lapland, Rovaniemi, Finland, 12 – 14 September 1997).

Movement for the Survival of Ogoni People (1992) *Ogoni Bill of Rights* (Port Harcourt: Saros International Publishers).

Okonta, I. and Douglas, O. (2001) *Where Vultures Feast: 40 Years of Shell in the Niger Delta*, (Ibadan, Nigeria: Environmental Rights Action and Friends of the Earth).

Osaghae, E.E. (1995) 'The Ogoni Uprising: Oil Politics, Minority Nationalism and the Future of the Nigerian State', *African Affairs*, Vol. 94, No. 376.

Otite, O. and Albert, I.O. (eds) (1999) *Community Conflicts in Nigeria: Management, Resolution and Transformation* (Ibadan: Spectrum Books for Academic Associates PeaceWorks).

'Proceedings of the Retreat on the Electoral Process and Violence' (2002) (Abuja: Office of the Secretary to the Government of the Federation, Presidency).

'Report of the 1st Presidential Retreat on National Security' (2001) (Abuja: The Presidency).

'Report of the Special Security Committee on Oil-Producing Areas' (2002) (Abuja: unpublished).

Ross, M. (2004) 'What Do We Know About Natural Resources and Civil War?' *Journal of Peace Research*, Vol. 41, No. 3.

—— (2003) 'Nigeria's Oil sector and the Poor' (paper prepared for UK Department of International Development, Nigeria: Drivers of Change programme, May 2003).

Shell Petroleum Development Company of Nigeria (2001) 'People and the Environment', *Annual Report* (Abuja: SPDC).

Shell Petroleum Development Company of Nigeria (2001b) 'Challenges of Gas Flare-out in Nigeria', SPDC Briefing Notes No. 4.

'Strategic Conflict Assessment: Nigeria (2003)' (Abuja: Institute for Peace and Conflict Resolution, The Presidency).

Turner, T. (1976) 'Multinational Corporations and the Instability of the Nigerian State', *Review of African Political Economy*, No. 5.

Watts, M. (1983) *Silent Violence: Food, Famine and Peasants in Northern Nigeria* (Berkeley, Calif.: University of California Press).

Watts, M. (2003) 'Economies of Violence. More Oil, More Blood', *Economic and Political Weekly*, Vol. 38, No. 48, 29 November 2003.

2 Drilling in deep water: oil, business and war in Angola

Philippe Le Billon

> It's fashionable to say that we are cursed by our mineral riches.
> That's not true. We are cursed by our leaders.
> (Raphael Marques, Angolan Journalist)[1]

Angolans tell a bittersweet story about the creation of their country. When God decided to make Angola, they say, He chose all that was best and most blessed in his store of natural riches: great rivers and heavy rains, rich fertile soil, vast tropical forests, great plateaux, mountains, and expanses of rolling savannah. God filled the ocean with fish, He buried fabulous diamonds in the soil, and huge oil reserves under the sea. And then, concludes the story, to compensate for this generosity, God peopled Angola with greedy men who could never agree to share the country's riches in peace, and instead ruined it by fighting.

In 2002, hostilities dating back to the independence struggle in the early 1960s finally came to an end. An optimist would argue that oil revenues greatly assisted the Angolan government in defeating UNITA rebel forces and now offer the hope of shared prosperity for all Angolans. While ranking 164 out of 175 in the Human Development Index, Angola's giant deep-water oilfields have become a magnet for the oil industry and Angola is now the highest recipient of foreign direct investment among the Least Developed Countries (UNDP 2003). I present in this chapter a more sober perspective based upon two visits to Angola, a vast literature supporting the idea of a resource curse, and numerous studies backing claims of embezzlement and mismanagement. Accordingly, I argue that the 'developmental' record of the oil sector in Angola has so far been abysmal, and suggest that it will remain so as long as the ruling élite fails to make a decisive transition to a more democratic and accountable governance.

Much stands in the way of such transformation. Oil revenues are limiting the leverage of local populations and international actors on the ruling élite. For decades, international oil companies, as well as diamond businesses and private banks, have profitably financed the bloodshed and can without doubt support a corrupt and repressive regime. New constraints and incentives are needed to change corporate and governmental behaviour in 'post-conflict' Angola. On a more positive note, some progress has been made in terms of transparency as international norms of oil governance are emerging following intense pressure over the past five years by advocacy organisations, international financial institutions, and some donor countries (for example Global Witness 1999, 2002a). Along with a generational shift among Angolan politicians and stronger demands for accountability on the part of Angolan civil society, these may help bring about a much-needed transformation of the oil sector in Angola and the region.

In this chapter, I first briefly present the history of hostilities in Angola, the oil sector and the political economy of oil dependence. I then turn to the role of foreign governmental and corporate actors, notably through the example of an oil-for-arms deal, and question the importance of the 'greed factor' in prolonging the conflict. I then discuss major efforts to end the conflict and bring about a better governance of the oil sector, before drawing some tentative conclusions.

THE LONG WARS: ANGOLA'S THREE PHASES OF HOSTILITIES

Angola has been in a chronic state of war ever since the Portuguese colonial project started in the sixteenth century with an attempt to wrest control from the local rulers (Henderson 1979; Pélissier 1977). Much of these hostilities revolved around the trading of slaves, and subsequently the control of land. Hostilities in the contemporary period date from the mid 1950s when socio-political movements, including Angola's main nationalist movement, the Popular Movement for the Liberation of Angola (Movimento Popular de Libertação de Angola – MPLA), launched a struggle to rid Angola of its colonial masters (Guimaraes 1998). The MPLA was formed in 1956 in the context of increasing anti-colonial struggles in Africa, after Portugal annexed Angola as a Portuguese province in 1951, and after the discovery of oil in 1955. The country remained trapped in conflict for virtually the whole of the rest of the twentieth century, passing through three distinct phases, and turning Angola into a veritable laboratory of war. Angola has suffered colonial and anti-colonial wars, the Cold War, wars motivated by domestic differences and by external powers, by ideology and by greed, conventional wars and guerrilla wars, civil wars and regional wars, and an ongoing war of secession. Angola's oil revenues came into play mostly during the third and final phase of the conflict as both UNITA and the MPLA faced declining support from foreign allies. However an understanding of all three phases is necessary to understand how this came to pass.

In its first phase, between 1961 and 1975, Angola's war was a classic struggle for national liberation from the Portuguese colonial power. Yet, unlike in Mozambique and Guinea-Bissau, several nationalist parties competed in this struggle. The MPLA was a socialist movement which emerged from the mixed-race, urban population, and the Umbundu ethnic group of central Angola, under the leadership of the poet Agostinho Neto and since 1979 by Eduardo dos Santos. Linked with Portuguese socialist groups and mobilising local unions, the MPLA's Marxism attracted the support of the Soviet bloc, including Cuba (Cahen 1989). Marxism also avoided the pitfall of a racially based nationalist ideology that would conflict with the *mestiços*, or white descendants, of the MPLA's intellectual élite and allowed for a linking with black workers and the poor of Luanda's slums. Despite rejecting any ethnic or 'tribalist' character it remained strongly affiliated – most notably through its 'popular defence' scheme – with Mbundu populations in and around the capital city of Luanda who represented 20 per cent of the population. The National Liberation Front of Angola (FNLA), headed by Roberto Holden, represented about 15 per cent of the national population and had a strong ethnic base among the Bakongo, located in the north-west.

While the leadership of the FNLA initially attempted to recreate the former Kongo kingdom through secession, it later moved to a national independence agenda and received the assistance of Western powers and Zaire. Finally, the National Union for the Total Independence of Angola (UNITA) emerged, headed by Jonas Savimbi, and comprising provincial *assimilados*, with a dominant ethnic base of Ovimbundu from the central highlands (*planalto*) who represented the largest ethnic group, with 35 per cent of the population. While these ethnic differences contributed, at least in the early stages, to defining the lines of Angola's conflict, they almost never served as a motivation for it. With time, however, Jonas Savimbi did increasingly portray UNITA as the party of the black Africans, struggling to free Angola from the domination of the white and mixed-race the MPLA.

The first phase of Angola's war ended when, following the Portuguese revolution of 1974, Lisbon hastily withdrew from its African colonies. Yet Angola's independence, in 1975, did not result in peace. The Alvor Accords signed in 1975 between the post-Salazarist Portuguese government and Angolan nationalist political parties to bring about an independent coalition government before holding national elections rapidly collapsed, as the different factions and their foreign supporters pursued a hegemonic agenda. Instead, the second phase of the conflict – between 1975 and 1991 – set in as Angola found itself sucked into both the Cold War, and apartheid South Africa's bid to destabilise neighbouring 'frontline' states. While the FNLA ceased to exist as a military force soon after independence following its defeat by MPLA and Cuban troops, hostilities continued between the MPLA and UNITA. With continued support from the Soviet Union and Cuba, the MPLA established a single-party, socialist government based in the capital Luanda. It allowed Namibia's South West Africa's People's Organisation

(SWAPO) and South Africa's African National Congress (ANC) to establish military bases inside Angola. Meanwhile, bolstered by the support of the United States and direct military involvement from South Africa, UNITA fought to dislodge the MPLA government. The ensuing civil war continued until May 1991, at its height raging in 15 of the country's 18 provinces, and pitting 50,000 Cuban troops against the élite units of the South African armed forces (Bridgland 1990).

With the end of the Cold War, and growing pressure on the apartheid regime in South Africa, the superpowers withdrew their support, the Cubans and the South Africans withdrew their forces, and in 1991 the MPLA and UNITA signed the Bicesse Peace Accords, briefly ending the fighting. The peace accords called for a ceasefire, demobilisation of the two armies, the holding of democratic elections, and the establishment of a UN mission to observe the process. The elections went ahead in September 1992, despite the failure to complete the demobilisation process. In the presidential ballot MPLA President José Eduardo dos Santos won 49.57 per cent of the vote against 40.07 per cent for UNITA leader Jonas Savimbi. In the legislature the MPLA won 54 per cent against UNITA's 34 per cent. UNITA refused to accept these results and accused the MPLA of vote rigging (Matloff 1997). Angola lurched into the third, and bloodiest, phase of its conflict between 1992 and 2002.

On 31 October 1992 fighting broke out in Luanda between UNITA and MPLA supporters. By the time it was over on 3 November, the battle for Luanda had claimed thousands of lives and driven UNITA out of the capital (Maier 1996). Within days UNITA's fiercely motivated and disciplined army had captured over 50 per cent of the country from the demoralised, poorly organised, and largely demobilised government forces. Significantly, they captured the country's rich diamond fields, in the north-eastern Lunda provinces. For the next decade UNITA funded its war effort with the sale of diamonds. The MPLA responded by using the proceeds from Angola's rapidly growing petroleum industry to rebuild its army. Angola's natural wealth fuelled its descent into war and abject poverty.

After two years of fighting, which at its height was estimated by the UN to have killed 1000 people each day, the post-electoral war ended with the signing of the Lusaka Peace Protocol on 20 November 1994. The Lusaka Protocol provided for a new ceasefire, the establishment of a large UN peacekeeping force, quartering of UNITA troops with a view to integrating some into the Angolan Armed Forces (Forças Armadas Angolanas – FAA) and demobilising the rest, and the participation of UNITA in a government of national unity.

Implementation of the accords proceeded painfully slowly, with both sides committing numerous ceasefire violations. Most significantly, despite pretending to demobilise its forces, UNITA in fact retained up to 30,000 combat ready troops.[2] After four years of 'neither war nor peace', Angola again began the descent into full-blown war in 1998. From March 1998 onwards violent attacks proliferated throughout the country, and UNITA reasserted its control over dozens of towns handed over to the government during the peace process. The post-Lusaka phase of Angola's civil war officially began in the first week of December 1998, when the government responded to UNITA provocation by bombarding UNITA's headquarters at Andulo and Bailundo and President dos Santos took the decision 'to wage war to gain peace'.

The ensuing conflict lasted until March 2002. The FAA launched two costly, unsuccessful offensives, before regrouping, rearming, and embarking on a third that ultimately defeated UNITA, but at immense cost to the civilian population. Employing scorched-earth tactics and the forced depopulation of large parts of rural Angola, it resulted in the displacement of at least 2 million Angolans, and the death by starvation of thousands of the civilians trapped behind UNITA lines. The war finally ended after Jonas Savimbi was killed in combat in February 2002. His subordinates, themselves on the verge of dying of starvation, agreed to a ceasefire within days of his death.

From 1992 onwards Angola's conflict was not motivated by any coherent ideology or ethnic grievance. The continued existence and resistance of UNITA provided the MPLA with justification for their part in the war, while UNITA cited the corruption of the MPLA, and the 'neo-colonialism' of international oil companies to justify their continued fight for 'national liberation'. In fact, throughout the 1990s, both sides were evidently motivated by a thirst for power. The major difference in their motivation appeared to be that the leadership of the MPLA craved power for the access to wealth which it delivered; whereas Savimbi demonstrated the characteristics of a genuine megalomaniac who desired power purely for its own sake. Or in simple terms, the MPLA used power to get money, while Savimbi used money to try to get power. Unfortunately for the people of Angola, the scale of the riches to which both sides had access was enough to fuel a sophisticated, large-scale and destructive conflict. With the end of the Cold War the political superpowers withdrew from Angola, only to be replaced by 'business superpowers'. Oil companies on the side of the MPLA and diamond companies on the side of UNITA competed fiercely for the rights to exploit Angola's mineral wealth. International arms dealers were content to supply both parties to the conflict with weapons in exchange for their mineral revenues. As a result a dreadfully destructive military stalemate persisted from 1992 to 2002. For their part the Angolan people appeared too traumatised and disenfranchised to halt a conflict which barely anyone desired.

Cumulatively, four decades of fighting have unmade and reshaped Angola, socially and physically. Most of the conflict took place in the countryside, depopulating rural areas and crippling a once vibrant rural economy. The country, which in 1975 was the world's fourth largest exporter of coffee, had few commercial coffee farms at all by 2002. Roads and bridges were systematically destroyed and the soil sown indiscriminately with landmines. The post-electoral war of 1992–94, however, centred mostly on the major cities of the interior, like Huambo, Kuito, Luena and Malange, reducing formerly elegant, bustling cities to shrapnel-scarred ghost-towns. Even those parts of the country which did not suffer directly from the fighting, like the southern cities of Lubango and Namibe, crumbled quietly under decades of poverty and neglect.

An estimated half a million people have died as a result of post-independence hostilities and at least a third of the total population of 13 million were displaced within the country, most abandoning their homes in the countryside and seeking refuge in squalid camps in the battered cities. A further half a million fled to neighbouring countries, where generations have grown up and grown old in refugee camps. Social and development indexes reflect this situation, with a Human Development rank of 164 out of 175 countries, an under-five mortality rate of 26 per cent and a life expectancy of 46 years. The gross national income is estimated at $1,890 per capita on a purchasing power parity basis,[3] a figure hiding high levels of inequality with 60 per cent of the population living below the poverty line.

Parallel with this, Angola also suffers from an ongoing secessionist conflict in the northernmost province of Cabinda which has tended to be eclipsed by the wider civil war. Cabinda is a small enclave, physically separated from the rest of Angola by a narrow strip of land which gives the Democratic Republic of Congo access to the Atlantic Coast. Since the 1960s a small separatist movement, the Front for the Liberation of the Enclave of Cabinda (Frente de Libertacao do Enclave de Cabinda – FLEC), and a number of splinter groups, have fought a low-intensity guerrilla war, first against the Portuguese and subsequently against the MPLA, to win independence for Cabinda. Where the role of oil in the MPLA–UNITA conflict is complex and nuanced, in Cabinda it is quite straightforward. Cabinda is Angola's most oil-rich province, accounting for 60 to 70 per cent per cent of the country's total current production and nearly all of its foreign-exchange oil earnings (EIU 2001). With a population of only 300,000, the revenues from this production would make an independent Cabinda one of the world's wealthiest developing countries per capita, with an annual tax revenue per capita of $18,000.[4] Conversely, the strategic importance of Cabinda's oil reserves to Angola has ensured that neither UNITA nor the MPLA would ever countenance relinquishing control over the province. Since the end of the conflict with UNITA, the FAA has directed its attention to the Cabinda conflict, with operations involving up to 30,000 troops. Both sides in the conflict have been responsible for numerous extrajudicial killings and torture in the province (Amnesty International 1998, 2004). In June 2002 the Bishop of Cabinda, Dom Paulino Madeca, called for the government of Angola, the EU and the UN to initiate a peace process that will free the people of Cabinda, whom he described as 'a persecuted people, a forgotten people, a people who are the victims of colonialism or maybe of the greed of third countries who wish to exploit their own resources'.[5]

THE OIL SECTOR

While most of Angola was thus being decimated by conflict, the country's oil sector was, paradoxically, booming. Angola's first onshore oil was produced in the mid 1950s, and the first offshore oil was produced from Cabindan waters in 1968. Offshore fields have since provided about 95 per cent of total oil production, insulating the industry from local communities and hostilities. By 1973 oil had overtaken coffee as Angola's biggest export. In 1976, following independence, the MPLA government founded the national oil company Sonangol (Sociedade Nacional de Combustíveis), and in 1978 a Petroleum Law was passed, decreeing that 'all deposits of liquids and gaseous hydrocarbons ... [belong] to the Angolan people.'[6] The law made provision for Sonangol to enter into joint ventures with foreign companies to secure the resources and expertise necessary to exploit the country's oil reserves. The first such joint ventures were established with the three foreign oil companies which had been working in Angola prior to independence: the Cabinda Gulf Oil Company (CABGOC) – a joint venture operated by Gulf Oil which subsequently became a subsidiary of Chevron – Texaco and Petrofina.

Sonangol then divided the waters immediately off Angola's coast into 13 exploration blocks, which foreign companies were invited to bid for. Each block was awarded to a small group of four or five different companies under a production-sharing agreement. In each case, one company was made the operator of the block, awarded the largest share of the equity, and made responsible for the largest share of the investment needed. The others were simply equity partners. Exploration in these blocks began from the early 1980s and some significant discoveries were made in Angola's northern waters, particularly by Chevron, Texaco and Elf. Apart from some minimal onshore production from the Soyo area, these shallow water blocks accounted for all of Angola's oil production until 2000, when Block 14 of CABGOC came online. In that year, Angola produced 746,000 bbl/d.

It was not until the late 1990s, however, that the international oil industry became truly excited by Angola's petroleum prospects. Following the development of new technologies allowing oil exploration in deeper waters in areas like the North Sea, Sonangol was able in the early 1990s to demarcate a further 17 exploration blocks, in depths of between 150 and 600 metres, immediately to the west of the initial 13 shallow water blocks. During this second bidding round the concept of signature bonuses was introduced, with companies being asked to make cash-down payments to Sonangol to secure the rights to explore the blocks on offer. Given the unknown qualities of these deep-water blocks, the bonuses paid were, with hindsight, extremely modest. Elf, for example, paid in the region of $10 million to secure the operatorship of Block 17, which by the end of the 1990s had become legendary in global oil circles.

After further technological advances, Sonangol in the late 1990s opened bidding on a further four exploration blocks, in ultra-deep waters, to the west of the other 'miracle blocks' 14 to 18. Following the deep-water discoveries, bidding for these blocks was frenzied. One of the blocks, 34, was awarded to Norsk-Hydro for about $400 million, under a special deal to help Sonangol develop operating expertise. Elf, Exxon and BP won the operatorship of the other three blocks after pledging signature bonuses of around $300 million each, at a time when oil prices were reaching a 25-year low. With exploration and development ongoing in both the deep and the ultra-deep blocks, it is estimated that around $2–4 billion will be invested in Angola's oil sector every year for at least the next ten years.

With a current production of 832,000 bbl/d, Angola remains in the minor league of oil producers, ranking as the 25th world producer with 1 per cent of world production. In 2003, oil exports represented a value of $8.5 billion, bringing $3.8 billion in fiscal revenue – or $277 per capita. Critics have argued that there is, however, no way of knowing if these figures are correct and have alleged revenue underreporting (Gary and Karl 2003). Government officials, in response, have pointed to the independent auditing of the oil sector by KPMG and the lack of support by the international firm for such allegations (see below). The country is currently the second largest producer in sub-Saharan Africa, after Nigeria. However, with recent discoveries brought into produc-tion, Angola could be reaching a production level of 2.5 million bbl/d by 2015. Although Nigeria's reserves remain about four times larger than those of Angola (9 billion barrels),[7] Angola could overtake that country and become sub-Saharan Africa's top producer. Given the exponential rise in Angola's known reserves in recent years, oil compa-nies see involvement in Angola as a key means of replacing their own reserves. Some companies also view Angola's deep waters as a key development and testing ground for pioneering new technology.

A further factor which encourages multinationals to do business in Angola is the modus operandi of Sonangol, which is widely reputed to be an impressively reliable and professional company, if a very hard bargainer. Sonangol has cleverly used the successive rounds of bidding and negotiation to divide and rule the foreign oil companies working in Angola, and to extract the highest payments and the most favourable terms possible from them. There is no question that in the Angolan oil industry it is the foreign companies which dance to Sonangol's tune, and not the other way around. Despite the chaos which prevails in most of Angola, Sonangol functions as a highly efficient state within the state. Besides its licensing, exploration, production and distribution branches, its drilling rigs, ships, construction yards, refinery and airline, Sonangol also operates its own shops, schools, kindergartens, clinics and sports teams. Only the company's employees have access to these services.

In total, Angola's oil industry employs only about 10,000 Angolans. It is in every way – physically, socially and economically – an extreme example of an enclave sector. Physically, most of the oil is produced offshore, loaded straight from the rigs onto tankers, and shipped off to international markets without ever coming into contact with Angolan terra firma. Until the early 1990s international oil companies, and oil service companies, kept their staff and installations in Angola to a minimum, preferring wherever possible to run their Angolan operations from overseas. Likewise, equipment destined for the production of oil in Angola was almost entirely manufactured and assembled outside the country. One of the few companies which did have significant installations in Angola, Chevron, maintained an enclave within an enclave: the company's Angolan operations ran from the Malongo camp in Cabinda, which is surrounded by mine fields and which expatriate staff are absolutely forbidden from leaving. In recent years, under pressure from Sonangol and the Angolan government, this has begun to change. All of the major oil companies have now invested in office space and accommodation for some expatriate staff in Luanda. Nevertheless, virtually all of the supplies necessary to their operations, from paper clips to Perrier, are shipped in from abroad. Even with this expansion of oil operations on Angolan soil, the industry is still present only in the coastal towns of Cabinda, Soyo, Luanda, Sumbe and Lobito, which were very rarely directly affected by the fighting. Had Angola's oil reserves lain onshore, in areas vulnerable to the fighting, it is highly unlikely that the war would have gone on for so long, although other forms of conflicts, as in the case of Nigeria, might have been more likely (Watts 2004).

Socially, many of the inhabitants of Angola's war ravaged interior are not even aware of the fact that their country produces so much oil. The oil industry remains a capital intensive and low employment sector. Furthermore, because the oil sector has been the only part of the Angola economy to grow since independence, and because the pay and opportunities provided by oil companies are so much better than in any other sector, the oil industry has sucked in the vast majority of the country's most qualified and able personnel at the expense of other sectors. Meanwhile, economically, the performance of the oil sector has been entirely unrelated to, and unaffected by, the performance of the wider economy and the state of the rest of the country

While agriculture and manufacturing collapsed as a result of both Portuguese mass departure at the time of independence and the wars, oil has continued to grow. Even in a time of low oil prices, such as 1998, the oil sector accounted for 61 per cent of GDP, and 74 per cent of government revenues. Thus an industry which employs less than 0.2 per cent of the active population, and which is barely present physically in the country, accounts for the lion's share of the country's income. The state's oil revenues are collected partly in the form of production share and of royalties, taxes and bonuses paid by international oil companies, and partly in the form of money raised through loans guaranteed against future oil production share.

This economic dominance is not unusual for oil economies. Yet, in contrast to many oil-dependent countries, Angola has much potential for achieving a diversified economy (Hodges 1993; McCormick 1994; World Bank 1991). Historically, this dependence has much to do with the departure of Portuguese settlers who operated most of the secondary and tertiary sectors, as well as the context of a continuous state of war. The MPLA, however, also came to rely on an enclave 'offshore economy' based on oil revenues and geared to finance the war and feed the army and a growing urban population of refugees. High oil prices from the mid 1970s favoured this option until 1986 when prices collapsed. By then, however, the dominance of oil had become structurally embedded in the Angolan economy. The continuation of the conflict, combined with ineffective government policies and reforms thwarted by political interference, prevented the development of a broad-based 'onshore' economy, resulting in rising debt as imports remained essential.

Attempts to break out of oil dependency have focused on recreating a manufacturing sector and transforming colonial agricultural estates into state farms, rather than supporting smallholder agriculture. This agricultural policy largely failed due to a lack of managerial skills, distrust of peasant farmers who were seen as politically hostile or unreliable, and inadequate technological inputs (Sogge 1994). Its main political consequence was to lessen governmental legitimacy among the rural population, to the (relative) benefit of UNITA. Angola's political geography thus came to be defined by the economic abandonment of the hinterland and its agricultural sector, with drastic consequences for the livelihoods of its population. This policy increased the vulnerability of the rural population and promoted further urbanisation – which grew from 18 per cent in 1975 to about 36 per cent of the population by 2003. Aside from this push effect and the impact of war, the urbanisation process was accelerated by the pull effect arising out of the creation of non-productive public employment and urban subsidies – in part a specific strategy of the government to lower social tensions (Gelb et al 1991). This policy of promoting urban 'social peace' has come under threat over the last decade as a result of the privatisation of the economy, structural adjustments lifting subsidies on fuel, and the forced displacement of poor people from the city centres to peripheral areas.

WAR, GOVERNANCE, AND THE POLITICAL ECONOMY OF OIL INDEPENDENCE

The MPLA government has faced considerable problems in asserting its sovereignty and legitimacy since independence. Militarily, UNITA progressively took over the hinterland in the 1980s and left the government only in control of the coast and main provincial towns, reflecting the duality of political power and claims for legitimacy. Politically, internal divisions within the MPLA resulted in a failed uprising in 1977 by partisans of a populist socialism and led to party purges and a consolidation of a presidential rule to oversee the interests of a *nomenklatura* (Hodges 2001). Theoretically a mass movement of socialist obedience, the MPLA was fundamentally an elitist movement that turned into a party apparatus after co-optation of, or violent confrontations with, competing groups. While an orthodox 'Marxist-Leninist' political line reigned, the personal convictions of party members 'were hidden [and] conflicts over policy direction and fights over group interests took the form of silent struggles for posts and privileges' (Messiant 1995). After initial reforms started in 1985, notably under pressure from leading Luanda families eager to develop private business interests, in 1990 the MPLA abandoned its references to Marxism-Leninism and the one-party system.

Despite constitutional changes towards a parliamentary democracy in the 1990s, the overall political structure remains one of personalistic rule by the president and his entourage, though this is less extreme than in the case of UNITA. Nominated by the president, most provincial governors rule their provinces as private fiefdoms, embezzling much of the budget through 'phantom' civil servants or overbudgeted public projects awarded to their private companies. Using the financial and institutional context created by the centralised control of the oil rent and allocation of state resources, President dos Santos acts as the tactical arbiter of a clientelist presidential regime. His relative victory in the September 1992 presidential elections reinforced his legitimacy and power, allowing him to distance himself from the MPLA, evict competitors from their positions and concentrate various mandates in his own hands, including at one point the function of prime minister.

The privatisation of most sectors of the economy in recent years has allowed the president's close relatives and cronies to take up economic stakes. People in the immediate presidential entourage are not the only ones, however, to seize economic opportunities. Many generals, in particular, have grown increasingly independent through diamond mining and trafficking, cattle trading, private security firms, the privatisation of state farms and real estate, or the import sector. President dos Santos' commitment not to run in the next presidential elections – which keep being postponed – may accelerate reforms and the institutionalisation of more democratic politics. Yet such a transition also raises the prospect of political unrest as competitors fight over the control of such a patrimonial regime.

Overall the state has disengaged itself from its role of social services' provider, despite the huge share of the economy coming under its control through the oil rent. As remarked by Eugenio Manuvakola, the President of UNITA 'Renovada' which integrated the peace process:

> the strength of [UNITA leader] Savimbi has come from the state's absence in the hinterland. It is not that Savimbi is strong, but that the state is weak; and it is weak because the state leadership is uninterested [in the population].[8]

Commenting on the state of local service institutions in rural Angola, Christoplos (1998:4) argues for example that 'Angola does not "lack capacity" to provide basic services. The government rather decided to abandon its own personnel. [Staff] have turned over the responsibility of making use of their civil service to NGOs and donors.'

Unsurprisingly, displaced people routinely mistook foreign aid for government services, and believed that the government is 'rich' and 'generous' since it appears to pay for (Médecins Sans Frontièrs) doctors and (World Food Program) maize. Resident populations are less credulous, however, especially those civil servants who depend on employment contracts from donors or petty corruption and user-fees to survive and provide basic services.

Criticism within and against the MPLA party has generally remained muted, despite improvements for independent media and political expression in the capital city (Human Rights Watch 2004a). Though some progress has taken place over the last decade in terms of freedom of opinion and public political opposition, arbitrary arrests and repression are still taking place, while populations remain at the mercy of arbitrary rule by a corrupt and politically immune *nomenklatura*. The government also finances most 'opposition' parties and rewards supportive members of parliament.

Oil-dependent economies tend to be characterised by poor governance, resulting in part from the drive to consolidate power, with the

---

Box 2.1 Between patronage and kleptocracy

Techniques of political control:

- Force and threats: use of military and paramilitary/popular force to quash protest (e.g. repression in 1977, 1978 State Security Law, 'Ninjas' force in 1991-92, military apparatus).
- Co-optation: patronage redistribution inside and outside MPLA (including the FAA and the subsidising of most 'opposition' parties and members of parliament).
- Blame and scapegoating: for governmental failings, especially economic ones (scapegoats include UNITA, Bakongo returnees, Lebanese and foreign traders, individual ministers).
- Façade democracy: most parties 'subsidised' by the state and many fake parties created and funded.
- Sanctions and threats: against journalists and researchers (e.g. journalist of Expresso fined, UNDP consultant persona non grata), companies (e.g. BP-Amoco threatened with contract cancellation because of transparency), and foreign governments which the MPLA judges meddle with Angolan oil, corruption, and arms (e.g. economic threats to France, breaking off diplomatic relations with Switzerland).

Techniques of economic appropriation:

Former mechanisms of central planning meant to achieve social goals became mechanisms for patronage:

- Foreign exchange: arbitrage and access to official exchange rate.
- Credit: access to credit at negative real interest rates.
- Contracts/Licences: award of state contracts, import and monopoly licences, concessions and commissions from foreign suppliers.
- Property: expropriation of formerly state owned businesses/property.
- Oil revenue and public budget: embezzlement and privileged access.

misappropriation of oil revenues instrumentalised to facilitate corruption. In Angola, the redistribution of oil revenues is largely mediated by the government, with revenue flows administered through both official state channels and parallel ones. This has two effects of significance with respect to livelihoods: first, it reduces the overall state budget available for social expenditure; second, it skews government expenditure towards privileged sectors and segments of the population.

This skewed redistribution must be viewed within the context of a worsening macro-economic situation since the 1980s. The overall macro-economic situation was characterised by fiscal deficits, balance of payment crises, repressed inflation, proliferation of parallel markets and an extremely distorted structure of relative prices and wages (Pereira da Silva and Solimano 1999). With negative oil price shocks in the second half of the 1980s, the government built up a large debt, first towards the Soviet bloc, and then towards Western banks.[9]

Unsurprisingly, a large proportion of the official Angolan budget was dedicated to military expenditure. Sustained combat against well-equipped South African and UNITA armies led to the construction of a capital-intensive war machine and made the army (FAPLA, now FAA) a priority recipient of budgetary allocations (Campbell 1996). Although oil revenues were not highly significant in military terms, given Soviet bloc assistance prior to 1989, they became crucial in the post-Cold War context as the government began mortgaging future oil revenues in order to purchase weapons on the international arms market. Since the failure of the peace process in late 1992, the MPLA has imported close to $5 billion worth of arms, mostly in 1993 and 1994 (Human Rights Watch 1994 and 1999). Arms procurement contracts provided considerable corruption opportunities (see below). This investment in the military apparatus possibly influenced the behaviour of the government in favour of a militaristic approach. A government military officer argued that, in contrast to UNITA, 'we always take losses, then recover. ... If we lose a tank, we pick up the phone and order another one. If UNITA loses one, it is more difficult.'[10] This strength also enticed the government into intervening militarily to root out support for UNITA and to support friendly regimes in Congo Brazzaville and the Democratic Republic of Congo since 1997, as well as in Namibia in 1999. Most recently, the Angolan government responded to a call for military assistance from President Gbagbo in Ivory Coast, bringing this former UNITA ally into the sphere of influence of Luanda.

In the post-Cold War period, military costs have been paid through public budget allocation: oil-collaterised short-term commercial loans passed directly through Sonangol, and signature bonuses from oil concessions. With the fall of oil prices in 1998, the government faced a renewed financial crisis at the time it was launching a new military campaign. The oil price recovery in 1999, signature bonuses amounting to $870 million for oil concessions, and the re-arrangement of a half-billion dollar loan by a Swiss bank have since eased the financial crisis and most of this windfall was absorbed by military spending (Human Rights Watch 1999).

As can be observed from Table 2.1, the proportion of social to military expenditure is low, and decreased significantly until 2000. Furthermore, remaining social expenditure is highly skewed towards privileged segments of the population. In 1995, for example, over a

Table 2.1 Oil sector in the economy and public finances (1992–2002)

	1992	1993	1994	1995	1996	1997	1998	1999	2000	2001	2002
Oil exports (million US$)	3759	2964	3074	3735	5071	4741	3091	4491	7120	5803	7677
Oil price ($ per barrel)	19	16	15.3	16.6	20.4	18.6	12	17	27	23	24
Oil and LPG in GDP (%)	36	40	57	56	58	49	39	61	61	54	56
Gvt. oil revenue (million $)	1578	1780	1518	1324	2625	2293	1506	2504	4098	3209	3349
Share of oil in	75.2	81.9	88.9	87.2	89.2	82	74	88	89.4	79.6	76.7
Gvt. revenue (%)											
Gvt. expenditure (% total)											
Social expenditure	23	21	9	14	10	13	11	5	15	20	16
Military expenditure	21	25	34	31	35	36	34	31	15	16	15

Source: IMF (1999, 2003), Hodges (2001, 2002); estimates for 2002.

third of the Ministry of Education budget was allocated to overseas scholarships. In the same year, $400 million was allocated to subsidies on petrol, electricity, municipal water, transport and housing, provided mostly to relatively affluent Angolans (Kyle 1998; UNICEF 1999). In 2001, about 12 per cent of the education budget was still allocated to overseas scholarships, equivalent to about half of the allocation to primary education (United Nations 2001).

In addition to skewing the redistribution of oil revenues via official government channels, revenues are redistributed through a variety of parallel channels. The main beneficiary has been the ruling élite and military apparatus: the 'oiligarchy'. Oil revenues are redistributed to a number of state and private companies and privileged sections of the population, through different mechanisms including embezzlement of public funds and privileged access to foreign exchange and credit (Ferreira 1995; Hodges 2001; Somerville 1986). A significant proportion of these funds fall directly under the control of the presidency through a variety of mechanisms, including 'signature bonus' payments from oil companies upon the awarding of oil concessions. Since 1996, the share of signature bonuses received by the presidency has been officially set at 55 per cent.

Official government revenue from oil has been erratic (35–60 per cent of gross revenue) and budgetary allocation largely non-transparent – with 'unclassified' government expenditure reaching $8 billion between 1999 and 2002, or 38 per cent of total revenue (IMF 2003). Preliminary results from a diagnostic study of the oil sector requested by the IMF as part of a Staff Monitored Program reportedly indicated that significant misappropriation of funds, running into the hundreds of millions of dollars, has been identified. A recent internal IMF report estimated that $4.2 billion had gone missing from state coffers between 1997 and 2002 (Human Rights Watch 2004b).[11] The $900 million reported missing for 2001 represented about three times the value of foreign humanitarian aid for Angola. Government officials have rejected such claims, however, arguing that weak institutional capacity in accounting had led to delays and poor reporting.

To some degree the highly centralised control of redistribution of oil revenues stems from the authoritarian nature of the MPLA regime. This authoritarianism cannot be solely or even primarily attributed to the mineral wealth of the country. Rather, significant factors include the personality of the leadership, as well as the nature of the Portuguese colonial regime and successive wars that have set individual political competitors in opposition to one another. While supposedly at the base a mass movement led by socialists, the MPLA has operated as a party apparatus under the control of its leader (the late Agostinho Neto and, since 1979, President dos Santos). From at least the mid 1980s, the regime has created a *nomenklatura* that formed the basis of a clientelist presidential regime.

Despite constitutional changes by the MPLA from single-party rule to a parliamentary democracy, and the holding of elections supervised by the UN in 1992, the overall political structure remains one of personalistic rule supported by allocation and accumulation of oil revenues.[12] As demonstrated by the behaviour of the elite, and its apparent contempt for the plight of population, this situation is also embedded in a deep-rooted class structure that transcended the departure of Portuguese settlers and the socialist rhetoric of the early MPLA movement. The disdain and social distance between many in the élite and the majority of the population is noticeable in everyday life in the wealthy parts of Luanda and in the lack of contact between politicians and their constituencies. Even the government's ombudsman in charge of social communication argues that 'people in the provinces only need five things: petrol, salt, soap, dry fish, and cassava.'[13]

The impact of 'oiligarchic' governance on politics, livelihoods and the military has been extensive. In terms of politics, although the regime has moved towards a constitutional democracy, citizens' representation is very limited. Members of parliament were selected, nominated and elected on a party basis, and the president and the government nominate provincial governors and municipality administrators. The only major non-armed opposition party, the FNLA, was co-opted and effectively collapsed. Criticism within the MPLA has generally been muted, in part due to the repression of dissent through the exile or co-optation of major players. The government finances most opposition parties and rewards supportive members of parliament (Hodges 2001). Major cash handouts, gifts and access to bank credit are made available to MPs supporting the regime. Support is not exclusive to MPLA members; for example, the Angolan parliament was popularly labelled the 'Audi-torium' as every MP was entitled to use a brand new Audi A6 – worth $70,000 and imported by a presidential crony. However, as a UNITA MP benefiting from this programme pointed out, the MP's salary is barely sufficient to service the car, implying the need for significant extra-salary sources of income. Most major private businesses include formal or informal joint ventures with members of the ruling élite. This partly explains why economic reforms initiated from 1987 onwards remained tepid and resisted by powerful vested interests within the ruling élite.[14]

Besides the impact of war, the macro-economic situation and poor governance have had significant and multidimensional impacts on the population. Key symptoms include the levels of poverty and income inequality. Poverty is widespread, and while there is a dearth of figures at a national level, studies of limited population samples suggest that between 60 and 80 per cent of households are living below the poverty line ($40 per month), and 12–33 per cent are living in extreme poverty ($14 per month) (IMF 1997). From 1995 to 1998 the wealth of the richest

10 per cent of the population increased by 44 per cent, while that of the poorest 10 per cent decreased by 59 per cent (UNDP 1999). Impacts on livelihoods have included a dearth of social services outside those provided by foreign donors and aid agencies, poor economic opportunities besides subsistence agriculture and petty informal trading, and high levels of insecurity and repeated displacements of large groups of people within government areas.

Although the government must be given due credit for its attempts at negotiation, particularly in light of an inadequate UN peacekeeping mission, the availability of oil revenues and the associated capacity to pursue a military campaign may have dissuaded it from pursuing all diplomatic options to their full extent. Moreover, the corruption and reduction and re-allocation of budgetary allocations entailed by pursuit of the military option, as outlined above, have served to entrench a *nomenklatura* within government structures whose interests are not aligned with those of ordinary Angolans. Furthermore, corruption also made the military less effective, thereby prolonging the conflict (Global Witness 2002b). The case of arms purchases through oil-backed loans in the mid 1990s illustrates that process. Even with the cessation of hostilities, critics reported that corruption on the part of senior political figures in charge of the demobilisation programme was jeopardising the quartering operations of UNITA soldiers and threatening the transition to peace.

WAR, GREED AND CORPORATE BEHAVIOUR

Although Angola's natural wealth was likely to constitute a major prize to the winning party and probably played a role in the strategic decisions of the belligerents and foreign backers, there is very little available evidence indicating that a scramble for Angola's resources significantly influenced the early phase of the civil war. From a Portuguese perspective, the military defence of colonial possessions had as much to do with the imperialist ideology of the Salazarist regime as the growing economic interests provided by the colony. Even fast rising oil revenues in the context of the 1973 oil crisis did not derail the independence process launched by the new Portuguese government. Although the nationalist parties undoubtedly realised that controlling the capital was key to power, Savimbi himself had underplayed the significance of oil to his supporters by declaring that 'the MPLA controls the capital, but in Luanda they produce only sand. Here [on the central plateau] we produce food' (Bridgland 1988:19).

The instrumentalisation of war to access oil and other resources was not systematic during the second phase of the conflict either. At a regional level, while Zaire eyed the oil resources of the enclave of Cabinda, the necessity of transporting Zairian and Zambian copper through Angolan railways actually dampened the conflict, with both countries withdrawing support for opposition parties in 1976. South Africa's military intervention in Angola was not so much motivated by a resource grab as by the understanding that the natural wealth of the country, and oil in particular, would provide a communist state with much greater independence from Pretoria than it had expected from a country as economically dependent upon South Africa as Mozambique.[15] If the US government did embargo the oil revenues generated under the MPLA by US companies, it relaxed this decision in 1976 and passed the Clark amendment that prohibited funding to UNITA until 1985 (Rodman 2001; Wright 1997). Similarly, the Soviet Union and Cuba did not undermine US and Western economic interests in the Angolan oil and diamonds sectors. While Cuba's strong involvement in the cobalt market may have given it incentives to intervene in favour of the rebellion in the cobalt producing province of Katanga/Shaba in Zaire during 1978, allegations by the Mobutu administration and the Carter administration that it did so remain controversial.

Oil and diamonds, however, came to significantly influence the course of the third phase of hostilities as foreign backing began to dwindle and ideological agendas waned. Oil funding the MPLA and diamonds funding UNITA is a simplistic yet relatively accurate reading of the Angolan war economy. Until recently, this division over natural resources was reinforced by the war, as the government lost control over diamonds, while oil remained out of reach of UNITA due to its mostly offshore location. Throughout the 1990s, this duality and complementarity of resources consolidated the MPLA and UNITA's respective political and military terrain. International resource-based business schemes were key to sustaining capital intensive armies when foreign state backing stopped in the early 1990s, and as such played a part in the belligerents' security dilemma and violent drive for power. Yet, despite UNITA losing its control of most major mining sites over the last four years and facing difficulties in converting its large diamond stock into fuel and weapons, the war did not end before the death of Savimbi.[16] Instead, UNITA shifted to guerrilla activities, in large part sustained by predation over civilians and commercial trade.

Testifying to the importance of diamonds in the second peace process, the position of Minister of Mines and Geology was first on the list of official postings granted to UNITA by the Lusaka Protocol. Yet the Protocol failed to provide any details on the management of the sector aside from the obligation to hand over UNITA-held territory to the government. Negotiated solutions failed and military offensives by the government towards UNITA mines in 1997 undermined the peace process. In 1997, Savimbi stated that UN sanctions 'would be regarded as an attack on UNITA to which it "was ready to respond"' (Human Rights Watch 1999). Isolated in the central eastern province of Moxico,

UNITA's leader reportedly died with a sizeable stock of diamonds and no one to trade them with, leaving most of his troops starving.[17] Tales of greed-driven rebels did not appear to match the emaciated faces of many hard-line UNITA commanders, who could have settled long ago in Burkina Faso or with other friendly regimes with their supposed diamond wealth. As mentioned earlier, if Savimbi was greedy his greed was for power, not simply money. How the greed factor may have played into the behaviour of government officials has been discussed above, although very little is yet known about the private wealth of the Angolan ruling élite.

Corporate practices and 'resource diplomacy'

Most resource corporations argue that they are neutral economic actors disengaged from the 'business of war' (Bray 1997). Angola demonstrates the contrary. With huge demand for arms and a wealth of mineral resources, this country became the 'Eldorado' of savvy businessmen juggling political relations, arms dealing, and natural resources brokering.[18] Because of the minimal disturbances caused by the war to an oil sector largely based offshore, most companies were unconcerned by hostilities and the human rights record of both parties. As put by an expatriate oil company manager:

> We, as well as [other oil companies], have proven that we can produce anyhow. The conflict does not matter so much for our activities, except if the whole country was in blood and flames, including Luanda. Even then, the price of petrol bothers us much more than the political situation.[19]

Most oil corporations justify their lack of initiative by arguing that they are working in a 'competitive environment', in which they cannot afford to take further political risks by supporting pro-peace reforms. Concentrating on their 'core business activities' – accessing fields and producing oil – they leave such tasks as budgetary transparency and accountability to international agencies like the World Bank and the IMF. This competition argument, however, is often one-sided: oil companies are not in competition when it comes to preventing political risks or reforms that might threaten their direct interests. For example, French corporations intentionally associate themselves with their US counterparts precisely to reduce political risks.[20] There is thus a double standard in matters of competition and risks, one concerning corporate interests, and the other concerning Angolan interests. In the absence of collective action by oil companies, risks exist for ethical initiatives by individual corporations. Having openly published its payments to the government, BP was threatened by the government oil company with contract termination that would have jeopardised billions of dollars in investment and future earnings.[21] As a clear warning, the letter was copied to all the other oil companies. About two months after the incident, BP hired a former Angolan Ambassador as its country executive vice-president, possibly to patch this gap in 'confidence', although a company official denied such a relation.[22]

While most companies have come under criticism for being 'silently complicit' with regard to allegations of corruption in the Angolan oil sector, most have sought to improve their reputation through supporting humanitarian initiatives. These initiatives deal with health, sanitation, educational sectors or domestic business-development sectors. In 1998, for example, the Chevron oil company made 28 grants, mainly for school and health services, totalling more than a million US dollars, thus making it one of the larger private aid agencies operating in Angola.[23] In 2001, Chevron sponsored the first Angolan trade mission to the United States. Some companies have also focused on the training of Angolan nationals, with Norsk-Hydro in particular setting up a joint venture with Sonangol to develop Block 34. Companies have also increased the physical presence of their staff in Angola.

Controversially, however, some foreign oil companies also directly provide goods and services, deducted from the companies' tax bills, to prominent figures or their philanthropic associations, such as the Eduardo dos Santos Foundation (FESA), which has been playing a growing role in extending presidential patronage in politics and promoting his personal public image (Messiant 1999). The payment by Chevron and the Cabinda Trust in 1998 was reportedly paid to ADPP (part of the Humana/Tvind Teacher Group), an organisation with close ties to the state oil company, Sonangol, whose director Morgens Amdi Petersen was charged in Denmark with fraud and embezzlement and deported from the United States in 2002.[24]

The controversial role of the oil industry in Angola dates back to the 1960s when, in the midst of a war of independence, the US company Gulf Oil – now within Chevron-Texaco – agreed to commercially exploit oil in Cabinda. US church groups and the MPLA denounced this corporate support for colonial and white minority rule in southern Africa.[25] Relations between oil corporations and the government established in Luanda have not changed: only the ruling élite has changed, the Portuguese being replaced in 1975 by the MPLA. Corporate managers continue to stress that 'we don't have a political role here, we make business with whoever is in power.'[26]

Ten international oil companies, from eight countries, are now working as operators in Angola, including all of the oil majors. Despite the war, Angola is perceived by companies as a secure investment and by governments as a reliable supplier. UNITA never acquired marine capabilities, and oil production was only once affected by the civil war, when UNITA attacks shut down onshore production in Soyo in 1993. Similarly, FLEC has never managed to hamper production from Cabindan waters, although the movement has kidnapped the employees of oil companies on several occasions. Besides being seen as physically secure, Angola is also perceived as politically stable and reliable, having had the same government ever since independence. This stability, however, was at least temporarily shaken during the 1991 peace process and resumption of the conflict, when some French and US interests believed that a UNITA electoral or military victory was possible. Along with internal divisions, this apparently led Elf and the French government to follow dual policies supporting both sides.

For companies and states wishing to diversify their sources of oil away from the Middle East, non-Muslim, non-OPEC Angola has also become particularly attractive. Thus, for example, in 2001 around 50 per cent of Angola's oil production was exported to the United States, accounting for around 4 per cent of all American oil imports.[27] On a visit to Cabinda in 1997 the then US Secretary of State Madeleine Albright pointed out that this was higher, as a percentage, than US imports from Kuwait immediately prior to the Gulf War (which had been only 1.6 per cent). Her comments appeared to be a thinly veiled warning to anyone planning to threaten those supplies, indicating the lengths to which the American government would go to secure them. Following the terrorist attacks on the United States in September 2001, the US administration sought to diversify its oil supply outside the Middle East, with West African oil a major target (Angolan oil represented 5.1 per cent of non-OPEC US oil imports in 2002). Since 9/11, President dos Santos has met with President George W. Bush twice; on the last occasion in May 2004 seemingly urging that President Bush 'turn a blind eye to delaying elections [until 2006] in exchange for oil and other promises of reform'.[28]

The Angolan government also considered that the access it allowed to oil should reflect the degree of the support (including military support) it received from foreign states. In the case of France, President dos Santos publicly stated to the new French ambassador that a Franco-Brazilian arms dealer, Pierre-Joseph Falcone:

> dealt with sensitive matters with the consent of the French authorities ... which were of great utility for Angola. We interpreted his action as a gesture of confidence and friendship on the part of the French State. For that reason, my government took decisions that permitted the spectacular growth in cooperation with France in the petroleum sector and in financial and economic areas.[29]

Angolan oilfields are indeed significant to TotalFinaElf, and indirectly to the French government, as Block 17 constitutes one of the largest oil reserves of the company, itself the biggest in France. Beyond these major economic players are a plethora of smaller companies, several of which have links to the Israeli political and security establishment. UNITA had similarly benefited from external support in relation to diamonds. Many Western businesspeople had supported Savimbi in the hope that the 'freedom fighter' would help them in return once in power. Reciprocally, Savimbi cultivated 'friendship' through donations of diamonds, including gifts to several regional rulers who in return extended diplomatic and arms-transiting facilities.

In all these aspects, the role of oil and diamonds in relation to the war went far beyond simple financial revenues. As in the case of other commercial dealings of strategic and political significance, these two resources also provided incentives in the fields of beneficial foreign relations and strategic support. If the death of Savimbi and the end of the conflict mark the beginning of a new era, commercial preoccupations will continue to dominate the diplomatic agenda for Angola. Peace, however, means that the government is facing increased pressure to account for the oil revenue. As argued by Alex Vines of Human Rights Watch, 'in the past [the Angolan government] used the war to deflect criticism but now they will find a great deal of international and domestic attention on the use of revenue.'[30]

BRINGING ABOUT TRANSPARENCY AND ACCOUNTABILITY AFTER THE WAR

International and domestic calls for greater transparency and a higher priority for social issues have undeniably marked the new 'post-conflict' era. The Angolan government has responded with a number of important measures, notably in terms of transparency and budgetary allocation. Oil revenues are now made publicly available through the Ministry of Finance; public accounts are more transparently managed through the Central Bank; the findings of an independent auditing of the oil sector have been made public; and some provinces, such as Cabinda, have also made public their expenditures. Internationally, the Angolan government has also expressed its interest in participating in the British-sponsored Extractive Industries Transparency Initiative, which sets international standards of transparency and good governance. Several provincial governors who had become an embarrassment for the regime were reappointed elsewhere, and technocrats were nominated in some key official positions. Even elections were scheduled for 2006, nearly a decade after the mandate of the current government technically ended, although as this book went to press they had been postponed once again. Critics of the regime, in any case, remain doubtful about the effects of these measures and pronouncements (Gary and Karl 2003; Global Witness 2004; Human Rights Watch 2004b; IMF 2004).

Oil production is scheduled to rise sharply in coming years, reaching 2 billion bbl/d by 2008. Government oil revenues will also increase (although not as fast as production, since oil companies recover their investments through a greater share of cost oil, and more revenues are absorbed by higher production costs for deep-water fields). Investments in other resource industries, such as diamonds, could strengthen this upward trend in governmental revenues as the peace starts to attract major investors. Given the current state of poverty of the population and minimal livelihood opportunities apart from subsistence agriculture and petty trading, the management of this revenue windfall will largely determine the broad development of Angola. In this respect, institution building and reforms with regard to revenue transparency, fair allocation and accountability are crucial, with the Angolan government, civil society, oil companies, donors and international agencies all playing a part.

The consolidation of the democratic process and a more open society in which an independent judiciary and media, as well as parliamentary functions and civil society, play an effective role in guaranteeing the protection of the most vulnerable in the population will continue to be a major priority. Much will depend in this regard on the nature of the political transition characterising possible elections in 2006 and change of personalities among the highest levels of the government. The most likely scenario, however, will be a preservation of the interests of the current ruling élite through the election of a 'protégé'. As demonstrated in several other countries, such political transition 'without change' risks becoming unstable if the new governmental team rapidly loses legitimacy among the population, as greater political competition and popular frustrations lead it to resort to increased repression.

Incentives by international financial institutions and donors will also be important in reforming the fiscal and budgetary framework. In this respect, these financial actors are likely to see their leverage even further reduced as oil revenues increase over the next six years (Hodges 2002). Efforts in this direction must therefore be made in the short term. Several analysts, in this respect, have called for strict aid conditionality with regard to reconstruction and development assistance, requiring the Angolan government to assume the main financial responsibility and to ensure transparency in public finances now that the war is over (Tvedten 2002). Even such selective conditionality faces its own dilemma, however. Poorly targeted international assistance in reconstruction and development does risk further entrenching the privileges and self-interest of the élite, through the corrupt financing of major infrastructure works and selective assistance to a private sector which sustains political cronyism. On the other hand, well-targeted reconstruction and development efforts by the international aid community can promote the emergence of a more politically independent middle class that will be most able to transform the Angolan polity and domestic governance in the long term. As some Angolan opposition politicians point out, it is only through economic independence that political freedom can be secured, and the emergence of viable business ventures outside of the key resource sectors is critical in this respect.[31] Perpetuating the economic dependence of Angola on the oil sector will only serve to prolong political patronage.

Compared with donors and aid agencies, oil companies may have greater room for manoeuvre as the number of offshore oil blocks open to future competition is reduced. Not only could international oil companies make concerted efforts to improve the social impact of the oil sector, but they could also join pro-change coalitions and initiatives in a more forthcoming way. Undoubtedly, the Angolan government has many other means of reining in companies wishing to press for reforms on transparency, but it cannot alienate all oil investors and operators. Progress in this regard should come from a joint reform of the financial reporting system – as proposed by the Extractive Industries Transparency Initiative – and a greater degree of accountability on the part of the Angolan government at all levels. Finally, better fiscal transfers from the oil industry will not solve the problems of underdevelopment and inequality in Angola. Access to land as well as fair access to education and economic opportunities will also prove essential.

CONCLUSION

Some tentative conclusions can be drawn from this study in terms of the relations between oil and the Angolan conflict, and their impact on the population. Arguably, the availability of oil revenues meant the Angolan ruling élite cared little about the collapse of the rest of the economy, in particular that of the hinterland. This had a negative impact on the population, which in large part was rural and depended on the agricultural sector and a trading network between the main coastal towns and the interior. It can also be suggested that to some degree the availability of oil revenues to a privileged and influential segment of the population made them indifferent to the continuation of the war. More generally, oil allowed the state to function as financially independent from the population and the rest of the productive economy, leading to a gap in citizen representation. Despite a relative capacity to serve the public interest, the state was largely absent and in any case mostly unaccountable, especially in rural areas. In turn, this institutional impact played in favour of UNITA and possibly prolonged the conflict. Oil revenues affected the structure and dynamics of state institutions, funding the system of presidential patronage and feeding what appears to be high-level corruption on a scale as massive as that of

Nigeria in the mid 1990s, although the level of evidence for embezzle-ment under President dos Santos is far lower than that for General Sani Abacha. The financial workings of the oil sector, with its concentration of revenues and quasi-exclusive offshore nature, also encouraged a lack of transparency, especially through oil-mortgaged loans and the opera-tions of Sonangol. The discretionary and secretive nature of decision making as well as competition between managing institutions resulted in 'creative' accounting, confusion, and possibly outright theft.

The vast amounts of money generated through the work and invest-ment of foreign companies also instilled a 'get rich quick' and 'money for nothing' mentality among many within the élite, resulting in lifestyles that the country cannot afford. This foreign involvement, and the bene-fits it generated for oil companies and the banking institutions, may also have curtailed international criticism of the government because of the economic stakes that were potentially involved. In this regard, the behav-iour of international oil companies, banks, and some donor governments reduced the leverage of the population and international actors who were demanding better governance of the oil sector.

Finally, the oil sector financed a military build-up that allowed for a military victory by governmental forces, although at a high cost to vulnerable populations. Beyond ending the war in Angola, this build-up also allowed the Angolan government to intervene militarily in the conflicts in Congo Brazzaville in 1997, the Democratic Republic of Congo in 1998, and Ivory Coast in 2002. Angola is also playing a growing role in the development of oil sectors in several countries in the region, such as São Tomé, Equatorial Guinea, Congo-Brazzaville and Gabon. The management of the growing oil revenue will thus not only be crucial to the development of Angola, but it may also have a significant influence on the future stability and prosperity of the region.

NOTES

1. Cited in Paul Salopek 'CEOs of War Bleed Angola', *Chicago Tribune*, 2 April 2000.
2. Reuters (Luanda), 1 June 1998.
3. All '$' = US dollars.
4. Calculation based on a 60 per cent tax return on production levels of 742,000 barrels per day (bbl/d) at $20 per barrel – a conservative estimate.
5. Cited in Timothy Bancroft-Hinchey, 'Cabinda: Call for International Help', *Pravda*, 22 June 2002.
6. Angolan Law No. 13/78. Promulgated 26 August 1978.
7. Figures for proven oil reserves vary from 5.4 to 25 billion barrels. Proven oil reserves for Angola are still listed at 5.4 billion barrels by the US Energy Information Agency (1 January 2006), whereas CIA fact book estimates are at 25 billion barrels. Sonangol lists liquid oil reserves at between 0.81 and 1.3 billion barrels – a 'conservative estimate', according to a special advertising site. The *Washington Post* figure stands at about 10 billion barrels – about a

third of the Nigerian oil reserves. See:
www.washingtonpost.com/wp-adv/specialsales/spotlight/angola/
article2.html
8. Interview with Eugenio Manuvakola, Luanda, 2001.
9. The debt towards the Soviet Union amounted to $1.6 billion for non-military and $4 billion for military supplies (IMF 1997).
10. FAA officer cited in Human Rights Watch, 1999.
11. The Economist, 'Measuring corruption', 26 October 2002. IMF reports cited by Human Rights Watch include: 'Angola: Staff Report for the 2002 Article IV Consultation' (2002:31–3); 'Angola: Staff Report for the 2002 Article IV Consultation' (2002:33); and 'Angola: Selected Issues and Statistical Appendix' (2003:107–9).
12. It should be noted that this tendency was more extreme in the case of UNITA, over which Jonas Savimbi maintained a totalitarian rule, unhesitatingly murdering dissenters and competitors, which resulted in significant defections from his movement and the creation of an alternative UNITA movement (so-called UNITA Renovada).
13. Interview with de Moraires, July 1998, Luanda.
14. For a detailed analysis of reform processes, see Aguilar (1999).
15. The South African Defence Force, however, did move into southern Angola to protect South African investments in the Cunene river hydroelectric dam (Guimaraes 1998).
16. UN sanction monitor, personal communication, Luanda, 2001 – name withheld.
17. Interview with Lopos do Nascimento, citing General 'Gato' Lukamba's wife, April 2002.
18. Only oil is discussed here. For more on the role of diamonds in the political economy of war, see Global Witness 1998 and Le Billon 2001, 2002.
19. Interview with oil corporation official, Luanda July 1998.
20. Interview with oil corporation official, Luanda July 1998.
21. Letter from Sonangol reproduced in Global Witness 2002b:41.
22. Interview with BP official, April 2002.
23. David Sogge, personal communication, September 2002.
24. Africa Confidential, 2000; see www.tvindalert.org.uk.
25. Gulf Oil covered about 30 per cent of the $54 m Portuguese military budget in the country. See Barnett and Harvey, 1972; CIC, 1972.
26. Interview with oil corporation official, Luanda, July 1998.
27. 'U.S. Crude Oil and Total Petroleum Imports from Selected Countries and Country Groups, Recent Months and Annual Averages for 1986–Present', http://www.eia.doe.gov/emeu/international/petroleu.html#USTrade.
28. Alexander's Gas and Oil Connection (2004) 'Angola and US meet for fourth time', News and Trends: Africa, Vol. 9, No. 11, 2 June 2004.
29. 'Remarks by His Excellency José Eduardo dos Santos, President of the Republic of Angola, on the occasion of the presentation of credentials by the new French Ambassador to Angola Luanda, 23 February 2001'.
http://web.archive.org/web/20030507054306/http://
www.angolamissionun.org/English/Mission_AtivDipl_002.htm,
last accessed on 7 November 2006.
30. Cited in Jonathan Leff, 'Will Angolans See Oil Wealth After Savimbi's Death?', The Namibian, 1 March 2002.
31. Interviews with the author, June 2001, Luanda.

BIBLIOGRAPHY

Africa Confidential (2000) 'Social Oil', *Africa Confidential*, Vol. 49, No. 18.

Amnesty International (1998) *Angola: Extrajudicial Executions and Torture in Cabinda* (London: Amnesty International).

—— (2004) *Annual Report 2004* (London: Amnesty International).

Aguilar, R. (1999) 'The Evolution of the New Private Sector: the Case of Angola', in Addison, T. (ed.) *Underdevelopment, Transition, and Reconstruction in Sub-Saharan Africa* (Helsinki: UNU/WIDER).

Aguilar, R. and Stenman, A. (1995) *Angola: Let's Try Again* (Gotenburg: Department of Economics, University of Gotenburg, Sida, Macroeconomic Studies No. 63).

Barnett, D. and Harvey, R. (1972) *The Revolution in Angola: MPLA, Life Histories and Documents* (New York: Bobbs-Merrill).

Beau, N. (2002) *La Maison Pasqua* [The Pasqua house] (Paris: Plon).

Bray, J. (1997) *No Hiding Place: Business and the Politics of Pressure* (London: Control Risk Group).

Bridgland, F. (1988) *Jonas Savimbi: A Key to Africa* (London: Hodder and Stoughton).

—— (1990) *The War for Africa* (Gibraltar: Ashanti).

Cahen, M. (1989) *'Vilas' et 'Cidades': Bourgs et Villes en Afrique Lusophone* ['Villages' and 'cities': villages and cities in Portuguese-speaking Africa] (Paris: L'Harmattan).

Campbell, H. (1996) 'Humanitarianism, War and the Recolonization of Angola', paper presented at the Chr. Michelsen Institute, Development Studies and Human Rights, Bergen, Norway, May 1996.

Christoplos, I. (1998) 'Humanitarianism and Local Service Institutions in Angola', *Disasters*, Vol. 22, No. 1.

CIC (1972) *Gulf Oil: Portuguese Ally in Angola* (New York: Corporate Information Center of the National Council of Churches).

EIU (2001) 'Angola, Country Analysis Brief', October 2001.

Ferreira, M.E. (1995) 'La Reconversion Economique de la *Nomenklatura* Pétrolière', *Politique Africaine*, Vol. 57.

Gary, I. and Karl, T. (2003) *Bottom of the Barrel: Africa's Oil Boom and the Poor* (Baltimore, Md.: Catholic Relief Service).

Gelb, A.H., Knight, J. and Sabot, R. (1991) 'Public Sector Employment, Rent Seeking and Economic Growth', *Economic Journal*, Vol. 101.

Global Witness (1998) *A Rough Trade: The Role of Companies and Governments in the Angolan Conflict* (London: Global Witness).

—— (1999) *A Crude Awakening: The Role of the Oil and Banking Industries in Angola's Civil War and Plunder of State Assets* (London: Global Witness).

—— (2002a) 'Publish What You Pay', press release (London: Global Witness, 13 June).

—— (2002b) *All the President's Men* (London: Global Witness).

—— (2004), 'Angola: Transparency Move Welcome but Serious Questions Remain', press release (London: Global Witness, 13 May).

Guimaraes, F.A. (1998) *The Origins of the Angolan Civil War: Foreign Intervention and Domestic Political Conflict* (London: Macmillan).

Henderson, L.H. (1979) *Angola: Five Centuries of Conflict* (Ithaca, N.Y.: Cornell University Press).

Hodges, T. (1993) *Angola to 2000: Prospects for Recovery* (London: Economist Intelligence Unit).

—— (2001) Angola: from Afro-Stalinism to Petro-Diamond Capitalism (Oxford: James Currey).

—— (2002) Angola's Economy: Perspectives for Aid Partners, in Tvedten, I. (ed.) Angola 2001/2002: Key Development Issues and Aid in a Context of Peace (Bergen: Chr. Michelsen Institute).

—— (2004) Angola, Anatomy of an Oil State (Oxford: James Currey).

Human Rights Watch (1994) Arms Trade and Violations of the Laws of War since the 1992 Elections (New York: Human Rights Watch).

—— (1999) Angola Unravels: The Rise and Fall of the Lusaka Peace Process (New York: Human Rights Watch).

—— (2004a) Unfinished Democracy: Media and Political Freedoms in Angola (New York: Human Rights Watch).

—— (2004b) Some Transparency, No Accountability: The Use of Oil Revenue in Angola and Its Impact on Human Rights (New York: Human Rights Watch).

International Monetary Fund (1997) 'Angola: Recent Economic Developments', IMF Staff Country Report No. 97/112 (Washington, D.C.: International Monetary Fund).

—— (1999) 'Angola: Statistical Annex', IMF Staff Country Report No. 99/25 (Washington, D.C.: International Monetary Fund).

—— (2003) 'Angola: Selected Issues and Statistical Appendix Series: Country Report No. 03/292' (Washington, D.C.: International Monetary Fund).

—— (2004) 'Statement by IMF Staff Mission to Angola. Press Release No. 04/155', 21 July 2004 (Washington, D.C.: International Monetary Fund).

Kyle, S. (1998) 'Angola: Current Situation and Future Prospects for the Macroeconomy', CAER Paper No. 25 (Cambridge, MA: HIID).

Le Billon, P. (2001) 'Angola's Political Economy of War: The Role of Oil and Diamonds 1975–2000', African Affairs, Vol. 100.

Le Billon, P. (2002) 'Thriving on War: The Angolan Conflict and Private Business', Review of African Political Economy, Vol. 90.

Maier, K. (1996) Angola: Promises and Lies (London: Serif).

Matloff, J. (1997) Fragments of a Forgotten War (London: Penguin).

McCormick, S. (1994) The Angolan Economy: Prospects for Growth in a Postwar Environment (Washington, D.C.: Center for Strategic and International Studies).

Messiant, C. (1995) 'MPLA et UNITA: processus de paix et logique de guerre' [MPLA and UNITA: peace process and logic of war], Politique Africaine, Vol. 57.

Messiant, C. (1999) 'La Fondation Eduardo dos Santos: à propos de l'investissement de la société civile par le pouvoir politique' [The Eduardo dos Santos foundation: the take-over of civil society by political powers], Politique Africaine, Vol. 73.

Pélissier, R. (1977) Les Guerres Grises: Résistance et Révolte en Angola, 1845–1941 [Grey Wars: Resistance and Rebellion in Angola, 1845–1941] (Orgeval: Pélisser).

Pereira da Silva, L.A. and Solimano, A. (1999) 'The Transition and the Political Economy of African Socialist Countries at War (Angola and Mozambique)', in Paulson, J.A. (ed.) African Economies in Transition, Vol. 2 (Basingstoke: Macmillan).

Rodman, K.A. (2001) Sanctions Beyond Borders: Multinational Corporations and US Economic Statecraft (Lanham, Md.: Rowman and Littlefield).

Sogge, D. (1994) 'Angola: Surviving Against Rollback and Petrodollars', in Macrae, J. and Zwi, A. (eds) War and Hunger (London: Zed Books).

Somerville, K. (1986) *Angola: Economics and Society* (London: Frances Pinter).

Tvedten, I. (2002) 'Angola 2001/2002: Key Development Issues and Aid in a Context of Peace', *Report R 2002:8* (Bergen: Chr. Michelsen Institute).

United Nations Development Program (1999) *Human Development Report* (New York: Oxford University Press).

—— (2003) *Human Development Report* (New York: Oxford University Press).

United Nations Children's Fund (1999) *Un Futuro de Esperanca Para as Criancas de Angola* (Luanda: UNICEF).

United Nations (2001) 'Memorandum on the draft text of the Interim Poverty Reduction Stategy Paper (I-PRSP)' (Luanda: United Nations System in Angola).

Watts, M.J. (2004) 'Antinomies of Community: Some Thoughts on Geography, Resources and Empire', *Transactions of the Institute of British Geographers*, Vol. 29, No. 2.

World Bank (1991) *Angola: An Introductory Review* (Washington, D.C.: World Bank).

Wright, W. (1997) *The Destruction of a Nation: United States' Policy Towards Angola since 1945* (London: Pluto).

3 Greed and grievance in Chechnya

Yahia Said

Since the collapse of the Soviet Union, Russia has fought two wars in Chechnya, the first lasted from 1994 to 1996 and the second, started in 1999, continues to date with sporadic violence. Thousands of Russian soldiers, and as many as 10 per cent of Chechnya's original population have lost their lives. A fifth of all Chechens have had to flee their homes.

The Russian military,[1] plagued with corruption and inefficiency, inadequate funding and weak political leadership, were unable to defeat the Chechen warlords in the first war and are unlikely to win outright in the current one. They have, however, inflicted widespread destruction, and almost all the victims have been civilians. The Chechen warlords, on the other hand, proved unable to win the peace. Kidnapping, highway robbery and terrorism continued to emanate from Chechnya even after the withdrawal of Russian troops and the signing of the Khazavyurt peace agreement in 1996.

The second Chechen war, unlike the first, was initially popular in Russia, so much so that it helped propel its main architect, Vladimir Putin, to the pinnacle of Russian power. Seven years on, more and more Russians are beginning to realise that this war cannot be won, short of annihilating the entire Chechen population. For Putin, who has built his legitimacy on efforts to reverse decades of state decline, the war has become a liability. Apart from a handful of warlords with links to international Islamic networks, available information suggests that most Chechens are yearning for a negotiated settlement, even if it does not lead to an independent Chechen state.

This chapter looks at the role of oil in the Chechen conflict, and asks whether the oil factor contributed to the causes of the war and whether oil has been significant in sustaining, exacerbating or mitigating the conflict.

Oil, as I argue, was for a long time the lifeblood of the war economy sustaining the conflict. Chechnya has a small oil industry with an estimated output of 40,000 to 80,000 barrels per day (bbl/d). A significant proportion of this industry was illicit, with the proceeds divided between the Russian military and the Chechen warlords.

Oil also contributed to the causes of war indirectly in two ways. First, US policy towards Caspian oil, and the Baku–Tbilisi–Ceyhan pipeline in particular, are perceived by parts of the Russian military and political establishment as a direct challenge to Russia's interests in the region. In this context of geopolitical competition, Chechnya acquires an added importance, making it much harder for Russia to seek compromise or accept international involvement in the resolution of the conflict. Second, like most countries in transition, Russia suffered not only from economic decline but also from a pervasive weakening of state structures and institutions. State weakness, which may have been exacerbated by a growing dependence on oil revenues, contributed to the beginning of the conflict, its intensity and persistence. Under Putin Russia seems to have reversed the decline of the Yeltsin years and dealt with some of the economic manifestations of oil dependence. Putin's authoritarian regime is reminiscent of the petro-states of the 1970s (Karl 1997). As such it may still sustain the conflict as a channel of patronage in response to rent seeking which would allow it to procrastinate on military reform. On the other hand the Chechen economy, and particularly the oil industry, is gradually emerging from the shadows with an increase in the relative size of legitimate oil production and export. This, perhaps more than any other development, offers the best hope for an end to the conflict.

In the following sections I will provide an overview of the two Chechen wars – their triggers and causes, as well as the factors that sustain the conflict. I will start with a description of the Chechen oil industry.

THE OFFICIAL CHECHEN OIL INDUSTRY

In a distant past Chechnya used to be the second largest oil producer in the Soviet Union after Azerbaijan. In the 1970s Chechnya produced 21.5 million tonnes of oil per year falling to 6 million immediately before the war. Today, official output stands at less than 2 million tonnes per year, or 40,000 bbl/d.[2] Illegal extraction is estimated at anywhere between an official estimate of 100,000 and 2 million tonnes per year. Even at this level, though, Chechen oil production is comparable to Russia's on a per capita basis.

One of the legacies of the Chechen oil industry was its large refining capacity, which has since been destroyed by war. Ironically the Grozny refinery, the largest in the former Soviet Union, was unsuitable for Chechen oil, which had to be shipped to a special refinery in Tuapse on the Russian Black Sea coast.

Given its decline and the war, the Chechen oil company Grozneft was not a sought-after prize in the scramble that led to the privatisation of the Russian oil industry. It remains state owned, with 49 per cent of its share controlled by the pro-Russian Chechen Interim Administration and 51 per cent by the Russian government-owned company, Rosneft.

Grozneft and its parent company Rosneft have been fighting a desperate battle against the Chechen Interim Administration, the Russian military, the warlords and the bootleggers to consolidate control over the industry and eliminate illegal siphoning and refining. Even the salaries for Grozneftgaz staff are sometimes commandeered by the Chechen rebels. Over the past three years there has been some progress on this front, with an ever larger share of Chechen oil being produced legitimately. Grozneft is also generating one of the most transparent sources of revenue and public services to the Chechen population.

TRIGGERS AND CAUSES OF THE FIRST CHECHEN WAR

The Chechen perspective

Dudayev's weakness

The Chechen nationalist movement was not dissimilar from its sisters which mushroomed across the Soviet Union during the latter's dying moments in the1980s, composed of former *nomenklatura*, members of the shadowy underworld of the 'second economy', and minor intellectuals. Thus the movement featured Zelimkhan Yanderbiyev, a little known Islamist poet who became vice-president during the first Chechen republic and briefly succeeded President Dudayev after his assassination. Leading intellectuals were usually too moderate for these movements. They had an affinity to Russia and a nostalgia for the 'golden days' of the Soviet Union. The movement also included Communist Party apparatchiks sensing the winds of change and positioning themselves for the post-Soviet era, like the former local Party Secretary Doku Zavgaev. It also included 'businessmen', as successful criminals liked to be called at the time, including Dudayev's First Deputy Prime Minister Khodja Akhmed Nukhayev, who was sentenced to 9 years in prison for allegedly running a protection racket in Moscow. In its early days the Chechen nationalist movement also included sundry activists such as environmentalists and human rights advocates.

Perhaps what distinguished the Chechen nationalist movement was the radicalism and brutality which dominated it from early on. There were other extremist nationalist leaders like Elchibey in Azerbaijan and Gamzakhurdia in Georgia but they were quickly overthrown. There are many reasons for Chechen nationalism to be more radical and violent than other Soviet-dominated groups, which are addressed below, but one reason could be found in the figure of its leader – Dzhokhar Dudayev. His ascent to the pinnacle of the Chechen nationalist movement was counterintuitive. He was the only Chechen to become a general in the Soviet airforce. He commanded a nuclear bomber wing, but this could just as well have acted to his disadvantage. Moreover, he had hardly ever lived in Chechnya, having served in various parts of the USSR, and was stationed in Estonia when he became the chairman of the Chechen National Congress in 1990. His wife was Russian and most importantly he belonged to an insignificant *teip*, as Chechen clans are called. Some argue (Lieven 1998) that it was his weakness that allowed the competing factions to choose him as a non-threatening compromise figure. If that was the plan it was a fateful mistake. From early on Dudayev sought to compensate for his weakness by adopting an extremist rhetoric which at times seemed irrational. This not only alienated the Russians and Yeltsin, who initially viewed Dudayev as an ally against Gorbachev and the remnants of the Soviet Union, but it also forced the most moderate elements out of the Chechen nationalist movement. Dudayev also sought to compensate for his lack of support within Chechnya by building a power base of criminals and freelance warlords. Nukhayev, the Vice-President, was serving a nine-year jail sentence in the Russian Far East and was transferred at Dudayev's request to Grozny in 1991 to assume his position (Khlebnikov 2003).

Dudayev's extremism, however, did not improve his popularity, and by the time of the first war his regime was on the verge of collapse (Evangelista 2002). After three years in power he had failed to deliver security or prosperity for ordinary Chechens; on the contrary, although he inherited one of Russia's poorest regions, the situation in Chechnya deteriorated significantly under his rule. With its oil industry in decline, and given the tensions between Dudayev and the Kremlin, it is arguable that Chechnya suffered even more than other regions from delays in the transfer of pensions and public sector wages from Moscow. However, at the same time Chechnya enjoyed an offshore tax status aimed at assisting underdeveloped regions and used by Moscow-based businesses as a tax-evasion mechanism. It also received oil export quotas from Moscow estimated at between $300 million and $1 billion for the period 1991–94 (Lieven 1998).[3] This, in addition to the repatriations from the Chechen mafia which at that time controlled Moscow, should have been sufficient to make the fewer than 1 million inhabitants of the region wealthy. The money, however, never reached ordinary Chechens. It is unlikely that Dudayev himself was corrupt but it is beyond doubt that he was surrounded by corrupt people.

At the start of the war Dudayev was facing serious challenges from three directions: a pro-Russian 'puppet' opposition, radical Islamists seeking a more religious and less corrupt regime, and moderates working for a peaceful arrangement with Russia. The outbreak of the war almost certainly saved his administration from collapse and forced the various nationalist factions to unite around him.

Ancient hatred

Chechnya's history is replete with brutal insurgencies against Russian rule, and even more brutal repression. The first clash between Russia and a coalition of northern Caucasian nations led by the Chechen Sheikh Mansur Ushurma started in 1785 as a response to Russian attempts to establish formal control over the region. In a pattern that would repeat itself in future confrontations, Sheikh Mansur was successful in the military campaign but failed to hold together his unruly coalition, which ultimately allowed the Russians to succeed. Russian control over the region was, however, nominal until the appointment of General Yermolov in 1816 as a Commander of the Caucasus with the task of pacifying the region. It was Yermolov who built Grozny (translated as 'terrible' in Russian) as a fort to intimidate the Chechens. His campaign ignited a 40-year-long Chechen revolt which was to be led in its latter part by Imam Shamil, the mythological figurehead of Chechen resistance. That campaign was not dissimilar from the current war in the brutality employed by both sides and the toll taken on the civilian population.

There were numerous other revolts after the defeat and capture of Imam Shamil in 1859, most notably after the collapse of the Tsarist regime in the period 1917–20. At the time some Chechens sided with the Bolsheviks against their former tormentors – the White Russians and Cossacks. But the Sufi religious leaders, who included Imam Shamil's grandson Said Beg, had no love for the communists and turned against them once the White Russians were defeated. The revolt was suppressed in 1921. In an emblematic move, even the Chechens who fought on the Bolshevik side were later executed by Stalin.

A relatively small Chechen revolt in 1940, in which some of the insurgents attempted to unite with advancing German forces, gave Stalin the excuse for a 'final' pacification of this unruly nation. In February 1944 he summarily deported the entire Chechen population of around 700,000 to the inhospitable steppes of Kazakhstan. Tens of thousands were killed, including all hospital patients and inhabitants of remote villages who would have slowed down the 'timetable' (Lieven 1998). Others died en route or upon arrival in Kazakhstan in the middle of the winter. It is difficult to overstate the deep scars left by Stalin's deportation on the Chechens. The brutality of the transfer was compounded by the unforgiving nature of the Kazakh steppe and the humiliations to which the Chechens were subjected in exile over the following two decades. It was not until 1957, after Stalin's death and the ascent of Khrushchev, that the Chechens were able to return to their homeland.

Ancient hatreds cannot in themselves explain the conflict or the brutality with which it has been fought, but they do offer a reservoir of narratives on which leaders can draw in their rhetoric.

The Russian perspective

'Small victorious war'

By the time of the war in Chechnya, Boris Yeltsin was in no better shape than his Chechen counterpart. He had squandered the political capital earned when he climbed the tank in defiance of the reactionary coup attempt in August 1991. In his subsequent quest to displace Gorbachev he had to strike alliances with anti-Soviet separatists like Dudayev. Former allies, including many Russian regional governors, sought payback by contesting Moscow's control and holding Yeltsin to his promise to give the regions 'as much sovereignty as they can take'.

The 'shock therapy' economic policies enacted by Yeltsin's 'young reformers' were more ideological than rational. They did little to prevent the collapse of the reeling economy inherited from Gorbachev, or to alleviate the damage caused by the collapse of the Soviet Union and the loss of captive markets in Eastern Europe. On Yeltsin's watch the economy contracted by half while hyperinflation wiped out the meagre savings of an impoverished population. The economic reforms exacerbated the social impact of the crisis, created opportunities for corruption and generally de-legitimised the transition process. Low oil prices and contracting output, in addition to poor tax collection and widespread embezzlement, meant that the state coffers were empty. The Red Army which Yeltsin inherited was robbed of its state, ideology, top-brass and purpose. To add injury to these insults, it had to contend with hunger as the military had to go for months without wages, rations or uniforms, not to speak of new equipment.

An alliance of communists and proto-fascist nationalists was emerging as the main challenge to Yeltsin's rule. They were advancing populist slogans of restoring national pride and social justice and combating corruption. A war may have seemed to offer a convenient diversion for Yeltsin and some of his military commanders, and an opportunity for rape and pillage for a frustrated army. The term 'small victorious war', often cited as the main justification for the war from the Russian side, is attributed to Yeltsin's Secretary of the Security Council at the time, Oleq Lobov (Lieven 1998).

Dudayev's extremist rhetoric

It is unlikely that Yeltsin intentionally went for war in Chechnya to save his regime from collapse and keep the army happy, but the context provided a disincentive for efforts to prevent war. That is not to say that others in the Yeltsin administration were not spoiling for a fight, including the Minister of Defence Pavel Grachev, Nationalities Minister Sergei Shakhrai and the president's Chief of Staff Sergei Filatov. Efforts to prevent war were further complicated by Dudayev's virulent rhetoric and provocative actions, which were more aggressive than those of other regional leaders who were pursuing similar agendas.

Dudayev resembled Palestinian leader Yasser Arafat in many ways. Both were returning exiles with no real domestic power base. Both had symbolic rather than real legitimacy – a weakness for which they had to compensate through a combination of unseemly alliances and bombast. Both presided over corrupt and authoritarian regimes although they may not have been corrupt themselves. Both seem to have walked away from good compromises. Like Arafat at Camp David in 2000, Dudayev inexplicably scuttled several openings for compromise in the weeks immediately before the war. Tatarstan, which is Russia's most populous Muslim republic, had obtained de facto independence, including passports, embassies and full control of its substantial oil industry. Dudayev could have obtained a similar deal if not for his virulent anti-Russian rhetoric and his style, which left little space for dialogue. He famously accused Russia of trying to destroy Chechnya with an 'artificial earthquake', called Yeltsin a 'leader of a gang of murderers' and a 'diabolical heir of a totalitarian monster' and declared that 'Russism is worse than Nazism' (Lieven 1998). Most provocatively he threatened to execute 19 Russian military personnel who were captured after a botched coup attempt by the pro-Russian opposition on 26 November 1994. He later retracted the threat and returned the soldiers, but war nonetheless started two weeks later on 11 December 1994. In a poll conducted by the Public Opinion Foundation (FOM) both leaders topped the list of politicians 'who behaved most inappropriately in the run up to the war'. Russians spread the blame evenly, with 27 per cent holding Yeltsin at fault and 24 per cent laying the responsibility on Dudayev (FOM 1994).

The geopolitical context

The beginning of the war coincided with a frenzy of geopolitical manoeuvring around Russia. Proposals for a Baku–Tbilisi–Ceyhan pipeline, which would ship newly discovered oil from Azerbaijan to Turkey and so bypass Russia, were perceived by many as an attempt to cut Russia off from the Caspian and its oil. The US administration at the time did not hide the fact that the pipeline and its policy in the Caucasus in general were aimed at loosening Russia's grip over the newly independent republics. Talking about the Baku–Tbilisi pipeline US Energy Secretary Bill Richardson said:

> This is about America's energy security, which depends on diversifying our sources of oil and gas world wide. ... It's also about preventing strategic inroads by those who don't share our values. ... We're trying to move these newly independent countries toward the West. ... We would like to see them reliant

on Western commercial and political interests rather than going another way. We've made a substantial political invest-ment in the Caspian, and it's very important to us that both the pipeline map and the politics come out right.[4]

The expansion of NATO to former Soviet republics was being mooted for the first time. The emergence of the US-backed Ukraine–Geor-gia–Azerbaijan axis was perceived as a serious provocation by the Russian establishment. An independent Chechnya would have fitted squarely into this axis. It would also have significantly diminished the possibility of transporting Caspian oil through Russia. Indeed the Chechens, by disrupting the Baku–Novorossisk pipeline, significantly weakened Russia's bargaining position over the 'Main Export Pipeline' route at a critical stage of the negotiation process.

The threat of Chechnya leading the Northern Caucasus out of Russia and thus cutting it off from the 'warm waters' of the Caspian and Black seas is the recurring nightmare of Russian geo-strategists, and of the traditional military establishment in particular. It is a constant narrative of the successive campaigns to pacify the region over the centuries. Indeed one of the main justifications used by the military for the Chechen war was that letting the region escape Russian control would amount to a betrayal of the thousands of Russian soldiers who had died fighting for it over the centuries.

This sentiment was, however, far from universal. Ordinary Russians, not to speak of the new intellectual and business élites, had no objection to Chechnyan independence, especially if the alternative was war. In a poll conducted by the FOM in 1998, 42 per cent of respondents suggested that Chechnya should get full independence, while 27 per cent suggested it should get a special treaty like Tatarstan and 18 per cent believed that it should remain an integrated part of Russia with no concessions (FOM 1998). This pattern changed dramatically over the following years, with a 2004 poll indicating that 48 per cent of Russians believe that Chechnya should remain within Russia (FOM 2004).

Crime and terror

The other recurring theme of Russia's wars in Chechnya is crime. Since they first came into contact with the Russians in the seventeenth century, the Chechens have raided their neighbours' settlements and transport routes for cattle and hostages. Putting an end to these raids was one of the main aims of Yermolov's campaign in the nineteenth century. In Soviet times, Chechens held a prominent position in the criminal under-world. A reputation for brutality, fierce clan loyalty and a safe haven in the lawless Chechen mountains were some of the advantages which helped them along the way. Chechen mafiosi had a moral advantage over their rivals. They believed that stealing state property and breaking Soviet law was an act of patriotism (Khlebnikov 2003).

By the time war broke out in 1994, Russia was engulfed in organised crime and violence. In this environment, crime associated with and emanating from Chechnya reached new heights. During that period Chechens had cornered the protection-racket market in Moscow – a considerable source of revenue since Moscow accounted for 35 per cent of the Russian economy. They were so powerful that they are credited with underpinning Moscow Mayor Luzhkov's ascent to power. One of Luzhkov's main lieutenants, Umar Dzhabrailov, has been banned from entering the United States on the grounds that he is allegedly implicated in organised crime and politically and economically motivated assassinations. [5]

Chechen control over the Russian underworld was nothing new, but the wave of kidnappings and hijacking raids that emanated from Chechnya in the period before the war presented a massive problem for the government. Numerous airplanes, trains and buses were hijacked by Chechen criminals throughout Russia. Often the hijackers would either take the hostages to Chechnya or escape there after collecting ransom. The hijacking of four buses in neighbouring Ingushetya in rapid succession in June and July 1994 is widely considered to be one of the main triggers of the war.

THE FIRST CHECHEN WAR 1994–96

Russia did not so much start the first Chechen war as gradually sink into it. The notoriously corrupt Minister of Defence Pavel Grachev (aka Pasha Mercedes) claimed that he could take Grozny in a couple of hours with a regiment of paratroopers (Gall and de Waal 1998). Many military commanders, including two deputy ministers of defence, were opposed to the war and felt that Russia was ill prepared. During the first weeks of the conflict the army was on the verge of mutiny, with many commanders refusing to obey orders. The ministries of Defence and the Interior had to bypass the chain of command to run the war. The various parts of the Russian military, underfunded, uncoordinated, incompetent and corrupt, made mistake after mistake and faced great losses from the first days of the war. Each disastrous engagement led to further entanglements as Russia poured in more and more men and equipment to 'rectify' the situation.

Russian forces soon started to vent their frustration, fear and anger at their lack of supplies on the civilian population. Contract soldiers, who were even less competent than conscripts when it came to combat, became notorious for terrorising defenceless Chechen civilians. From the first indiscriminate bombing raids on Grozny to the massacre of dozens of civilians in the village of Samashki in October 1999, civilians were the main casualties of the war.

There are widely differing accounts of the casualties in both Chechen conflicts. The State Statistical Office estimates Chechen and Russian civilians killed in Chechnya during the first war at 30,000–40,000. The human rights group Memorial sets the number at 50,000. The second war is estimated by Memorial to have cost 25,000 civilian lives. It estimates total war casualties including rebels and Russian military at 90,000.[6] By contrast Taus Jabrailov – a Chechen MP who tracks the war's body count – sets the number at 160,000 (Uzzell 2005).

In response to the invasion and army brutality, the Chechens buried their differences and mounted a successful two-year campaign to oust the Russian forces. While enjoying both the military and moral high ground, Chechen fighters showed no more regard for civilian lives and property than their Russian counterparts. They terrorised those whom they regarded as Chechen collaborators as well as Russian civilians in neighbouring regions. On 14 June 1995 Chechen Commander Shamil Basayev drove two truckloads of Chechen fighters 40 miles into Russia, past numerous checkpoints, and seized the maternity hospital in the town of Budyonovsk, along with several hundred hostages whom he threatened to kill if Russia did not withdraw its forces from Chechnya. During that incident he executed several wounded Russian military captives. Most of the 90 casualties of the raid were civilian. Russian Prime Minister Chernomyrdin had to comply with most of the hostage takers' demands, including the initiation of negotiations on a ceasefire and safe passage.

The Chechen campaign culminated in August 1996 with a humiliating defeat for Russian forces and the fall of Grozny. Negotiations and the withdrawal of Russian troops followed shortly afterwards. Following the wisdom of the time, the Khazavyurt agreement of September 1996 left the final status of Chechnya open, to be determined five years later. In May 1997, the newly elected Chechen President Maskhadov and Yeltsin signed the 'Treaty on Peace and the Principles of Mutual Relations between the Russian Federation and the Chechen Republic Ichkeria'. The treaty renounced the use of force and determined that relations between Chechnya and Russia should be 'in accordance with the generally accepted principles and norms of international law'[7] – a de facto recognition of Chechen independence.

THE PEACE THAT LED TO WAR: TRIGGERS OF THE SECOND WAR

The Chechen perspective

The Khazavyurt peace agreement of 1996 was in reality an uneasy truce. Hawks in the Kremlin and the Russian military did everything in their power to make the Chechens pay for the humiliating defeat. Significant resources were needed for reconstruction after a devastating war, but instead Chechnya was left under a virtual blockade. Promised reconstruction aid never came through, diverted through mismanagement and corruption as well as by intent.

Various attempts at breaking Chechnya's political and economic isolation were thwarted by the Russian establishment. They included the Caucasus Common Market, an initiative developed by Vice-President Nukhayev. The idea of building a common market akin to the European model involving Chechnya, other Northern Caucus republics, Azerbaijan and Georgia had such illustrious backers as Jacques Attali, the first President of the EBRD, former US national security adviser Zbigniew Brzezinski and former British Prime Minister Margaret Thatcher. Russian oligarch Boris Berezovsky, who was deputy secretary of the Russian Security Council at the time, was also lobbying for large energy projects involving Chechnya.

Without a viable economic base, moderate Chechen President Maskhadov had no chance of delivering relief to his citizens or imposing his authority on the unruly warlords who had helped him to win the war. Chechens increasingly felt that their victory was pyrrhic. It did not bring any noticeable improvement in their living conditions nor did it rid them of Russian domination. This provided an opening for extremist warlords, led by Shamil Basayev, to pursue their own economic and political agendas, armed with the experience and equipment amassed during the war.

Hostage taking and highway robbery in Chechnya and the neighbouring regions were on the rise again, culminating in the kidnapping on 1 May 1998 of Valentin Vlasov, the Russian President's envoy to Chechnya. Another development during the interwar period was the discovery by some of the most prominent Chechen warlords of Wahabism – the radical branch of Islam associated with the Saudi Royal family and Al Qaeda. Independent observers could never substantiate Russian military claims that large numbers of Afghan *mujahideen* and Arab nationals fought alongside the Chechens during the first war. Relations with the *mujahideen*, and Al Qaeda in particular, were however established and expanded during the interwar period.

Links to international Islamic networks, including Al Qaeda, may well have been another way of making money for the Chechen warlords. The kidnapping and subsequent murder of British telecommunications engineers, and the gratuitous slaughter of six Red Cross nurses, are acts that could have been paid for and inspired by Al Qaeda. The warlord allegedly responsible for both incidents, in response to journalists wondering about the motive for beheading the telecoms engineers despite the offer of ransom by their company, claimed that he could lose more in Al Qaeda funding if he let the Westerners go. With hindsight, even the synchronised 1999 apartment building bombings, which effectively triggered the second Chechen war, carry an eerie resemblance to Al Qaeda atrocities. The Al Qaeda ideology, in combination with the need to break Russia's stranglehold on Chechnya, provided a justification for raids into neighbouring republics; the Chechen warlords were pursing the liberation of the entire Caucasus as the only way to liberate Chechnya.

The Russian perspective

The Chechens were not the only ones unhappy with the peace. The Russian military was left with the bitter taste of defeat at the hands of a tiny rebel army. Shortly after the first Chechen war a narrative evolved within the military along the following lines: 'The army was dragged into a losing war by corrupt and cowardly politicians and then betrayed with capitulation before it could finish the job.' This myth still resonates. The need to let the army 'finish the job' this time around is one of the major obstacles to ending the war.

The coordinated attacks on three apartment buildings in Russia, which left more than 300 people dead, and a desperate invasion of neighbouring Dagestan by Chechen rebels in August 1999 served as the official triggers for the second Chechen war as far as Russia was concerned. The bombings were the last straw in the context of continuing hostage taking and other Chechen crimes committed in neighbouring Russian regions. The raid into Dagestan, unlikely as it was to succeed, touched a raw nerve with the Russian establishment. It raised the prospect of rebellion in the entire region.

Regardless of motives and justifications, the war had a remarkable impact on the career of Vladimir Putin: the former KGB operative was plucked from obscurity to become President Yeltsin's successor. Putin's legitimacy during the handover period and in the crucial first months of his presidency was built entirely on the war. The regime change in Russia which followed from the second Chechen war, including Putin's meteoric rise to power and the consolidation of the power of the military and security establishments within the Russian state, led many to believe that Putin and his allies staged the apartment bombings and the Dagestan raid, or at least failed to act upon warnings about them, with the explicit purpose of igniting a second war (Dunlop 2002). This is hard to believe, but such conspiracy theories are understandable since, towards the end of the first Chechen war, it became harder and harder to distinguish between the two sides of the conflict. The Russian military and their Chechen allies used the same methods and displayed the same brutality as their Chechen opponents. Most Chechen warlords, as well as their Russian military counterparts, could be bought for the right price. That was best demonstrated later in the arrest of the Radio Free Europe reporter Andrei Babitsky by Russian forces who claimed that he was handed over to Chechen warlords. The reporter claimed that he was held all along by Russian forces posing as Chechen warlords.[8]

THE SECOND CHECHEN WAR, 1999 TO DATE

The second Chechen war was meant to undo the damage caused by the first conflict to Russia's pride, and that of its military. It was to be conducted using 'US-style' overwhelming force (80,000 Russian troops against 3000 rebels by most estimates) and precision bombing, while taking the utmost care to avoid Russian casualties. Unlike the first war, conducted under the banner of 'restoring constitutional order', this one was an 'anti-terrorist operation' which can have no legitimate opponent or a negotiated settlement. The idea, as Putin put it, using Russian high school slang, is to 'lock the Chechens into the toilet stall and give them a good drubbing'.

When the war started, Russia's leading human rights advocate and erstwhile human rights commissioner under Yeltsin, Sergei Kovalev, stated: 'We borrow NATO methodology while acting on the basis of Milosevic's ideology.'[9] He went on to accuse the Russian military of planning to commit genocide in Chechnya, since this is the only way the war can be fought. This prophecy has been borne out by the actions of the Russian military, which has conducted the second Chechen war with the same mixture of incompetence, corruption and brutality as the previous one. According to various sources, over 25,000 Chechen civilians are estimated to have been killed and a similar number have gone missing in this round of hostilities, mostly as a result of Russian 'mopping up' operations. Between 100,000 and 200,000 people have been displaced, out of a total pre-war population of less than a million (Uzzell 2005). Visitors to Chechnya describe scenes of devastation not seen since the grinding battles of the Second World War.

Seven years into the war Russia is in no better shape than it was on the eve of its defeat in the first conflict. Russian military casualties are estimated at 10,000, more than three times those of the previous war. The rebels seem to have total freedom of movement in any part of Chechnya and, most ominously, throughout the North Caucasus. Not a month goes by without spectacular operations leading to the destruction of Russian heavy equipment and aircraft and the murder of high-ranking officers. Chechens are succeeding in shooting down Russian helicopters, reminding observers of the critical point in the Afghan war when the *mujahideen*, equipped with Stinger missiles, overturned the strategic advantage of the Soviet Army.[10]

The Russians, however, have succeeded in recruiting some Chechen allies this time around. Most prominent among them was Akhmet Kadyrov, the Mufti of Chechnya during Dudayev's time who was elected President in September 2003 and assassinated by the rebels in May the following year. His son Ramzan is being groomed for succession. The Kadyrovs have their own militia – the self-styled 'defence forces of Chechnya' – of more than 1000 men. The force, mostly comprised of former rebels, is pursuing its own economic and political interest and conducting its own human rights violations.

Another Russian ally is Sulim Yamadaev, a warlord in the first war who now commands the 'Vostok' special operations battalion which is directly attached to the Russian Ministry of Defence. Vostok is comprised exclusively of former warlords and has earned notoriety for reprisals against civilians. In July 2005 the battalion was involved in a mopping-up operation in the village of Borozdinovskaya which resulted in the abduction of eleven villagers, widespread destruction and the mass exodus of the villagers to neighbouring Dagestan. The Russian authorities first tried to cover up Vostok's involvement in the event but seem to have reconsidered this position as it became apparent that the attack was ethnically motivated against the predominantly Avar inhabitants of the village.[11] Apart from the prospect of ethnic civil war in Chechnya itself, the various warlords seem to have succeeded in dragging some of the neighbouring regions into the conflict. Over the first half of 2005 there were numerous attacks in Dagestan, Ingushetia and Kabardino-Balkaria involving both Chechen and local fighters. Russia's fear of a regional conflagration seems to have become a self-fulfilling prophecy.[12]

One significant difference from the previous war is the news coverage in Russia. This is partly a result of Putin's clamp-down on independent journalists and media outlets not controlled by the Kremlin. It is also partly a self-inflicted wound by the Chechens. The abduction and occasional murder of many Russian journalists, including those who were sympathetic to their plight during the first war, means that few Russian journalists are prepared to cover the war today. Those that do enter the war zone face threats from both sides of the conflict.

ELEMENTS SUSTAINING THE CONFLICT

The first Chechen war was widely unpopular from the very outset. More than 60 per cent of Russians opposed the war only weeks after it started in 1994. The ratio of those opposing the war to those supporting it was reversed at the outset of the second war in 1999. Today, more and more Russians are convinced that there is no military solution to the conflict and that a peaceful settlement should be reached, even if it leads to Chechen independence.

Putin, whose ascent to power was built on the second Chechen campaign, remains popular but receives his lowest performance ratings on the subject of the war. In another FOM survey conducted in 2002, 61 per cent of Russians described Putin's reign as mostly successful but

Table 3.1 Attitudes to the war

'Do you approve of the conduct of the Russian military in Chechnya?'				
	1999	**2000**	**2001**	**2002**
Yes (%)	64	53	42	30
No (%)	23	34	46	48

Source: FOM 2002b.

identified the continued conflict in Chechnya as his main failure (FOM 2002a). Many in Russia believe that the war is being perpetuated by corrupt officers who are making a living out of the conflict.[13] Indeed, before the terrorist attack on the Moscow theatre in 2002 there were hints that Putin was beginning to explore the possibility of a peaceful settlement in Chechnya, including the floating of a peace initiative by former Prime Minster Evgenyy Primakiv, a person closely associated with Putin.[14] However, all such attempts were abandoned in the face of the brutal terrorist attacks on the Moscow theatre in 2002 and the school in Beslan in 2004, and the success of Chechen warlords in spreading the conflict to neighbouring regions.

The picture is not very different on the Chechen side. Before his murder, Aslan Maskhadov, the elected Chechen president, had offered to start unconditional negotiations with any willing Russian official. He even hinted at a readiness to abandon demands for full independence.[15] Shortly before his assassination in March 2005, Maskhadov had declared a unilateral ceasefire which was uniquely adhered to by all warlords. It went unanswered by the Russian government.

The Wahabi warlords who constitute the 'party of war' on the Chechen side are not popular among ordinary citizens. Their brutality has not been limited to Russians but has extended to those Chechens who are deemed to be collaborating with the occupiers. The warlords are blamed by many ordinary Chechens for needlessly provoking the second war. The extremist Wahabi rhetoric promoted by the likes of Movladi Udugov is alien to most Chechens, who espouse a more forgiving interpretation of Islam and whose overriding desire is to see an end to the conflict and military brutality.

So what are the reasons behind the continuation of the conflict, despite the fact that both populations and their leaders seem to be edging towards compromise?

Military brutality legitimating Chechen extremism

Not a day passes without gruesome revelations of Russian military brutality against the civilian Chechen population. Killings, rape, torture and kidnapping are carried out systematically by all branches of the Russian security services operating in Chechnya, and now increasingly by their Chechen allies. These actions are motivated by greed, frustration and sheer sadism, but they are also typical of most counter-insurgency operations throughout history. They have made it almost impossible for Chechens to live in the presence of the Russian military ever again.

Although most of the violence against civilians in the conflict is perpetrated by Russian troops, the Chechen warlords have done their share to alienate the Russian public. Terrorist attacks, hostage taking, kidnapping, slave labour and highway robbery have fed into pre-existing prejudices against the peoples of the Caucasus and are making co-existence between Russians and Chechens ever more difficult. Indeed, the escalating brutality on both sides is threatening to turn the war from a political conflict into an ethnic one.

Mutually beneficial war economy

There is one thing that Chechens and Russians, ordinary citizens and analysts all agree on. They all believe that the continued conflict is economically motivated. The war has created its own self-sustaining economy, including groups which can only maintain themselves through it. These groups include Russian officers, and contract soldiers and Chechen warlords fighting on both sides of the conflict (Evangelista 2002). The war economy is comprised of many elements which feed into each other and create a relation of mutual dependence and benefit between the warring parties. This has led analysts to allege that the Russian Military Intelligence (GRU) has been warning the most notorious Chechen warlord, Shamil Basayev, about possible attacks in order to sustain him as the main excuse for the continued war.[16]

The following points illustrate some of the main elements of the Chechen war economy.

Checkpoints

The Russian military are known to collect between $1 and $10 per person at checkpoints. There are hundreds of checkpoints throughout the small republic, even though most military commanders agree that they are useless from an operational perspective. The rebels bypass them during the day. During the night they are convenient targets. When he attacked the maternity hospital in Budyonovsk in 1995, Basayev claims to have paid $9,000 in bribes to Russian military manning the checkpoints on his way which allowed him to smuggle two truckloads full of armed rebels deep into Russian territory. The military is resisting repeated directives from Moscow to dismantle the checkpoints. Moreover, the various Russian power structures and the pro-Russian Chechen administration are competing with each other over who controls the checkpoints, thus providing an indication of their true purpose.[17]

Looting

During 'cleansing' raids, allegedly aimed at flushing out rebels hiding among the civilian population, a 'door tax' of up to $5,000 is collected by the Russian forces. Non-payment is punished by kicking in the door of the offender's home and looting it.[18] Another approach used during these operations is to arrest all men and demand a ransom of $100–$200 per head for their release. This approach is usually employed in villages engaged in the illegal extraction and refining of oil (see below), who can afford to pay.[19]

Hostage taking by both sides

At any point in time there are several thousand missing Chechens who have been kidnapped by both sides, as well as several hundred Russian soldiers and several dozen Russian civilians seized by the Chechens. People are also being kidnapped from neighbouring republics, including Ingushetia and Northern Ossetia. Hostages are not only exchanged for ransom but also kept for slave labour (Tishkov 2004; Politkovskaya 2001). Even the bodies of killed Chechens or Russian soldiers are routinely kept for ransom. Ransom payments peaked in the 1990s, when Russian billionaire Boris Berezovsky was channelling tens of millions in US dollars to secure the release of high-profile hostages, including government officials and prominent journalists. It is then that Al Qaeda was alleged to have paid millions for the beheading of British telecoms workers.

Russian government spending

Allocations for the reconstruction of Chechnya, as well as other expenditures to maintain the 80,000 strong Russian presence in the Republic, are the subject of ongoing turf battles between the Defence Ministry, the Ministry of the Interior, the Federal Security Service, the President of the Interim Chechen Administration and his Prime Minister. Not a month goes by without a new intrigue by one of these parties aimed at seizing a larger piece of the cake. Needless to say, only a fraction of these allocations ever reaches the designated beneficiaries, be they ordinary Russian soldiers or the citizens of Chechnya.

Illicit extraction and refining

There are 776 oil wells and 26 processing plants, in addition to the Baku–Novorossisk pipeline, all of which are tapped for oil, oil products and parts. There is a cottage industry of up to 3000 illegal refineries throughout Chechnya – many located in people's back-yards. There are ongoing battles among warlords and strongmen from all sides for the distribution and redistribution of each of these resources. The refined products are shipped in hundreds of tankers a day along known 'oil roads' to neighbouring Russian regions. The various branches of the Russian security forces 'tax' the process at every stage, retaining as much as 50 per cent of total proceeds. For example, tankers are charged a $200–300 fee by the military in exchange for free passage or even an escort to their destination. The military are sometimes alleged to have bought bootleg gas and diesel to replace fuel supplies sold in Russia at a higher price (Politkovskaya 2001).

The main source of value sustaining all these activities is oil. There are no reliable figures about the Chechen oil output, but an estimate could be based on the last recorded output in 1991 of 4 million tonnes per year, or 80,000 bbl/d. It is highly unlikely that this output level has been maintained to this date, after ten years of war and abuse. If it had been, Chechnya would have earned $1.7 billion for its oil in 2005, assuming a price of $60 per barrel. But even if output was reduced to a fraction of 1991 levels, there would still be enough revenue to keep 10,000–15,000 Russian officers and Chechen warlords financially motivated. If other sources, such as Russian government transfers and ransom payments, are added a clearer picture begins to emerge to explain how the conflict has been sustained for so long. Oil usually stops flowing in situations of total chaos, like those reigning in Chechnya over the past ten years. This creates an incentive for competing parties to avoid descent into anarchy in order to sustain revenues. But Chechen oil is a special case, since it is particularly suited for looting. It is close to the surface and is very easy to distil into gasoline.

The experience of the last truce

A Russian withdrawal from Chechnya today along the lines of the Khazavyurt peace agreement is unlikely to result in anything different from what occurred the last time hostilities ceased. The warlords need to be disarmed and Chechnya needs an alternative economic base and a vast reconstruction budget. Both Maskhadov and the Russian military have failed to rein in the warlords in the past. Meagre reconstruction monies, directed into the republic during the past war and today, are regularly embezzled somewhere along the way from Moscow to Grozny. Even if reconstruction efforts were managed by an international party, there would still be a need to provide security. The likelihood of the UN offering, and Russia accepting, an international force to keep the peace is at best remote.

International factors

Two elements of the international community's approach towards the conflict in Chechnya are contributing to its continuation.

First, Russia seized on the events of 11 September 2001 to legitimise the war in Chechnya and brush off any criticism of human rights violations. The international reaction to Russian brutality, whether during the first or second war, was always muted. It is understood in Russia that no matter what happens in Chechnya, there will be no major international intervention akin to what happened in the Balkans. Although the situation in Chechnya deteriorated after 9/11, the Western – and especially American – approach to the war on terrorism makes it hard for critics to condemn Russia for its actions without leaving themselves open to charges of hypocrisy. The Russian authorities, aware of this dilemma, have exploited the new international climate to the fullest, exaggerating the links between the Chechen warlords and Al Qaeda and seeking to present Russian actions in Chechnya as part of the global war on terrorism. Since 11 September 2001, Putin has been promoting a new 'special relationship' with Washington based on realpolitik, prompting some in Russia to recall the Yalta model and the carving up of spheres of influence between the Soviet Union and the West after the Second World War. Many Russian politicians and entrepreneurs are promoting the idea of Russia as an alternative supplier of oil to Western markets, in place of Saudi Arabia and OPEC. This proposition assumes that Russia should be given a free hand to control oil supplies not only on its territory but also in the Caspian and even Iraq.[20]

Second, as long as Russia continues to perceive a threat to its interests in the Caucasus and Central Asia, it will be very hard for any Russian politician to allow an independent Chechen state or a meaningful international role in settling the conflict. The United States, despite the new relationship between Presidents Bush and Putin, continues to compete with Russia at the geopolitical level – especially in the Caucasus and Central Asia. Russia has yet to reconcile itself to the Baku–Tbilisi–Ceyhan pipeline.

THE PEACE EFFORTS

International intervention in the conflict has not been entirely negative. Europe in particular has applied considerable pressure on Russia to limit human rights violations. Prior to 9/11, Russia's membership in the Council of Europe was all but suspended. Both the Council and the Organization for Security and Co-Operation in Europe (OSCE) continue their efforts to monitor and report human rights violations in Chechnya and pressure all sides for a negotiated settlement, albeit ineffectually. These efforts are, however, undermined by the position of the

United States and to a lesser degree the UK, which have significantly toned down their criticism of Russian actions in Chechnya since 2001. The contrast between the Anglo-American approach and the European approach was highlighted in the aftermath of the Moscow theatre hostage crisis in 2002. The United States and the UK expressed unqualified support to the Russian government for its handling of the crisis, and refused to make any link between the terrorist act and Russia's own behaviour in Chechnya. Most European countries, however, saw the terrorist act as proof of the futility of seeking a military solution to the conflict, and as an opportunity to call for negotiations and an end to human rights violations by both sides.

There are numerous local and international grassroots efforts aimed at documenting the conflict and the human rights violations, helping the victims and mediating between the two communities and their political representatives. These include human rights organisations like Memorial, Soldiers' Mothers and Human Rights Watch, and lobby groups like the American Committee for Peace in Chechnya founded by Zbigniew Brzezinski and Alexander Haig. Courageous Russian journalists like Anna Politkovskaya, Maria Eismont and Andrei Babitsky have taken considerable risks to report the truth about the conflict. Indeed Politkovskaya – who had presciently said: 'People sometimes pay with their lives for saying aloud what they think' – was murdered in Moscow in October 2006.

RUSSIA AS A FAILING STATE: THE YELTSIN ERA 1991–98

Economic decline and increasing dependence on oil

In the seven years between the collapse of the USSR and the 1998 crisis, the Russian economy contracted by 50 per cent. Over the same period the government incurred a massive public debt, predominantly to Western investors. The government was issuing short-term securities to finance revenue shortfalls caused by failing tax collection, a shrinking economic base and low oil prices. Low inflation, a stable exchange rate and a flood of foreign funds did nothing to prevent insolvency. Ultimately, the government was unable to rollover its debts, prompting a stampede by foreign investors and forcing a default and a devaluation of the currency in August 1998.

During this period the export-oriented oil and gas industry increased its share of GDP. At the end of Yeltsin's reign, oil and gas accounted for 22 per cent of Russia's GDP and 50 per cent of its exports. The total share of natural resources, including other minerals and timber, in the country's export revenues is now in excess of 80 per cent. Due to the demonetisation of the Russian economy over the period from 1991–98, dependence on oil and gas revenues has increased as a percentage of government revenues, amounting to 30 per cent in 2000 (EBRD 2001).

State weakness

Russia's economic decline and increasing dependence on oil revenues were accompanied by a pervasive erosion of state structures and institutions. As a consequence, Yeltsin's Russia shared many of the typical characteristics of a failing state.

Patronage and predation

Tax collection and tax reforms are among the most challenging issues faced by Russia since the collapse of the Soviet Union. Under Yeltsin, efforts to improve tax collection always seemed to end with the government going back to the oil and gas sector for more taxes, fees and duties. Successive governments have repeatedly postponed other structural reforms. From 1991 to 1998 Russia made no progress on reforming the judiciary, the army, social security, agriculture or natural monopolies.

Patronage in Russia flows through various channels and in various quantities, depending on the target constituencies. The infamous oligarchs first emerged as the recipients of government loans and loan guarantees, at fixed interest rates.[21] During a period of hyperinflation, this amounted to a 'privatisation of the central bank's seigniorage stream' (Dabrowski et al 2000). Later patronage took place on an even larger scale. In the 'loans for shares' privatisation scheme, the bulk of the country's resource wealth was transferred to the same oligarchs in exchange for nominal amounts of money. Other channels of rent distribution were less exclusive. The Russian Olympic Committee and the Orthodox Church were for a long time the country's largest cigarette importers, benefiting from an exemption on import duties. Energy prices inside Russia are several times lower than world prices, creating an indirect transfer of resource rents, mostly to old Soviet industries.

Since the collapse of the USSR, Russia has been running down the systems for the provision of public goods inherited from the Soviet Union. Health care, education, transport and social security are near collapse, as evidenced by the steep decline in life expectancy, growing illiteracy rates, non-payment of social security entitlements and numerous tragic accidents. Especially critical is the condition of the army and police, who in the absence of public funds are acting as free agents, often in the service of criminal groups. Many of the excesses of the Russian police and military in Chechnya can be explained by the catastrophic lack of funds.

The blurring of the boundaries between economics and politics

Unlike most oil-dependent countries, Russia privatised much of its oil industry. The oil companies, however, remain dependent on the Kremlin in several ways. First, the government maintains tight control over the export pipeline, the lifeline for all oil companies. Second, the questionable legitimacy of the transfer of most of these companies to private hands means that the new owners' freedom to exercise their ownership rights is limited. Selective application of the law has been used by the Kremlin to punish unruly oligarchs or to support one against the other. The expropriation of Russia's largest oil company, Yukos, and the jailing of its owner, Mikhail Khodorkovsky, amply demonstrate this point. Before Yukos, the government transferred the assets of Chernogorneft, a large oil company, from an oligarch associated with former President Yeltsin to one aligned with President Putin, through the selective use of bankruptcy procedures. Gazprom, which effectively controls the entire Russian natural gas industry and is one of the largest corporations in the world, is still state controlled. It embodies all the traditional ills of state-owned energy companies in other oil-dependent countries. Russians refer to it as the state within the state. It is no coincidence that Viktor Chernomyrdin, Gazprom's long-time head, who was its minister when it was a Soviet ministry, was also the longest-serving prime minister under Yeltsin.

Concentration and personification of power instead of the rule of law

Ten years of transformation succeeded in dismantling the Soviet system and weakening the state, but did not reduce its central role in Russian life. Within the state, it seems that power is being consolidating in the institution of the president. Yeltsin and his reformers introduced formal democratic institutions and forms of government against stiff opposition, only to undermine these very institutions through greed, fraud and arrogance. Political parties continue to be established without a popular base or an ideology, with the express purpose of being the 'party of power'. Yeltsin routinely bypassed parliament through presidential decrees, buying and otherwise discrediting individual MPs and entire factions. There are so many electoral irregularities at all levels that people are beginning to lose faith in democracy as a concept.

Declining capacity to prevent, manage and resolve conflict

In the past decade Russia has been involved in half a dozen conflicts along its periphery, and two in Chechnya. Following the 1970s petro-state model, it is arguable that Russia is using the conflict as a way to satisfy rent seeking among high-ranking officers which cannot be met by the state. In this particular case, Chechnya is being used as a patronage channel to keep the army top brass happy, thus allowing the government to procrastinate on the enormous task of military reform.

BEATING THE CURSE? 1998 TO THE PRESENT

The distortion that dependence on oil and gas exports caused in the Russian economy was first acknowledged in the aftermath of the 1998 crisis (Illarionov 2000). Today, most Russian economists agree that Russia exhibited symptoms of Dutch disease both prior to and after the 1998 financial crises, and continues to do so today. In particular the continuing growth in real wages and real exchange rates have had a detrimental impact on the competitiveness of the remaining traded-goods sectors of the economy (for example agriculture and manufacturing). Constant fluctuations in oil prices also undermine long-term planning, especially when it comes to the government. Grigorii Yavlinsky, a leading opposition figure, compares the Russian economy to an 'addict who gets high when oil prices go up and suffers from withdrawal when they go down'.[22]

After the 1998 crisis the Russian government attached a much lower priority to inflation than its predecessor had, concentrating more on keeping the exchange rate under control. What followed exceeded all expectations. The combination of a looser monetary policy, low exchange rates and high oil prices sent all sectors of the Russia economy into a boom. In 2001 industrial production grew by 10 per cent and total GDP by 8 per cent, making Russia the fastest-growing economy in Europe. Spectacular growth has continued, putting Putin on course to fulfil his pledge to double the size of the Russian economy in ten years. The Russian stock market has been the best performing in the world for several consecutive years, signalling a return of investors despite the all-too-recent default. Significantly, economic growth over the past four years has been accompanied by a surge in productivity, prompting some analysts to conclude that it is not just an oil boom (Breech 2002).

Not all the windfall from the oil prices and the devaluation has been consumed. Russia used some of it to boost the Central Bank Reserve and some to accelerate debt payments, which should help 'sterilise' oil revenues and prevent Dutch disease. The devaluation of 1998 and the favourable situation on the world oil markets gave Russia a badly needed respite to tackle some of the deeper structural problems inherited from the Yeltsin regime. Over the past six years serious efforts have been made to reverse the disintegration of state institutions, and to build new ones. The unruly regional governors have been reined in. Efforts at reforming the tax system and improving tax collection are bearing fruit. The oligarchs continue to exert influence on government but to a lesser degree than before. Progress has been made on judicial reform, land reform and the restructuring of social insurance. The first steps are being undertaken to reform the so-called natural monopolies, including the energy distribution grid, the railways and even Gazprom.

Many observers doubt the sincerity, sustainability and efficiency of these reforms, pointing to continued and pervasive corruption. A study by the Moscow-based INDEM think tank estimates that bribes paid by various private agents run at 12 per cent of GDP.[23] They also point to the continuing war in Chechnya, Putin's clamp-down on independent media and political opposition, and lack of progress on the critical issue of military reform.

CONCLUSIONS

Russia went to war in Chechnya for a number of reasons. Some of them were legitimate, such as the need to stem the tide of crime emanating from the renegade republic. Others are understandable, such as the reaction to perceived geopolitical threats from the West in the shape of the Baku–Tbilisi–Ceyhan pipeline. There were also mundane reasons such as the personal loathing between Yeltsin and Dudayev. The catastrophic condition of the Russian state, and particularly the military establishment, also contributed to the beginning of hostilities and to the way the war was conducted. The legacy of the collapse of the Soviet Union, bungled shock-therapy reforms and growing oil dependence at a time of low oil prices brought the Russian state to the verge of collapse at the outset of the first Chechen war. Over the past six years Russia has managed to leverage high oil prices to reverse some of the damage of the Yeltsin years. It seems to have found remedies to some of the manifestations of the oil curse, but it still suffers from others, in particular the tendency towards authoritarianism and patronage. Indeed Russia seems to have stepped back from state collapse and into the petro-state model of the 1970s. This does not bode well for the prospect of a peaceful resolution in Chechnya.

Once the war started other factors emerged to sustain the conflict, including war profiteering and brutality towards civilians by both sides. Oil plays a key role in profiteering, as the Russian military and the Chechen warlords seem to be jointly running an illicit oil business of up to 40,000 bbl/d in Chechnya.

There are reasons for optimism even in this area, however. The Chechen official oil company Grozneft, a subsidiary of the state-owned Rosneft, has managed to increase legitimate oil output and export at the expense of the wildcatters in the face of intimidation, sabotage and even murder at the hands of all benefiting parties, including the Russian military, the pro-Russian Chechen administration and the rebels.

There are also grounds for pessimism. Faced with declining popularity at home, Chechen warlords seem to be succeeding in spreading the conflict to other parts of the North Caucasus, including Dagestan, Ingushetia and Ossetia. They have established closer ties with transnational extremist networks and are perpetrating Al Qaeda-type outrages, as in the case of the Moscow theatre hostage crisis and the school siege in Beslan. These developments, and the assassination of the moderate elected Chechen President Maskhadov, leave virtually no space for a negotiated settlement. With the exception of some laudable efforts by the Council of Europe, the OSCE and to some extent the EU, the international impact on the war has been negative; the West has fed into Russia's geopolitical insecurities and turned a blind eye to its human rights violations under the pretext of the 'war on terror'.

NOTES

1. Note on terms used:
   Oil: unless specified, is used to refer to both oil and natural gas.
   Russian military: unless specified, is used to refer to troops and other armed personnel under the command of the Ministry of Defence, Ministry of the Interior and the Federal Security Service, as well as those operating under the control of the Russian-allied Chechen Interim Administration.
2. Y. Stroiteleva, 'Peak of Oil Extraction in Chechnya Will be Reached Next Year', *Izvestya*, 29 April 2004.
3. All '$' = US dollars.
4. Kinzer, S. (1998) 'On Piping Out Caspian Oil, US Insists the Cheaper, Shorter Way Isn't Better', *New York Times*, 8 November 1998.
5. R. Schleinov, 'Serial Victims', *Novaya Gazeta*, 7 November 2002.
6. www.memorial.ru, last accessed in June 2002.
7. As cited by Radio Liberty/Radio Free Europe, 31 August 2000 : www.rferl.org.
8. The claim that they had exchanged him for two captured Russian soldiers appeared to be an attempt to discredit Babitsky as a collaborator. A video of the 'handover' was produced, which was later shown to be a forgery. In fact, he was held by Russian forces or their Chechen allies throughout the incident. C. Fitzpatrick, 'Babitsky Claims Photo Reveals His FSB Captor', *Uncivil Societies, Radio Free Europe/Radio Liberty*, 26 June 2000: http://www.rferl.org/reports/ucs/2000/06/7-290600.asp, last accessed 7 November 2006.
9. Cited on www.memorial.ru, last accessed 2002.
10. According to Pavel Felgenhauer, 'Military Dossier', *Moscow Times*, 2002.
11. L. Fuller, 'Chechnya: Does Outrage over Borozdinovskaya Sweep Presage Change of Russian Tactics?' *Radio Free Europe/Radio Liberty*, 24 June 2005: http://www.rferl.org/featuresarticle/2005/06/ 487f4546-26f3-4a08-bb79-e72166328b8d.html, last accessed 7 November 2006.
12. L. Fuller, 'Is it Too Late for Peace Talks in Chechnya?' *Radio Free Europe/Radio Liberty*, 11 Feb 2005: http://www.rferl.org/featuresarticle/2005/02/ a27fc076-66c2-415e-9b32-eea692f08d2d.html, last accessed 7 November 2006.
13. FOM and VTSIOM polls: 1994, 1999 and 2002. See: www.bd.english.fom.ru and www.krotov.info/engl/abbrev/vtsiom.html.
14. *Washington Post*, 5 October 2002.
15. www.iwpr.net, last accessed 13 June 2002.
16. Radio Free Europe/Radio Liberty Analysis: 'Has Chechnya's Strongman

Signed His Own Death Warrant?'
http://www.rferl.org/featuresarticle/2005/03/
533b2aa8-dfbd-4837-9dfe-ec64e3206aa6.html,
last accessed 7 November 2006.
17. *Novaya Gazeta*, 11 June 2002.
18. *Chechenpress*, 24 June 2002.
19. www.iwpr.net, 6 October 2002.
20. Interview with Gregorii Yavlinsky, leader of opposition party Yabloko, 2002.
21. In Russia these oligarchs are mostly private businessmen who occasionally acquired official positions in government but mostly exercised significant behind-the-scenes influence over government decisions in ways which resulted in their further enrichment.
22. Interview with Gregorii Yavlinsky, 2002.
23. *The Independent*, 23 May 2002.

BIBLIOGRAPHY

Breech, A. (2002) 'Goldman Sachs Russia Weekly Report' (Moscow: Goldman Sachs).

Dabrowski, M., Gomulka, S. and Rostowski, J. (2000) *Whence Reform? A Critique of the Stiglitz Perspective* (London: LSE Centre for Economic Performance).

Dunlop, J. (2002) 'Putin and Berezovsky Comment on 1999 Provocation', *Chechnya Weekly*, Vol. 3, No. 30.

European Bank of Reconstruction and Development (2001) 'Transition Report' (London: EBRD).

Evangelista, M. (2002) *The Chechen Wars: Will Russia Go the Way of the Soviet Union?* (Washington, D.C.: Brookings Institute Press).

FOM (Public Opinion Foundation) (1994) 'List of Politicians Who Behaved Most Inappropriately in Relations to Events in Chechnya is Led by Dudayev and Yeltsin' (Moscow: FOM). www.english.fom.ru, last accessed October 2005.

—— (1998) 'Now Russia and Chechnya Are Debating the Issue of Chechnya's Status. Each Side is Suggesting its Options. With Which of the Proposals Listed Below Do You Agree?' (Moscow: FOM), www.english.fom.ru, last accessed October 2005.

—— (2002a) 'Putin's Main Failure – "Chechnya Is Not Quieting Down"' (Moscow: FOM). www.english.fom.ru, last accessed October 2005.

—— (2002b) 'Support for the Actions of Russian Military Forces in Chechnya Is Steadily Declining' (Moscow: FOM). www.english.fom.ru, last accessed October 2005.

—— (2004) 'On the Status of Chechnya' (Moscow: FOM). www.english.fom.ru, last accessed October 2005.

Gall, C. and De Waal, T. (1998) *Chechnya: Calamity in the Caucasus* (New York: NYU Press).

Illarionov, A. (2000) 'World Rents, External Debt and Economic Growth: The Government Failed in Solving This Puzzle'. www.Polit.ru, last accessed October 2001.

Karl, T.L. (1997) *The Paradox of Plenty: Oil Booms and Petro-States* (Berkeley: University of California Press).

Khlebnikov, P. (2003) *Razgovor c Varvarom* [Interview With a Barbarian] (Moscow: Detektivpress).

Lieven, A. (1998) *Chechnya: Tombstone of Russian Power* (New Haven: Yale University Press).

Politkovskaya, A. (2001) *Dirty War: A Russian Reporter in Chechnya* (London: Harvil).

Tishkov, V. (2004) *Chechnya: Life in a War Torn Society* (Berkeley: University of California Press).

Uzzell, L. (2005) 'Dzhabrailov: 160,000 People Killed in Two Chechen Wars', *Chechnya Weekly*, Vol. 6, No. 32.

4 Oil and conflict: the case of Nagorno Karabakh

Mary Kaldor

> Only yesterday a fat Armenian tried to tell me that the Christian Maras Church in Susha was five thousand years old. 'Don't tell such tall stories,' I told him. 'The Christian faith is not yet two thousand years old. They can't have built a Christian church before Christianity was even thought of.' The fat man was very hurt and said reproachfully: 'You are, of course, an educated man. But let an old man tell you: The Christian faith may be only two thousand years old in other countries. But to us, the people of Karabakh, the Saviour showed the light three thousand years before the others. That's how it is.'
>
> (Kurban Said, *Ali and Nino*)

Before the war in the early 1990s, Nagorno Karabakh had a population of around 180,000. Since then, some 15–20,000 people have been killed and over a million people have been forced to flee their homes in Armenia and Azerbaijan as well as Nagorno Karabakh. The population has probably fallen by half. Yet the small mountainous province still claims an exaggerated importance, casting a pall over politics and society in the whole Transcaucasus region.

The conflict began in the late 1980s when the region was still part of the Soviet Union; ethnic cleansing on both sides started in the period 1988–91. The main fighting took place in 1992–94 and a ceasefire was initiated on 12 May 1994. Since then the conflict has been 'frozen'. The ceasefire holds but there has been little or no progress towards a resolution. Indeed, the term 'frozen' is probably a misnomer: the conflict is more like a festering wound. Nagorno Karabakh has become a 'black hole', a source of continued tension between Armenia and Azerbaijan, a haven for organised crime and extreme ideologies, a place of longing for thousands of refugees and displaced persons and a form of legitimation for the weak states of the region.

The main conclusion of this chapter is that oil did not play a significant role in the early phases of the conflict. It was one of several factors that help to explain Russian policy towards the region, and it contributed towards financing the Azeri war effort. But oil has been a salient factor in the current 'no war/no peace' situation. It has influenced the character of the Azerbaijani state, which is typical of an authoritarian oil state, needing the conflict as a way to explain lack of openness and laggard development while avoiding the risks of actual war. And, especially since 9/11, it has influenced the behaviour of outside powers that compete for power in the region. In other words, Azerbaijan could be viewed as a petro-state on the verge of becoming a predatory state. There is a real risk that 'old war' thinking on the part of outsiders, that is to say, geopolitical competition in the South Caucasus, could exacerbate 'new war' tendencies in the region, and especially in Nagorno Karabakh.

In this chapter, I will briefly describe the character of the conflict over Nagorno Karabakh. Then I will analyse Azerbaijan as a petro-state and discuss the role of outside powers. In the conclusion, I will set out some possible policy directions.

THE 'NEW WAR' IN NAGORNO KARABAKH

The conflict is about the status of Nagorno Karabakh. The region was made an autonomous region (*oblast*) within the Azerbaijan Republic by the Soviet Union in 1921, although the majority population was Armenian. The Soviet of Nagorno Karabakh voted to secede from Azerbaijan and join Armenia in 1988, and this demand became the central plank of the Armenian national movement that developed in the last days of the Soviet Union. Conversely, keeping Karabakh within Azerbaijan became equally important for the emerging Azerbaijani national movement. In addition, the demand was taken up by those, like Andrei Sakharov and Yelena Bonner, who favoured democratisation and interpreted the Karabakh cause as a democracy issue.

At present, Nagorno Karabakh is de facto independent, although financially dependent on Armenia, and also controls some 14 per cent of Azerbaijani territory. Both Karabakh and Armenia are under blockade from Azerbaijan and Turkey. For Armenians, the Karabakh cause is viewed in terms of the principle of self-determination, while Azerbaijanis argue that territorial integrity is the overriding international principle. In addition, both sides claim that the region has an important symbolic and cultural importance for them, as the quotation at the beginning of this chapter indicates.

> For Armenians, Karabakh is the last outpost of their Christian civilisation and a historic haven of Armenian princes and bishops before the Eastern Turkic world begins. Azerbaijanis talk of it as a cradle, nursery or conservatoire, the birthplace of their musicians and poets.
>
> (De Waal 2003:3).

Among Western commentators, there is a tendency to interpret the conflict in Nagorno Karabakh in terms of 'centuries-old tradition' (Forsythe 1996) or the revival of 'dormant tensions' (Kechichian and Karasik 1995). It is true that in the early twentieth century, there were bloody episodes between what were then called Tartars and Armenians, largely fomented by outside powers. It is also the case, as everywhere, that the history of the region is littered with stories of brutality. But, at the same time, the melange of languages, ethnic groups and religions gives testimony to a history of tolerance as well. Indeed, what is striking for visitors to the region are the common features – similar cultural practices, shared assumptions and values, prevalent ways of thinking. As Herzig puts it:

> A true melting pot for the many cultural currents that have flowed in from all around, the South Caucasus possesses distinctive, if not uniform, characteristics in its popular and material culture, characteristics which overarch the ethnic, linguistic and religious diversity of its people.
>
> (Herzig 1999:2).

I argue that the war in Nagorno Karabakh is typical of a 'new war'. It cannot easily be categorised as 'international' or as 'civil'. Technically, it was 'civil' up until the collapse of the Soviet Union and became 'international' after the establishment of two independent states – Armenia and Azerbaijan. In practice, it is both local and global, involving a host of global actors such as Russian mercenaries, Armenian diaspora volunteers and Afghan *mujahideen*, not to mention international agencies and NGOs like Christian Solidarity, chaired by Baroness Caroline Cox. Likewise, it cannot easily be categorised as state or non-state. The war involved fractions of the Soviet army, volunteer militias and paramilitary groups, and criminal gangs as well as the newly established armies of Azerbaijan, Karabakh and Armenia. It is best explained in terms of the break-up of the Soviet Union and the struggle among competing networks for the remnants of the state apparatus. These networks used the ideology of extreme nationalism to mobilise popular support.

The South Caucasus region has historically been part of competing empires – Russia, Turkey and Iran. It is worth noting that although the Azeri people speak a Turkic language, they were always Persian Turks rather than Turkish Turks.[1] Turkish-speaking tribes date back to the twelfth and thirteenth centuries when Turkish dynasties began to rule Iran. Although the rulers adopted Persian, the tribespeople continued to speak Turkish. Most of what is now Azerbaijan was part of Iran until the early nineteenth century, and this explains why the dominant religion is Shi'ite Islam rather than Sunni like the Turks'; some two-thirds of the Azeri people still live in present day Iran. Although there have historically been Armenian and Georgian kingdoms, there was never an Azerbaijani state before the twentieth century, although there were smaller Khanates consisting of different Azeri tribes. The Russians occupied the whole region from the early nineteenth century. During this period the towns of Baku, Yerevan and Tblisi were very cosmopolitan, and the dominant urban groups in all three towns were the Armenians.

For a brief period after the First World War, the three countries became independent. Then the Bolsheviks took over and established the Transcaucasian Socialist Republic, which lasted until 1937. The story of Nagorno Karabakh is typical of the way in which nationalism was constructed in the Soviet period, which has been described by a number of scholars of the Soviet Union (See Suny 1993; Kaiser 1994; and Rakowska-Harmstone 1974). The Soviet Union was organised, like Yugoslavia, into a complicated hierarchical system of administrative units. Each unit was given a titular nationality usually linked to the dominant ethnic group (the titular nation was not always dominant; in Abkhazia, for example, the Abkhaz accounted for only 17 per cent of the total population). Language and culture were promoted, although political expressions of nationalism were suppressed.

Armenian nationalism dates back to the nineteenth century. The genocide of Armenians in 1915 by Turkey and the creation of modern-day Armenia have contributed to a nationalism that is often compared with Zionism. Like the Jews, the Armenian diaspora is scattered world-wide. Visiting Yerevan, the modern-day capital of Armenia in the 1930s, Arthur Koestler described the city as a 'kind of Tel Aviv where the survivors of another martyred nation gathered to construct a new home' (De Waal 2003:76). Genocide Day, 24 April, was marked annually even in Soviet times.

Azeri nationalism, on the other hand, did not really exist before 1918, when Azerbaijan was briefly independent. However, the Soviet administrative framework fostered a sense of nationalism, even where it had not existed earlier. National arguments were used by local communist leaders when bidding for resources from the centre. The various academies concerned with history, ethnography, or art and architecture, were able to conduct nationalist debates under the cover of the obscurity of their esoteric subjects. As one Karabakh activist put it: 'The Soviet Union did not exist from the beginning of the 1970s! Different republics existed. One republic fought with another and so on. They were not interested in humanitarian ideals' (De Waal 2003:136). Another Russian commentator noted that 'when Gorbachev finally discarded the worn-out Marxist verbiage, the only language that remained was the well-honed and practised language of nationalism' (Yury Slezkine, quoted in De Waal 2003:143).

The descent into war has to be understood in terms of the erosion of the monopoly of violence in the Soviet Union. On the one hand, Soviet bases in the Caucasus began to act relatively autonomously and to support different factions. On the other hand, paramilitary groups made their appearance all over the region. Some were criminal groups engaged in banditry of various kinds, especially hostage taking, for private gain. Others were fanatics in search of a cause and an adventure. A series of massacres and population expulsions on both sides (in Sumgait and Baku against Armenians, and in Khojaly against Azeris) created a sense of fear and insecurity that helped to mobilise people around the nationalist demands, and to provide an umbrella to unite or legitimise these disparate fighting groups. A key role was played by Russian forces, which intervened on various sides both to foment and to end the violence in 1994. Whether these forces were acting autonomously (they depended on local recruits) or whether they were acting under instructions from Moscow may never be known.

Azeri refugees testify that Armenian hardcore nationalists, 'the bearded ones', played a prominent role in the initial round of violence. Even if the initial clashes were undertaken spontaneously by disparate groups, Erik Melander argues that:

> the subsequent waves of ethnic cleansing in both Armenia and Azerbaijan would have been impossible without substantial planning and centrally organised efforts. ... For example, Rafael Kazaryan, a member of the Karabakh committee, claims that he helped organise the expulsion of the Azeris from Armenia.
>
> (Melander 2001:64)

Melander also interviewed Zhanna Galstyan, one of the paramilitary leaders in Karabakh. He explained that it was necessary for the paramilitary groups to secure lines of communication within Nagorno Karabakh, and that this necessitated the capture and destruction of Azeri-inhabited villages. This idea, that political control depends on the expulsion of those with a different nationality 'spread as the scale and intensity of the conflict increased' and was 'converted into a deadly ideology by fears of pre-emption and memories of past bloodshed' (Melander 2001:65).

A key event in the escalation of the conflict was Operation Ring, carried out by then Soviet forces. Operation Ring involved units of the Soviet 23rd Motorised Rifle Division, together with Azeri special police and internal security troops, in massive operations against Armenian villages near the border with Nagorno Karabakh in the north. 'Officially, the purpose was to neutralise illegal guerrilla formations in the area; but in practice Operation Ring amounted to systematic ethnic cleansing' (Melander 2001:68). A Soviet observer noted that the tactics were very similar to those used by the Soviet army in Afghanistan, tactics that were to be repeated in Chechnya. The main fighting took place in the period 1992–94. On both sides, the war was fought by a combination of former units of the Soviet army and freelance brigades and militias. At one point, soldiers from the same division, the 23rd, were fighting each other. Former Soviet soldiers joined the fighting either because they were also nationals or for economic reasons.[2] In terms of military experience and skills, Armenia had the advantage because many more of the army officers and men were Armenian. Approximately 20–30 per cent of the officers and 60–80 per cent of the Soviet troops based in Armenia were Armenian.

In addition to former Soviet troops, many volunteer groups were formed. Some were criminal gangs. Others were fanatics. In Armenia, they were called *djogads* (hunter's groups) or *fedayeen*, meaning fighters willing to sacrifice themselves for the cause. They were joined by volunteers from the American-Armenian diaspora.[3] On the Azerbaijani side, some independent entrepreneurs established their own brigades with Russian help. The most notorious was Suret Husseinov, who organised a coup against the nationalist President Elchibey in June 1993, which paved the way for the return to power of the veteran communist leader Heydar Aliyev. In addition, villagers organised themselves in self-defence units. These volunteer groups were complemented by Russian mercenaries and Afghan *mujahideen*. Reportedly, after a visit to Afghanistan by the Iranian Deputy Interior Minister in July 1993, some 1000 Afghan *mujahideen* from the Iranian backed Hezb-I-Wahdat were recruited (See Kechichian and Karasik 1995). Both sides had access to equipment left behind by the departing Soviet forces, with Azerbaijan inheriting more material than Armenia. However, the Russian government 'compensated' Armenia for its supposed military inferiority in deals arranged between Presidents Lev Ter Petrosian and Yeltsin, as came to light in evidence given to the Russian Duma in 1997.

By the end of the war, both sides had established 'real' armies (Ter Petrosian, quoted in De Waal 2003). In Karabakh the Minister of Defence, Serge Sarkisian, now Minister of Defence in Armenia, and the military commander, Samvel Babayan, were able to forge the various paramilitary groups into an effective fighting force.[4] In Azerbaijan, Aliyev disbanded the independent brigades and established an army mainly based on inexperienced press-ganged recruits. Despite huge efforts, this force was not able to recover territory lost to the Karabakh army, which by the end of the war had succeeded in occupying a large part of Azerbaijan's territory. In addition to the territory of Nagorno Karabakh, it captured the territory connecting Nagorno Karabakh to Armenia, known as the Lachin corridor.

The strategy of the armed forces was very similar to that of the Serbs in Croatia, Bosnia and Kosovo. They would shell villages with heavy artillery until the irregular forces withdrew. They would then occupy the villages and towns, expel the civilian population, and loot and destroy all the buildings. The town of Agdam, for example, had been the richest town in Azerbaijan, with a population of some 40–50,000. Along with several villages it was totally destroyed in the fighting, with not a building left standing.[5] Over the whole period between 1989 and 1994, some 200,000 Armenians fled Azerbaijan, mostly to Armenia and Nagorno Karabakh, but some 45,000 to Russia; 185,000 Azeris and 11,000 Muslim Kurds were forced to leave Armenia; 47,000 Azeris were forced to leave Nagorno Karabakh; and 500,000 to 600,000 were expelled from the occupied territories (Herzig 1999). The ratio of Armenian to Azeri casualties is said to have been 1:8 and the ratio of destroyed weapons was 1:20.

The financing of the conflict was also typical of a 'new war'. Because of the collapse of the official economy and because, in any case, taxation had been centralised in the Soviet era, there was almost no official funding. On the Armenian side, funding was almost entirely war-related – diaspora support, Russian military assistance, loot and pillage, contraband trade (especially petroleum products) and hostage taking. As a consequence, post-war Armenia has inherited a large shadow economy whose operation depends on a continuing atmosphere of war. On the Azeri side, the government was able to commandeer crude oil from the Azerbaijan State Oil Company (SOCAR) either for use at the front or for sale, but it did not have diaspora support or, after 1992, Russian military assistance. Because they were losing, the Azeris were not able to take advantage of loot and pillage on the same scale; but hostage taking and contraband trade remained important.

In May 1994, a ceasefire was brokered by Russia, under the auspices of the Commonwealth of Independent States (CIS). In Armenia, especially, the war had established the networks that were to dominate the state structures in the post-war period. On the Armenian side, Ter Petrosian, who had led the Armenian national movement as a broad coalition including former communists and nationalists, was overthrown by the so-called Karabakh party after he tried to reach a peace agreement in 1997. Robert Kocharian, the former President of Karabakh, is now the President of Armenia and Serge Sarkisian became Minister of Defence. Just as in Karabakh, Sarkisian is considered 'the real power in the land'. The Ministry of Defence is a conduit for receiving both diaspora support and Russian military assistance, and it controls a variety of instruments of patronage including licences for petrol stations, cigarette sales and public transport.

In the case of Azerbaijan, Elchibey, leader of the Azeri Popular Front that won power in the first elections in 1992, was overthrown the following year by Husseinov, possibly with the help of Russian military forces. Heydar Aliyev, the First Secretary of the Azerbaijan Communist party during the Brezhnev era, was installed in power.[6] Aliyev had been dismissed by Gorbachev and had rebuilt his power base in Nakchivan, where he had spent the years since being replaced in Baku. His network is known as the 'family'. After his death in 2003, he was succeeded by his son Ilham. If the Ministry of Defence has been the key instrument of the Karabakh party's rule in Armenia, it is SOCAR, which was taken under the direct control of Heydar Aliyev, that serves a similar function in Azerbaijan. As Mutalibov, the Soviet-installed President of Azerbaijan in the period before the main fighting, put it:

> A power struggle is going on. ... No measures will be of any help so long as the Karabakh map is a bargaining chip in the political game being played out by the Azerbaijan clans, groupings, and individuals waging bitter power struggles.
>
> (Kechichian and Karasik 1995:61)

These 'clans, groupings and individuals', what I call networks, are not throwbacks to the past, to ancient tribal or ethnic formations. Rather they constitute alliances consisting of *nomenklatura* networks from Soviet times, families and clans, and criminal groups that emerged in the latter days of the Soviet Union. They have forged a common identity through the war, and constructed or reconstructed a national idea out of the fears and hostilities that were created as a consequence of ethnic cleansing.

Since the ceasefire, the conflict has been immobilised or 'frozen', providing a long-term obstacle to democracy. Despite early progress in economic and political reforms, Armenia suffers from pervasive militarisation and from economic isolation; the borders with both Turkey and Azerbaijan are closed. In both countries, the dominance of the Karabakh issue blocks democratic debate and the growth of civil society. On both sides there are huge numbers of refugees and/or displaced persons (DPs), and both sides manipulate them for political purposes. On the Armenian side, it is argued that refugees should be integrated and only DPs (Azeris from the occupied territories) should be allowed to return. Within Armenia, the strategy has been forcible integration. This has sometimes included forced conscription, something forbidden under the Geneva Conventions. The degree of integration tends to be used for political purposes. Thus refugees were encouraged to vote in the referendum on independence but were not allowed to vote in the 1996 elections when it was feared they would vote against the ruling party.

On the Azerbaijani side, the opposite approach has been adopted. The continued existence of large numbers of displaced persons, living in tragic conditions, offers a constant reminder of the occupation of Azerbaijani territory and the possibility of a future war of liberation. At least 92,000 are still in camps and most live in isolated conditions (see

ICG 2005a). Very little is done to help the DPs; indeed humanitarian assistance from international organisations is creamed off or 'taxed'. Every day, speeches by Aliyev about his devotion to the DPs cause are shown on television. But the DPs have no self-organisation and by no means all of them welcome the rhetoric.[7]

There have been many attempts to broker a peace both during and after the war. Perhaps the most important were the talks in Key West, Florida, in 2001. Although it is claimed that both sides were close to an agreement, the content of the talks has never been made public. During 2005, the foreign ministers of both sides were involved in new efforts to reach agreement through regular meetings, known as the Prague process (see ICG 2005b).

The key reason for the failure at Key West and for the low hope of success in the Prague process is less the difficulty of reaching agreement and more the weakness of the two sides. Each time the leaders get close to agreement, more radical groups threaten their positions. The fact that talks have tended to be secret and top-down, and that political leaders use the nationalist card for legitimation, makes it difficult to mobilise public support for a peace agreement and to outflank the radicals. On the Armenian side, the ruling network needs the war to justify the militarisation of society and the use of sources of income linked to militarisation. Ter Petrosian was overthrown because he tried to reach a peace agreement. In 1999 two more moderate leaders, Vazken Sarkesian and Karen Demirchan (the former Communist party boss) were elected Prime Minister and Speaker of Parliament respectively, but they were both assassinated six months later. On the Azeri side, the argument that Aliyev ended the war and brought stability was key to his legitimation. The continuing conflict provides an excuse (repeated like a mantra by all officials) for not tackling Azerbaijan's deep-seated problems. Moreover, among opposition networks there are groups who use the war argument – the need to liberate the occupied territories – in the struggle for power.

AZERBAIJAN AS A PETRO-STATE

Azerbaijan has a very similar political structure to Armenia and a number of other post-Soviet countries, although it has special characteristics that result from oil dependence. Both countries could be described as 'post-totalitarian' states where the leadership tries to control every aspect of society and economy through patronage or *nomenklatura* networks. In Armenia, the important instrument of political control is the Ministry of Defence; in Azerbaijan, it is the state oil company SOCAR. As the former Azerbaijan foreign minister put it: 'They use their diaspora; we use our oil' (quoted in Karagiannis 2002:47).

Typical features of the new post-totalitarian dictatorships are: dominant leaders who establish or maintain their position through some kind of electoral process and control the main political institutions; control over the electronic media, especially television; widespread bribery and corruption; widespread human rights violations; and strong security measures. Independent-minded observers sometimes argue that the situation in these societies is worse than in communist times. It is certainly true that material conditions for the mass of the population are much worse: inequality, increases in mortality, unemployment and lack of public services are all visible aspects of everyday life. On the other hand, these regimes are not totalitarian; although governments, ruling parties, and security services try to control all aspects of social life, increased openness, international liberalisation and outside pressure for democratisation mean that NGOs, independent media and critical intellectuals survive, albeit precariously.

Elections in Azerbaijan have been characterised by widespread irregularities – multiple-voting, ballot-stuffing, intimidation and so on. Heydar Aliyev died in December 2003 and the subsequent elections, which brought his son Ilham to power, were so fraudulent that large numbers of people came out on the streets to demonstrate. The demonstrations led to severe repression in which thousands were injured, one person killed and hundreds of opposition leaders arrested. A further round of parliamentary elections in 2005 was also associated with repression of the opposition and widespread irregularities.

There is no separation of powers in Azerbaijan. Parliament is totally under the control of the president. There is no constitutional court. The opposition political parties are persecuted, particularly the Popular Front and the small, semi-legal Islamic Party. The headquarters of the Popular Front in Baku were occupied by the police for several years and a number of its deputies have been arrested. Some were accused of possessing weapons and some have been beaten and tortured. The leader of the party, Elchibey, died in August 2000 and the party subsequently split. The government has also used the 'war on terror' to clamp down further on the Islamic Party and to arrest its leaders.

In general, there are widespread human rights violations in Azerbaijan and widespread reports of torture. The state largely controls the media. In addition to state television there is a private channel owned by the Aliyev family. There are a few independent newspapers and radio stations, mainly Radio Liberty, but there is also censorship and magazines have been closed down. The magazine *Monitor*, for example, was closed down after publishing articles containing analysis of the use of torture, particularly against political opponents, and of the corrupt clan networks on which Aliyev's rule is based. There are very few NGOs in Azerbaijan. Only 120 had been registered by 1998 and many of these were government sponsored. Genuinely democratic NGOs face all kinds of obstacles in trying to get officially registered.

The use of oil in Azerbaijan has a long history.[8] In the late nineteenth century, an oil industry was developed by the Nobels and the Rothschilds and, by the turn of the century, Baku was the second-largest oil producer in the world. In Soviet times, the importance of Baku declined both because of the strategic decision to develop other oilfields and because of new discoveries, especially in Siberia. In the last three decades oil output has been declining because of lack of investment, although Baku became a major manufacturer of oil equipment for the whole Soviet Union. Between 1975 and 1995 production dropped by nearly half, from 17 million tonnes per year (roughly 340,000 bbl/d) to 9 million. Since 1998, oil output has begun to rise again as a consequence of foreign investment.

There are essentially three important arrangements for the exploitation of oil and gas: SOCAR, the state oil company; AIOC (Azerbaijan International Operating Consortium), dominated by BP; and the Shah Deniz gas field company, also dominated by BP, with Turkish and Iranian participation. The Shah Deniz gas field is expected to sell natural gas to the Turkish market although it is not yet yielding revenues. Azerbaijan produces, as of 2004, 15 million tonnes of oil per year (300,000 bbl/d). Nine million are produced by SOCAR and 6 million by AIOC, in which SOCAR has a 10 per cent share. In the future, SOCAR's 9 million is expected to decline to 7 million as a result of lack of investment, while the 6 million produced by AIOC is expected to rise to 25–35 million.

Azerbaijan is much more dependent on oil than in Soviet times. Moreover, it is exhibiting classic signs of Dutch disease (see Table 4.1). The manufacturing sector has collapsed. In 1999, productivity was 10 per cent of its level in 1990; this was the consequence of the war, the establishment of frontiers closing off the Soviet market and the opening up of trade to much more competitive imports. Light industry was at 6 per cent of its 1990 level. Agriculture also collapsed as a result of loss of inputs, loss of markets, and the selling off of collective farms, which was virtually completed by 2000. Construction is increasing faster than the oil sector but it is still below 1990 levels. Tax revenue is very low, amounting to some 15 per cent of 1990 levels (see Table 4.2). Indeed it is lower than any post-Soviet republic except Georgia, Tajikistan and the Kyrgyz Republic. Approximately a third of tax revenue is made up of taxes and royalties from SOCAR. Some 47 per cent of the population live in poverty, while 8.8 per cent live in extreme poverty (IMF 2005).

Unlike other petro-states, Azerbaijan did not increase spending by much under Heydar Aliyev, although fiscal discipline is much less tight than appears. This is owing to huge off-budget subsidies – mainly to gas and electricity – amounting in 2002, according to the IMF, to some 27 per cent of GDP. (Some efforts have been made under IMF pressure

Table 4.1 Azerbaijan: structure of GDP (percentage shares)

	1997	1998	1999	2001	2002	2003
Oil and gas Sector	10	11	20	25	31	31
Non-oil/gas industry and construction	27	34	19	13	12	19
Agriculture	20	18	16	15	14	13
Other	43	47	43	42	40	37

Source: IMF 2002 and 2005.

Table 4.2 Tax revenues in Armenia and Azerbaijan and in selected former
  Soviet Republics (percentage share of GDP)

	1995	1996	1997	1998	1999	2000 (est.)
Armenia	12.7	12.9	16.3	16.9	19.3	17.7
Azerbaijan	10.4	14.2	17.0	15.0	14.0	14.6
For comparison:						
Estonia	38.4	37.0	37.4	37.0	36.3	35.6
Russia	27.5	27.6	28.4	25.5	32.1	36.1
Ukraine	34.8	34.7	35.6	32.6	32.1	30.5

Source: IMF 2001.

to increase transparency and reduce subsidies.) The fact that spending remained rather stable is partly to be explained in terms of the current climate of international economic thinking. In the 1970s, state-led development was a popular policy and petro-states tried to 'sow the petroleum' through state-led industrialisation (see Karl 1997), while nowadays, privatisation and macro-economic stabilisation are considered more prudent economic strategies. But this level of spending also reflects the preoccupation with maintaining control. In a period when economic development is likely to be led by the private sector, it offers a threat to the controlling position of the president. Under Ilham, military spending has increased but it is still only 60 per cent of military spending in Armenia.

SOCAR is the main instrument for political control. It is a typical Soviet-type enterprise, currently employing 78,000 workers, which combines a governmental regulatory function with commercial production. It is responsible for negotiating agreements with foreign companies, such as AIOC or Shah Deniz, as well as undertaking its own exploration, production, refining and sales. SOCAR answers directly to the president.[9]

In effect, political control blocks commercial development in various ways. First, deals are undertaken according to political criteria. Particularly important in this respect are the deals with Russia. The decision in October 1995 to use both the Baku–Novorossisk and the Baku–Supsa pipelines was motivated by concern to maintain good relations with Russia. It was agreed that SOCAR's crude oil exports would go through the Baku–Novorossisk pipeline, which meant that they would be mixed with lower-quality Siberian oil and sold to Russia at prices below the world average.

Second, revenue from SOCAR is used both to fund the budget and to fund personal projects of the president. SOCAR is both the largest single tax payer and the largest debtor. The main reason for the debt is the delivery of crude oil to other ministries, such as agriculture or energy, which do not pay for it. The IMF is currently demanding greater transparency; it wants these debts to be counted as subsidies on the budget. Only exports, which account for between 40 and 50 per cent of the total output, are paid for in real money. And of those hard currency earnings, roughly 60–70 per cent goes to the government in taxes or help-in-kind.

A related problem is corruption. Being part of the 'family' is an opportunity for personal enrichment. Three sorts of activity are vulnerable to corruption: investment, refining and sales. As a consequence of the collapse of the Baku oil-machinery sector, oil machinery is now imported. As with exports, it is the contract with importers and exporters that offers the easiest way to include 'special payments'. Sales, investment and the two oil refineries which produce refined products, often for export, are under the closest control of the president's office. SOCAR's 9 million tonnes per year translates to 25,000 tonnes of oil per day. Of this, 10,000 are exported through the Baku–Novorossisk pipeline; 10,000 go to the domestic market and 3000–5000 go to the two refineries to be transformed into oil products (lubricants, petrol, etc.) mainly for export.

Corruption has to be understood as part of the functioning of the political system – the way patronage networks are sustained.

> The holder of any government position that gives control over economic resources (budget allocations, privatisation, tax or customs receipts, regulatory responsibility for an industry, foreign aid or loans, etc.) or means of coercion (policing, border controls, 'protection', etc.) is in a position to become the centre of such a network.
>
> (Herzig 1999:21)

Thus a position in government is not a job or an opportunity for public service; rather it is a way to take part in the distribution of favours. *The*

Economist reported that a position in government in Azerbaijan could be bought for $50,000 (cited in Karl 1999).

SOCAR is the main source of tax revenue. A State Oil Fund (SOFAR) has been established, which will absorb the oil revenues accruing to Azerbaijan from AIOC and Shah Deniz, both profits and taxation. As of 2004, the fund had $860 million, drawing on Azerbaijan's share of costoil.[10] This is expected to rise to some $10 billion in the next decade. The theory behind the establishment of SOFAR, according to its Executive Director, Samir Sharifov, is to avoid 'Dutch disease' – to insulate oil revenues from the government budget and so maintain fiscal discipline.

SOFAR is directly under the control of the president. However, international agencies have been influential in its establishment and scrutinise the fund carefully. Its mandate specifies that the funds can be used for humanitarian and infrastructure projects and for economic projects approved by an independent international economist. Up to 2004, expenditure consisted of housing and resettlement of DPs in the area adjoining the occupied territories – a project jointly funded by the World Bank, the EU and UNDP; Azerbaijan's share of the Baku–Ceyhan pipeline, a sum estimated at $220 million; and budgetary support. This pattern of expenditure has been heavily criticised by NGOs, who argue that the fund should be reserved for 'relieving poverty and improving social, environmental and public health conditions' (Caucasus Environmental NGO network; www.oilfund.az). According to BP, the fund accurately reflects revenues paid so far; it may be somewhat high as it includes some $100 million in profitoil.[11]

Thus, what is happening is that oil funds are being removed from the government budget. Although they will be announced in parliament, as yet, there is no provision for public scrutiny, let alone approval of how funds are spent. This is under the control of the president, though there is strong pressure from international economic agencies. In addition, as part of its policy of social responsibility, BP is attempting to increase the transparency of revenue management. There are also local NGOs which have established a coalition called Increasing Transparency in the Extractive Industries. An MOU on increased transparency was signed by the government, local companies and a coalition of NGOs in November 2004.[12]

Thus it can be concluded that oil revenues immeasurably strengthen the position of the president and his patronage 'family' network. The existence of the oil instrument, combined with repression, blocks any alternative groupings or political alliances based on autonomous and substantive interests. The rent from oil compensates for declining tax revenue but does not increase public legitimacy because of the personalised favour system. The consequence is pervasive political apathy. 'The most troubling feature of the Southern Caucasus' writes De Waal, 'remains the wide gulf between distant and unpopular rulers and their embittered citizens' (De

Waal 2002). In these circumstances, the formal democratic process does not offer a mechanism to challenge Aliyev's rule or, indeed, to reform the political system. As a consequence, conflict, both in emphasising the Karabakh bargaining chip and actual violence, is the main way in which opposition groups can compete for power. Aliyev has kept military spending low, probably to prevent any political threat from the security sector. Although the army is large, most reports say that it is not effective and that it is poorly equipped compared with the Karabakh armed forces (see Table 4.3). The Karabakh army has built strong fortifications along the border with Azerbaijan, so any attempt to liberate the occupied territories is likely to fail. But any lasting solution is also blocked because of the form politics takes in Azerbaijan; and there is always a risk that some groupings could see advantage in a chaotic situation in the aftermath of Aliyev's rule.

There is, however, a potentially important offsetting factor. This is the fact that oil revenues are derived from the global economy. Azerbaijan's increasing oil dependence means that there is both much greater interest in the country internationally, and probably greater sensitivity to international opinion within Azerbaijan. As AIOC and Shah Deniz increase in importance, that sensitivity may grow. Thus the behaviour of outside players – states, companies and international organisations – can influence the evolution of Azerbaijan's internal development.

THE ROLE OF OUTSIDE PLAYERS

The most important states are Russia and the United States, although Turkey and Iran also play a significant role. There are also a range of

Table 4.3 Armed forces and defence expenditure in Armenia, Azerbaijan and Karabakh

	Armed forces, personnel (2000)	Defence expenditure (US$mil., 1999)	Defence expenditure (share of GDP, 1999)	Tanks (2000)	Other armoured vehicles (2000)	Artillery pieces (2000)
Armenia	41,300	159	8.6%	102	168	229
Azerbaijan	72,100	203	4.5%	220	135	282
Karabakh	10-20,000	n.a.	n.a.	316	324	322

Sources: IISS 2001; IMF 2001, 2002.

international institutions – economic institutions like the IMF, the World Bank and UNDP, and political/security institutions like the OSCE, the European Union, the Council of Europe and NATO.

Russia is probably the most powerful actor in the region. In the aftermath of the fall of communism, Russian policy was chaotic, with various bits of the state apparatus pursuing their own agendas. Although Russian military forces in the area appear to have had a high of degree of autonomy, it does seem likely that the conflicts in the region (Abkhazia and Ossetia as well as Nagorno Karabakh) were manipulated for political purposes. As a consequence of the conflicts, radical anti-Russian nationalists were defeated in both Azerbaijan and Georgia and former communist leaders brought back to power. Both countries joined the CIS in 1993 after the return of Aliyev and Shevardnadze. And Georgia agreed to the presence of Russian bases. In Azerbaijan, Russia has retained control of the Gabala early-warning radar station.

In the period after 1994 it is possible to identify two broad contradictory directions in Russian policy towards the region, though there is still a lot of irregular foreign policy activity.[13] One is espoused by the 'traditionalists', those people largely in the military and in the Ministry of Foreign Affairs who regard the region as part of Russia's sphere of influence and who believe that Western companies are about to 'plunder the Russian Caspian Sea' (Shoumikhin 1999). It is argued that the main purpose of the coup which overthrew Elchibey in 1993 was to prevent him from signing a deal with Western oil companies. In November 1993, after Aliyev came to power, a number of significant deals were signed with Russia and the deal with foreign oil companies was renegotiated. In the final 'deal of the century' which established AIOC, signed in September 1994, the Russian oil company Lukoil acquired a 10 per cent share of AIOC. Nevertheless there was considerable opposition from the traditionalist camp. The Russian ambassador to Azerbaijan, Valter Shonia, said:

> we have had 200 years of cooperation with Azerbaijan. Any politician denying the reality of Russian power is not going to stay long in his office. Russia is interested in cooperation with the West over Azerbaijan, but if there are attempts to unseat Russia, there will be unpleasant consequences.
>
> (Quoted in Nassibli 1999:111)

Part of the argument used to oppose the deal had to do with the status of the Caspian Sea. According to treaties signed in the nineteenth century between Russia and Iran, the coastal states have a ten-mile jurisdiction over coastal waters, with shared jurisdiction over the rest of the sea. The traditionalists argued that the 1994 deal was illegitimate because it made use of offshore oilfields. The signing ceremony in September was attended by Lukoil and the Russian Ministry of Energy. Despite that, the Russian Foreign Ministry held a press conference at the same time, condemning the deal as illegitimate (see Forsythe 1996). Even after the deal was signed, the traditionalists continued to oppose the presence of Western companies in the region. For example, the Moscow-based Institute for Defence Studies produced a document in 1995 entitled 'Conceptual Provisions of the Strategy for Counteraction of Major Threats to the National Security of the Russian Federation'. It argued:

> the most important task is not allowing the realisation of the Caspian oil contract in its present form. In this case it would be expedient to implement a set of measures ... including, if necessary, the use of force in order to stop any activity of foreign companies in the former Soviet part of the Caspian until its legal status is defined; *to apply pressure on the Baku regime, for example, by creating threats of fragmentation of Azerbaijan and [an] Armenian military offensive on Gyandza and Vevlakh.*
> (quoted in Karagiannis 2002:41; italics added)

In 1998, the Russians agreed to the division of the seabed but not the surface of the Caspian Sea according to national jurisdictions. This would put natural resources under national jurisdictions, but allow Russia to retain freedom of movement. Since then, the increasing presence of NATO in Azerbaijan, through the Partnership for Peace (PfP), and of the United States, through various military exercises and most recently the training of border guards to help prevent terrorism, has provided more fuel for the traditionalist position.

The other direction of foreign policy is captured in a group known as the 'realists' or 'pragmatists'. These include the Russian oil sector, which argues that the Russian economy needs access to Western companies for technology and know-how and that political stability is good for business. According to a leading researcher, Yakov Pappe:

> The oil business ignores Russia's attempts to pressure her southern neighbours into submission. ... [T]hey are much more interested in getting their share before the final division takes place. Consequently, they have much more respect for the national ambitions of the 'Near Abroad' countries.
> (quoted in Shoumikhin 1999:138).

The moderates or realists have agreed to work with the OSCE in trying to solve the Nagorno-Karabakh conflict. Russia is one of the three co-chairs of the so-called Minsk Process along with the United States and France.

In practice, these two directions are not so clear cut or distinct: the oil entrepreneurs are closely interlinked with the military, and different positions are expressed by different groups at different times.

A similar schizophrenia characterises US policy. The United States began to focus on the region only after the signing of the 'Deal of the Century' in the mid 1990s. One view, which has been strengthened under the Bush administration, especially after 9/11, is that oil is a key component of national security and that the Caspian region can represent an important alternative source of oil to the Middle East (see Klare 2002). The establishment of bases in Central Asia and frequent joint military exercises are all viewed as part of a strategy designed to ensure friendly regimes in the area. Both Russia and Iran are viewed as potential threats to American interests in the Caspian region. The other view, which was promoted in the State Department during the Clinton years, holds that what matters is stability achieved through democratisation and conflict resolution. The United States has been very supportive of Azerbaijan's civil society and been an active player in the 'Minsk process' (named after a planned conference – which in fact did not take place – in Minsk under OSCE auspices to resolve the Nagorno Karabakh conflict). It hosted the talks in Key West, Florida, in early 2001 where agreement was nearly reached. This line of policy holds that the so-called Great Game, the competition for spheres of influence, is over. Strobe Talbott, as Deputy Secretary of State, epitomised this view arguing that: 'What is required now is just the opposite, for all responsible players in the Caucasus and Central Asia to be winners' (McGuinn and Mesbahi 2000:200). A US State Department spokesman said the 'US does not believe in spheres of influence' (ibid:201).

This schizophrenic US policy is well illustrated by the pipeline issue. Pipeline capacity was insufficient for the new oil and, throughout the 1990s, a debate raged about where to site a new pipeline. On the one hand, the US position was that that Russia and Iran should be excluded from the route. Probably, the most economical option was to build a pipeline to Iran, where the oil could be 'swapped' for Iranian oil and shipped through the Persian Gulf. Another option, especially for the early stages, was to use the existing Baku–Novorossisk pipeline, upgraded and reversed (since it formerly was used for Russian oil imports to Azerbaijan). Instead the Americans favoured a new Baku–Supsa oil pipeline (through Georgia to the Black Sea) and the Baku–Ceyhan pipeline (to the Turkish Mediterranean). As Kazakhstan President Nursultan Nazarbayev put it in February 2000: 'You could get the impression that what is to be built is not a purely civilian structure, but something that constitutes the dividing line between good and evil' (De Waal 2002). In the event both Baku–Supsa and Baku–Novorossisk were chosen in order to please both Russia and America, although the latter pipeline is hardly used for AIOC oil. The Baku–Ceyhan pipeline was chosen as the primary carrier.

At the same time, the Americans argued that the shortest route for the Baku–Ceyhan pipeline would be through Nagorno Karabakh and argued that it would be a 'peace pipeline'. According to John Manesca, the US negotiator for the Nagorno Karabakh conflict:

> If Azerbaijan does not seize on the possibility of building the pipeline across Armenia, Nagorno Karabakh and Nakchivan to the Turkish Mediterranean, it will be wasting a unique opportunity for ending the conflict over Nagorno Karabakh on acceptable terms. Once a decision is made to route the pipeline elsewhere, this opportunity will be lost forever. No other possible route could offer such benefits to both Azerbaijan and Turkey. It would be truly a peace pipeline.
>
> (Karagiannis 2002:43)

This proposal was, however, rejected by Armenia (possibly under Russian influence). According to Gerald Liaridian, the advisor to Kocharian, 'it would be a mistake to think that from a desire to correct the route of the oil pipeline, Armenia would agree to concessions that could lead to the destruction of security' (ibid:45). There was also resistance in Azerbaijan since the pipeline would have broken the blockade of Armenia.

In practice, the two US approaches are contradictory. There is no way that a settlement of the Nagorno Karabakh conflict can be reached without a serious commitment from Russia and perhaps also Iran and Turkey. For example, the Russians and the Americans could have jointly pressured Armenia and Azerbaijan to accept a 'peace pipeline'; but as long as Russia was excluded from the pipeline, this was unlikely to happen. It may be the case that the Russian traditionalists are sufficiently strong to torpedo any peace efforts in the interests of maintaining the conflicts as a political lever for Russian interests in the region. On the other hand the national security approach of the United States, especially bases and military exercises, strengthens the arguments of the Russian traditionalists. What the Americans see as war games, the Russians see as a prelude to further engagement.

The international organisations have the potential to play a different role, strengthening the cooperative elements in the policies of states, but all too often they merely reflect the positions of the dominant member states. The role of the IMF and the World Bank has already been mentioned. Both organisations have been instrumental in setting up the state oil fund and in influencing how the fund will be spent. The IMF is playing an important role in insisting on transparency of budgeting. UNDP has developed a poverty reduction strategy for Azerbaijan, which the various international organisations and companies hope can be applied through the state oil fund.

On the political side, the main organisation is the OSCE. The OSCE has offices in both Baku and Yerevan, aimed at promoting democracy. In addition, the Minsk process is the main conduit for negotiating a settlement in Nagorno Karabakh. Membership of the Council of Europe has also, to some extent, been a spur to democratic reform, at least before Azerbaijan and Armenia were admitted. A variety of legislation was passed in order to qualify for membership, relating both to human rights and democracy. Now the Council of Europe has a permanent presence in Azerbaijan, monitoring the situation concerning human rights with particular attention to political prisoners. The European Union's TACIS programme and NATO's PfP have also played a role in training and professionalisation.

These organisations, particularly the political ones, have the potential to link up with the nascent civil society and exploit Azerbaijan's sensitivity to international opinion. They could act as surrogates for democracy – a way of counter-balancing and putting pressure on the ruling circles. In the absence of any domestic separation of powers, international institutions, through their links with civil society, could offer an alternative mechanism for accountability. Although civil society groups are weak, there have been efforts to construct links between Armenia and Azerbaijan at the level of civil society and to engage in conflict prevention efforts. Some efforts along these lines were made soon after the ceasefire – for example, the Helsinki Citizens Assembly (hCa) has branches throughout the Transcaucasus. A peace caravan was organised throughout the region in the summer of 1992, and this resulted in the establishment of a peace zone in the Kazakh-Echevan region. Through combined pressures, local hCa groups were able to secure the release of over 500 prisoners of war and hostages. There are current efforts among young people and town councils to cross borders but they receive little support from the OSCE and other organisations.

The problem is that international institutions have been very weak. Not only has the OSCE failed to find a solution to the conflict, but its efforts to encourage democratisation have also been flawed. In particular, the failure to criticise the elections in 2003 in both Armenia and Azerbaijan has had a detrimental effect on the public perception of both the OSCE and the Council of Europe. In Armenia, recently, the new Russian Head of Mission said that Armenia was making good progress towards democracy and gave a positive assessment of the country's media and electoral process, despite the flawed nature of the elections and the fact that the only independent TV station is still off-air. Moreover, there is no cooperation between the OSCE offices in the two countries. The two offices do not engage in cross border activities and, therefore, do not currently facilitate confidence-building measures (CBMs) between the populations of the two countries.

Some of the oil companies also pursue policies of social responsibility.

For example, BP is engaged in three main areas. One is security and human rights, for which BP has drawn on the lessons learned in Colombia. BP's security guards are recruited and trained according to the Code of Conduct drawn up by the US State Department and the FCO. The code insists that the same principles are also respected by local companies, in this case BOTAS, the Turkish company responsible for pipeline construction, as well as other subcontractors. The second area is revenue management. BP publishes revenues regularly and intends to post them on its website. It also has a 'loosely formed intention' to publish other types of payments. The company is starting English courses for journalists as well as courses in technical language associated with the oil business, for example 'What are production-sharing agreements.' The third area is sustainable capacity-building to 'sow the petroleum'. BP has established an Enterprise Centre in its former office in Baku's old town. The idea is to lower the entry barrier for local suppliers through training in tender processes and ethical standards, the provision of Internet connections, and a database of local and international businesses. BP is also supporting community development at the Sangachal onshore receiving terminal (three villages) and along the route of the pipeline.

However, as International Alert has pointed out (International Alert 2002), social responsibility is not the same as conflict prevention. As long as the oil companies avoid directly addressing the issue of conflict prevention, their efforts at social responsibility will have a marginal impact.

FUTURE DEVELOPMENTS

Nagorno Karabakh is extremely isolated. Perhaps as much as half of the Armenian population has left, in addition to the forced departure of Azeris during the war. Estimates of the remaining population vary. In Azerbaijan, they claim there are only 40,000 people left in Karabakh. The OSCE estimates between 60,000 and 100,000.

Views remain trapped in a time warp of the early 1990s. People, especially officials, insist that the right to national self-determination is the most important human right and that independence is not about economics but about the preservation of a pure national culture. Society is heavily militarised: the army may have as many as 20,000 troops – mostly Armenians from Armenia. According to the Ministry of Defence they are 'volunteers' who are paid $100 a month. Yet many talk of regular Armenian units composed of conscripts being sent to Karabakh. The Minister of Defence is confident of the ability to defend Karabakh; what is important, he says, is the 'moral spirit of our army'. The aggressive rhetoric of Aliyev, he added, helps to raise this moral spirit.

Formally, Karabakh is a democracy. But, like Armenia and Azerbaijan, it is a highly authoritarian, cosmetic version of 'democracy'. Politically, there is in-fighting among the leadership. The former Minister of Defence, Babayan, who used to be the power in the land, is now imprisoned. The press club is protesting about control of the media. Economically, Karabakh is not viable. Two-thirds of its income comes from the Armenian state budget. The Armenian diaspora provides support for infrastructure and humanitarian assistance, houses, hospitals, education for the children of officers, publishing and water supplies. After 9/11, this assistance fell by a factor of five.

Because it is unrecognised, Karabakh has no international relations. However the Foreign Minister has established what is known as CIS 2, namely relations among similarly unrecognised small states – Abkhazia, South Ossetia, and Transdinestr, but not Chechnya. She described this new forum as a 'spiritual alliance' among those who believe in the principle of national self-determination.

Like Nagorno Karabakh, Armenia is isolated and heavily militarised – defence accounts for 30 per cent of the budget. The shadow economy accounts for roughly half of GDP. The Karabakh syndrome can be understood as a way of blocking democratic development. 'It shadows everything,' says the head of the local OSCE office. According to one local human rights activist, 'defence' is not just physical; it is psychological as well. It affects the mentality of people, who believe that human rights, especially the national right, have to be protected by force. The economy is deteriorating under the blockade from Azerbaijan. Armenia is becoming more and more dependent on Russia. Recently, a debt-equity deal was signed with Russia; three-quarters of Armenia's debt to Russia was cancelled in exchange for Russian control of military and industrial facilities from Soviet times. The general mood is passive and pessimistic. One in three young people leave to find jobs elsewhere or to escape conscription.[14]

The conflict is slowly squeezing Armenia, killing Karabakh through isolation. Although many fear that in the post-Heydar period there may be attempts to take back the occupied territories for political reasons, this does not seem imminent, despite increases in military spending. If Ilham's position becomes more fragile, however, this could lead to unpredictable measures. The main immediate risk is a growing fissure between an increasingly prosperous Azerbaijan, at least in Baku, and an impoverished, militarised Armenia, leading to bitterness and despair that could be used by authoritarian leaders to block democratic development. Karabakh and Armenia could become 'black holes' like Abkhazia and Transdinestr and even Afghanistan under the Taliban – a source of criminalisation and extremism. In the longer term, when oil revenue declines again, Azerbaijan is likely to face all kinds of unpredictable, chaotic forms of violence.

I have argued that the main obstacle to reaching a peace agreement is the weakness of the states in the region. Both Azerbaijan and

Armenia are rentier states; Azerbaijan is dependent on oil and Armenia is dependent on the diaspora and on Russian military assistance. In these circumstances, politics is about controlling access to resources and the main instruments of control are repression and an extremist ideology. Any leader who tries to make peace risks losing control.

This situation is compounded by the geopolitical competition between outside players, especially since 9/11. The importance of oil in shaping top-down approaches is well illustrated by the differing behaviour of external actors towards the elections of 2003. In Georgia, there was widespread international support for civil society and for the demonstrations protesting against the fraudulent character of elections, which led to the fall of Shevardnadze in the rose revolution. Nothing of the kind happened in Azerbaijan. There was no widespread condemnation of the violence, no pressure on the government and inadequate support for civil society.

In the long run, this policy of shoring up weak states and competing for influence over them will ricochet. The new pipelines are vulnerable in the event of renewed violence; the Baku–Tbilisi–Ceyhan pipeline passes only a few kilometres from the borders of Nagorno Karabakh. Yet precisely because these weak states are dependent on external finance, there are real possibilities for influencing the situation in a different way. International organisations could play a much more active role in pushing for more cooperative approaches by outside powers. They could pursue more bottom-up approaches, helping to strengthen civil society, facilitating cross-border movement, involving civil society to a much greater degree in the peace process, and increasing the transparency of the peace process so as to stimulate public discussion and mobilise greater public support. Of course, they would also need greater capacity for implementation. The OSCE has never had the wherewithal to put together a truly multinational peacekeeping force; nor are they capable of mobilising sufficient resources for reconstruction.

What is needed is above all, a change of mindset. The members of international organisations need to understand that oil can never be secured through traditional geopolitical approaches, through 'old war' thinking, and that serious efforts to achieve what has become known as human security are also the only way to secure energy supplies in the future.

NOTES

1. The name Azerbaijan means land of fire, after the Persian word *azer* meaning fire. It was the centre of ancient Zoarastian Persian culture. The name referred to burning oil, mentioned by many travellers, including Marco Polo.

2. According to Leila Yusunova, Deputy Azerbaijani Minister of Defence during the war: 'You know how many officers came from the Soviet Union? Clever, educated officers, rocket specialists, signallers – they were left completely without salaries. ... Their children and families were here, they had no salary, nothing. Do you think they listened to Moscow? What Moscow? Money alone decides everything' (quoted in De Waal 2002:201).

3. The most famous was Monk Melkonian, a Californian archaeologist, known as Avo. He forbade his men to drink or loot and was killed in June 1993.

4. Sarkisian was a former Intourist guide and used to be active in the Communist Party and the Komsomol. He attended the same KGB Academy in Leningrad as Putin and Aliyev. In an interview in the summer of 1993, Sarkisian explained that since the Soviet equipment was divided up in June the war had become more sophisticated, with missiles, artillery and aviation. He claimed that all the Soviet equipment in Karabakh had gone to the Azeris but his forces had captured some of it. Asked whether he really had an army or just bands of volunteers, he said he was trying to create a regular army and that this was much easier now that there was 'real war'. 'In a real war with tanks and helicopters, formerly independent military forces are willing to join together.'

5. Seen during a visit, 1999.

6. There is a striking parallel here with Georgia, where the radical nationalist Gamsakhurdia was overthrown and Shevardnadze installed in power in similar post-independence chaos.

7. 'Tell Aliyev that thanks to his love we are dying,' one DP said to me when I visited a refugee camp in 1999.

8. Reports of Baku oil date back to the sixth century BC. A Venetian traveller in 1543 reported: 'Upon this side of the sea there is another city called Bachu whereof the sea of Bachu taketh name, near unto which there is a mountain that casteth forth black oil, stinking horribly, which they, nevertheless, use for furnishing their lights and for the anointing of their camels twice a year' (Gökay 1999:4).

9. Ilham was, until recently, the vice president of the company. One executive told me that from 8 in the morning till 12 at night, the president's office calls continually.

10. 'Costoil' refers to a portion of produced oil that an operator applies on an annual basis to recover defined costs. Azerbaijan's share is 10 per cent of what remains after AIOC has recovered its capital expenditure.

11. 'Profitoil' refers to the amount of production, after deducting costoil production allocated to costs and expenses, that will be divided between the participating parties and the host government under a production-sharing contract.

12. See www.revenuewatch.org and www.eititransparency.org.

13. For example, the well-known businessman Boris Berezovsky became deputy secretary of Russia's Security Council in 1997. He travelled around to meet the leaders of the region in his private plane with no diplomats present, effectively 'privatising' Russia's foreign policy (De Waal 2003).

14. All the volunteers in hCa's Vandzor office were women; the boys were either in the army or had left to avoid being drafted.

BIBLIOGRAPHY

Amirahmadi, H. (ed.) (2000) *The Caspian Region at a Crossroad: Challenges of a New Frontier of Energy and Development* (New York: St Martin's).

Beblawi, H. (1990) 'The Rentier State in the Arab World', in Luciani, G. (ed.) *The Arab State* (London: Routledge).

Caucasus Environmental NGO Network (CENN) www.cenn.org, last accessed October 2005.

Collier, P. and Hoeffler, A. (2001) *Greed and Grievance in Civil War* (Washington, D.C.: World Bank).

Croissant, M.P. and Aras, B. (eds) (1999) *Oil and Geopolitics in the Caspian Sea Region* (Connecticut and London: Praeger).

De Waal, T. (2002) 'Reinventing the Caucasus', Institute of War and Peace Reporting, www.ipwr.net, last accessed June 2005.

De Waal, T. (2003) *The Black Garden* (New York: New York University Press).

Delay, J. (1999) 'The Caspian Oil Pipeline Tangle: A Steel Web of Confusion', in Croissant, M.P. and Aras, B. (eds) *Oil and Geopolitics in the Caspian Sea Region* (Connecticut and London; Praeger).

Economist Intelligence Unit (EIU) (2001a) *Azerbaijan: Country Profile 2001* (London: Economist).

—— (EIU) (2001b) *Georgia, Armenia: Country Profile 2001* (London: Economist).

—— (EIU) (2002a) *Azerbaijan Country Report* (London; Economist).

—— (EIU) (2002b) *Georgia, Armenia: Country Report* (London: Economist).

Forsythe, R. (1996) 'The Politics of Oil in the Caucasus and Central Asia', *Adelphi Paper 300* (London: IISS).

Gökay, B. (1999) 'History of Oil Development in the Caspian Basin', in Croissant, M.P. and Aras, B. (eds) *Oil and Geopolitics in the Caspian Sea Region* (Connecticut and London: Praeger).

Herzig, E. (1999) *The New Caucasus: Armenia, Azerbaijan and Georgia* (London: Royal Institute of International Affairs).

International Alert (2002) 'Conflict Prevention in Azerbaijan': www.international-alert.org, last accessed July 2004.

International Crisis Group (2005a) 'Nagorno Karabakh: Viewing the Conflict from the Ground', *Europe Report No 166* (Brussels and Tbilisi: ICG).

—— (2005b) 'Nagorno Karabakh: A Plan for Peace: Europe Report No 167'.

International Institute of Strategic Studies (IISS) (2001) *The Military Balance 2000–2001* (London: IISS).

International Monetary Fund (2001) *Republic of Armenia: Recent Economic Developments and Selected Issues: IMF Country Report No. 01/78* (Washington, D.C.: IMF).

—— (2002) *Azerbaijan: Selected Issues and Statistical Appendix: IMF Country Report No.02/41* (Washington, D.C.: IMF).

—— (2005) *Azerbaijan Republic: Selected Issues: IMF Country Report 05/17* (Washington, D.C.: IMF).

Kaiser, R.J. (1994) *The Geography of Nationalism in Russia and the USSR* (Princeton, N.J.: Princeton University Press).

Karagiannis, E. (2002) *Energy and Security in the Caucasus* (Routledge: London).

Karl, T.L. (1997) *The Paradox of Plenty: Oil Booms and Petro-States* (Los Angeles and London: University of California Press).

Karl, T.L. (1999) 'The Perils of the Petro-State: Reflections on the Paradox of Plenty', *Journal of International Affairs*, Vol. 53, No.1.

Kechichian, J.A. and Karasik, T.W. (1995) 'The Crisis in Azerbaijan: How Clans Influence the Politics of an Emerging Republic', *Middle East Policy*, Vol. 4, No 1–2.

Klare, M.T. (2001) *Resource Wars: The New Landscape of Global Conflict* (New York: Henry Holt).

—— (2002) 'Global Petro-Politics: The Foreign Policy Implications of the Bush Administration's Energy Plan', *Current History*, Vol. 100, March.

Luciani, G. (ed.) (1990). *The Arab State* (Routledge: London).

McGuinn, B.R. and Mesbahi, M. (2000) 'America's Drive to the Caspian', in Amirahmadi, H. (ed.) (2000) *The Caspian Region at a Crossroad: Challenges of a New Frontier of Energy and Development* (New York: St Martin's).

Melander, E. (2001) 'The Nagorno-Karabakh Conflict Revisited: Was the War Inevitable?' *Journal of Cold War Studies*, Vol. 3, No. 2.

Nassibli, N. (1999) 'Azerbaijan: Oil and Politics in the Country's Future', in Croissant, M.P. and Aras, B. (eds) *Oil and Geopolitics in the Caspian Sea Region* (Connecticut and London: Praeger).

Rakowska-Harmstone, T. (1974) 'The Dialectics of Nationalism in the USSR' *Problems of Communism*, Vol. 23, No. 3.

Sachs, J.D. and Warner, A.M. (1995) 'Natural Resource Abundance and Economic Growth', *National Bureau of Economic Research Working Paper 5398* (Cambridge, Mass.: National Bureau of Economic Research).

Said, K. (1937) *Ali and Nino* (London: Vintage).

Shoumikhin, A. (1999) 'Russia: Developing Co-operation on the Caspian', in Croissant, M.P. and Aras, B. (eds) *Oil and Geopolitics in the Caspian Sea Region* (Connecticut and London: Praeger).

Suny, R.G. (1993) *The Revenge of the Past: Nationalism, Revolution, and the Collapse of the Soviet Union* (Stanford: Stanford University Press).

Yergin, D. (1990) *The Prize: The Epic Quest for Oil, Money and Power* (New York and London: Simon and Schuster).

5 The conflict in Aceh: struggle over oil?

Kirsten E. Schulze

The province of Aceh is located on the northern tip of the island of Sumatra, on the periphery of the Republic of Indonesia. Although an integral part of the state since 1945, Aceh set itself apart from the rest of the country by its religious devotion and its history. It was the only part of Indonesia that had existed as an internationally recognised independent state, a Muslim sultanate, before the republic's establishment and Acehnese identity reflected this. It was also the only part of the archipelago never to have been totally conquered and subdued by the Dutch. As far as the Acehnese were concerned it was the inability of the Dutch to reoccupy Aceh after the Second World War that provided Indonesia with a territorial base from which to wage war against the Netherlands Indies colonial administration. It was Acehnese money that enabled Indonesia to buy its first two planes and launch its diplomatic offensive to gain international support in its struggle for independence. And after natural gas was discovered in 1971, it was Aceh that was subsidising the development of the rest of the republic. At the same time, however, the Acehnese believed that they had received little if any recognition by Jakarta of their contribution to the Indonesian national project. In fact, most would argue that the only attention paid to Aceh came in the form of troops sent in to quell anti-centrist sentiments, which had resulted from Jakarta's lack of appreciation and understanding as well as repeatedly broken promises.

Unsatisfactory centre–periphery relations were at the heart of two major insurgencies in Aceh. The first, known as the *Darul Islam* rebellion, erupted in 1953 under the leadership of Daud Beureueh. It followed Aceh's incorporation into the province of North Sumatra in 1951 and was triggered by differences over the role of Islam and the reneging by President Sukarno on promises of special status. The conflict was eventually brought to an end in 1959 through a negotiated agreement that conferred upon Aceh special status or *daerah istimewa*. This provided the province with autonomy in matters of religion, *adat* or customary law, and education. The second insurgency started in 1976 under the leadership of Hasan di Tiro and was brought to an end through negotiations in January to August 2005. Like the *Darul Islam* rebellion it was triggered by unsatisfactory centre–periphery relations, namely the removal of special status in all but name. However, unlike Daud Beureueh, who wanted to transform all of Indonesia into an Islamic state rather than secede from it, Hasan di Tiro sought Acehnese independence. Also unlike the *Darul Islam* rebellion, the second insurgency had a distinct economic dimension, ranging from popular grievances over exploitation to opportunities for enrichment. Both were directly, but not solely, linked to the discovery and extraction of natural gas.

This chapter will look at the role natural gas played in the second Aceh insurgency. The key question is to what extent the struggle between the Free Aceh Movement, or *Gerakan Aceh Merdeka* (GAM), and the Indonesian government was over this resource rather than about sovereignty and ideology. This will be explored by looking at the impact of the discovery of gas on Acehnese society, the impact of subsequent economic development policies, GAM's perception of the extraction of Aceh's natural resources and, finally, the role natural gas played in prolonging the conflict.

It will be argued here that the nature of the conflict in Aceh was primarily ideological. It was a violent clash of competing and mutually exclusive nationalisms as defined by the protagonists: GAM and the Indonesian government. Ultimately, it was a war over territory and sovereignty. Neither GAM nor Indonesia would have been willing to forego their claim to Aceh if it were resource-poor rather than resource-rich. Indonesia literally equated a possible secession of Aceh with the disintegration of the state as a whole. Similarly GAM saw the liberation of Aceh not only as freeing a population from oppression and restoring true ownership of the land, but as striking at the heart of the 'neo-colonial Javanese Indonesian empire' – and causing it to unravel.

That does not, however, mean that natural resources did not play an important role. Indeed, without understanding the 'natural gas dimension' it is impossible fully to understand the conflict. To begin with, the roots of the conflict are inextricably intertwined with the discovery of liquefied natural gas (LNG) (Kell 1995), the Suharto 'New Order' regime's management of its exploitation, and the distribution of the resultant economic benefits (Robinson 2001). Key here is that the benefits of the LNG boom accrued above all to the central government, foreign companies, and non-Acehnese Indonesians, and that so little of locally generated revenues were spent locally. This provided a fertile breeding ground for rebellion. For GAM and many Acehnese, the LNG industry epitomised everything that was wrong with Jakarta – over-centralisation, crony capitalism, corruption, and ultimately repression to safeguard those élite interests.

Moreover, natural gas is crucial to understanding the dynamics of the violence. In simple terms, GAM equated the extraction of natural gas with neo-colonial exploitation by Jakarta and thus saw it as legitimate to target oil companies as agents of neo-colonialism. In order to safeguard the flow of natural gas, the Indonesian government repeatedly sent in security forces to create a safe corridor and to crush the insurgents. Human rights abuses committed in this process created a link between the military and the oil industry – Mobil Oil Indonesia, Inc. (later Exxon-Mobil Oil Indonesia, Inc. – EMOI), Pertamina and PT Arun – not only in the view of GAM but also of large parts of Acehnese society. This, in turn, provided the insurgents with further legitimacy to target these companies as well as the soldiers assigned by the government to guard the gas production and processing facilities in Aceh. It also provided GAM with scores of willing recruits.

In addition to influencing the dynamics of the conflict, natural gas also contributed to prolonging it. Every step in the development of the greater Lhokseumawe industrial area created additional Acehnese grievances over unequal distribution of the benefits, contracts and jobs. Moreover, since 1999, the extortion by GAM of the oil companies, third-party contractors and the population adjacent to EMOI's production operations, as well as the kidnapping for ransom of oil workers and executives, financed the increase in the movement's military capacity. The natural gas industry also provided individuals in GAM, the Indonesian security forces, and the Aceh provincial government with real or perceived opportunities for personal enrichment, undermining both GAM's Acehnese and Jakarta's Indonesian nationalist projects. Granting Aceh special autonomy in 2001 as part of a dysfunctional peace process only increased the scramble for the spoils.

THE ARUN GAS FIELD, PERTAMINA AND MOBIL OIL

The exploration in Aceh for what initially was oil and later turned out to be natural gas started in 1968 and was part of a broader policy by President Suharto to stimulate the Indonesian economy after the turbulent events of 1965, which had brought him to power. At the time, the population of Aceh numbered just over 2 million – today 4.4 million – of whom 98 per cent were Muslim and 71 per cent were farmers.

The exploration and extraction of oil and gas in Aceh, as in the rest of Indonesia, is governed by production-sharing contracts (PSCs) which divide physical production, after allowing a portion to be retained for the recovery of pre-production and production costs (Barnes 1995:42). Unlike in the concession system, which basically gives all production to the concessionaire so that the oil or gas becomes property of the concessionaire at the wellhead, and the state obtains all revenue from royalty or tax, under the PSCs the state retains sovereignty over the natural resources. All production, including crude stored at export terminals, is the property of the government, with the state company as its agent (Barnes 1995:43). As Public Affairs Manager for EMOI located in Jakarta, Bill Cummings, put it: 'ExxonMobil has contractual rights under the PSCs to produce gas but does not own the facilities or equipment in Aceh. Everything related to gas production in Aceh belongs to the government of Indonesia that contracted Exxon-Mobil to operate the Aceh fields under PSCs.'[1]

The production-sharing ratio of the first generation of PSCs for oil was on a basis of 65/35 in favour of the government. This was renegotiated in 1976 to a ratio of 85/15. The production-sharing ratio of PSCs for natural gas generally differed from those for oil in recognition of higher up-front costs. The original contracts were signed on a basis of 70/30, and for gas produced in deep-water on a basis of 55/45 (Barnes 1995:111).

While the PSC was not introduced until 1966, it was in many ways the product of Indonesia's colonial history, with sovereignty over natural resources as the key issue. Dutch colonial rule had focused on the extraction of the archipelago's natural resources for the sole benefit of the Netherlands, inflicting hardship and sometimes near starvation on the peasant population (Barnes 1995:3). Indonesia's founding fathers were moulded by this experience in no uncertain terms. It prompted the first president Sukarno to advocate a highly individualist, radically non-aligned, anti-colonial and anti-imperial policy, which was reflected in the 1955 Bandung Conference and the 1963 confrontation with Malaysia. The policy also included a freeze on oil concessions to foreign corporations and the 1958 nationalisation of Dutch-owned enterprises. The latter gave birth to Indonesia's national oil company Pertamina which traces its origins to 'when PT Permina was incorporated under the aegis of the Indonesian army to operate the country's recently nationalised North Sumatra fields' (Vaughan 1998:68) and was, until the 1975 Pertamina crisis, headed by Lieutenant General Ibnu Sutowo.

In 1960, President Sukarno, taking his cue from other leaders in the non-aligned movement such as Egypt's Gamal Abdel Nasser, embarked upon a process of nationalising the oil industry through Law 44, which was ratified by parliament in 1961. This law decreed that 'oil and gas mining is conducted only by the state, and only a state enterprise is authorised to engage in oil and gas mining on behalf of the state' (cited in Vaughan 1998:69). Under this law three companies were authorised to oversee Indonesia's oil operations: Permina and two new companies, Pertamin and Permigan.

Foreign oil companies, which had operated in Indonesia since the 1890s when it was still the Dutch East Indies, were now only able to obtain exploration and production concessions. Their marketing, refining and shipped assets were transferred to the Indonesian state following negotiated restitution.

The events of 1965, the placing under house arrest of President Sukarno and the rise to power of Major General Suharto brought further change. First, the new regime opened the country to exploration by a large number of foreign companies because oil production was in decline (Bresnan 1993:164). Indonesia's annual growth averaged only 2 per cent (Barnes 1995:18). Second, the Indonesian oil industry was centralised. In 1966, Permigan was dissolved and its assets were turned over to Permina and Pertamin. On 20 August 1968, Suharto promulgated a decree combining the two remaining companies into one: Pertamina. In the same year, Indonesia embarked upon a business relationship with Mobil Oil Indonesia, Inc. (MOI), which was awarded a PSC operatorship in the province of Aceh with a production-sharing ratio of 65/35.

Over the next three years MOI seismically explored B Block and drilled 14 wells without result. Then the Arun natural gas field was discovered in 1971, with recoverable gas reserves estimated at 13 trillion cubic feet and 1 billion barrels of liquids (ExxonMobil 2001:2). The Arun Field was found to be eleven miles long and three miles wide with a maximum thickness of 1080 feet (Vaughan 1998:82) – at the time Asia's largest natural gas field. The B Block in which the Arun Field was situated also comprised the South Lhok Sukon A and D fields, which were estimated to hold more than 500 billion cubic feet of natural gas. Just to the south was the Pase Block. And finally, there was the North Sumatra Offshore Block with reserves of more than 1.2 trillion cubic feet of gas (Vaughan 1998:98–9).

In 1973, two years after the discovery of the Arun Field, Pertamina director Ibnu Sutowo committed Indonesia to the delivery of 130 shiploads of LNG to Japan, an agreement which he saw as the solution to Indonesia's debts (Vaughan 1998:83). And in 1974, construction began on the gas liquefaction plant PT Arun on the outskirts of Lhokseumawe from where the LNG would be shipped to Japan.

Under Ibnu Sutowo's auspices, PT Arun was formed as a joint-venture, owned 55 per cent by Pertamina, 30 per cent by MOI, and 15 per cent by the Japanese Indonesia LNG Co. (JILCO), which had provided an estimated 85 per cent of the investment capital (Barnes 1995:115). The LNG would be processed at cost, with all revenues netted back to the wellhead where profits would be split by Mobil and Pertamina according to the 35/65 PSC terms (Vaughan 1998:89).

In 1977, the first Arun Field work cluster went online, and by October of that year some 600 million cubic feet of gas a day were being produced (Vaughan 1998:91). In 1978 Mobil started up the second Arun Field cluster, and on 9 September 1978 President Suharto formally opened the Arun LNG plant in Lhokseumawe. A couple of weeks later the first LNG cargo was shipped to Japan. After the third Arun cluster went online in 1982 and the fourth in 1983, LNG was also exported to South Korea.

The LNG boom resulted in the establishment of a number of petrochemical industries in Lhokseumawe. In 1983, the ASEAN fertiliser plant began operating. Shortly afterwards the Iskandar Mudar fertiliser plant also began production. In 1986 the first gas was delivered directly to these two downstream industries. This was followed two years later, in 1988, by the first gas delivery to the PT Kertas Kraft paper plant.

The highest point of production was reached in 1992, and it has been in decline ever since. In 1997 the 3000th cargo of LNG was sold from the Aceh gas fields, and in 2002 118 cargos were delivered to Pertamina's LNG customers in Japan and Korea.[2] In the meantime, on 30 November 1999, Exxon Corporation and Mobil Corporation merged to form ExxonMobil, in Indonesia becoming ExxonMobil Oil Indonesia Inc. (EMOI). In June 2002, Indonesia established a new regulatory agency for oil and gas, *Badan Pelaksanaan Minyak dan Gas* (BPMIGAS), reducing Pertamina's role to LNG seller only.

Today, EMOI holds a 100-per cent contractor share and operates the Arun, South Lhoksukon A and D, and Pase on-shore fields as well as the North Sumatra Offshore Field under PSCs managed by BPMIGAS. EMOI is also a non-operating contractor for A-Block in Aceh through its affiliate Mobil A-Block Inc, which has 50-per cent ownership.

SUHARTO'S DEVELOPMENT POLICY

Philippe Le Billon in his analysis of the ecology of war argued that 'the likelihood of political secession increases when "outsiders" are perceived to extract "local" resources without sharing the wealth, and when local populations are displaced by the extractive industry or suffer from its environmental costs.' (2001:4) A closer look at the development policies – or, arguably, the developmentalist ideology – under President Suharto's New Order regime from 1967 until his fall in May 1998 shows a clear link between the discovery and exploitation of the Arun natural gas field and popular discontent, which, amongst other factors, translated into support for GAM. Aceh's main grievances revolved around four issues: first, centralisation; second, modernisation and socio-economic dislocation; third, enclave development; and fourth, lack of mobility and poverty.

Centralisation

Since the independence of Indonesia, oil and gas revenue has been vital for building the new republic and, like other production states, Indonesia suffered from the 'paradox of plenty' (Karl 1997) and the 'resource curse' (see Ross 1999; Sachs and Warner 1995) – albeit to a lesser extent and less rapidly as its economy was more diversified. Nevertheless, the availability of rent had postponed the development of a broader tax base and had also encouraged over-centralised political power, enclave development, and strong networks of complicity between public and private sectors (Karl 1999:34), leading to crony capitalism and corruption. Centralisation was reinforced by two developments in the mid

1970s: first, the oil boom, which ensured that oil and gas revenue became the engine of Indonesian national development (Bresnan 1993:164); second, the Pertamina crisis of 1975, which ensured that 'ideas about decentralisation were stillborn' (Bresnan 1993:190).

Political and economic centralisation became the key to the survival of the Suharto regime. Economic centralisation, in particular rent derived from natural resources, underpinned the regime through patronage and clientalism. It reinforced an ideologically driven political centralisation, which had characterised Indonesia almost from the beginning. Under Sukarno centralisation was the by-product of his anti-colonial, anti-imperial and quasi-Marxist approach to both politics and economics, which had resulted in nationalisation. His successor Suharto equated decentralisation with federalism and federalism with disintegration. Conversely, centralisation was seen as the means to protect the unity and integrity of the state and as an integral part of the nation-building effort. National Indonesian identity was emphasised over regional, tribal or religious loyalties, and all policies, including development, were drafted with the greater national good in mind. More often than not this came at the expense of regional development, especially in the outer islands. And as the wealth and power gap between ruling and ruled increased, so did the frustration in these marginalised areas.

The impact of Suharto's centralisation policy on Aceh cannot be overstated. Politically, it revoked in all but name the special autonomy status Aceh was granted in 1959 as part of the conflict resolution process to end the *Darul Islam* rebellion. It denied space and expression to a people with a strong sense of identity derived from religion, culture and a long history of independence. Economically, centralisation meant that while Aceh had since 1980 contributed between $2 and $3 billion annually to Indonesian exports (Dawood and Sjafrizal 1989:115), the people of Aceh received few benefits from the exploitation of Aceh's gas wealth as the revenue flowed to the centre and from there to the rest of Indonesia. Only a small amount of Aceh's export surplus was 'recycled' in the form of central government expenditure in the province.

Modernisation and socio-economic dislocation

Centralisation was not the only policy to have negative impacts on the Acehnese. Modernisation, too, held the seeds of popular discontent, especially in the Lhokseumawe area where it was accompanied by dislocation, industrialisation, foreign corporations, and the influx of non-Acehnese migrant workers.

Until the discovery of natural gas, Aceh's economy was mainly agricultural. In the late 1960s, however, the economy started to be transformed, first by the restoration of political and economic normal-ity after the *Darul Islam* rebellion, and later by the exploitation of natural gas reserves. This turned Aceh into a province with one of the highest per capita GDPs and into a major foreign exchange earner (Dawood and Sjafrizal 1989:107). In 1971, the province's per capita GDP was 89 per cent of the national average; by 1983 it had increased to 282 per cent (Dawood and Sjafrizal 1989:6, Table 1.1). Between 1971 and 1979 Aceh underwent rapid development, peaking in the years 1978–79. The annual rate of growth from 1975 until 1984 was 7.6 per cent, and from 1984 to 1989 was just under 5 per cent. Aceh's manu-facturing sector grew at an average rate of 13.7 per cent and the percentage of the province's GDP derived from oil and gas rose from 17 per cent in 1976 to 69.9 per cent in 1989 (Ross 2003:14).

This rapid pace of development was welcomed by the Aceh Gover-nor of the time, Muzzakir Walad, but the Acehnese population was 'woefully unprepared for the arrival of the modern industrial complex.'(Kell 1995:26) As Kell pointed out, as late as the mid 1970s there was not even a technical high school in North Aceh. Not surpris-ingly, at grassroots level the efforts at industrialisation were viewed with suspicion. Mobil's exploration geologist Sudhyarto Suwardi, who was in charge of drilling the A-1 well at Arun, recalled that 'the local Acehnese people were not very happy to have exploration going on in their area and were hostile to outsiders' (quoted in Vaughan 1998:74). Local suspicion turned into resentment, fed by the belief that too few Acehnese were being employed by the new project and that '"outsiders" had gained a disproportionate share of the benefits of industrial growth.' (Amnesty International 1993:4)

Foreigners and Javanese took many of the higher-paying jobs as the Acehnese often lacked the required technical and educational qualifi-cations. This situation was further exacerbated by the unrealistic expec-tations of the villagers. As a local military commander in the 1980s, Sofian Effendi, recalled:

> I had a lot of contact with Arun and Mobil. They tried with community development but there was a problem with skills. The Acehnese did not have the skills for the good jobs. There was resentment in the villages next to Arun and Mobil, so I asked them to employ more Acehnese but their education was just too low. It was a real mismatch – a real problem. When I talked to villagers they said they wanted to be managers. And they complained that they didn't get those jobs. What made things worse was that those same villagers had no electricity and would sit in the dark next to the brightly lit Arun and Mobil complex.[3]

Local firms more often than not could not compete. Hasan di Tiro himself was convinced that he had been the victim of unfair competition. In 1974, he lost out to Bechtel on a bid to build one of the pipelines (Ross 2003:12). This, no doubt, added a personal twist to GAM's grievance with respect to Mobil and Bechtel. Even at the lower levels of employment, the Acehnese faced the competition of some 50,000 migrants from other parts of Indonesia who, attracted by the energy boom, had come to Aceh in search of work. Added to this were Javanese transmigrants, who were settled in Aceh by the Suharto regime. In 1998, oil and gas accounted for 65 per cent of Aceh's GDP and 92.7 per cent of its exports. However, it only employed one-third of one per cent of the province's labour force (BPS Aceh 1999 as cited in Ross 2003:19).

In 2003, as far as the villagers next to EMOI were concerned, the picture had not changed significantly. As one resident of Nibong Baru village adjacent to Cluster II explained: 'Only one percent of this area are employed with Exxon and then only in jobs like drivers and security guards. All skilled work is from outside this area.' While there was some development, in the eyes of the villagers there was nowhere near enough and not of the right kind. In the words of another villager, it was a case of 'if the village asked for a buffalo Exxon would give it a duck.'[4]

Last, but certainly not least, there were the 'side effects' of industrialisation and modernisation and their destructive impact on the local culture and value system. One of these side effects was the process of rural–urban migration to the Lhokseumawe area. Between 1974 and 1987, North Aceh's population rose from 490,000 to 755,000 (Ross 2003:15). Greater Lhokseumawe was unable to absorb these numbers and its infrastructure and social services quickly became overstretched. Added to this was the dispossession of local farmers, the forcing of fishermen from their traditional occupations without providing alternative employment, increasing prices and serious pollution (Amnesty International 1993:4). Dislocation, unmet expectations, unemployment, social jealousy and urban poverty placed considerable strains on Aceh's social fabric. This was further compounded by the emergence of 'prostitution, gambling, alcohol, drugs, and strong-arm thugs,' which the Acehnese associated with the military (Riklefs 2001:388) but also, rightly or wrongly, with the Javanese migrants. The Lhokseumawe industrial complex took on 'the obtrusive character of a high-income, capital-intensive, urban, non-Muslim, non-Acehnese enclave in a basically low-income, labour-intensive, rural, Muslim, Acehnese province.' (Emmerson 1983:1234) The consequent volatile mixture of resentments often resulted in sporadic violence such as the August 1988 bombing of a hotel in Lhokseumawe after repeated complaints by the local community that it was being used as a prostitution centre, and the March

1989 destruction of a military-owned building in which a circus, considered offensive by local Islamic leaders, was due to perform (Amnesty International 1993:4).

The perceived attack on traditional and devoutly Muslim Acehnese culture by a modernisation process driven by the secular government in Jakarta and Western oil companies, and the un-Islamic behaviour of transmigrants provided the spark to set alight the grievances over the distribution of high-paying jobs and gas revenue. While it did not result in an Islamic revolution, as in Iran, GAM and the movement's construction of Acehnese nationalism were no less a reaction to modernity (Aspinall 2002:3–4).

Enclave development

The population of Aceh, and North Aceh in particular, was on the frontier not only of modernity but also of economic inequality. This inequality had two dimensions. First, Aceh contributed substantially towards the national GDP but government expenditure in the province was not above average. Virtually the entire gas revenues accrued to Jakarta either through the PSC between MOI and Pertamina or directly through Pertamina itself (Dawood and Sjafrizal 1989:115). The Acehnese as a whole did not benefit markedly. Second, the few local benefits from the energy boom were sector specific, thus creating inequality both within Aceh and between Aceh and Jakarta. These were mainly spin-offs such as construction and transportation, as well as investment in downstream user industries such as fertilizer (1989:115). Foreign investment further reinforced this picture. Looking at the situation in the mid 1980s, Dawood and Sjafrizal noted that, while there was substantial foreign investment in Aceh outside the oil and gas sector, 'the number of realised projects – three – has been disappointingly small, and the investment is concentrated almost entirely in chemicals. Up to June 1986, $132 million of the $141 million was invested in the ASEAN Aceh Fertiliser plant' (1989:114). Manufacturing output doubled between 1980 and 1984 and a number of large industries – ASEAN fertiliser plant, Iskandar Muda fertiliser plant and Kraft paper factory – joined MOI, Pertamina and PT Arun. Yet, while 'the share of Aceh's GDP rose more than fourfold over the period 1975–84, outside the oil and gas sectors … structural change was quite limited.' (Dawood and Sjafrizal 1989:111) In 1985, 14 years after the discovery of the Arun Field, Aceh's agricultural sector share of 71 per cent was still one of the highest in Indonesia, while its mining, manufacturing, construction and transport sector share of 8.6 per cent was one of the lowest (Hill and Weideman1980:14, Table 1.5). Lhokseumawe had become a highly industrialised city while the rest of Aceh, outside of its capital Banda Aceh, remained a largely underdeveloped rural backwater with inadequate infrastructure. The pressure on the social fabric of

Acehnese society increased further as the residents in the industrial zone were accused of driving up prices in local markets. Price hikes of staple foods thus coincided with the decline of per capita income in the outlying rural areas (Kell 1995:17).

Lack of mobility and poverty

What is striking when looking at Aceh in comparison to other parts of Indonesia is that Aceh until recently was by no means a poor province and the living standard in Aceh, both rural and urban, was always comparatively high. Provincial data taken from the national socio-economic survey or *survei sosial ekonomi nasional (Susenas)* and prepared for the World Bank (2002) shows that Aceh in 1980 had only 11.7 per cent urban poor and 11.2 per cent rural poor while, for example, in Maluku 51.7 per cent of the urban population and 52.4 per cent of the rural population lived under the poverty line. In fact, living standards in Aceh were higher than those in the neighbouring province of North Sumatra, which had 31.8 per cent urban and 15.1 per cent rural poor (Booth 1992:348). What is equally striking, however, is that Aceh barely improved between 1980 and 1987. Data for 1987 from the Central Statistics Bureau, or Biro Pusat Statistik (BPS), reveals that while the urban poverty rate in Maluku dropped to 10.2 per cent and in North Sumatra to 8.6 per cent, and the rural poverty rate dropped to 36.3 in Maluku and 9.2 per cent in North Sumatra, in Aceh the drop was negligible. In 1987, the proportion of the urban population living under the poverty line was 9 per cent and that of the rural population 8.9 per cent.[5] Of all of Indonesia's provinces, Aceh ranked lowest in terms of mobility, and this was during the boom years of the Arun Field before production peaked in 1991.

The lack of mobility of the 1980s turned into poverty in the 1990s when Indonesia's economy went from boom to bust, hitting rock bottom with the 1997 Asian economic crisis. In Aceh, this was further exacerbated by the destructive impact of the counter-insurgency operations from 1989 to 1998 on the local economy. In 1998, the provincial economy contracted by 5.3 per cent and another 2.9 per cent in 1999 (ICG 2001:5). In 1999, Aceh's unemployment figure rose to 30 per cent, with the highest unemployment in the areas most affected by the conflict: Pidie, East Aceh and North Aceh (ICG 2001:5). In 2002, the World Bank estimated that only half of Aceh's population had access to clean drinking water and electricity. In 2003, according to Governor Abdullah Puteh, approximately 40 per cent of the population or some 1,680,000 Acehnese lived below the poverty line.[6] This number was double the 1999 figure of 886,809, and four times that of 1996, when the total number of poor was 'only' 425,600 (Sukma 2004:32). Indeed, in 2003, Aceh officially became the poorest province on the island of Sumatra and the second poorest in Indonesia as a whole.[7]

It is not surprising that the way Aceh was developed under the Suharto regime translated into discontent, especially when measured against high popular expectations from the discovery of natural gas. In Acehnese eyes, the province was being bled dry for the benefit of Jakarta, and resentment quickly took on ethnic overtones, translating into 'stealing' from the Acehnese to 'give' to the Javanese. The Acehnese grassroots felt exploited and trapped. Mutually reinforcing political and economic centralisation ultimately created broad popular discontent upon which GAM was able to draw. The slippery slope from lack of mobility into poverty for the average population contrasted sharply with the corruption of the Jakarta élite, which brought the students onto the streets in May 1998, ultimately bringing down the regime. There is no doubt that GAM's resurgence in 1989 and again in 1999 can be linked, in the former case, to Acehnese grievances against the LNG revenue sharing between the Aceh provincial government and the central government as well as the migrants and, in the 1999 case, against the LNG revenue sharing, the migrants, the economic crisis and military repression (Ross 2003:32).

THE ESTABLISHMENT OF GAM AND THE TARGETING OF MOBIL

The Aceh Sumatra National Liberation Front (ASNLF), which became locally known first as *Aceh Merdeka* and later as *Gerakan Aceh Merdeka* (GAM), was established in October 1976. Its founding father was Hasan di Tiro, grandson of Teungku Chik di Tiro, hero of the anti-colonial struggle against the Dutch. Di Tiro was born in Aceh on 4 September 1930. At the age of 20, he left Aceh to study in the United States, where he also worked at the Indonesian Mission to the United Nations. In 1953 he resigned his post in support of Daud Beureueh's *Darul Islam* rebellion. Thereafter he continued to work as a businessman until he returned to Aceh on 30 October 1976 in order to fulfil his historical obligation as a member of the di Tiro family, namely to fight for the restoration of Acehnese independence.[8]

GAM's ideology was one of national liberation aimed at freeing Aceh from 'all political control of the foreign regime of Jakarta' (Aceh Sumatra National Liberation Front 1976). GAM saw its struggle as the continuation of the anti-colonial uprising that erupted in response to the 1873 Dutch invasion and subsequent occupation of the sovereign Sultanate of Aceh. Contrary to official Indonesian historiography, GAM maintained that Aceh did not voluntarily join the Republic of Indonesia in 1945, but was illegally incorporated. GAM's reasoning was twofold: first, Aceh was an internationally recognised independent state, as exemplified by the 1819 Treaty between the Sultan of Aceh and the United Kingdom of Great Britain and Ireland or the 1824 Anglo-

Dutch Treaty. Sovereignty should therefore have been returned to the Sultanate of Aceh rather than the Republic of Indonesia (di Tiro 1980:11). Accordingly di Tiro argued that:

> Aceh has nothing to do with Javanese 'Indonesia'. The Netherlands declared war against the Kingdom of Aceh, not against 'Indonesia', which did not exist in 1873; and 'Indonesia' still did not exist when the Netherlands was defeated and withdrew from Aceh in March 1942. And when the Netherlands illegally transferred sovereignty to 'Indonesia' on December 27, 1949, she had no presence in Aceh.
>
> (di Tiro 1995:2)

Second, the people of Aceh were not consulted on the incorporation of Aceh into Indonesia and thus their right to self-determination was violated (di Tiro 1995:12–13). These premises were reflected in GAM's re-declaration of independence on 4 December 1976, which declared illegal the transfer of sovereignty 'by the old, Dutch colonialists to the new, Javanese colonialists' (Aceh Sumatra National Liberation Front 1976). GAM's aim as stated on its webpage in 2002 was 'the survival of the people of Aceh Sumatra as a nation; the survival of their political, social, cultural and religious heritage which are being destroyed by the Javanese colonialists' and to reopen 'the question of decolonisation of the Dutch East Indies alias "Indonesia"' (see Aceh Sumatra National Liberation Front, no date).

While the overall aim of GAM was an independent Acehnese state and GAM's ideology was above all one of national liberation, it comprised a number of ideological sub-currents, one of which directly related to the 'protection' of Aceh's natural resources from the 'neo-colonial exploitation' of the 'Javanese' government in Jakarta and foreign corporations. [9] This ideological sub-current was arguably linked to the fact that di Tiro himself had lost out to Bechtel in a bid for building a pipeline for MOI in 1974 (Robinson 2001:223). Other Acehnese businessmen who lost in the competition for lucrative contracts to either foreign contractors or outsiders with good political connections in Jakarta became the strongest supporters of GAM (Robinson 2001:223). This put GAM on a collision course with the emerging energy industry in North Aceh and allowed the movement to see MOI (later EMOI) as an active player in the conflict.

For the first 15 years GAM articulated its opposition to the extraction of Aceh's natural gas in anti-capitalist and anti-Western language. GAM leader Hasan di Tiro, in his diary covering the first three years of the movement from 1976 until 1979, clearly illustrates this. For instance, on 4 December 1976 when di Tiro 'redeclared' Aceh's independence, he stated that Aceh:

has been exploited and driven into ruinous conditions by the
Javanese neo-colonialists. ... [T]hey have put our people in
chains of tyranny, poverty, and neglect ... while Aceh, Sumatra
has been producing a revenue of over 15 billion US dollars
yearly for the Javanese neo-colonialists.

(di Tiro 1984:17)

On 15 June 1977, he lamented that 'our country has been laid bare by
the Javanese colonialists at the feet of the multinationals to be raped'
(1984:77). And on 15 August 1977, he wrote about the 'actions taken by
our forces in Kuala Simpang, Langsa and Pangkalan Susu regions to
close down foreign oil companies and to prevent them from further
stealing our oil and gas' (1984:87). His diary entry for 16 October 1977
recounts how in a GAM cabinet meeting the decision was made to safeguard Aceh's natural resources 'that are being increasingly plundered
by the Javanese and their foreign cohorts, especially our oil and gas'
(1984:107). Four days later, on 20 October 1977, GAM leafleted the
Lhokseumawe industrial complex calling upon all Americans,
Australians and Japanese employees of MOI and Bechtel:

to pack and leave this country immediately, for the time being,
for we cannot guarantee the safety of your life and limbs. Your
employers, Mobil and Bechtel, have made themselves co-
conspirators with Javanese colonialist thieves in robbing our
unrenewable gas resources for their mutual advantage. We, the
National Liberation Front of Aceh Sumatra, the protector and
the defender of the rights of the people of this country are
duty-bound to stop this highway robbery of staggering
proportion perpetrated by the Javanese colonialists, aided by
Mobil and Bechtel. If you stayed, you are liable to get shot by
stray bullets aimed at Javanese mercenaries who are all around
you in civilian clothes, in every hook and nook of this place.

(GAM leaflet quoted in di Tiro 1984:108–9).

Just over a month later, in early December 1977, three foreign contractors for Bechtel, an American and two Koreans, who were involved in
the construction of Arun Field Cluster III, came under attack. Di Tiro's
diary entry for 6 December 1977 records this incident as follows:

An American worker was reportedly killed and another
wounded by stray bullets in the fighting between our forces
and the Indonesian colonialist troops. This was the sort of
thing we have been trying to avoid for months. It was
precisely in order to avoid such an incident that we had

issued a public announcement in October 1977 advising American and other foreign workers to leave the area temporarily because we cannot guarantee their safety in the event that fighting might take place between Acehnese Sumatran defenders and the Indonesian Javanese invaders, which is inevitable. Unfortunately, however, they have totally ignored our friendly warning although it was issued repeatedly.

(di Tiro 1984:125–6)

However, Bechtel's doctor at the time recalled events differently. According to him there was no evidence of a gun battle, only an armed attack on the unarmed foreign contractors. The Koreans fled the scene, hid in the rice paddies and survived the incident. The American was shot dead. Sofian Effendi, commander of Special Forces unit *Nanggala* 16, which was operating in the area at the time, claims that the killing was carried out by GAM troops under a local commander, most likely without authorisation by di Tiro.[10]

The attack did not succeed in intimidating foreign workers or in stopping the construction of the natural gas facilities, and GAM continued to see the company as a target, as di Tiro's diary shows. On 1 May 1978, he wrote that 'US policy is to insure that colonialist regime in power against our just interest, in order that American companies like Mobil Oil Corporation can buy and sell us in the international market' (1984:178). In December 1978, he stated that 'the NLF [GAM] forces in East Aceh, Pase Province, attacked the enemy troops near the LNG complex in Paja Bakong area in accordance with our policy to protect our gas resources from being stolen by the Javanese invaders and their foreign accomplices' (1984:208).

When di Tiro and other GAM leaders went into exile in 1979, GAM's focus shifted to gaining international support for its cause. This resulted in a significant reduction in attacks on MOI, PT Arun and other 'targets' in the Lhokseumawe industrial complex for two reasons. First, until the 1989 return of the guerrillas from Libya, GAM was generally less militarily active on the ground in Aceh.[11] Second, from 1989 until 1998 it was primarily engaged in fighting the Indonesian security forces. Consequently, MOI operations until 1999 were reasonably secure.

The fall of Suharto in May 1998 and the push for reform resulted in the withdrawal of so called non-organic Indonesian troops, which are centrally recruited, under operational command, and not part of the territorial structure. The consequent security vacuum allowed GAM to reorganise, recruit and increase its military capacity. As a result, GAM activity against MOI, PT Arun and Pertamina facilities and personnel once again increased. In May 1999, gunmen claiming to be from GAM took over MOI's Pase Cluster for several hours and demanded money.[12] In March 2001 EMOI was forced to stop production from the four onshore gas fields it operated and to evacuate workers after a general deterioration in the security situation and the specific targeting of its workers, which came to a head in the latter half of February.[13] On 6 May 2001, while EMOI was closed down, GAM cut a 16-inch condensate pipeline, and on 20 May it interrupted the 20-mile, 42-inch underground gas pipeline between the Arun Field and the PT Arun LNG plant, thus rendering a restart of production impossible (ICG 2001b:9). GAM was also believed to have been responsible for firing at aircraft transporting EMOI workers and hijacking the company's vehicles, as well as stopping and burning buses and planting landmines along roads to blow them up.[14] Bill Cummings, EMOI Public Affairs Manager in Jakarta, described the security situation as follows:

> Starting in May 1999 there was a general increase in brigandry in our area of operations. Between May 1999 and the onshore shutdown in March 2001, acts of vandalism increased and over 50 vehicles were hijacked from public roads. In 2000, two chartered airplanes carrying ExxonMobil workers were hit by ground fire. In one case in March 2000, a gunman on the back of a motorcycle fired at the plane as it was taxiing to the terminal in Point A, the Arun Field control centre, wounding two passengers. Through a news story in a local newspaper a few days later, GAM claimed responsibility for the attack. Also in 2000, there was an increase in small-arms fire directed at the facilities. GAM occasionally acknowledged responsibility to local reporters for some of the attacks but we have no first-hand knowledge of who was responsible. In the weeks leading up to the onshore shutdown in 2001, our personnel were repeatedly targeted. There were several incidents where unknown gunmen fired on our chartered buses and vans carrying workers. In a couple of cases buses were emptied of occupants and burned. For years buses were used to transport employees between the Arun Field and the nearby town of Lhokseumawe where many of them live. That targeting of our employees during travel was a serious concern to management and impacted the provision of company transportation services to local employees. Small arms, grenades and occasionally even mortars were regularly fired into the facilities EMOI operates in Aceh. Local newspaper reports claimed GAM was responsible and they said they were firing at soldiers but the risk to the EMOI workforce was significant and eventually intolerable.[15]

While ExxonMobil was able to reopen its operations in July 2001, it remained a target of both extortion and sporadic violence. On 21 December 2001 one of the local workers of a contractor of EMOI was shot dead in a GAM attack on a bus transporting staff from Lhokseumawe to Lhoksukon.[16] On 21 August 2003 a rocket propelled grenade exploded at Point A, the control centre for the Arun Field, at around 7 a.m. The grenade, which had been one of two set up to fire from a home-made timer-triggered launcher, had been aimed at the front gate at the time when most workers enter the complex for work. As the grenade fell short of its

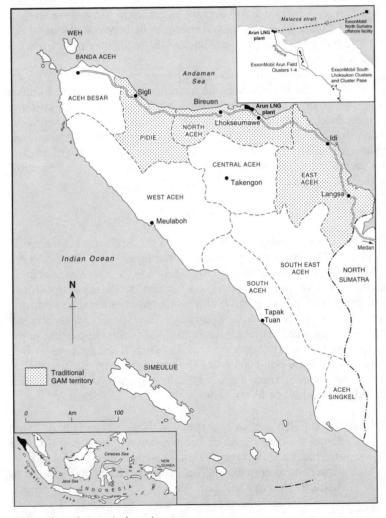

Aceh and north-west Indonesia

target, there were no injuries to personnel or damage to the facilities. The second grenade, which had failed to go off, was aimed in the direction of the aviation fuel storage tank and ExxonMobil's planes and helicopters.

INDONESIAN COUNTER-INSURGENCY OPERATIONS AND 'VITAL OBJECTS'

Indonesia's response to the threat posed by GAM to the 'vital objects' of the Lhokseumawe industrial complex, the threat of separatism and the threat of social unrest resulting from both political and economic griev-ances came in the form of repeated counter-insurgency operations. Not surprisingly, military activity became increasingly focused on areas of economic significance, and there is no doubt that natural gas was a key factor in Indonesian decision making and the security approach toward Aceh since 1977.

There were four major military campaigns and several police opera-tions between the discovery of the Arun natural gas field and the 2005 peace agreement. All focused on North Aceh, East Aceh and Pidie, and all included the establishment of a safe corridor for the Lhokseumawe industrial complex. Two were directly triggered by GAM actions against the energy sector. The other two were more indirectly linked but undoubtedly part of the greater gas–security–insurgency dynamic as the following discussion will show.

Nanggala intelligence operations, 1977–79

The first counter-insurgency operations in the Aceh conflict started in October 1977, almost a year after the establishment of GAM and ten months after di Tiro declared Aceh's independence. The *Nanggala* intel-ligence operations as a whole were a response to the separatist threat. (The term *Nanggala* refers to both the operations themselves and the Special Forces units that carry them out.) However, in a more immedi-ate sense they were a direct reaction to GAM leaflets appearing in the Lhokseumawe area calling upon MOI and Bechtel foreign personnel to leave as they were no longer safe. The commander of the first Special Forces *Kopassandha* (now *Kopassus*) unit, *Nanggala* 16, Major Sofian Effendi, recalled his orders as follows:

> The aim of *Nanggala* 16 was to win the hearts and minds of the people because Hasan di Tiro was advocating separatism. We also had to protect the foreign investment from Mobil Oil. We were sent to counter di Tiro's concept. GAM had started to distribute pamphlets and leaflets so we also distributed pamphlets and talked to the people in mosques.[17]

Nanggala 16 was reinforced by *Nanggala* 21, which arrived in Aceh in December 1977 and was headed by First Lieutenant Sjafrie Sjamsoedin. Not surprisingly, this additional unit was sent in following the shooting dead of the American contractor. As Sjafrie Sjamsoedin recalled:

> There were several attacks against the new LNG project. It was still under construction in Matang Kulie–Point A13. Arun was also still being built. So when *Aceh Merdeka* carried out an attack on the foreigners we were scared and realised they needed more protection. Three foreigners were attacked and we needed a quick response to show that the state had control over the situation. The decision was taken to send in the Special Forces to handle the situation. ... The main objective was to neutralise the situation, restore security to enhance the construction of the LNG project and to destroy *Aceh Merdeka*.[18]

The link between the *Nanggala* operations and the threat to the 'vital objects' was direct and clear. The operations were concluded in 1979 when security around the Lhokseumawe industrial complex had been restored and di Tiro had fled into exile.

Daerah Operasi Militer, 1989–98

The second attempt to crush the insurgency started in the mid 1990s with the *Kolakops Jaring Merah*, or Red Net Operations, more conventionally referred to as military operations area or *daerah operasi militer* (DOM). Unlike the first counter-insurgency operations, this move was not directly linked to a threat against MOI or the PT Arun LNG plant. Instead, it was a response to GAM's re-emergence in 1989 as a much more credible military force following the return of guerrillas from training in Libya. Upon their return to Aceh, they reorganised their troops, trained local volunteers, purchased better military equipment and emerged as a much more effective force (Schulze 2003:245).

That does not, however, mean that the 'gas factor' was absent from the overall decision-making process. Indeed, Aceh's technocrat Governor Ibrahim Hassan repeatedly expressed fears that the deteriorating security situation would affect 'vital objects' such as the Lhokseumawe industrial complex. Although neither MOI nor the local military commander recall any specific threats to the natural gas operations, Hassan claimed that development initiatives had already been brought to a halt and proceeded to ask for a military solution (Sukma 2004:5; see also Sulaiman 2000:78).[19] The governor's request was further endorsed by the Central Planning Board, *Bappenas*.

In response, in July 1990 some 6000 non-organic troops were sent into Aceh, including *Kopassus*, to join the 6000 territorial troops already there. Launched with the object of crushing the rebels in six months, DOM lasted until 1998 and was only lifted after the fall of Suharto.

Operasi Pemulihan Keamanan dan Penegakan Hukum, 2001–03

The third counter-insurgency campaign, like the first, can be directly linked to a threat to the natural gas production. After the fall of Suharto, the lifting of DOM and the withdrawal of non-organic troops, a security vacuum emerged which GAM quickly exploited. Insurgents returned from Malaysia, others were released under President B.J. Habibie's amnesty, guerrillas were recruited, and GAM pushed into 'new' areas of Aceh. In this second re-emergence of GAM, a local commander by the name of Ahmed Kandang, who was based just outside Lhokseumawe, became a key figure.

On 2 November 1998, under his leadership, GAM captured and tortured two Indonesian soldiers. In response, 23 suspected rebels were arrested. A week later, on 15 November, a state-owned radio station was burnt. The police then arrested 43 people believed to be helping Kandang. On 27 December, Kandang's men abducted seven soldiers returning by bus from Medan to Lhokseumawe after the Christmas holiday and executed them.[20] This marked the beginning of a new cycle of violence and counter-violence.

The turning point came with another one of Kandang's activities. In early 2001, Kandang started sending letters demanding taxes to all of the industries in the greater Lhokseumawe area. When EMOI refused to pay, he threatened to shut down their operations. He proved true to his word, and on 9 March 2001 EMOI was forced to halt onshore production and to evacuate workers.[21] On the day of the shutdown Indonesia's defence minister, Mahfud MD, and the Indonesian military (TNI) commander, Admiral Widodo, announced new military operations against GAM. Almost immediately troops were sent in to protect the facilities being operated by EMOI. In the context of the ongoing economic crisis it was imperative to get production going again as soon as possible. The shutdown cost Indonesia $100 million per month, reaching a total of $400 million in foreign exchange earnings by the time the security conditions had sufficiently improved for EMOI to resume its activities.[22]

A month after the shutdown, on 11 April 2001, President Abdurrahman Wahid issued Presidential Instruction 4 launching a new Operation for the Restoration of Security and Upholding the Law or Operasi Pemulihan Keamanan dan Penegakan Hukum (OKPH).

Operasi Terpadu, May 2003 to August 2005

The fourth major counter-insurgency effort came with Presidential Decree (kepres) 28, which placed Aceh under martial law on 19 May

2003 and provided the legal framework for the Integrated Operation (*Operasi Terpadu*). Like DOM, this operation was primarily a reaction to the increase in GAM's military capacity. It followed three years of intermittent negotiations between the insurgents and the Indonesian government, in which the gap between GAM's position of 'nothing but independence' and Jakarta's position of 'anything but independence' could not be bridged. Moreover, the ceasefire immediately preceding the declaration of martial law was exploited by GAM to expand its membership from about 3000 in 2001 to about 5000 in 2003.[23] The liberation movement disabled an estimated 80 per cent of Aceh's government through a combination of intimidation and the establishment of a GAM shadow-government structure. It also openly raised 'taxes', a large part of which came from the Lhokseumawe area where GAM targeted the large industries, contractors, civil servants, and the villagers (see below on the criminalisation of GAM). This money, in turn, was used to buy weapons, increasing its arsenal from some 1500 to 2300 guns.[24]

DILEMMAS OF SECURITY: MOBIL, SECURITY AND HUMAN RIGHTS ABUSES

When MOI became the contractor under the PSC for Block B in Aceh in 1968, the province was peaceful and there was no reason to believe that it would erupt into the conflict that wracked it from 1976 to 2005. Like other PSCs for foreign oil companies and mining companies operating in Indonesia, Mobil was contractually limited to the extraction of the resources. Pertamina on behalf of the state took on responsibility for everything else, including security. When the first threats were issued against MOI and Bechtel in 1977, Pertamina relied upon the Indonesian security forces to protect the Arun Field and PT Arun LNG operations, as the military by law was responsible for the protection of all national assets. While MOI paid Pertamina, which in turn paid the military for this security, decisions about the deployment of troops were out of MOI's control.

The dilemma faced by MOI is evident when looking at the DOM period 1989–98. In the face of potential GAM attacks, MOI needed security for its clusters, its personnel and the 30-km-long pipeline road. However, the same military guarding the Lhokseumawe industrial complex was also carrying out reprisals against villages believed to have provided logistical help or sanctuary to GAM (Amnesty International 1993:6). The approach was heavy-handed and included a systematic 'campaign of terror designed to strike fear in the population and make them withdraw their support from GAM' (Kell 1995:74) as well as arbitrary arrest and detention, torture, 'disappearance' or summary execution (Amnesty International 1993:6).

MOI had few choices. Primary resource exploitation activities, unlike manufacturing, cannot be relocated. Moreover, at the time 25 per cent of Mobil Corporation's worldwide income came from Arun. If it had shut down its Aceh operations, the effect on the company would have been substantial. That also placed it in a position where it had little leverage to argue against what was going on. As an adviser to a different multinational energy company facing the same challenges explained: 'Until 1998, if the military came in and said "I want to borrow your bulldozer", this wasn't a request. They'd take it anyway and if an individual said something they'd revoke your work permit.'[25] The situation was further complicated by the fact that there was little real information about what was happening. Aceh during DOM was a closed area, rife with rumours, steeped in fear, yet deceptively tranquil. In fact, it was only after the fall of Suharto that Indonesia's media revealed the extent of human rights abuses perpetrated in Aceh between 1990 and 1998. Provincial government accounts from late 1998 recorded that between 1989 and 1992, 871 people were killed outright by the army, 387 were missing who were later found dead, and another 500 were listed as disappeared and never found (Human Rights Watch 2001:8). Amnesty International (1993:8) in 1993 estimated that some 2000 civilians had been killed. Care Human Rights forum estimated that 16,375 children had been orphaned.[26] Indonesia's national human rights organisation, Komnas HAM, registered an estimated 7000 cases of human rights violations during DOM.[27]

Not surprisingly, the quest for justice became central to Aceh's budding civil society in the more liberal atmosphere of *reformasi*. One of the focal points of the new Acehnese human rights groups became EMOI, payments to the TNI, and the question of corporate responsibility. For instance, KontrasAceh (2000) alleged that during DOM, MOI had made its operated facilities (all facilities and assets are owned by Pertamina and the government of Indonesia) available to the security apparatus 'which then was proved to have perpetrated many human rights violations in Aceh'. For this, according to KontrasAceh, 'moral, political, and legal responsibility lies with ExxonMobil for its involvement in humanitarian crimes in Aceh' (2000). The organisation further alleged that these abuses were still going on and that EMOI was funding the very soldiers who were responsible. Thus EMOI was implicated in human rights abuses against the civilian population in Aceh, as the company paid the Indonesian security forces. 'The amount of money spent on operational personnel of TNI/Polri amounts to almost Rp 5 billion per month. ExxonMobil also gives a daily allowance of Rp 40,000 (about US$4) for each soldier, transport facilities, offices, posts, barracks, radio, telephone, mess, etc.' (2000). A more emotional account was given by Lhokseumawe resident Cut Zahara Hamzah at Exxon Mobil Corporation's annual shareholder's meeting in 2002:

In 1998, at the fall of the tyrannical regime of General Suharto we found out that your Company had been financing the military operation in Aceh since 1989. ExxonMobil had provided the facilities for the Indonesian military to torture, rape and kill our kinsfolk. It had paid the salaries of soldiers who burnt our houses and robbed our properties. ... In fact, all the atrocities are still going on this very moment. The soldiers are still being paid by this Company of yours and the soldiers are still killing civilians, raping women, pillaging and burning villages around the ExxonMobil complex, in the name of protecting your Company.[28]

With respect to the allegations that EMOI funded the Indonesian military, the company's Public Affairs Manager Bill Cummings explained that 'we do not pay the army directly but we do pay Pertamina for our share of routine services such as customs, harbour fees and security. But until 1999–2000 there was not much need for extraordinary security.'[29] While soldiers did patrol the clusters just inside the perimeter fence in response to the deteriorating security in 2000, this was at the behest of Pertamina, which has been contractually in charge of the security for all facilities since 1968. Moreover, after repeated GAM threats, soldiers now secure the facilities from outside the premises only. Cummings explained that the increasingly insecure operational environment in Aceh posed a dilemma. 'We, of course, want stability and safety for our personnel.' However, 'the deployment of security forces in Aceh is a matter for the government of Indonesia to decide.' He also stated that 'ExxonMobil is opposed to any form of human rights abuses by any person or organisation. ... [And] we have voiced our concerns on this issue on many occasions to representatives of the government of Indonesia.'[30] He also suspected that GAM decided to target EMOI not only because of the exploitation of natural resources but also because it provides them with international attention. Looking at patterns of violence and allegations over the last few years, he concluded that:

It seemed that whenever GAM had its back to the wall they would release to local newspaper accounts of 'ExxonMobil soldiers' perpetrating human rights violations. We couldn't confirm most of these reports at all, let alone determine who was responsible for them. And if they did happen, how can anyone tell the difference between soldiers transiting across the 50 miles of North Aceh in which EMOI conducts its gas production operations, and those assigned by the government of Indonesia on an exclusively defensive basis to protect all of its vital industries in North Aceh, including the Arun Field? In any case they are not ExxonMobil soldiers but government soldiers. But with such allegations GAM got what they wanted – international media attention at EMOI's expense.[31]

On 11 June 2001, the case of EMOI in Aceh and corporate responsibility was taken to court to shed light on the allegations and counterallegations and determine whether ExxonMobil bore corporate responsibility. The International Labour Rights Fund (ILRF) filed a complaint for equitable relief damages on behalf of seven Acehnese men and three Acehnese women against Exxon Mobil Corporation in the United States District Court for the District of Columbia. Exxon Mobil Corporation, PT Arun and EMOI, along with its predecessor MOI, were accused of 'complicity in the Aceh atrocities'. According to the ILRF, ExxonMobil bore corporate responsibility as it not only was aware of the 'brutality of both the Suharto regime' and the Indonesian military at the inception of the Arun Project but supported financially, logistically and materially the 'pervasive and systemic human rights violations perpetrated upon innocent non-combatant villagers of Aceh by the TNI troops specifically hired to provide "security" for the Arun Project.' (ILRF 2001:15) On 29 July 2002, the State Department's legal adviser issued a non-binding opinion that the 'adjudication of this lawsuit at this time would in fact risk a potentially serious adverse impact on significant interests of the United States, including interests related directly to the on-going struggle against international terrorism.'[32] The case is still pending.

Irrespective of whether or not Exxon Mobil Corporation or EMOI bore corporate responsibility, some sections of the Acehnese population – and certainly GAM – were convinced it did. This allowed the insurgents to charge EMOI with an additional crime. Not only did the company collaborate in the neo-colonial exploitation of Aceh but it was also complicit in the security forces' violence against the civilian population. This, amongst other reasons, explains why GAM stepped up its activity against EMOI after 1999. GAM believed that EMOI's (operated) facilities were used as a military base during DOM and 'also as torture camps'.[33] GAM further claimed that TNI troops based at EMOI-operated facilities were carrying out 'massive military operations' against the surrounding villages in the North Aceh subdistricts of Tanah Luas, Matang Kuli, and Meurah Mulia.[34] That made EMOI a legitimate target. As GAM spokesman Isnander al-Pase explained in 2002:

> The general principle is the government of the State of Aceh prohibits all activities that lead to the exploration of its natural resources by foreign powers, especially if such exploration is the source of revenue for the enemy Indonesia. The Hague and

Geneva Laws recognise the right of warring parties to eliminate those economic facilities of the enemy that can be used to
strengthen the muscle of the military.[35]

On a subsequent occasion when asked specifically about EMOI, he
stated that 'ExxonMobil is a legitimate target in war. Why? Because it
helps the opponent's military and now Exxon is housing a military base
within its complex.'[36]

FROM GRIEVANCE TO GREED: THE EXPANSION AND CRIMINALISATION OF GAM SINCE 1999

Paul Collier and Anke Hoeffler in their analysis of greed and grievance
in civil war concluded that 'rebellion is not explained by motive, but by
the atypical circumstances that generate profitable opportunities'
(2001:2). In another study for the World Bank, Collier argued that 'civil
wars occur where rebel organisations are financially viable' and that
rebellion is 'more like a form of organised crime' (2001:1). A closer look
at GAM shows that while this does not hold true for the initial outbreak
of the insurgency in 1976, or even GAM's resurgence in 1989, it does go
a long way toward explaining GAM's rapid expansion in membership
after 1999 – and again the natural gas factor cannot be overlooked.

When GAM was established in October 1976, it was a highly idealistic and ideological organisation whose leadership comprised doctors,
engineers, politicians, and businessmen. Its followers, many of whom
had fought in the *Darul Islam* rebellion, were driven by the repeated
broken promises of Acehnese autonomy. The organisation maintained
its predominantly ideological character until the end of DOM. The
subsequent withdrawal of non-organic TNI troops provided GAM with
an opportunity to expand not only its membership but also its territorial base. This brought two new categories of recruits: first, those who
had been victims of DOM, who were motivated by revenge, and saw
GAM as a means to settle scores with Jakarta and the security forces;
second, those who saw GAM as a means for personal economic gain.
They included local thugs or *preman*, petty criminals, and unemployed
youth. The former category mainly joined from GAM's traditional territory of Pidie, North and East Aceh – areas hit hard by counter-insurgency operations; the latter joined from GAM's new territory, areas
which had not been so much affected DOM: West Aceh, Central Aceh,
South-East Aceh, South Aceh, and Aceh Singkel.

Both elements of recruits diluted GAM's ideological character and
added an intensely personal element to it. Yet, while the victims of
DOM popularised GAM's struggle and thus lent legitimacy to its cause,
the *preman* undermined the movement's credibility. Their actions
revealed how thin the line had become between a political movement

which needed to extract funds to increase its military capacity in order to further its ideological agenda, and members of a movement who were using the GAM 'label' as a cover for personal greed. Whether the aim was to finance an increase in GAM's military capacity or whether it was to line individual pockets, the Lhokseumawe industrial complex played a key role, albeit indirectly, in keeping the conflict going.

GAM had three main sources of revenue: first, taxation/extortion; second, foreign donations; and third, crime, drugs, and kidnapping.[37] The first and the third directly targeted the oil industry, third party contractors and the population adjacent to the Arun Field clusters. GAM levied an Aceh State tax or *pajak nanggroë* on all elements of society. According to senior GAM negotiator Sofyan Ibrahim Tiba, *pajak nanggroë* was not new:

> It has been collected since GAM was established by di Tiro and it is based on Islam. In Islam if there is a struggle there is *infaq*. But now that Aceh is no longer struggling for an Islamic state it is called *pajak nanggroë*. It was changed from *infaq* to *pajak nanggroë* with the Humanitarian Pause in 2000. But it has only recently become an issue because the Indonesian government has made it an issue.[38]

GAM believed it had the right to tax all parts of Acehnese society and GAM Pase commander Sofyan Dawod did not think the majority of the population minded:

> The Indonesian government has the right to tax and so does GAM. But the Acehnese do not object to our taxes while they do object to paying taxes to Indonesia, because that money is then used to send troops and kill them while we use the tax to defend them.[39]

According to Dawod, the level of taxation depended on the project or the salary. There were two bases for taxation, first taxation of the profit, which he claimed was around 2.5 per cent, and, second the value of the project. Additional contributions were sought for holidays – *hari raya* – and Dawod claimed these were used for Acehnese orphans. For instance, ExxonMobil was asked for a special *Idul Adha* 'holiday allowance' of Rp 250 million. According to Dawod, farmers and teachers did not pay taxes, 'but we do ask for a voluntary contribution of one day's earning per month. We also ask for donations from Aceh's wealthy to help society, to cover state functions and expenses, and also to buy weapons.'[40]

GAM particularly targeted merchants in Aceh Besar, many of whom were ethnic Chinese, contractors in the Lhokseumawe industrial area,

Javanese transmigrants, particularly those in the coffee plantations of Central Aceh, and civil servants. The hardest-hit area, however, was the Lhokseumawe industrial complex. This area was under GAM's Samudra Pase finance section, which included a special sub-section for 'vital projects'. The importance of the industrial complex to GAM can be seen by the fact that Lhoksukon alone had three tax collectors.

From mid 1999, EMOI experienced not only an increase in general violence against its workforce and facilities but also an increase in extortion attempts by people claiming to be GAM. GAM tax collectors with mobile phone contact numbers were identified in faxed letters, and some communications asked the company to pay certain taxes to GAM. As Cummings explained, 'these letters supposedly from GAM asked for money. We have never knowingly paid money to anyone with GAM. However, we do not know the political affiliations of the over 3000 Acehnese workers involved in EMOI's business operations in Aceh'.[41] The suspicion that GAM either was 'inside' or had access to 'inside information' was echoed by foreign and local contractors. One foreign contractor, who did not want to be named, related how GAM demanded 5 per cent of his profits. Often these demands came by text message to his mobile phone. He changed his number twice, and within two weeks GAM had his new number. Also, GAM seemed to be fully aware of his travel schedule. He never once got a 'tax demand' when he was in Jakarta or overseas. But as soon as he landed in Lhokseumawe, GAM would be in touch. He further said that while he was only asked for 5 per cent, his local third-party contractors were being issued with demands of up to 20 per cent. And while he had the privilege of being able to stay in the protected compound in the industrial complex, and thus had the luxury of not paying the 'taxes', his local staff did not. Moreover, GAM seemed to know exactly on which day salaries were paid, the amount of the salary, and which third parties had been awarded contracts.[42] In fact, several local contractors spoke about a GAM list, and how once a contractor had made it onto the list, there was no escaping short of leaving Aceh forever.

According to the *Jakarta Post*, GAM generally demanded around 10 per cent of the contract value from local contractors[43] As one such contractor in Gedung Blangpria near Lhokseumawe described:

> I have been asked several times for money by GAM. From contractors they demand 12 per cent of the contract value. Most people here don't agree with GAM but they are afraid because they have guns. If you are asked for money and you don't give it you will be shot a day later, especially if you are a government employee. Or you get kidnapped and they ask the family for money. Sometimes they ask you specifically to donate money to buy a weapon. It all depends on your economic status.[44]

Villages in the vicinity of the Lhokseumawe industrial complex were also harder hit by GAM's village tax, presumably due to the assumption that they benefited either through employment or developmental assistance. After the signing of the Cessation of Hostilities Agreement (COHA) in December 2002, every village was asked for Rp 35 million to buy weapons.[45] In contrast, villages in GAM's traditional stronghold area were asked for Rp 10 million, and those in new, non-traditional areas such as South Aceh for Rp 9 million.

Kidnapping was another means for raising funds. During 2000–01, GAM kidnappings increased to such an extent that it was feared that the movement was undergoing a process of criminalisation similar to that of Abu Sayyaf in the Philippines. According to EMOI's Public Affairs Manager Bill Cummings, between May 1999 and March 2001 over 50 vehicles were hijacked.[46] Kidnappings again surged after Aceh was placed under martial law in May 2003. By March 2004, some 300 Acehnese civilians had been taken hostage by GAM. While some of the kidnappings were ideologically motivated, such as the detention of students believed to be informers for the TNI, young women for dating Indonesian soldiers,[47] or the detention of journalists for 'biased reporting', and village heads (*keucik*) in need of 're-education', most kidnappings were for ransom, with the targets being either local legislators, businessmen, or oil workers.[48] For instance, in early 2001, GAM kidnapped a senior executive of PT Arun and demanded $500,000 to release him.[49] In late August 2001, six Indonesian crewmembers from the *Ocean Silver* were abducted by GAM, which demanded $33,000 for their release.[50] In April 2002, three oil workers contracted to Pertamina were kidnapped. One was released the following day; for the other two, GAM wanted a ransom of Rp 200 million.[51] On 2 July 2002, it was reported that nine crewmen servicing the offshore oil industry were kidnapped from their ship the *Pelangi Frontier*.[52] After Aceh was placed under martial law on 19 May 2003, kidnappings increased. This included the abduction of an engineer for PT Arun, for whom GAM demanded a Rp 60 million ransom payment.[53]

Both taxation and kidnapping also contributed to GAM's fragmentation and the emergence of warlordism. Unsurprisingly one of the key fiefdoms was North Aceh, where there were repeated disjunctures between the GAM leadership, in exile in Sweden, and the area commander, Sofyan Dawod. For instance, in 1999–2000 the official GAM policy was one of not attacking foreign companies (Ross 2003:27). Yet during this period EMOI-operated facilities were repeatedly attacked. Similarly in 2001, it was speculated that the official GAM leadership decided to shut off the gas flow in order in order to preserve the resources in the belief that independence would be achieved by November that year, but local GAM leaders wanted gas production resumed as the shutdown had deprived them of a source of income from taxation and extortion.[54]

GAM was, of course, not the only player in this conflict whose aims were undermined by greed and whose members succumbed to the temptation of resource riches. Rent-seeking individuals and groups could also be found in the TNI and the police, and their 'economic' behaviour too alienated exactly those people whose hearts and minds they sought to win in order to protect the unity and integrity of the state. Geoffrey Robinson in his analysis of the New Order's policy toward Aceh described them as 'military mafia', soldiers who enrich themselves by 'serving as enforcers, debt-collectors, security guards, and extortionists' (2001:223).

More extensive research on military 'business' interests was conducted by Lesley McCulloch. She documented the extent of security forces 'businesses' in the formal, informal and illegal economy in Indonesia as a whole in several studies (see, for example, McCulloch 2000). This dates back to the founding of the republic and the fact that even today the official defence budget only covers about one-third of minimal operating costs (ICG 2000). Salaries, too, are extremely low, leaving the military with no choice but to seek off-budget finances. In Aceh, such income was derived above all from illegal logging, marijuana trafficking, arms sales, protection rackets, car smuggling and extortion at checkpoints (McCulloch 2000:30). Some of this activity, in particular protection and extortion, was intense in the Lhokseumawe area and clearly benefited from LNG-related industries. And then there was, of course, the formal payment for security via Pertamina and later BPMIGAS under the PSC, which EMOI was contractually obliged to make and which from 2001 amounted to something like $6 million annually. At the same time, however, security forces' 'businesses' were far more diversified, and consequently it is difficult to link them directly to the 'gas aspect' of the conflict in the same way that GAM was linked.

ATTEMPTS AT RESOLVING THE CONFLICT: POLITICAL DIALOGUE, 2000–03

With the fall of Suharto and end of the New Order in May 1998, resolving the conflict in Aceh became one of Indonesia's key priorities. President B.J. Habibie initiated the first changes in Aceh policy by lifting the status of DOM and withdrawing non-organic military forces, and this was followed by a public apology by General Wiranto for the trauma experienced at the hands of the security forces. Habibie's successor, President Abdurrahman Wahid, took this policy one step further by embarking in January 2000 upon a political dialogue aimed at finding an end to the conflict in Aceh. While the Indonesian government saw this dialogue as an alternative to its previous reliance on the security approach to manage the violence in the province, GAM saw it as an additional tool in its struggle for independence.[55] This process was facilitated by a Swiss-based NGO, the Henry Dunant Centre, through its head office in Geneva as well as a local office in Banda Aceh. Yet while there were numerous staff, delegates and committees in Aceh, the actual negotiating took place outside of Indonesia at the insistence of the exiled GAM leaders, who feared they might be arrested or killed if they entered Indonesia and, more importantly, because internationalisation was key to their political strategy.[56]

The first fruit of the negotiations was the 12 May 2000 Humanitarian Pause, which was a ceasefire accompanied by the establishment of two joint committees – one on humanitarian action and one on security modalities – and a monitoring team. Although the implementation of the Pause lacked commitment from both sides and violence actually escalated, it was extended until 15 January 2001 as the Moratorium on Violence and then renamed Peace through Dialogue. The negotiations broke down in all but name in July 2001 when the Indonesian government 'froze' the Security Modalities Committee and GAM's Banda Aceh-based negotiators were arrested and jailed.[57]

The talks resumed in February 2002, with Indonesia now under a Megawati government. A new element, foreign 'wisemen', was added, most notably retired US Marine general Anthony Zinni and former Thai foreign minister Surin Pitsuan. At the same time, however, Indonesian security operations continued and were stepped up following an ultimatum on 19 August from the Coordinating Minister for Security and Political Affairs, Susilo Bambang Yudhoyono, demanding that GAM accept special autonomy. Throughout October, the TNI encircled GAM troops in several North Aceh locations, and in November it laid siege to the village of Cut Trieng. To this exercise in compulsion, or 'stick', a 'carrot' was added in the form of a promised economic rehabilitation of Aceh by the United States, EU, Japan and the World Bank should another agreement be reached. On 9 December 2002 the Cessation of Hostilities Agreement (COHA) was concluded.

The COHA called for the cantonment or storage of GAM weapons, the relocation and reformulation of the role of the Indonesian security forces, and the establishment of peace zones. It also set up a Joint Security Committee (JSC) under the leadership of Thai Major General Thanongsak Tuvinian, for which 50 Thai and Filipino soldiers would work alongside 50 GAM and 50 TNI personnel. The first signs of trouble came when GAM failed to meet the February deadline for the cantonment of its arms. This was followed by the TNI's refusal to relocate, and the paralysing of the JSC through TNI-inspired systematic attacks on all its offices outside of Banda Aceh. By April the COHA was dead in all but name. Efforts to resuscitate it at a meeting in Tokyo on 18 May 2003 collapsed when GAM refused to agree to the government's demands that it recognise Indonesia, accept autonomy, and relinquish its struggle.

The following day, on 19 May, the Indonesian government placed Aceh under martial law and launched *Operasi Terpadu*.

The main achievement of the Geneva peace process was the two ceasefires. Yet, neither of the these was fully adhered to by either side. In fact, throughout the peace process as a whole, GAM and Indonesia officially and unofficially carried out military operations against each other in parallel with the talks. This was partially in order to increase their leverage at the negotiating table but also because there were elements on both sides who continued to believe in a military solution, as well as elements who were not interested in a settlement as that would damage their 'business' interests.

Overall, the Geneva peace process saw more failures than achievements and it has even been argued that the Acehnese would have been better off without it, as it polarised the people through its zero-sum structure. Civil society did not have a voice of its own but was only involved in the dialogue as appointees of GAM or the Indonesian government to the various committees. They were forced to choose sides, eroding the middle ground as a result. The process also failed to build confidence and trust between the two negotiating parties and, above all, it failed to bridge the gap between GAM's position of 'nothing but independence' and Indonesia's position of 'anything but independence.'

STOKING THE GREED: DECENTRALISATION AND SPECIAL AUTONOMY

The backdrop to the dialogue between GAM and the Indonesian government was a national decentralisation process with provisions for broad arrangements of special autonomy for the restive provinces of Aceh and Papua. However, rather than underwriting the dialogue, the local political and business élite started a scramble for resources, leaving the average Acehnese behind once again as the main losers. In fact it will be argued here that the failure to deliver effective and accountable regional government fundamentally undermined the prospects either of resolving the conflict through negotiation or of managing it through counter-insurgency operations. A properly implemented autonomy package would have gone a long way toward addressing the original grievances of the Aceh conflict. Yet, as the cynics like to point out, corruption is the only thing that has been successfully decentralised in post-Suharto Indonesia.

In April 1999, under President B.J. Habibie, the Indonesian parliament adopted Law 22 and Law 25 on decentralisation, aimed at forestalling the rise of separatism, especially in those regions which are resource-rich. Accordingly these laws, which did not come into effect until the beginning of 2001, devolved extensive governmental powers to the regions. They also allowed regional and local governments to retain some of the net income from the exploitation of natural resources, including 15 per cent from oil, 30 percent from natural gas, and 80 per cent from timber. In addition Aceh, under Law 44, was given autonomy with respect to culture, religious affairs and education.

In August 2001, under President Megawati Sukarnoputri, special autonomy was given to Aceh under Law 18/2001, which formally changed the province's name to *Nanggroe Aceh Darussalam* (NAD). While this was not officially part of the negotiation process, Indonesia considered autonomy as a concession with the hope that GAM would lay down its arms and give up its struggle for independence. Special autonomy allowed for the introduction of Islamic Law, but most importantly, the law gave Aceh control over 70 per cent of its oil and gas revenues for the next eight years. Rather than alleviate some of the grievances of the people, however, the devolution of power and above all the control over resources resulted in local legislators counting their chickens before they hatched.

At the time Acehnese legislators estimated that Aceh would receive $500 million a year while foreign development experts expected the sum to be closer to $240 million a year (ICG 2001a:6). In December 2000, Aceh governor Abdullah Puteh expressed his interest in joint-ownership in EMOI and stated that Aceh's provincial government wanted to control shares in every strategic company.[58]

One problem with the implementation of autonomy, which became effective in 2002, was GAM's opposition to it. A far greater obstacle, however, was the provincial government itself and came in the form of lack of transparency and accountability, corruption, mismanagement, and lack of development. In 2001, more than Rp 1118 billion in humanitarian aid money was misappropriated.[59] According to Acehnese civic leaders and political activists, in 2003 an estimated Rp 5.5 trillion ($654 million) was squandered by provincial officials on corrupt projects.[60] On 8 October 2003, Aceh's *Serambi* newspaper reported that the provincial government had admitted to the misuse of funds for humanitarian assistance during the Integrated Operation.

A closer look at the activities of Aceh's governor Abdullah Puteh provides a glimpse, but nowhere near the whole picture, of the challenges faced by the Indonesian government in addressing this issue. His first purchases following the devolution of power included an eight-seat Ukrainian-manufactured helicopter for personal use at the price of Rp 12.6 billion,[61] which is about four times the price the Indonesian military paid for a similar aircraft. Puteh also established an airline, Seleuwah NAD Air, partly owned by the province and partly by a Malaysian investor. Some Rp 10 billion in public funds were poured into Seleuwah NAD, only for it to go bankrupt amidst allegations of mismanagement six months later.[62] On 1 May 2003, the newspaper *Sinar Harapan* published a list of Aceh's corrupt projects which, in addition to the above-mentioned, included corruption and mark-up in the purchase of a speedboat for Rp 8.6 billion, misuse of Rp 100 billion flood assistance money, misuse of Rp 43.7 billion aid money from Pertamina, a Rp 10 billion project in the Kampung Jawa area of Banda Aceh whose contract was awarded without tender, lack of transparency in the use of UN flood assistance of more than Rp 176 million, and last but not least the purchase of an official car for Rp 1.83 billion, more than three times the price of the cars of Puteh's cabinet ministers.

Moreover, whatever development did take place fell into the category of 'prestige' projects. For example, a small airport was built in the Central Aceh city of Takengon while the only road that connected this area, its residents and its merchants to the coast remained almost impassable due to landslides. Another such project was the Banda Aceh harbour where, in addition to a breakwater and pier for the boat to Sabang, the foundation was laid for a three-story shopping mall with a hotel – and then the allocated Rp 80 billion ran out. Not surprisingly, most rural Acehnese believed that NAD was only for the élite in Banda Aceh. The lack of community involvement in the design and execution of development projects ensured that the majority of the Acehnese remained as alienated from the provincial government as they had been from Jakarta. In fact, the average Acehnese did not see a change in their every day lives from the time of Suharto's authoritarianism and centralisation to the post-Suharto democratisation and decentralisation. So why not try independence? And it is exactly this alienation to which GAM negotiator Amni bin Marzuki attributed the movement's virtual doubling of membership between 2002 and 2003:

> There is the distrust of Jakarta, which, of course, goes back to before NAD. But the people wanted to give Jakarta another chance to give Aceh real autonomy and welfare. But there are no changes and the Acehnese people have not benefited at all – only *Pemda* [the regional government]. GAM's new members come from the villages but also from the cities. Before, the urban population thought they were untouched. But not now – when there is no electricity, no water and credit is not working, they are disappointed.[63]

The regional government's lack of interest in real autonomy – and thus its inability to deliver benefits from the devolution of power in 2002 and its failure to use Aceh's resources to underpin the peace process – was only surpassed by the lack of political will to address this issue. Until the second martial law period in November 2003, Aceh's police claimed they had insufficient evidence for an investigation into the corruption; indeed, Aceh's provincial prosecutor stopped legal proceedings into the misuse of the Pertamina money. The regional legislature, which had the authority to file a complaint against Abdullah Puteh, chose to accept his accountability speech on 13 October 2003. The president, who could have removed the governor, had not done anything anywhere to clamp down on corruption and chose not to act against Puteh for a combination of reasons; these included 'bad timing' with the upcoming elections, fear of the political fall-out, and allegedly good connections between Puteh and the president's husband, Taufik Kiemas. Not surprisingly the vacuum in local government was quickly filled by GAM's shadow civil service. With an estimated 80 per cent of Aceh under GAM control and with the insurgents openly raising 'taxes', another military operation became virtually inevitable. Aceh was placed under martial law in May 2003 and counter-insurgency operations continued until the peace agreement in August 2005, four months after Puteh was finally sentenced to ten years in prison for corruption.

THE TSUNAMI AND THE HELSINKI PEACE PROCESS

On 26 December 2004, Aceh was struck first by an earthquake and then by a tsunami which took over 200,000 lives. This natural disaster paved the way for another round of peace talks, starting with calls for the Indonesian government and GAM to set aside their differences and return to the negotiating table. The international community also sent clear signals to Jakarta that relief and reconstruction funds would flow more freely if the situation on the ground was stable. GAM, which had been pushing for a resumption of the talks since May 2003, immediately seized upon the tsunami to push for new negotiations. These were needed as the counter-insurgency operations had destroyed GAM's civilian government structure and reduced its military capacity. Moreover, the exiled GAM leaders faced a challenge to demonstrate their continuing relevance. Not surprisingly, they quickly integrated the natural disaster into GAM's strategy of internationalisation. In fact, the tsunami did in minutes what GAM had failed to achieve since 1976: it put Aceh on the map and raised international interest in the conflict. Most importantly, the sheer scale of the human tragedy provided a face-saving opportunity for already existing secret, back-channel talks to go public.

Back-channel talks between the exiled GAM leadership and the Indonesian government started after the election of Susilo Bambang Yudhoyono as Indonesia's new president in September 2004. These contacts focused on a political solution in which GAM explored alternatives to independence. In parallel, Indonesian Vice President Jusuf Kalla initiated talks about an economic solution with GAM in Aceh. In November 2004, Kalla, Aceh governor Abdullah Puteh, Aceh businessman Rusli Bintang, Acehnese Information Minister Sofyan Djalil, and

Major General Syarifudin Tippe (the former Aceh deputy commander) went to Malaysia to meet with GAM members M. Daud Syah and Karim Yusuf, who claimed to represent GAM Aceh commander Muzakkir Manaf. This was followed by another meeting in Batam. A memorandum of understanding was reached on economic compensation, according to which each GAM regional commander would receive 10 hectares of land and Rp10 billion; lower ranking GAM would get between two and five hectares of land and between Rp 1 and 10 billion; all of the oil revenue in East Aceh would accrue to GAM, which would also receive 1000 hectares of land for religious schools, and two airbuses and 15 smaller planes for its own airline. GAM would manage local government and Aceh's electricity.[64]

Manaf was not directly involved in these talks but he was aware of their content and, according to one GAM source, he agreed, providing that all 17 regional commanders and the exiled leadership approved. Underlying Kalla's initiative was the notion that the conflict could be resolved purely economically, bypassing a political solution. However, when the tsunami hit, Indonesia felt under pressure to revive the political negotiations and thus the back-channel political contacts were merged with Kalla's economic initiative and his group became the core of the Indonesian delegation.

The Helsinki process started in January 2005 and was facilitated by former Finnish president Martti Ahtisaari and the Crisis Management Initiative (CMI), a Finnish NGO. The first meetings focused on aiding relief and reconstruction. It was not until the second round in February that it became clear that two important changes had occurred within GAM's approach to negotiations. First, GAM was willing to discuss arrangements other than independence and, second, GAM wanted to establish a political party. GAM had rejected both during the 2000–03 Geneva talks.

According to GAM, during this second round the Indonesian delegation agreed to set aside special autonomy while GAM set aside independence. Between the second and third round, on 23–4 March, one of GAM's foreign advisors, Australian academic Damien Kingsbury, flew to Jakarta and met with Kalla's team – Justice Minister Hamid Awaluddin and Dr Farid Hussein – to explore GAM's idea of self-government. GAM's position as put forward by Kingsbury was as follows: it wanted full TNI withdrawal from Aceh, full police withdrawal from Aceh, the security vacuum to be filled by 5000 foreign military monitors from Western countries, the establishment of an indigenous police force comprising GAM and others, change in legislation so that GAM could form a political party, immediate elections, full revenue of all resources in Aceh, a special passport, new identity cards, and for Aceh to have its own flag and anthem.[65] Indonesia would retain sovereignty.

In the third round economic matters were addressed, and in the fourth round security arrangements. While there were few difficulties on economic issues, the fourth round saw some backtracking on the Indonesian side. Most notably, the Indonesian delegation reverted to its 'old' position, insisting on special autonomy, and started emphasising the informal nature of the dialogue. As Minister of Defence Juwono Sudarsono pointed out, informality meant that if the talks failed the government would not be held responsible.

While the peace process went fairly well, a number of stumbling blocks emerged. From the beginning the Indonesian government was split on the resumption of talks. Indeed the driving force was clearly the vice president, backed by Yudhoyono. Foreign Minister Hassan Wirayuda and Coordinating Minister for Security and Political Affairs Widodo Adisucipto were initially critical of the talks, and the TNI and parliament rejected negotiations outright. The rejection by the latter two in particular was of great importance as parliament was needed to change legislation and the TNI would be crucial to the success of any security monitoring arrangements.

Parliament rejected the possibility of rescinding the special autonomy legislation and amending the electoral law. Legislators feared that local parties would open Pandora's box and that a compromise would lead to the formation of ethnic and religious parties everywhere, ultimately resulting in the fragmentation and disintegration of the state. Moreover, as Fuad Bawazier, deputy head of the PAN party, explained, to hold 'local elections is the same as a referendum. ... The DPR [parliament] must oppose the negotiations.'[66]

Security arrangements were equally problematic. Both GAM and the Indonesian security forces contained ideological hardliners as well as individuals who benefited economically from the conflict. So even if security arrangements could be agreed upon, implementation could have proved difficult. Critically, beyond any security arrangements there was a more fundamental issue, namely that GAM only wanted a ceasefire while Indonesia wanted a permanent end to the conflict and the disarmament of GAM. Both positions were unsurprising. Indonesia wanted the Aceh conflict to be over once and for all, with Aceh remaining under the republic's sovereignty. The TNI, moreover, feared that GAM would only exploit a ceasefire to rearm, recruit and regroup, as the guerrillas had done during the 2000 Humanitarian Pause and the 2002 COHA. GAM clearly saw these negotiations as a stage, and any form of agreement short of independence as a half-way house. The conflict was not over and weapons might still be needed. As GAM Information Minister Bakhtiar Abdullah stated at the closing of the second round when the notion of self-government was introduced: 'To be clear, GAM has not given up independence.'[67] Nevertheless, GAM and the Indonesian government signed a memorandum of understanding on 15 August 2005, and the Aceh conflict has since ceased to be fought by military means.

CONCLUSION: CLASH OF IDEOLOGIES OR CONFLICT ABOUT 'OIL'?

Returning to the question of whether the conflict in Aceh was about oil, there is no doubt that resources played a critical role. A comparison of North Aceh where the LNG facilities are located with other districts shows that this district suffered the highest number of dead and wounded, offices and schools burnt, and homes and businesses destroyed (BPS, cited in Ross 2003:35). It was also home to both the Indonesian military's operational headquarters in Lhokseumawe and had the strongest GAM presence in both membership and weapons.

The link between the conflict and the natural gas resources can be found in four key factors. First, GAM likened the extraction of oil and gas to neo-colonial exploitation, in line with its view that Aceh was illegally occupied by the forces of the Javanese neo-colonial government in Jakarta. That allowed GAM to see EMOI as a collaborator with and PT Arun and Pertamina as representatives of neo-colonialism and thus as among its 'legitimate targets'.

Second, and closely related, the oil and gas industry is considered a vital asset of the state and the state has tended to equate securing this asset with sending more troops, especially when threatened with insurgency. This created a direct link in the minds of the people as well as GAM between the troops and the behaviour of the troops on the one hand, and on the other the domestic and foreign oil companies. The fact that the TNI received an estimated $6 million annually from the companies for its services only exacerbated this issue and allowed some to assert that the conflict in Aceh was being kept going by Indonesian military business interests.

Third, the exploration, extraction and liquefaction of the natural gas, as well as the construction and maintenance of the infrastructure, provided work for a large number of local contractors. GAM specifically targeted these contractors as well as employees and even the companies themselves for extortion. Alongside kidnapping for ransom of company personnel, this system of 'taxation' provided GAM with the money necessary not only to keep the insurgency alive but, since 1999, to expand its membership fivefold and to increase its military capacity.

Fourth, the uneven development of the economy and infrastructure, the modernisation process, and the fact that throughout much of the conflict in Aceh most of the gas and oil revenue went to Jakarta with little return, contributed to popular grievances that nurtured secessionist sentiments. This gave credit to GAM propaganda that if Aceh were independent every Acehnese would be rich and Aceh would be as wealthy as Brunei.

These four factors illustrate a compelling link between the conflict and resources; they were a determining factor in the dynamics of the violence and the location of most of the armed contact, and served to prolong the insurgency. Nevertheless, the struggle in Aceh was and remains above all ideological in nature. It erupted over political grievances resulting from unsatisfactory centre–periphery relations, which had failed to recognise Aceh's cultural, religious, and historical particularities. These grievances preceded the discovery of natural gas, and adequately addressing them in the near future will determine the survival of the memorandum of understanding. In the meantime, the Arun gas field is expected to 'run dry' by about 2014.

NOTES

1. Interview with Bill Cummings, Public Affairs Manager, ExxonMobil, Jakarta 19 March 2003.
2. Interview with Bill Cummings, 19 March 2003.
3. Interview with Lt.-Gen. (ret.) Sofian Effendi, Jakarta, 25 September 2003.
4. Both quotes from interview with residents of Nibong Baru, Nibong Baru, 20 April 2003.
5. BPS, Pengeluaran untuk Konsumsi Penduduk Indonesia per Propinsi, 1987 as cited by Booth (1992:348).
6. *Antara News Agency*, 28 October 2003
7. *Sinar Harapan*, 31 March 2003.
8. Interview with Hasan di Tiro, GAM leader, Norsborg, Sweden, 22 February 2002.
9. For a detailed discussion of all sub-currents see Schulze (2003:246–51).
10. Interview with Lt.-Gen. (ret.), Sofian Effendi, Jakarta, 25 September 2003.
11. According to GAM, between 1986 and 1989 an estimated 1500 soldiers underwent guerrilla warfare training in Libyan camps. Interview with Malik Mahmud, GAM Minister of State, Norsborg, Sweden, 23 February 2002.
12. Interview with Bill Cummings, Jakarta 19 March 2003.
13. *The Jakarta Post*, 24 April 2001.
14. *Sydney Morning Herald*, 3 April 2001.
15. Interview with Bill Cummings, Jakarta 19 March 2003.
16. *Asian Political News*, 24 December 2001.
17. Interview with Lt.-Gen. (ret.) Sofian Effendi, Jakarta, 25 September 2003.
18. Interview with Maj.-Gen. Sjafrie Sjamsoedin, TNI spokesman, Cilangkap, 4 September 2003.
19. Interviews with: Bill Cummings, Jakarta, 10 April 2003 (comments on MOI); Lt.-Gen. (ret.), Sofian Effendi, Jakarta, 25 September 2003 (on the local military perspective. For Hassan's claim see *Republika*, 12 August 1998.
20. *Serambi*, 4 November, 16 November and 30 December 1998.
21. *Jakarta Post*, 24 April 2001.
22. *Far Eastern Economic Review*, 16 August 2001.
23. Interview with Indonesian Army Chief, General Ryamizard Ryacudu, 5 April 2003.

24. Interview with General Ryamizard Ryacudu, 5 April 2003.
25. Interview with an advisor to a multinational energy company, Jakarta, 7 November 2003.
26. Cited in *Far Eastern Economic Review*, 19 November 1998.
27. Cited in *Suara Pembaruan*, 26 November 1999.
28. Testimony on 'ExxonMobil, Involvement in Human Rights Abuses in Aceh', made at the 120th Annual Meeting of Shareholders of the ExxonMobil Corporation in Dallas, Texas, USA, on 29 May 2002 by Cut Zahara Hamzah, Board Member of the International Forum on Aceh.
29. Interview, 19 March 2003.
30. Interview, 10 April 2003.
31. Interview, 19 March 2003.
32. Department of State (2002) The Legal Adviser, Re: *Doe et al v. ExxonMobil et al*, 29 July 2002.
33. Press Release, Aceh-Sumatra National Liberation Front, Central Bureau for Information, 4 June 2001:2.
34. AGAM Field Report, 8 February 2002.
35. Phone interview with Isnander al-Pase, GAM spokesman, 15 September 2002.
36. Interview, 19 April 2003.
37. For a more detailed discussion of all aspects of funding see Schulze (2004).
38. Interview with Sofyan Ibrahim Tiba, Banda Aceh, 21 April 2003.
39. Interview with Sofyan Dawod, GAM Pase Commander, North Aceh, 19 April 2003.
40. Interview with Sofyan Dawod, 19 April 2003.
41. Interview with Bill Cummings, Jakarta, 19 March 2003.
42. Confidential interview with foreign contractor to ExxonMobil and PT Arun, Medan, 17 April 2003.
43. *The Jakarta Post*, 4 February 2003.
44. Confidential interview with local contractor, Gedung Blangpria, North Aceh, 22 August 2002.
45. *Far Eastern Economic Review*, 30 January 2003.
46. Interview, Jakarta, 19 March 2003.
47. *Agence France Presse*, 15 May 2002.
48. *Joyo Indonesian News*, 28 May 2002.
49. *Tempo*, 20 March 2001.
50. *Associated Press*, 29 August 2001.
51. *Dow Jones Newswires*, 6 May 2002.
52. *Agence France Presse*, 15 May 2002.
53. *Agence France Presse*, 21 November 2003.
54. Interview with Bill Cummings, Jakarta, 19 March 2003.
55. Interview with Malik Mahmud, GAM Minister of State, Norsborg, Sweden, 22 February 2002.
56. Interview with Sofyan Ibrahim Tiba, GAM senior negotiator, Banda Aceh, 21 April 2003; interview with Amni bin Marzuki, GAM negotiator, Banda Aceh, 24 June 2001; interview with Hasan di Tiro, GAM leader, Norsborg, Sweden, 22 February 2002.
57. For a full discussion of the peace process see Aspinall and Crouch (2003).
58. *Ibonweb.com*, last viewed 15 December 2000.
59. *Sinar Harapan*, 1 May 2003.
60. *Far Eastern Economic Review*, 9 October 2003.

61. *Far Eastern Economic Review*, 9 October 2003.
62. *The Wall Street Journal*, 3 October 2003.
63. Interview with Amni bin Marzuki, GAM negotiator, Banda Aceh, 18 April 2003.
64. Interview with confidential Acehnese source, Jakarta, 20 March 2005.
65. Discussion with Damien Kingsbury, Jakarta, 23 and 24 March 2005.
66. *Kompas*, 7 June 2005.
67. Statement on the Helsinki Peace Talks by ASNLF/GAM Spokesman Bakhtiar Abdullah, at the close of the talks, 23 February 2005.

BIBLIOGRAPHY

Aceh Sumatra National Liberation Front (no date) 'Aims of the ASNLF', www.asnlf.com/asnlf_int/politics/aimsoftheasnlf.htm, last accessed 7 November 2006.
Aceh Sumatra National Liberation Front (1976) *Declaration of Independence of Aceh-Sumatra*, 4 December 1976.
Aceh Sumatra National Liberation Front (1995) 'Denominated Indonesian', an address by Tengku Hassan di Tiro, President Aceh/Sumatra National Liberation Front, before UNPO General Assembly, The Hague, 20 January 1995.
Amnesty International (1993) *'Shock Therapy': Restoring Order in Aceh, 1989–1993* (London: Amnesty International).
Aspinall, E. (2002) 'Modernity, History and Ethnicity: Indonesian and Acehnese Nationalism in Conflict', *The Review of Indonesian Malaysian Affairs*, Vol. 36, No. 1.
Aspinall, E. and Crouch, H. (2003) *The Aceh Peace Process: Why it Failed*, Policy Studies 1 (Washington, D.C.: East West Center).
Barnes, P. (1995) *Indonesia: The Political Economy of Energy* (Oxford: Oxford University Press/Oxford Institute for Energy Studies).
Booth, A. (1992) *The Oil Boom and After: Indonesian Economic Policy and Performance in the Suharto Era* (Singapore: Oxford University Press).
Bresnan, J. (1993) *Managing Indonesia: The Modern Political Economy* (New York: Columbia University Press).
Collier, P. (2001) *Economic Causes of Civil Conflict and their Implications for Policy* (Washington, D.C.: World Bank).
Collier, P. and Hoeffler, A. (2001) *Greed and Grievance in Civil War* (Washington, D.C.: World Bank).
Dawood, D. and Sjafrizal (1989) 'Aceh: The LNG Boom and Enclave Development', in Hill, H. (ed.) *Unity and Diversity: Regional Economic Development in Indonesia since 1970* (Singapore: Oxford University Press).
Department of State (2002) *The Legal Adviser, Re: Doe et al v. ExxonMobil et al*, 29 July 2002 (Washington, D.C.).
di Tiro, H. (1980) *The Legal Status of Acheh-Sumatra under International Law* (Stockholm: The National Liberation Front of Acheh-Sumatra).
—— (1995) 'Denominated Indonesian', An address by Tengku Hassan di Tiro, President Aceh/Sumatra National Liberation Front, before UNPO General Assembly, The Hague, 20 January 1995.
—— (1984) *The Price of Freedom: The Unfinished Diary* (Stockholm: Ministry of Education, ASNLF).

Emmerson, D.K. (1983) 'Understanding the New Order: Bureaucratic Pluralism in Indonesia', *Asian Survey*, Vol. 23, No. 11.

ExxonMobil (2001), *ExxonMobil in Indonesia*, brochure.

Hill, H. (ed.) (1989) *Unity and Diversity: Regional Economic Development in Indonesia Since 1970* (Singapore: Oxford University Press).

Hill, H. and Weideman, A. (1989) 'Sectoral Distribution of the Labour Force, 1980', in Hill, H. (ed.) *Unity and Diversity: Regional Economic Development in Indonesia since 1970* (Singapore: Oxford University Press).

Human Rights Watch (2001) 'Indonesia: The War in Aceh', *Human Rights Watch Report*, Vol. 13, No. 4.

International Crisis Group (2000) 'Keeping the Military Under Control', *Asia Report No. 9* (Brussels and Jakarta: ICG).

—— (2001a) 'Aceh: Can Autonomy Stem the Conflict? *Asia Report No. 18* (Brussels and Jakarta: ICG).

—— (2001b) 'Aceh: Why Military Force Won't Bring Lasting Peace', *Asia Report No. 17* (Brussels and Jakarta: ICG).

International Labour Rights Fund (2001) *Complaint for Equitable Relief Damages vs ExxonMobil Corporation, ExxonMobil Oil Indonesia Inc, Mobil Corporation, Mobil Oil corporation, and PT Arun LNG Co.* (Washington, D.C.: ILRF).

Karl, T.L. (1997) *The Paradox of Plenty: Oil Booms and Petro-States* (Berkley: University of California Press).

—— (1999) 'The Perils of the Petro-State: Reflections on the Paradox of Plenty', *Journal of International Affairs*, Vol. 53, No. 1.

Kell, T. (1995) *The Roots of Acehnese Rebellion, 1989–1992* (Ithaca, N.Y.: Cornell Modern Indonesia Project).

KontrasAceh(2000) *Pernyataan Pers, ExxonMobil terlibat pelanggaran HAM di Aceh* [ExxonMobil denies human rights abuses in Aceh] (Banda Aceh: KontrasAceh).

Le Billon, P. (2001) 'The Political Ecology of War: Natural Resources and Armed Conflicts', *Political Geography*, Vol. 20, No. 5.

McCulloch, L. (2000) 'Trifungsi: The Role of the Indonesian Military in Business', Paper for the International Conference on 'Soldiers in Business: Military as an Economic Actor', Jakarta 17–19 October 2000.

Riklefs, M.C. (ed.) (2001) *A History of Modern Indonesia since c.1200*, 3rd edn (Houndsmills, Basingstoke: Palgrave).

Robinson, G. (2001) 'Rawan is as Rawan Does: The Origins of Disorder in New Order Aceh', in Anderson, B. *Violence and the State in Suharto's Indonesia* (Ithaca: Southeast Asia Program Publications, Cornell University).

Ross, M.L. (1999) 'The Political Economy of the Resource Curse', *World Politics*, Vol. 51, January.

Ross, M.L. (2003) 'Resources and Rebellion in Aceh, Indonesia', Yale World Bank project on 'The Economics of Political Violence', unpublished manuscript.

Sachs, J.D. and Warner, A.M. (1995) 'Natural Resource Abundance and Economic Growth', *Development Discussion Paper No 517a* (Cambridge, Mass.: Harvard Institute for International Development).

Schulze, K.E. (2003) 'The Struggle for an Independent Aceh: The Ideology, Capacity, and Strategy of GAM', *Studies in Conflict and Terrorism*, Vol. 26, No. 4.

Schulze, K.E. (2004) *The Anatomy of the Free Aceh Movement*, Policy Studies 2 (Washington, D.C.: East West Center).

SIRA (2001) *Laporan dan Investigasi Khusus: Kontinuitas kekerasan TNI/Polri PT ExxonMobil terhadap warga sipil* [Report and special investigation: continuation of the ExxonMobil police and military violence against the civilian population] (Banda Aceh: SIRA).

Sukma, R. (2004) *Security Operations in Aceh: Patterns and Dynamics*, Policy Paper 3 (Washington, D.C.: East West Center).

Sulaiman, M.I. (2000) *Aceh Merdeka: Ideologi, Kepimpinan dan Gerakan* [Free Aceh: The Ideology, Leadership and Movement] (Jakarta: Al-Kautsar).

Vaughan, R. (1998) *Mobil in Indonesia: 100 Years and Generations to Go* (Hong Kong: Oceanic Graphic).

World Bank (2002) *Promoting Peaceful Development in Aceh*, Background Paper for the Preparatory Conference on Peace and Reconstruction in Aceh, Tokyo, 3 December 2002.

6 Oil and armed conflict in Casanare, Colombia: complex contexts and contingent moments

Jenny Pearce

This chapter is about the complex relationship between oil and armed conflict in Colombia and the role of the national and local state, multinational corporations and armed and civil actors. It is based on a case study of the department of Casanare, where one of the largest discoveries of crude oil reserves in Latin America in two decades was made in 1991 and exploitation took place under the operational leadership of British Petroleum (BP, later BP-Amoco).[1] Over the next decade or more, as well as being a major oil-producing region, Casanare became the site of multi-polar militarisation. The armed forces of the state, guerrilla groups of the left, right-wing paramilitary groups and criminal mafias have been responsible for gross human rights violations. Civilian institutions have been undermined by extortion and threats. Oil revenues have delivered a bonanza for the region, but despite significant infrastructural advance, oil has not brought development in the sense of a self-sustaining economic progress able to meet the needs of all the population in the department. Instead, people have lived in permanent fear and insecurity. The future looks bleak at the time of writing (2004), as oil reserves diminish and new exploration in the Niscota region has yet to reveal its potential.

This chapter, nevertheless, argues that it was not inevitable that oil should play the role it has ended up playing in the Colombian conflict. There were contingent contextual moments when appropriate action might have prevented the transformation or intensification of conflict resulting from the discovery of oil. BP-Amoco recognised this in the wake of a damaging international media campaign accusing it of collusion in human rights violations. The corporation embarked on a new approach. However, it is argued that this is weakened by the policy environment at the national level. Sustainability cannot be guaranteed without a coherent and consistent national state peace and development policy, as opposed to erratic government initiatives that swing between peace discussions with selected groups and military and authoritarian solutions.

Unlike many regions of the global South where oil is found, Colombia has a relatively sophisticated level of institutionality. It has a constitutional framework, a significant middle class and highly educated professional sector and policy-making élite. It therefore offers possibilities for action which are inconceivable in some other contexts. Once the predation capacity of armed groups reaches a certain point, patterns of conflict can be transformed very rapidly beyond the control of even the most sophisticated policy interventions. The challenge is whether it is possible to prevent the rise of organised predation through extortion before it becomes more the norm than the exercise of authority by civilian institutions, and in turn contaminates and undermines those institutions.[2] Colombia's sophisticated level of institutional development compared with many states of the South, and its highly educated policy makers, suggest that in the evolution of internal war it may be that policy failure, of will and of omission, account for missed opportunity as much as does the presence of economic resources.[3]

The first part of the chapter will explore the evolution of that war in Casanare, and identify the contingent contextual moments when appropriate policy intervention might have prevented the multi-polar militarisation of the department. The second part will look at the oil-producing corporations, in particular BP-Amoco, and how they have responded to the security and developmental challenges of producing oil in Colombia and of their responsibilities to the oil-producing communities.

OIL IN CONTEXT: THE DYNAMICS OF 'BOON AND BURDEN' IN THE OIL-PRODUCING REGION OF CASANARE

> Over almost a century and a half, oil has brought out both the best and worst of our civilization. It has been both boon and burden. ... Its history has been a panorama of triumphs and a litany of tragic and costly mistakes. It has been a theatre for the noble and the base in the human character. Creativity, dedication, entrepreneurship, ingenuity and technical innovation have coexisted with avarice, corruption, blind political ambition and brute force. ... Much blood has been spilt in its name. The fierce and sometimes violent quest for oil – and for the riches and power it conveys – will surely continue so long as oil holds a central place.
>
> (Yergin 1991:788)

Before the oil bonanza of Casanare was revealed, Colombia had experienced a previous bonanza in neighbouring Arauca, also part of the Orinoquia region. Like Casanare, Arauca was a frontier territory before oil was discovered, with minimal state presence or attention. There were in fact many similarities between the two departments at the time of oil discovery. Casanare was a province of Boyacá until it became an administrative district or *intendencia* like Arauca in 1973, and a department in 1991. Like Arauca, it was a disarticulated territory in which no clear pole of economic development had emerged to shape the region before oil was discovered. De facto power resided in cattle ranchers of the plains, or *llanos*.

However, in the case of Arauca, that power had been contested by a strong peasant resistance. The core of this was the settlers of the *piedemonte* or foothills around Sarare in the 1970s, where they had at first received support from the Agrarian Reform Institute (INCORA). When this was withdrawn through a shift in national agrarian policy, the settlers began to organise themselves and some significant civic strikes took place in the 1970s. At this moment the remnants of the National Liberation Army (ELN) guerrillas, dispersed after the military defeats of the 1970s, arrived in Sarare. They established the Domingo Lain Front and built strong connections with the disaffected settlers. When oil was discovered and a pipeline had to be rapidly built between Arauca and the coast in 1984, the ELN was well situated to extort a deal from the construction company, Mannesmann, and from the multinational oil corporation, Occidental, which was responsible for oil production in the region.

In the absence of appropriate state intervention, extortion of the oil industry and the misappropriation of the oil royalties which began to flow to the region in the mid 1980s transformed and militarised the social and political conflicts of Arauca. Colombian legislation gives the province and the municipality where an oil well is located a 9.5 per cent and 2.5 per cent share of the royalties respectively. Arauca was a huge territory with a very small population of around 100,000 people when oil was discovered in 1983.[4] When the Caño Limón well came on stream in 1986, it generated a bonanza for a very poor and very sparsely populated region, calculated at $195 million over five years for the regional government, or *intendencia*, at 1980s prices, as well as royalties for the municipalities where the oil is located. This large amount of resources became available to a territory where politics was still a struggle for personal accumulation of wealth and power based on relationships with vote-delivering clients. The weakness and venality of local institutions and the growing power of armed groups, in particular the ELN guerrillas, meant that oil revenues failed to bring serious benefits or sustainable development to the people of Arauca.[5] By the early 1990s, the most populated foothills region of the department had been turned into a strong base of the ELN and its militaristic Domingo Lain Front, and an extremely lucrative source of revenue for the guerrilla group. A national state with a clear analysis of the national problematic and a commitment to equitable and peaceful development should have been able to recognise what was unfolding in Arauca.

There are at least four key actions that might have avoided the process through which social co-existence in the region became mediated by armed actors indirectly funded by the oil industry:

- Adequate state protection of the new pipeline and oil installations, provided by security forces trained to respect human rights. This might have made it unnecessary for Occidental/Mannesmann to offer a deal to the ELN.
- State action to:
  - build effective political institutions
  - promote political and social adjustments to demographic change and land pressures
  - protect the space for citizen action against corruption
  - challenge the clientelist political practices which preserved the dominance of traditional parties and political/landowning élites.
- Promotion of effective judicial institutions capable of implementing the rule of law and protecting citizens threatened by armed groups.
- An action plan for the proper use of royalties within the context of the developmental needs of the region, implemented by a legitimate political authority capable of rising above particularist interests and basing itself on what could be recognised as a commitment to a 'common good'.

The failure to act appropriately in Arauca was one major error. A second, was the failure to apply lessons learned to the neighbouring department of Casanare, with allowances for the many peculiarities of that department

British Petroleum began exploration in Casanare in 1987 and the Cusiana and Cupiagua fields in the municipalities of Tauramena and Aguazul were discovered in the following two years.[6] (The two municipalities are within 7 kilometres of the processing facilities.) Commercial production of oil from Cusiana began in September 1992.[7] BP had very little experience of drilling in populated regions with a weak state presence and a history of violence and conflict, and during the years 1990–98, it made a number of critical mistakes in its approach to the region. The company has embarked on a very distinct strategy since then, but it is very difficult for a high-profile multinational to recover its reputation after mistakes, while the conflict in the region has been transformed in favour of armed power of all kinds.

In drawing upon the Arauca experience, BP had extracted only the surface story rather than the complex underlying sub-plots. However, even if it had fully appreciated these, it would not have helped the company to simply read off the situation in Arauca and 'apply the lessons' to Casanare. In addition, the Arauca situation had already reached a critical point by 1990. The presence of the oil industry had transformed the character of the conflict in that region; few could remain immune from this corrupting process, and many who tried lost their lives.[8]

The situation in Arauca would inevitably have consequences for Casanare, but Casanare had many of its own particularities, and knowing these well was probably the only way to manage the impact of oil. The Colombian state should have been in a position to alert the multinational to the context and its responsibilities. But policy makers and political élites had their minds on the oil revenues, which in the course of the 1990s would compensate for the decline of traditional exports such as coffee and reduce the public sector deficit in a decade in which the internal armed conflict reached unprecedented levels of intensity. Ironically, oil revenues also contributed indirectly to the intensification of that conflict.

There are two parts to the Casanare case study that follows. The first will trace the rise of what is called a process of multi-polar militarisation in the department, and its relationship to territorial claims, rent seeking and wealth accumulation. The second explores how this militarisation interacted with civil life and institutions, particularly after the arrival of oil. By 1998 the interaction between the two had resulted in a situation reached by Arauca in 1988 – that is, armed domination of civilian political and social life – although in Casanare this took forms of its own.

TERRITORY, RENTS AND ACCUMULATION: ECONOMIC FACTORS IN THE MULTI-POLAR MILITARISATION OF CASANARE

BP drew the lesson from Arauca in the early 1990s, that it should not make any deals with the guerrillas. It turned to the Colombian armed forces, which had a long history of human rights violations, for protection.[9] But it failed to draw an important additional lesson from Arauca, about the way oil interacted with the pre-existing patterns of political and social life. In Arauca, guerrillas had manipulated these patterns and forged implicit and sometimes explicit alliances with competing political élites in order to gain de facto control over oil revenues. The particularities of these pre-existing patterns would be different in Casanare, but should have been taken into account in terms of the way the discovery of a huge oilfield would impact on them.

The war in Colombia evolved in new ways in the 1990s. On the one hand the ELN and the Revolutionary Armed Forces of Colombia (FARC) enjoyed a new lease of life, the ELN through its strategic focus on oil and the FARC through its involvement in drugs. The rent-seeking element was vital for both, and by the end of the 1990s would become more important than strategic military objectives for an ELN that was struggling to survive. The FARC saw rent seeking as a means to further its territorial claims and respond to the paramilitary expansion of the 1990s. The paramilitaries had their origins in private armies which were formed in the 1980s to enable élites to defend themselves from guerrillas in the face of what was seen as the failure of the armed forces.[10] These became known as self-defence groups. In Arauca, the first such group appeared in Saravena in 1993, a vigilante group known as the Saravena Self-Defence, or *Los Encapuchados* (The Hooded Ones). It targeted unionised workers, particularly members of the peasant organisation (ANUC) and political opposition leaders.[11] A number of local and regional self-defence groups emerged at this time in different conflict zones, including Casanare. They were facilitated by legislation in 1994 to authorise the *Convivir*, civilian armed groups that were supposed to support the army in preventive, defensive and intelligence work. The abuses committed by these groups led to the revocation of this legislation, but by then self-defence or paramilitary groups had multiplied. In many cases, the armed forces colluded with or actively encouraged these groups.[12]

At this time BP, like the Colombian state, saw the threat to oil extraction in Casanare as coming exclusively from the guerrillas, whose presence was not as strong as in Arauca but was clearly growing. The position was understandable given the experience of Arauca, the fact that the ELN had publicly declared that the oil industry was a military target, and that the guerrillas were clearly enemies of the Colombian state. But it misjudged the complexity of politics in Casanare, and failed to understand that the ELN was only one of a number of armed actors with interests in the region, and only one of the problems the oil industry would face. While the paramilitary right did not formally target the oil industry, its abuse of the civilian population and criminal extortion of local BP contractors had serious implications for BP and the militarisation of Casanare. In the course of the 1990s, oil interacted with a variety of agendas of at least four organised armed groups seeking territory, rents and accumulation for a number of distinct purposes.

The department of Casanare is a disarticulated territory, whose central economic axis and identity had not been formed before the arrival of oil. The region is normally divided, rather like Arauca, into a plains area, the *llanos* proper, and the foothills or *piedemonte* region, itself divided between the Andean slopes, or *cordillera*, above 1000 meters and the foothills themselves. As in Arauca, the foothills are the most densely populated area. Eleven of Casanare's 19 municipalities are located there.[13] In the *llanos* extensive cattle ranching predominates, in the *piedemonte* small peasant farming. The Cusiana-Cupiagua field is located right in the midst of this *piedemonte*. In the south around Villanueva, there is an important agro-industrial area based on African palm and rice production, as well as a traditional ranching and an illegal drugs processing economy.

In Casanare each of these socio-economic spaces has a story to tell with respect to the war, independent of as well as interacting with the arrival of oil. Another 'reading' of Casanare is an ongoing process to determine the 'Casanare identity', which would shape the future of the department. This had never emerged clearly from the natural topography, dispersed settlement patterns or from a commodity capable of generating wealth through commercialisation to outside markets. Cattle ranching in Casanare has never been a highly productive or lucrative sector, partly because of the poor communications, the difficulties of transporting cattle to national markets and general lack of investment. Since the 1930s, the one road between Aguazul, Yopal and Sogamoso (Boyaca) had been passable only in the summer. Ranchers from the south sought alternatives; the road to Villavicencio via Barranca de Upía, once the bridge over the river Upía was built, linked them to the Meta and ultimately to a route to Bogota.[14] In the late 1970s, African palm gave a new economic impetus to Villanueva and set it further apart from other areas of Casanare. Just over a decade later, oil shifted the centre of gravity towards the central region and the capital of the department, Yopal. Oil was not a commodity owned by local interests, but a source of rents, around which the political élite could develop a Casanare project 'a la Yopaleño'.[15] But this has not gone unchallenged. The south maintains its own project, which is being built through various forms of illegal accumulation and a paramilitary army that has sought to build its social base amongst the population of the area. The growth and consolidation of Yopal with the rise of oil has meant, however, that it cannot be ignored, and at least part of the logic of the paramilitary expansion of the 1990s is about control over the department's future, not just about the defeat of the guerrillas. The following section looks at the rise of each of the armed groups in Casanare.

The cattle ranching families of the *llanos* dominate the landowning structure of Casanare, which consists primarily of large and very large properties. Of the total land area, 48 per cent belongs to just 492 properties (1.8 per cent of all properties) in farms over 1000 hectares. In contrast, 90 per cent of properties between them cover only 22 per cent of the land area; 28 per cent of properties comprise less than ten hectares. The rich landed families, which one historian calls 'dynasties' (Pérez Ángel 1997), form a *llanera* culture characterised by a long history of violent expulsion and subjugation of the

Indians who originally inhabited the region, which continued into the twentieth century.[16]

Some Indians may have survived by accepting acculturation and joined the growing mixed or *mestizo* population of daily paid workers on the estates, or landless poor. These were the foot soldiers, argues Pérez Ángel, of the violent conflicts of the *llanos*, of which the civil war or *Violencia* of the 1950s was the most bloody. During and after the *Violencia*, a wave of small farmers from Boyaca came to Casanare in search of land and peace. They found neither. Most of this colonisation to Casanare was spontaneous, and unlike in Arauca, there was no systematic INCORA-like programme of support and land titling. The peasants arrived in a region where state presence and infrastructure were minimal, settling in the higher Andean slopes and the foothills, wherever they could find a piece of land.

The FARC guerrillas began visiting communities in the *piedemonte* of Casanare in the mid 1980s and the ELN established its armed presence in the municipalities of the *cordillera*, such as La Salina, Recetor and Chámeza a few years later.[17] The guerrillas came to control some of these population centres and the people learnt to regard them as the authority in the town. Today, displaced people from these municipalities are murdered simply because of the place of origin shown on their identity card.[18] The guerrillas chose these locations partly because of their isolation and their importance as a logistical rearguard, partly because of the *focista* vision of acting as a catalyst to mobilise the poorest peasants against their servitude, and partly because of the ELN's strategic interest in the oil industry.[19] From its strongholds in the communities it controlled, the ELN began its attacks on BP's exploration and production facilities in the region in the early 1990s. The ELN's Jose David Suárez and Domingo Lain Fronts also infiltrated the social and political life of many other municipalities of the *piedemonte*, turning them into spaces that would be contested by all the armed groups of the department.

The idea of 'Araucanising' Casanare may have been a tactical vision of the ELN, but it would prove more complicated in Casanare, a department twice the size of Arauca with a distinct history and socio-political composition and a relatively more diversified economy. Although oil came to dominate the Casanare economy, the department never became an oil enclave like its neighbour.[20] The ELN was unable to build a tactical alliance with independent politicians within the dominant Liberal Party, although like all the armed groups it has infiltrated the electoral processes in order to tap into municipal and regional revenues through successful candidates. Even its military actions against the oil installations were containable by mid 1997–98.[21] The mass civic actions of Arauca could not be replicated amongst the less organised peasants of Casanare, although the ELN probably tried to intervene in some of the land struggles and community struggles against BP that took place in the early 1990s.[22] As the ELN grew militarily weaker in the late 1990s, it directed its attention to its need for funds, primarily through kidnapping and extortion of oil contractors, and taxing local businesses and individuals.

The FARC established three of its 33 Fronts in Casanare in the mid 1990s, the 28th and 45th Fronts in the north and the 38th Front in the south. This was less out of interest in the oil industry than for the drug-trading corridors that linked the producing areas it controlled in the Meta to markets elsewhere. It was forced out, however, of Monterrey, Villanueva and Sabanalarga. But its interest in the strategic territorial importance of Casanare, which connects strong areas of FARC influence in the Meta and Arauca, increased. There is a rumour that the FARC commander, Mono Joyo, ordered his troops to rescue Casanare in the late 1990s after it had virtually fallen under paramilitary control. The FARC escalated its military presence and actions, displacing the ELN from some areas of the *piedemonte*, challenging paramilitary control and organising regular *paros armados* ('armed strikes') when no traffic on the vulnerable main communications route through Yopal was permitted. It also blew up the electricity pylons and twice left Yopal without electricity for long periods in 2001 and 2002.[23]

The paramilitaries of Casanare have their origins in the cattle ranching families of the *llanos*, who have traditionally controlled land and wealth in the department and have strong family links with the neighbouring department of Boyaca. During the post-*Violencia* years, lawlessness, cattle theft and invasions of estates were rife. Protecting estates of sometimes 10,000 hectares was very difficult without state security forces. This led the ranchers to create their own armed guards.[24] In the 1980s, a rural force of the Colombian intelligence service, the Departamento Administrativo de Seguridad (DAS-Rural) was created in Casanare, and its training school in Aguazul specialised in cattle theft. The men whose livelihoods centred on defending the cattle ranches were probably the embryo of what one Casanareño described as '*paramilitarismo criollo*' (Creole paramilitarism).

The paramilitary project in Colombia grew out of the sense that 'if you have land you have rights'; Castaño, founder of the united paramilitary group the United Self-Defence Forces of Colombia (AUC), refers in his book to the many fiefdoms with armed power in the regions, among them 'el de los ganaderos de Yopal' (Castaño 2001:199) – the one belonging to the ranchers of Yopal, the capital.[25] The links between paramilitary groups and large landowning interests are very clear. The municipalities where 80–99 per cent of the land is in the hands of large and very large properties are today heartlands of paramilitary power in Casanare: Orocué where large estates make up 99 per cent, San Luis de Palenque at 96.2 per cent, Trinidad 94.8 per cent, Maní

89.5 per cent, Paz de Aríporo 89.6 per cent, and Hato Corozal 97.2 per cent (DANE/IGAC 1999:226). All are strategic municipalities close to the border with Arauca, where the FARC launched a major offensive in 2000.[26] The extensive territory controlled by the paramilitaries in the plains through their relationship to the ranchers has given them a strong base from which to erode and eliminate guerrilla influence in the *piedemonte* foothills, and they rapidly became the ascendant force in Casanare. By the late 1990, only the FARC seriously contested their dominance.

The paramilitaries are not, however, a united front in Casanare. There are at least two, perhaps three paramilitary groups.[27] The Autodefensas Unidas de Colombia: Norte y Centro del Casanare is supported by Castaño's own paramilitary group, the Auto Defensas de Cordoba and Uraba. It is a kind of mercenary army of people from outside the department who see themselves as part of the great national conflict; they are seeking resources to help them with this larger-scale project and stem the FARC expansion into the territory. They operate in the northern open territory and frontier region with Arauca. They are reported to have a presence in eleven of Casanare's 19 municipalities, with a strong presence in Yopal, and their aim is to take control of La Salina, Sácama, Nunchía and Támara, where the guerrillas have strong influence (Corporación Excelencia en la Justicia 2001).

The other paramilitary group is the Autodefensas Campesinos del Sur de Casanare, reputed to have been founded in the south of Casanare around Villanueva, Monterrey and Tauramena by Victor Carranza, an emerald dealer convicted of drug smuggling. Carranza had local links with traditional cattle ranchers of the region. In the 1980s, young men from the area went to work in the emerald mines and the coca laboratories of Guaviare and Vichada, absorbing some of the most violent cultures in Colombia and investing their money in land and laboratories back home. Private armies were set up to guard these acquisitions. These municipalities of the south are reputed to have some of the largest cocaine laboratories in Colombia. Carranza himself began buying land in various municipalities of Casanare in the 1980s. Alejandro Reyes has calculated that 43 per cent of Casanare's municipalities have seen land purchased by drug traffickers (Posada 1997, 1998). Some traditional ranchers were happy to sell up, given the situation in the region, particularly at the prices the drugs traffickers were willing to pay. The boundary between legal and illegal economic activities was gradually erased in the south and a semi-mafia type economy emerged, whose élite were ready to confront the growing guerrilla threat in the region.[28] These were the origins of the Autodefensas del Sur, formally founded in 1995 but with antecedents in the late 1980s.[29] Carranza himself has been in prison for a number of years and his precise relationship to the paramilitary group he helped found is not clear. It is known that a major internal dispute and change of command took place within the Autodefensas del Sur in 2000, which led to the murder of Victor Feliciano, a drug trafficker and landowner, together with his entire family, and the subsequent rise of the much feared paramilitary commander known as HK.[30]

Local people see the paramilitaries as criminals and killers who have created an atmosphere of terror.[31] Where criminality begins and ends with these paramilitary groups is not easy to judge, and a number of criminal gangs also operate in Casanare. But the levels of violence and crime in the department increased notably from 1990 and particularly after 1998. There is a suggested (Collier and Hoeffler 2001) correlation between the shift to a qualitative and quantitative escalation in the violence around 1998, shortly after the completion of the Cupiagua production facilities, and the end of major employment opportunities in the oil industry's construction works.[32] In 1996, there had been 231 murders in Casanare and 21 kidnappings, with 41 murders in Yopal alone, and 73 in Aguazul;[33] in 1997 the figure was 262, with 46 kidnappings and 217 displaced people. The Defensor (people's ombudsman) described the situation in an interview with the author in 1997 as a 'dispersed massacre', in that killings were selective and individual, disguising the growing numbers. By 1998, the figure reached a new peak of 322, declining only slightly to 257 in 1999 and 309 in 2000, making a total of 888 for the three years 1998–2000.[34] In 29 cases, there were massacres that involved multiple murders; ten of these were attributed to the paramilitaries and two to the guerrillas. Seventeen were carried out by 'unknowns'. The number of kidnappings over the three years was 147, of which the guerrillas were responsible for 97, the paramilitaries for 26, and common criminals for 24. An indication of the rise in fighting is the estimated figure of 4084 displaced people over the three years, with the figure doubling every year (Defensoria 2001).

By the end of the decade, civilian authority and civilian space in Casanare struggled to maintain room for manoeuvre in the face of the territorial and rent-seeking competition of the armed groups. The 16th Brigade of the armed forces was mostly engaged in the defence of the oil industry; the police were on the frontline against guerrilla attacks in municipalities; in the capital police had to deal with the paramilitary presence and were swamped by the everyday violence and criminality. All the armed actors are present in Yopal, although the paramilitaries dominate. A growing number of displaced people from the conflicts in other municipalities also arrive destitute in the capital. Some have been the victims of land seizures by paramilitaries.[35] While 80 per cent of displaced people are from within the department, a further 20 per cent come to Yopal fleeing the conflict elsewhere in Colombia. There are few places of safety anywhere in Colombia today.

CIVIL INTERACTION WITH THE MULTI-POLAR MILITARISATION OF CASANARE

What role did the discovery of oil play in the militarisation of Casanare? At one level, that story has been told. It offered the opportunity for rent seeking. However, that does not explain the contingent contextual factors that enabled this rent seeking to take place, or how military actors were able to absorb, marginalise and eliminate civilian democratic ones. A distinction also has to be made, however, in that although the arrival of oil can generate conflict for a number of reasons, this does not make it a source of armed conflict, except in exceptional circumstances. In Casanare the social conflicts generated by oil and the misuse of oil revenues by weak local institutions ran in parallel with the rise of armed groups. The latter began to overwhelm the fragile but by no means non-existent civilian and democratic dynamics. Poverty and inequality had created resentments in Casanare long before the oil industry arrived; by 1995, the average income per capita in the department was $930, compared with $1850 for Colombia as a whole, and 47 per cent of the population did not have their basic needs met.[36] It took a surprisingly small number of armed men to intervene in this environment and reshape it, reinforcing the importance given here to their interactions with civilian processes. Although statistics are by no means reliable and the figures are only indicative, the study by the Corporación Excelencia en la Justicia in 2001 cites an approximate number of 340 armed insurgents of the FARC and around 100 for the ELN in Casanare; the police of Yopal quoted a figure of 500 paramilitary members.[37] The army, on the other hand, has around 3000 troops in Casanare.

This section will look at how civilian life has become militarised through these interactions. A prevention strategy for Casanare would have had to prioritise unequivocally the strengthening of its civilian, judicial and democratic forces. While the Colombian national government began to decentralise in the late 1980s, and took some steps to open up participation in the 1991 Constitution, these initiatives were not accompanied by a simultaneous programme of institutional strengthening.

Oil had a clear impact on the demographics of Casanare, whose population was 89,186 in 1973. The largest town was Yopal, with a population of 24,517 (DANE 1986). By 1994 the population had reached 150,000, with 27,499 in Yopal, rising in 2001 to 300,000 overall and in Yopal to 79,521 (Gaviria et al 2002). An estimated 47 per cent of population growth was concentrated in the two oil municipalities, Tauramena and Aguazul, and Yopal. A population that was 70 per cent based in rural areas in 1990 was only 53 per cent rural in 2001.[38] Yopal's rate of growth is similar to that of Arauca, and those of Aguazul and Tauramena comparable to Arauquita and Cravo Norte in the neighbouring oil-producing department (Dureau and Florez 2000). The process of constructing an oil production facility is the most labour-intensive period for the oil industry, in which infrastructure is built and services required for skilled and unskilled labour. Labour requirements decline considerably once production starts. The key years for Casanare were 1993–98 when the final phase of the extension of the installations (Centro de Facilidades de Producción or CPF) of Cusiana took place and of the CPF in Cupiagua was completed. Expectations of a bonanza in Casanare were created through headlines in the national newspaper.[39] An estimated 12,000 jobs were created between 1994 and 1996, and at this time some 80 people a day were arriving in Casanare. In the first six months of 1996, 6000 people arrived in Yopal, 1800 in Aguazul and 2300 in Tauramena (Gaviria et al 2002). By 1996, 58 per cent of the population of Tauramena, 20 per cent of Aguazul's and 14 per cent of that of Yopal were working directly for the oil industry, and many others were indirectly associated through services in restaurants, hotels and domestic labour. A great deal of the unskilled labour is hired on 28-day contracts, and the fence-hangers or *malleros* hang outside the perimeter fence competing for these contracts. Alfredo Molano conveys the lives of the *malleros* in his oral history of Casanare:

> I came home from Ibagué. There they told me about the Cusiana project. I went down there and to Tauramena. ... On the fence one suffers a lot. There are days that start without hope, others that go by without anything happening. ... Cusiana is a Disneyland, but few manage to shake hands with Mickey Mouse. As time goes by things become clearer: Cusiana is a vicious circle, a place from which people do not escape. Everyone talks of the 'boom' but if people are not living the boom, who is it for? As we are now, only the trader achieves it; the opportunist is the only one that lives and enjoys it. ... But the other side of the boom, which is unknown, is that of suffering. Cusiana is also a sick worker who has to go to the well with a fever; it is the 15-year-old kid in love with the engineer; it is the boy hit by a tractor who is dying in hospital; it is the cheque sent to the wife each month so that she has everything she needs and then one day, he gets home and finds the clothes hanging on a peg because the lady has gone off with another man. Here, on the other side of the boom, you live off dreams and you hear everyone's regrets.
>
> (Molana 1995:106–8)

Salaries in the oil industry were so much higher than elsewhere, that the 28-day system was one of a number of rationing mechanisms for labour.[40] Workers were not allowed to reapply for a contract for three months.

Similar rationing occurred among contracts for services, which were in the hands of the neighbourhood councils, or Juntas de Accion Communal. Numerous conflicts have arisen around these service and labour contracts.[41] One of the tensions has been between the native population and the incomers. Fedesarrollo's study of the impact of the oil industry on Casanare found that the migrant workers there tended to come from higher socio-economic strata than most migrants to the large cities of Colombia, and to have a higher level of education than the native population (Gaviria et al 2002:20). The migrants were able to gain access to any work requiring higher skills than the local population, generating huge resentments and demands for access to more skills training locally.

These resentments grew considerably after the completion of the construction phase of the installations and the decline in job opportunities, and it is at this moment that the paramilitaries tried to intervene and 'support the communities'. In 2002, the body of a migrant oil worker for Petrobrás, the Brazilian company which has a small well in Mani, was discovered, marked with the words 'muerto por sapo' (killed for being a grass), but people believe he was killed by the paramilitaries as a message to other migrant workers.[42] Local politicians have begun to talk of the 'Casanarisation' of the region, meaning that jobs should only be for local-born people. The decline in employment prospects has had another impact on the armed conflict as there is a pool of potential recruits for the armed groups amongst the unemployed. The armed groups offer subsistence and the paramilitaries offer regular payment.

Behind these resentments is the transformation of a time-honoured if impoverished form of life by the arrival of oil. A study in 1995 of socio-cultural transformations in Tauramena records how in the 1980s 'it was once a town lost in the llanos' with only seven streets and a park.[43] The author of the study watched while four discotheques were set up in two months and the musical tastes of young people shifted to rock. The diet of the people began to change towards tinned food; the traditional platano (banana) was no longer found in local markets and began to be imported.[44] Rural dwellers began to drift from the land. Prostitution increased, and shook a region known for its conservative family structure and values, and the migrants were also blamed for this. In a public forum in the early 1990s to discuss the impact of oil, the peasants' association, the ANUC, complained to the Ecopetrol representative about the 'attack on and destruction of the family unit by the floating population known as the twenty-eighters, who are brought in by the oil companies instead of giving jobs to people native to the area. This results in the introduction of depravity, drugs and immorality, the effects of which have been seen with the first AIDS cases in Yopal hospital' (quoted in Celis 1994:125). The rise in alcoholism, crime and violence in the early 1990s in the context of an ineffective judicial system contributed to the sense of unfettered social change and insecurity.

In addition, there is evidence of a very high level of intra-family violence that has also contributed to the generalised insecurity and breakdown of affective relationships. This cannot be traced directly to the oil industry, but may have some connection with the generalised rise of fear and violence in the department, and its impact on masculine identities in particular. In 1997, the Instituto Nacional de Medicina Legal y Ciencias Forenses (National Institution of Legal Medicine and Forensic Sciences) carried out a survey which showed Casanare had one of the highest levels of intra-family violence in the country. It had 171 cases for every 100,000 inhabitants, compared with 144 on average at the national level, with a very high level of matrimonial violence. By 2000, this was 151 cases per 100,000 inhabitants; the rate in Aguazul was between 3.0 and 3.9 times the national average, and in Yopal between 2.0 and 2.9 times (Corporación Excelencia en la Justicia 2001). Daily life changed for the people in the oil towns of Casanare, and by the early 1990s social action to protest at disruptions and potential damage to community life was mounting. The mishandling of these social protests was to cost BP its reputation locally, nationally and internationally and it has found it hard to recover. It remains exposed to further claims arising out of these years and subsequently, by individuals and groups who realised that a multinational can be vulnerable to reputation loss. It is here that an oil multinational becomes an actor in the conflictive processes that inevitably emerge when oil is found in a poor and peripheral region such as Casanare. A company of such size and power becomes the focal point of myriad distinct complaints, some justified and others not.

Social organisation was weak in Casanare in the 1980s, in contrast to the mobilisations of the settlers in Arauca, but it was not non-existent. By the 1990s, the peasant association, ANUC, had an estimated 35 organisations at the village and municipal level in Casanare.[45] While it helped organise a number of land invasions, it did not have the mass base it built in some other regions. Between 1989 and 1993, there were efforts to revitalise it through the leadership of Carlos Arrigui. This coincided with the rise of the oil industry in the region, the growing ELN presence in the *piedemonte*, the establishment of the 16th Brigade of the armed forces, charged with defending the oil industry, and the appearance of an organised response from the right.

Another form of social organising which grew stronger in these years was the forming of Juntas de Acción Comunal, or neighbourhood councils. These grew from 502 in 1988 to 888 in 1998, excluding the juntas of Villanueva (Galindo León and Jáuregui 1998:69). The juntas would become one of the main mechanisms for BP's relationship with the communities. In addition, the idea that oil would bring new developments to communities and that BP was willing to help with social projects led a number of communities to organise their own community development associations. These associations also became involved in protests about the impact of oil on their environment. An example would be Asoccocharte, an organisation of twelve hamlets in the village of Unión Charte, between Aguazul and Yopal.[46] Another example is that of the Asociación Comunitaria para el Desarrollo Agroindustrial de El Morro (ACDAINSO, the Community Association for the Agro-industrial Development of El Morro). It is interesting to note that while the armed groups discussed above are dominated by male actors, women figure prominently in the arena of the juntas and the community associations.[47] The erosion of safe space to participate in civic activity in Casanare has been a particular loss for women.

The difficulty for poor communities struggling around legitimate social demands in Casanare, as elsewhere in Colombia, was not only that the guerrillas tried to infiltrate and influence these struggles but that the armed forces and right-wing paramilitary groups did not distinguish between such legitimate social struggles and support for the guerrillas. In the political culture of Colombia, powerless and vulnerable communities have great difficulty forging strong and independent organisations. They are quickly seen as a clientele for the electoral purposes of political leaders and, as the militarisation of Casanare progressed, for the interests of armed groups. In turn, these communities often seek interlocutors and mediators who can help them pursue and present their demands. Community action can be easily discredited in these conditions. Community organisation is often weakened through the divisions created, and the murder of community leaders leaves a lasting legacy of resentment that can lay the basis for ongoing conflicts, particularly when the murder goes unpunished. The murder of Carlos Arrigui in April 1995 is an example; the murder came just over a year after he had led El Morro in a civic strike against BP. Although the Procurator General investigated the circumstances surrounding Arrigui's murder, the report does not reflect a very thorough investigation.[48] It concluded that the murder was probably the responsibility of the security forces and a result of Arrigui's community activities, and indeed an army intelligence officer, Luis Alfredo Soler Gomez, was arrested. The officer was later seen 'living comfortably in the army barracks' in 1998.[49]

BP's relationship with ACDAINSO and the community of El Morro is an example of the complexities and risks surrounding social organisational dynamics in Colombia – one which should have been better understood by the company. Around 1993, the community of El Morro, which is situated in the midst of La Floreña, a small oilfield in an early phase of exploration at that time, began to protest about damage to the road used by the community from the machinery and trucks driving up and down to reach the wells and the seismic tests taking place in the area. The report of the Defensoria on the case stated that the main complaints from the people were that 'dynamite is placed around the rivers, ravines and springs, drying up the water source in many cases, fracturing the earth, felling the forests and affecting the fauna' (Defensoria del Pueblo 1998). It found that the community was also facing other problems, such as the location of an army base in its midst to defend the wells, and that the army was responsible for water contamination and leaving rubbish in the peasants' fields. The report also pointed out that the communities themselves had originally upset the fragile ecosystem of the area when they deforested the land in order to settle it and clear it for farming.[50]

The El Morro community is a *corregimiento* of Yopal, a community of six hamlets with a population of 1500 people. The community are mostly colonisers from one of the poorest municipalities of Labranza Grande in Boyaca. The Colombian think tank Fedesarrollo included El Morro in its study of the impact of oil on Casanare and identified it as a community in a 'poverty trap'. Despite considerable infrastructural development since 1994 and the tarmacking of the road following an agreement with BP, El Morro stands out today for the exceptionally low level of education of adults and children and the high levels of child labour, around 20 per cent (Gaviria et al 2002). The hopes of this community that oil could offer a way out of this poverty trap, its frustrations as such hopes failed to materialise and its sense of powerlessness in the face of large-scale and poorly understood transformations around them were behind the civic strike that took place in January 1994.

BP made a critical mistake at a key point in the evolution of the conflict of Casanare by failing to understand the wider implications of the actions of this very small community. Its relationships with the community at this time were based on an old-fashioned benevolent paternalism, while it concentrated strategically on the security of the enterprise.[51] This was in the hands of the Colombian armed forces and a private security company, Defence Systems Colombia (DSC), part of the multinational security company, Defense Systems Limited. Following the civic strike, a number of community leaders were threatened. It was alleged that BP security employees were filming and photographing community leaders and meetings, and handing the pictures to the army.

These allegations, together with the murder of Arrigui, came to the attention of the British press. Between 1996 and 1998, BP became headline news in the UK press, the subject of at least two major television documentaries, a visit from a European Parliament delegation, human rights protests in the UK, a debate in the House of Lords and a report by Human Rights Watch (1998).[52] An investigation by the Public Prosecutor, or 'Fiscalía', published on 10 January 1998, found no evidence to substantiate the allegations against BP and the company was exonerated.[53] Several new allegations were made against BP and DSC in 1998 concerning police training and the security of the OCENSA pipeline, and against BP for environmental infringements.[54] An inter-agency group of UK NGOs (Save the Children Fund, Oxfam, Christian Aid, CAFOD and CIIR) was set up to engage in a dialogue with BP around these allegations. The international focus on BP's role in Casanare contributed to a major rethink in the company around its handling of the situation (see below). In the meantime, the armed groups extended their predatory advances. A qualitative shift in the conflict took place, as growing paramilitary control led to the FARC offensive, while the ELN's military decline led them to extend their efforts at extortion through kidnapping and 'taxing' local contractors.

The main political actors in Casanare were traditionally a political élite who expected to control electoral positions in the key municipal and departmental offices and make the personal gains that accompanied this. It was not a respected institutionality, but it was the only one there was and it enjoyed some legitimacy for that reason alone. In the late 1980s, the Colombian government promoted a decentralisation process aimed partly at opening up political participation. This included the direct election of mayors in 1988. But it was a decentralisation to weak institutions and to a political sphere characterised by the patron–client relationship that was easily manipulated, as we saw in the case of Arauca. This did not mean that everyone who attempted to represent the communities was caught up in corruption. An emphasis on contingent contexts is that they require, in this discussion of the political arena, discrimination between those committed to a public interest, those who would be committed if the incentives were right, and those with only personal interests in mind. In Casanare, there are examples of all of these. But what is clear is that the space to be neutral and act for the public interest became more and more restricted as armed actors increased their power over civilian ones, who were now in charge of the oil revenues that started flowing to Casanare from 1993.

The precise relationship between the rise of armed groups, oil revenues and the agendas of political élites is not easy to untangle. In order to get elected, candidates have to make deals with armed groups, particularly the paramilitaries but also the guerrillas, in the municipalities they control. These deals involve access to the revenues of the municipality after the election and refusal to comply means death. Two mayors of Aguazul have been murdered and many live under permanent threat. Many politicians, up to and including the departmental governor, live in a state of ambivalence between a wish to carry out their political duties and their need to appease the armed groups around them.[55] Oil royalties, it can be argued, weakened rather than strengthened Casanare's fragile political institutionality.

Oil produced very high levels of growth in Casanare (CRECE 1995). Between 1995 and 1998 Casanare received 33 per cent of the total royalties distributed to oil-producing regions, compared with 28 per cent to Arauca, and 7 per cent to Meta, Huila and La Guajira; by 2000 Arauca's share had declined to 12 per cent, whereas those of Casanare had risen to 35 per cent.[56] Between 1994 and 1998, the aggregate value of the department's contribution to National GDP increased to 2 per cent while in Arauca it declined from 1.1 per cent to 0.7 per cent (Gaviria et al 2002). The structure of production was transformed; agriculture and cattle diminished considerably in their economic contribution to GDP, but African palm production and cattle were nonetheless still significant economic activities. The contribution of agriculture and cattle to the departmental GDP decreased, from 10 per cent and 50 per cent respectively in 1985, to 9 per cent and 11 per cent in 1993, while oil rose from 12.5 per cent to 45 per cent.

The Fedesarrollo study of the impact of oil on public finances in Casanare illustrates the potential and the dangers of the income the region began to receive, particularly the municipalities of Aguazul and Tauramena (Gaviria et al 2002). These municipalities came to depend on royalties for 45 per cent of their income (in contrast, non-oil-producing municipalities of a similar size depended on the national government for between 65 and 90 per cent of their income). At the departmental level, the contribution of royalties to total income was even more significant than at the municipal level, rising from 70 per cent in 1996 to 74 per cent in 2000. In addition to the royalties, the rise in commerce between 1991 and 1996 was very high and became an important source of municipal and departmental taxation revenue (and indirectly, for extortion by armed groups).

Casanare ended up with the highest investment resources per capita in the country, 30 times those of the poorest departments of Chocó and Vichada, and similar to that of a relatively wealthy department such as Cundinamarca. Considerable infrastructural investment was made with these royalties and Fedesarrollo found that public services and educational coverage were, by 2002, not very different to those of other large towns in the country. The quality of education remains a problem and the informal nature of much unemployment has affected affiliation to the national health programme and pensions. But while provision of and access to basic services has improved markedly, these soon become taken for granted as people search for improved employment and income. Casanare has not achieved sustainable human development despite its oil bonanza: 'There is no development, only infrastructure,' was the view of a group of women I interviewed in Yopal.[57] And even with the improvements in infrastructural development, Casanare cannot officially account for the massive $800 million it has received in royalties from Cusiana/Cupiagua between 1993 and 2000.

The audited royalties accounts of the department for 2001, prepared by the Contraloria Departmental de Colombia (2002), are very revealing on the investment profile. The municipality of Aguazul, for instance, spent 41.3 billion pesos in 2001, of which 7.6 billion went on roads, and 5.2 billion on debt servicing, compared with 3.1 billion on the agriculture and production sector. The armed forces, it is interesting to note, receive 5 per cent of the amount designated for road building to fund their security role in keeping them open.[58] Another problem with the expenditure on infrastructure is the quality of the works and the tendency for companies to charge inordinately high prices. It is never clear whether these sums include the *vacuna*, or tax, to one or other armed group, as is often claimed to justify these costs. Corruption undoubtedly accounts for a considerable loss in royalty revenue. Fedesarrollo found that with the resources it received, the municipalities of Casanare could have easily achieved 100 per cent coverage of health, education and basic sanitation by investing only the resources of the years 1998 and 1999 (Gaviria et al 2002).

In addition to corruption and the siphoning of resources to armed actors, an economic bottleneck disrupts resource flows when a sudden influx of oil revenues reaches a department with a weak existing resource base. This is because current account expenditure increases at a greater pace than the total resources or existing savings. Increased revenues from royalties ironically led to greater indebtedness at the municipal and departmental level, and an inability to generate savings which might reduce the ever greater dependency on royalties. Any major downward shift in oil prices could create a major problem of short-term insolvency, which in the climate of Casanare could be very dangerous.

The 1998 Plan for Casanare produced by the departmental Planning Administration acknowledged the profound institutional weakness in the department: 'The department currently lacks a functioning and accountable structure which would enable it to provide the decision-making processes for planning and management' (Departamento Administrativo de Planeación 1998:27). Yet while this was acknowledged in 1998, that year marked an escalation in the levels of violence and extortion. Interviews in 2001 and 2002 with the main institutions charged with introducing accountability and legality into Casanare found them all under tremendous pressure from the volume of cases and from the threats they received from armed groups.[59] The Defensor had to go into exile in October 2000 after a bomb was placed under his car. In May 2001, the paramilitaries ordered two 'fiscales', or prosecutors, to present themselves in Tauramena. After they failed to do this at the second demand, they were told that one of the fiscales would be shot.[60] The Procurator General was in despair at his inability to investigate all the cases that came to him, and even when he did carry out investigations he could not take the cases to court, due to threats on him and the Fiscal.

Civilian authority had been greatly undermined in Casanare by the late 1990s. Nevertheless, there were still voices and organisations that were trying to keep the civilian space open. This chapter has argued that there were contingent moments when institutional and social decomposition might have been avoided or at least mitigated. To achieve this, it would have been vital to support those voices and organisations from the very moment oil was discovered.

By the late 1980s there was a generation of young professionals who were concerned with the development of the region. They were prepared to act independently of the traditional élite political families and challenge their clientelist political culture. Some founded NGOs, such as Cemilla in Yopal and the Fundación para el Desarrollo de Upía in Villanueva. The latter had proposed a participatory regional approach to the development of Casanare in the early 1990s to over-come disarticulation and fragmentation. A space for participation from different social sectors and organisations would, it was argued at the time, offer a strong local interlocutor to the oil industry as 'the weaker the community, the worse is the impact of oil.'[61] The Barco government's Programme Nacional de Rehabilitación (National Rehabilitation Programme, or PNR), which targeted the conflictive areas of Colombia, had been applied in Yopal in 1991 and had been supportive of partici-patory approaches. The governor at the time supported the idea and Consejos de Participación (Participation Councils) were set up between 1992 and 1994. However, the councils were closed by the next governor of the department, and the PNR was abandoned by a later national administration.

Many of this generation of professionals have come to occupy key roles in the institutions of government as well as in the private sector and the Chamber of Commerce. They have remained committed to the department despite the war and could, they argue, have been the core of an alliance to construct a more sustainable institutionality based on a region-wide development strategy. Many feel that the national state undermines rather than strengthens such capacity. The Contraloría (auditor) in charge of investigating corruption finds that rather than giving greater support for him to exercise his investigative role, the government cuts his budget and seeks to establish a new outside body to audit the departmental Contralorías. 'Strengthen us!' he entreated in an interview.[62] A strategic national plan of institutional strengthening in Casanare would have also prioritised the judiciary and included regu-lar support from national teams when local people are threatened. Impunity positively fosters violence.

A serious pre-emptive plan for Casanare should have involved a recognition of the importance of the grassroots, developmental, women's and environmental groups to the democratic process in the department. This would have required effective security for citizens and measures to ensure that the security forces, in particular the armed forces, were them-selves accountable to the rule of law and not above it. The widespread belief and considerable evidence that the army has colluded with the paramilitaries in cruel actions against social activists, and prioritised the defence of the oil industry over the civilian population, has created a great deal of cynicism towards the security forces of the state. Civilian security is guaranteed for no one, and those who try to keep an independent voice frequently risk their lives. Nevertheless, there are still social activists in Casanare who dare to speak out. The march to the central square in Yopal in November 2001 by some 50 women to commemorate the International Day of Non-Violence Against Women illustrates that, despite the militarisation of Casanare, some are prepared to defend the civilian space no matter what the risks may be.

Finally, regional institutions should have been prepared for the influx of royalties, and established transparent and democratic mechanisms of accountability and decision making. The royalties have been a major source of indirect predation by armed groups and the weakening of local authority structures. In 2002 the government was considering the option of re-centralising control of the royalty payments. This would have ensured central government expenditure on education, health and other local social and infrastructural expenditure. The proposal was a response to the evidence of corruption and ineffective local administration, but also called into question the high percentage of royalties that go to the oil-producing regions. There is some logic to guaranteeing the redistributive and appropriate use of revenues centrally, although this depends on the capacity of the central government, which must remain doubtful in Colombia. But this belated proposal is likely to create a renewed crisis in Casanare, and my interviews in 2002 revealed that it was already provoking political unrest as local élites and professionals alike contested the erosion of power and room for manoeuvre it would imply. Casanare has not yet achieved anything resembling sustainable development, they argued. While there is considerable infrastructural development, royalties should now be redirected towards the productive sector.[63]

This chapter argues that policy failure at the level of the national government has contributed to the opportunities for predation by armed groups in both Arauca and Casanare. An antagonistic interaction emerged between the civil and non-civil processes in the regions, which led ultimately but not inevitably to the triumph of the latter over the former. A considerable financial boom took place in regions with weak and poorly prepared institutions, disarticulated territories and clientelist political practices. Expected and real revenues created new socio-economic dynamics which institutions could not handle. At the same time, armed groups began to make use of the opportunities for predation which opened up, and interacted with the civilians who controlled the fragile institutions, made vulnerable by the lack of shared norms which underpinned them. Gradually the non-civil processes made inroads into the civil world, corrupting political representatives, killing and threatening independent social activities and siphoning resources to strengthen armed confrontation. In an investigation into the judicial system in Casanare, the department was described to a team of interviewers as being in a state of 'co-government' with armed groups (Corporación Excelencia en la Justicia 2001:39). This weakening of civil order was not a one-off but an evolving process, in which the national government might have intervened to prevent an outcome that became obvious in Arauca by 1988 and in Casanare a decade later: a level of militarisation of civilian life which would be very difficult to reverse. But if one can attribute policy failure to the national government, what might one attribute to the main multinational company operating in the region? And how has the oil industry responded to the dilemmas of extracting oil in such a complex, militarised environment?

BEYOND THE PERIMETER FENCE: THE OIL INDUSTRY AND NEW RESPONSES TO THE CONFLICT

From defence of the oil industry to security of the oil-producing community

Policy failure in Colombia has often been as much due to a policy vacuum as to misguided policies. It could be argued that this is very evidently the case with respect to the oil industry. In the 1980s Occidental adopted the easier, but ultimately highly damaging, policy of offering a deal to the ELN in order to protect its oil interests. This was partly a result of the lack of any state direction that would have made the company accountable to a national policy environment or provided alternative forms of security. By the late 1990s, individual companies and the Asociación Colombiana de Petroleo (Colombian Petroleum Association, ACP) had been forced to develop their own approach to the protection of their industry. In doing this, they have tried to make a distinction between defending the industry, and the security of the industry in its *entorno*, or socio-political environment. This has involved them engaging actively with the communities and political structures around them.

The ACP was founded in 1965 but did not develop a clear set of strategies for the industry as a whole until the 1990s. Different policies were implemented in different regions and by individual companies, and a military and defensive approach dominated. The association or *Gremio* as is it called in Colombia, is a relatively weak pressure group compared with the historic power of the coffee producers federation. As oil has overtaken coffee as the country's major export, the ACP has not been able to replicate that power; this is partly explained by the number of foreign companies within the association and the sensitivities about such companies trying to exert political influence over areas of Colombian national policy. As the Colombian government has gone into overdrive to attract foreign investment, many new companies of varying size have come to Colombia; an estimated 70 were operating by 2002 (Ecopetrol 2002). The capacity of these companies to deal with the violent environment in which exploration and production must take place in Colombia varies a great deal. BP Amoco cannot be compared with some of the small companies which do not have the resources to develop sophisticated monitoring of environmental impact or to pay for the same level of protection by the armed forces. But nor are they such high-profile targets as a huge multinational like BP. The ACP has begun to foster some coherence amongst the different kinds of companies operating in the sector.

The ACP has made serious efforts over the last five years to persuade the state to develop a coherent security policy, as well as forging its own. It was evidently not possible to protect the whole length of a 490-mile pipeline. It only takes two or three people to blow it up. In addition, when companies are asked to pay the armed groups, they need a strategy and a framework with which to respond.[64] The ACP has been trying to develop such a framework, to offer a coherent and shared ethical approach that is agreed across the industry, including foreign companies, Ecopetrol, oil workers and contractors. Ecopetrol has developed its own parallel discussion, but worked closely with the ACP.

The ACP has promoted national forums, and the establishment of regional Mesas de Trabajo (Work Tables) which bring together the different companies exploring and producing in particular regions and Ecopetrol.[65] In the course of the 1990s, but particularly in the years 1999–2002, they were established with varying levels of permanence.[66] Companies have responded as the situation has grown increasingly serious for both the petroleum sector and energy sector as a whole.

By 2001, in its first forum in Paipa, the sector was recognising that it faced three serious threats from armed groups: to the security of its employees and contract workers, to its physical infrastructure and to its profitability. The armed groups saw the industry as an opportunity for extortion, pressure and the expression of political demands. The industry considered itself to be in the middle of the confrontation between the guerrillas and self-defence groups for control of wealth production in the regions (oil, coca, opium, electricity generation, ranching, mining and industry), control of strategic corridors, with pressure put on the government to agree to specific demands by means such as the destruction of electricity pylons and local armed strikes. Companies faced increasing costs related to the security of infrastructure and people, repairs, transport, prevention and legal services. Labour relations had deteriorated, project implementation had been delayed and the economic competitiveness of the sector was deemed to be at risk.

The idea of regional committees emerged first in the Central and Alto Magdalena in 1991. Hocol was a leading player in the process in this region. This company, which was owned by Shell until 1992, is Colombian registered but has shareholders from Saudi Arabia and elsewhere. Shell's withdrawal forced the company to face up to its environment in a new way as before 1992, there was a feeling that Hocol merely implemented a schema which had been developed overseas.[67] The policy it adopted in the 1990s, and the experience of BP that is discussed below, reinforce the argument that when Colombian professionals are involved in the policy development process, they have both more knowledge and more at stake in 'getting it right'.

Hocol had a long history of some 40 years of operating in FARC-controlled territory in Huila. Local people had been incorporated into the business from early on, and the company thus had a fairly strong acceptance in the region before conflict escalated. In 1991, during the discussion about its new constitution, the company began to accept the idea of business ethics; at the same time, it recognised the need for a state of law in Colombia and its own obligations to support that. Hocol's outreach to the community had emphasised leadership training, which had assisted political formation in the community and enabled the local people to resist manipulation of party political bosses by the FARC. A reasonable co-existence had been forged, in which the autonomous civilian space appears to have maintained more integrity than is the norm in Colombia.

The situation began to deteriorate when the FARC got involved in the drugs industry and when its members began to appear in uniform and evolve into an army rather than a group of armed peasants. The company had to develop a policy towards extortion and other threats. When the company suffered its first armed attack in 1992, it was easily able to resist it and the local people themselves marched against the increase in violence. By 1998, however, the situation had evidently worsened, and the company was attacked in 1999 and again in 2001, when 100 armed men broke into one of the most important installations. Although the FARC dominated the territory, by this time the paramilitaries were regularly invading, and common crime and violence were mounting amidst rising unemployment and population displacement.

In the meantime, the company had begun to shift its social outreach. It began to develop a programme with its contract workers and to involve the community as a stakeholder in strategies to deal with the dynamics of militarisation. It did not wish to work with the army or the police, and as a small company it could not afford a costly arrangement with the state security forces anyway. It did seek more help from the state. In the absence of such help, it has sometimes taken the decision to wait rather than go into production, a decision recently taken in regard to an exploration bloc in Caqueta, in the heartland of FARC territory. The company does not have a security department, but analyses scenarios. It has developed a *cultura de auto cuidado*, or a culture of self-awareness and protection, amongst its employees, to encourage sensitivity to the security situation and anticipation of dangers, such as that of kidnapping. It has identified some critical principles: a non-paternalistic approach, working with the community, not substituting for the state, working for sustainability, and a tripartite strategy between state, community and company (ACP 2001). The company has spent a year preparing to operationalise a new bloc in Casanare, which has involved an almost anthropological approach of 'getting to know how Casanare thinks'.[68]

These ideas have fed into the evolving approach of the ACP. The tripartite strategy is different from the 'social works' approach of the past, in which the company built what it thought the community wanted, such as a school. It might then find that the state would not or could not provide teachers. The new framework of *gestión social*, or social management, aims to involve the community as well as other local actors in all stages of the process of defining local needs. This framework should not, argues the ACP, be a tool for improving security. It should be a genuine effort to promote peaceful co-existence in cooperation with all the communities in the area of oil exploration or production.

Nevertheless, the success of the strategy, argues the ACP, still depends on the state. The petroleum sector cannot divorce itself from national processes, and the work of regional committees and Ecopetrol is heavily dependent on the evolution of the war and the peace process. An Arab company that debated between strategies based on *gestión social* only, the army and police only, or both, opted for the first. Sixteen of its employees were subsequently kidnapped, and it has since sought to involve the departmental governor in a protection strategy.

As kidnappings, attacks, bombs and dynamiting have increased, the issue of physical protection alongside the community outreach and partnership building strategy remains critical for the industry. Without the rule of law, effectively administered by state institutions, the industry remains very vulnerable. It has urgently sought action from the government, to support beleaguered institutions operating in the midst of the conflict and to provide the objective conditions for security. Each oil-producing region varies in the degree to which its local institutions function. Huila retains some institutional infrastructure while Arauca has lost much of this, and what remains has been severely affected by the loss of royalties due to pipeline damage. 'We can't replace the state, but the state must give protection,' argues Alejandro Martínez, Executive President of the ACP.[69] But without an appropriate response from the state, the oil industry feels it has to act on its own.

However, while the industry now has its ethical practices, regional committees working with Ecopetrol and its *gestión social* approach, it lacks a plan for security, which will depend on effective state institutions. The aspiration is that improved and genuine relationships with communities will to some extent defend the companies that work with them, but the risks remain high. The ACP is convinced, despite the risks, that the security of the oil well cannot be divorced from the security of the community as a whole. Oil wells cannot be protected through military means alone; a greater guarantee is that judges are able to do their work and that there are institutions to control corruption.

Efforts to persuade the national government to focus on this institutional effectiveness as a guarantor of security have led the oil industry association into a broader political role, despite the tensions that arise both with the foreign companies in its midst and from its own historic weakness as an association. This shift towards such advocacy of its interests suggests that business in Colombia is having to change its traditional assumptions that the state was there to provide the macro-economic stability and social order that would allow the private sector to get on with its tasks of accumulation. This led it to allow the political class to control the state apparatus through the clientelist practices that we have already explored. The evident weakening of the traditional political parties in Colombia has eroded that distancing mechanism for business interests. The business sector has had to become more proactive in proposals for overcoming the crisis, and to present its views on the future of Colombian society, just as the guerrillas and paramilitaries and other civilian associations do. Whether the association will be able to develop this engagement further is uncertain. It was not consulted about the issue of US protection of the pipeline, and recognises the danger of the United States being seen to come into Colombia to protect its own, making it more legitimate to attack the oil industry as a whole. The strengthening of the armed capacity of the state with US assistance, and the pursuit of a military solution to Colombia's war, also entail the danger that the state will confuse and weaken the other agenda of restoring legitimacy and effectiveness to Colombia's institutions, the agenda that the ACP at least identifies as the priority need for the country and for the oil sector in particular.

For the ACP, security for the industry has come to mean more than its defence. A proactive, sincere and ethical engagement with the world outside the perimeter fence has been seen as a vital component of operating in a climate of violence. It is unclear how well this nuanced and sensible strategy for the longer-term vision of a democratic and equitable Colombia will survive if the United States and the Colombian government succeed in strengthening the military responses of the state without simultaneously strengthening the civilian ones. The final section of this chapter looks at how BP has dealt with this dilemma in the context of Casanare.

BRITISH PETROLEUM IN CASANARE: FROM 'SPLENDID ISOLATION' TO STRATEGIC PARTNERSHIP

By the mid 1990s, BP was forced to recognise that however unjust it felt the accusations against its role in Casanare to be, as a huge and power-ful multinational in a poor and violent region it would be held respon-sible for much of what happened there. To its credit, it has had a serious rethink of its entire strategy and has acknowledged mistakes. The Chief Executive, John Browne concluded in his 1998 Elliott Lecture at St Anthony's College, Oxford:

> We've been accused in the last couple of years of being associ-ated with serious human rights and environmental problems in Colombia. We've taken these allegations very seriously and gone through a very thorough process of investigation, inter-nal and external. Having been through that process I'm convinced we were not guilty of the sort of wilful misconduct of which we've been accused. We made mistakes, but I don't believe they were deliberate and we've learned from them. One of the things we've learned is that we can't stand aside from the problems of the communities in which we work. We can't try to operate in splendid isolation and cut ourselves off from local realities behind a security fence.[70]

The Inter-Agency Group of Oxfam, Christian Aid, CIIR and CAFOD, which also investigated the events surrounding the allegations against BP in 1998, did not find evidence of 'wilful misconduct'. However, it concluded that BP had allowed its security concerns to dominate its understanding of the dynamics of the region:

> [It] chose not to know what is happening in Casanare and listened to apparently 'natural allies' such as the armed forces and political élites. Reluctance to acknowledge that their own security personnel might have been too close to the armed forces or that intelligence operations amongst civilians to protect a pipeline might result in extra-judicial killings, have exposed BP to charges of complicity in abuses.

> (Unpublished report of a field visit to Casenare by the Inter-Agency Group 1998:61)

BP may also have been ill-advised by the British Foreign Office, which until the latter part of the 1990s did not acknowledge the importance of army and paramilitary violence in Colombia. As the *Financial Times* wrote: 'The oil company sees the guerrillas behind many protests; while local people see BP protected by fortresses and behind armed guards and working with the army'.[71]

The company had never ignored its social responsibility in the region, but its policy had been based on a form of benevolent paternalism, under which it responded to social demands without any strategic vision, and tried to build good relationships with local politicians and professionals through invitations to London. An evaluation visit by a team of three people from the World Bank in 1998 reviewed how BP had factored social concerns into the development of its operations. It found that, as early as 1992, the company was helping communities to identify their development needs and priorities. Since 1993, it had a 'robust Community Affairs Policy dealing with interactions between the company and its stakeholders in Casanare' (Davy et al 1998:21). A community affairs budget of $29 million between 1993 and 1997 financed a wide range of social investment activities to meet community expectations and, at its peak in 1997, the company was employing some 32 people to deal with community affairs. BP and its partner oil companies had established a local NGO, Amanecer, to administer credit and other social programmes. Nevertheless, the evaluation recognised that 'not all the approaches in Casanare to develop a relationship of mutual benefit to the company and its stakeholders have been successful' (Ibid:29). The evaluating team particularly emphasised the importance of BP building 'effective partnerships between government, BPXC and civil society' (Ibid:30). Internally, BP went further than this evaluation. In a document on Corporate Affairs Management (BP 2002) it identified four important lessons:

- The company cannot work in isolation from the rest of the region and offer direct investment only in the areas of operation.
- The department's long-term sustainable development can only be achieved by effective planning and better-trained leaders both in the community and the local governments.
- As a member of the community, BP cannot extricate itself from the conflict that affects everyone in Casanare. In sum, BP's security concerns go hand in hand with those of the community.
- Ecopetrol as the state partner of the operation has a role to play. BP should embrace that interest

By 1998, BP was downsizing its community affairs staff in posts within Casanare and devolving responsibility for community affairs to operations managers so that it became central to their concerns. The World Bank evaluation team warned about the need to maintain a team capable of communicating with local people and partners. BP did in fact appoint a particularly strong Bogota and Casanare team to take forward their new approach to the department. A notable feature of this team is that, as well as individuals with particular knowledge and experience in Casanare, it includes people with considerable prior experience of working with the PNR rehabilitation programme for conflict zones introduced by President Barco in the late 1980s. This Colombian team has a deep knowledge of the country and a strategic vision which reflects their understanding that they are citizens of Colombia, with responsibility to their country as well as the multinational they work for. 'We are talking about our children's patrimony', as BP's Manager for Corporate Affairs expressed it.[72]

This team presents its strategy in terms of four levels of activity. The first is the establishment of a baseline of reliable and up-to-date data. It commissioned a study by the Colombian think tank Fedesarrollo, on the evolution of the social and economic development of Casanare, which was published in 2002. The second is the creation and implementation of strategic partnerships; the third is managing the conflict; and the fourth, preparing for the future. The latter refers to exploration in Niscota, which will affect the municipality of Nunchia in Casanare, an even poorer municipality than Aguazul and Tauramena when oil was discovered, as well as Paya in Boyaca. BP is making a serious effort not to repeat its errors with Cusiana-Cupiagua, and if oil is discovered in Nunchia it will be the test for its new approach to working in conflict.[73] These four levels reflect also a statement of longer-term commitment by BP to Casanare, and its recognition that it must play a role in the future of the region from which it has profited through the extraction of oil. Rather than extract the oil and abandon the region, BP has expressed its commitment to work with the state, community/civil society and the private sector to ensure that oil revenues are used for the development of the region and that it prepares responses to the reduction in those revenues:

> BP's future is inextricably linked to Casanare's. How the region manages the challenges of reduced revenues within a conflict zone in the coming years will impact on oil development, present and future. Given this scenario, it would not seem wise, both from a business and social perspective, to sit back and watch as the neighbourhood deteriorates.
>
> (BP Corporate Affairs Management 2002:10)

The building of strategic partnerships has been one of the key means by which BP has sought to become a key player amongst many others in the region. The oil industry should, in this conception, collaborate with others in building towards shared goals, rather than act as a 'cow to be milked' as it is often seen. That attitude towards the oil industry has diverted attention and interest in state building both locally and nationally. BP's strategic vision has led it to promote what is known as the Grupo Gestor, a development task force involving key institutional actors in the region. The group meets to construct a consensus around a participative and sustainable development plan for Casanare and the recovery of democratic governance.[74] To achieve this goal, BP is now working with some of the professionals referred to above, those that remain committed in some form to an integral human development approach and occupy important positions in local governmental and private sector institutions. It seeks to build a coalition of local leaders who could foster social consensus and a regional cultural identity, and comprehend the multiple challenges at the economic, institutional, environmental, political and social levels. In concrete terms, the Grupo Gestor began at the end of 2001 to discuss how a regional development plan, or *plan de ordenamiento territorial*, might be the focus for strategic thinking and cooperation between state, private sector and community, with an emphasis on enhancing the transparency and efficiency of public investment.

At the same time, BP is working to strengthen the capacity within society to monitor institutions and to develop new leadership at other levels of society. It has supported a school for leadership, worked with women from Casanare through productive projects, women's rights and political participation, and with youth through music and theatre projects. It has placed particular emphasis on the strengthening of the judicial system, and has promoted the Justices of Peace programme in Nunchia, Yopal, Aguazul and Tauramena; this programme is working to develop legitimate ways for resolving daily conflicts which would take months in the formal legal arena. In the same spirit of improving relationships with local communities in oil-producing areas, it has promoted a Neighbourhood for Development programme. BP continues to fund specific productive, health and infrastructural projects, but it now has a strategic programme rather than projects that respond to particular demands of the most vociferous communities and individuals.

In the process, there is evidence of some shift in the meaning of security, although the 16th Brigade still defends BP's infrastructure. Following criticism after the events of the mid 1990s, the company has made explicit its concern with human rights protection, and promoted training of the armed forces in International Humanitarian Law under the 1998 agreement between Ecopetrol and the Ministry of Defence for the protection of oil installations. It has taken the auditing of this agreement much more seriously and committed itself to greater transparency. Nevertheless, although accusations of human rights abuse against the army have declined, most believe that there is still tolerance of, if not active collaboration with, the paramilitaries.

Events since the fieldwork for this chapter were completed suggest that the security dynamics around oil exploration areas in conflict zones remain highly problematic. Mathew Gitsham (2003) describes the way BP opted to work with the army to create a 'military ring' around the village of Morcote, the chief beneficiary of any potential royalties from the Niscota exploration. This was to protect the community from incursions from any armed groups. However, his interviews with Ecopetrol revealed that there were neighbouring municipalities, such as Pisba Paya and Labranzagrande, which also hoped to benefit from royalties in Boyacá. Paramilitary groups have targeted these munici-palities, which are outside the military ring, in an effort to gain a foothold in the area. BP could not persuade the Colombian government to extend the military-ring model, which is very expensive.

BP has recognised that reliance on the protection of armed men is not enough. It has begun to identify its own security with that of the security of civilians in Casanare. It has made this clear in statements, such as 'violence against the community is a threat for everyone' (BP Corporate Affairs Management 2002:7), a notable change from the 1990s when its prime concern was defence of the oil industry against guerrilla attack. More than this, it has publicly condemned violent actions, joining with others in Casanare and identifying itself as a co-citizen in this respect. This represents significant a change from the past, particularly given the escalation in the conflict and that fact that BP personnel are often shot at when travelling in helicopters, contract workers have been kidnapped and executed, and it is impossible for them to safely have a cup of coffee in Yopal without some protection on hand.[75]

However, BP's new approach is not without its problems and contradictions. It is too early to judge whether the company can effec-tively become a partner in the development process of Casanare; other members of the partnership have been severely weakened by the violence of the previous decade, while BP is still seen as a very power-ful actor. This imbalance has created tensions in the idea of 'partner-ship'. The company has tried to prevent itself being sucked into a state-like role by building relationships where possible with state insti-tutions, such as the Departamento de Planeación, or National Planning Department, and ensuring that it works closely with the state oil company, Ecopetrol, in the region. But Ecopetrol still sees itself as the junior partner in many respects. Its perception is that the power of the multinational to define an agenda in the region is much greater than its own and gives the multinational a role which should properly be that of the state company.[76] A similar sense that BP promotes an agenda that should by right be taken forward by local actors also weakens the rela-tionship BP is attempting to build with the local professional class. In the context of Casanare, many find it hard to see how the strategic and participatory departmental planning process that BP is promoting can be realised in practice while people still do not share a common vision of Casanare and violent armed groups are intent on fighting over the spoils the department has to offer.

At the level of communities BP found it difficult to overcome the mistrust generated from past mistakes, although an opinion poll it commissioned in April 2001 suggested that it was now beginning to do so (cited in BP Corporate Affairs Management 2002:3). It is still heavily criticised by environmental groups and by communities who expect employment opportunities to decline. Associations of unemployed workers are emerging in some communities, while some of the women who led the struggles against BP and then learnt to negotiate with the company have lost positions in the Juntas de Acción Comunal to a new leadership of individuals who aim to defend particular interests. The levels of fear are such that many no longer want to stand for president of the juntas. A community leader from a rural community of Aguazul explained how much had been gained from the negotiations with BP, but she now recognises that some young members of the community became lazy waiting for their turn to get their labour contracts. She felt that the community had not shared its bonanza enough with other municipalities.[77]

Violence and the climate of terror have torn apart the weak social fabric of Casanare and made BP's initiatives extremely difficult to implement. The company remains vulnerable to those wishing to damage its reputation, and it is difficult to distinguish genuine grievances from the opportunistic and malicious. However, it is also clear that BP has played a very important role in opening up space for those who are interested in building a more peaceful and equitable Casanare. Most people will also recognise that while there is some resentment towards the powerful multinational, its power has begun to be used also to open up opportunities for debate about the problems of the department that would otherwise have been difficult to set in motion.

BP has taken a risk by coming out from behind the perimeter fence. Some would argue that it has had no choice. International monitoring has forced it to look at its role differently. The weakness of the national government has left it no choice but to build its own agendas for the department in cooperation with other actors. Ultimately it is defending its commercial interests in a more appropriate way. However it is infinitely preferable that, in pursuing its commercial interests, a multinational should assume some responsibility for the territory it profits from. It is a marked advance from backing corrupt and repressive regimes as the oil industry once did. It is also an advance from 'choosing not to ask questions' as BP did in its first period of engagement with Casanare.

The danger is that the strategy will not produce quick results. It is an approach that involves patient and time-consuming daily contact with a large number of individuals and groups. It requires sensitivity to the conditions in which most people struggle to survive, and an ability to distinguish genuine from opportunistic collaboration. It depends on the local people gaining greater confidence, overcoming fear and mutual distrust in order to rebuild the social fabric and take back the power appropriated by the armed groups. It involves humility on the part of BP, and recognition that the future of Casanare will depend not on its vision but on the emergence of a new civil order, based on locally determined social and political processes.

In the meantime the pursuit of military solutions by the national government, supported by the United States, might offer another option to this painstaking work begun in Casanare. It can only be hoped that the vision of oil company security based on stronger and more effective institutions and democratic participation and part-nerships will be realised before the temptation to pursue a military and authoritarian path overcomes it. A military solution to the prob-lems of Colombia has been the road taken by President Alvaro Uribe since 2002, with considerable backing from the UK as well as US governments, alongside efforts to strengthen Colombian institutions. A process of negotiations with paramilitary groups was initiated in 2003 but, significantly, this has been resisted by the paramilitaries of Casanare. In April 2004 Uribe went to Casanare for a security coun-cil meeting in Yopal provoked, it seems, by the failure of the para-militaries of Casanare to comply with the paramilitary ceasefire as well as by formal complaints that they were extorting money and jobs from Casanare's municipal authorities. He met with the Gover-nor, the 17 mayors and the Defensor of Casanare. *El Tiempo* reported that:

> it is the first time that there has been a denunciation concern-ing the pressure by paramilitaries on mayors and local author-ities in order to obtain jobs and participation in municipal budgets, a practice common amongst the guerrillas, which even forced the government to freeze royalties to Arauca last year and to establish a rigorous monitoring of public finances in that department.[78]

This chapter has documented the long history of paramilitarisation of Casanare, and the collusion of local landowners and the armed forces of the state in that process. It has shown that the paramilitaries have been systematically eroding civil political processes in Casanare for many years. The violence and extortion of other armed groups, notably the left-wing guerrilla movements, has also been discussed, although by the beginning of the new millennium their influence was much weakened, at least in Casanare. The unwillingness of the paramilitaries to negotiate with the state, the ongoing human rights abuses (115 persons were selectively killed in Yopal between January and March 2004) and the fear which grips the population is the outcome of accumulated policy failure at best and collusion at worst by the national state of Colombia. [79] The impact of this failure/collusion is felt most intensely by the civilian population. In April 2004, Amnesty International published its report on the human rights situation in Arauca, which since the history discussed at the beginning of this chapter has deteriorated into one of the worst situations of violence in a violence-torn country.[80]

When the focus is only on the armed actors, the national policy context is not factored in and the changes demanded of the Colombian state by human rights organisations working in Colombia for nearly two decades are ignored. In contrast BP-Amoco, a major multinational oil corporation, has begun to recognise the complex nature of the conflict in Casanare and the complex solutions it requires. It has moved away from a simplistic attribution of all the region's problems to the guerrillas of the left, while not underestimating the problem that they also represent. It has recognised the significance of supporting local civilians willing to work against corruption and for the rule of law. Will the Colombian state do the same?

CONCLUSION

This case study of Casanare illustrates the dilemmas that confront multinational oil companies when they enter a region without full knowledge and understanding of the socio-political environmental context. They can contribute unwittingly to the escalation of the predatory dynamics already in play as a result of prior policy failure. In the course of the 1990s, oil companies operating in Colombia were forced to acknowledge the importance of these socio-political environmental factors and seek options for manoeuvre in the midst of deepening violence. British Petroleum in Casanare was one of the first to recognise that it needed to recognise early mistakes and look 'beyond the perimeter fence'.

The case of BP-Amoco in Casanare illustrates the shift that has begun to take place, albeit unevenly, in multinational oil company thinking and behaviour. It illustrates how one multinational company is confronting and adapting to the instability and dangers of extraction in the post-Cold War world. This in turn raises issues around local–national and state–global economic dynamics. In regions once known as the Third World, the state and nation-building project was still incomplete at the time when economic forces were liberated from the direction of the state in both ideological and real policy terms. The dominant economic philosophy stressed the positive contribution to national and global economic growth that is made when markets allocate resources freely and the private sector pursues its interests without interference. Subsequent thinking has brought the state back into the picture for governance purposes, but the task of 'good governance' has proved very elusive in contexts where the normative basis for co-existence in a territory is weakly developed – that is, there is no positive value invested in building the conditions for living together.

The failure of the national and local state in Colombia to build, promote and defend a basis for co-existence allowed the oil resources of first Arauca and then Casanare to interact with the socio-political environment in a way that contributed to decomposition rather than articulation of social forces around a governance project. Ineffective and undemocratic local, national and international regulatory institutions do not foster legal forms of economic accumulation and much less so in situations of war.[81] The lack of a central redistributive authority, acting in a recognisable sense in terms of the 'common good' of the society, has had a profoundly negative impact on conflict in the global South.[82] In Casanare it enabled oil to contribute to the multi-polar militarisation of the territory rather than its integration around a development project for the good of everyone.

In situations like these, multinational companies in the extractive sector, where location is determined not by the market but by the terrain and its mineral deposits, have to adapt or face the consequences. Unwilling to get dragged into violent and politically complex environments, many have chosen the easier route of appeasement through dollars with few questions asked. Oil multinationals have often relied on this approach and a local militarised state to provide stability, no matter what the cost to human rights. International monitoring has begun to make this a very costly path in terms of public relations and image, while national armies, where they exist, have proved less and less effective in the face of self-financing armed groups.[83] The more difficult route has been to explore the world 'beyond the perimeter fence' in a serious way and to develop policies that will involve engagement in a dangerous environment. The danger is of slipping by default into 'state-like roles'.[84] The question remains whether a multinational oil company, accountable not to the citizens of the country of operation but to overseas shareholders, and for its economic not its political performance, should or can take this path. Still less clear is whether it is the only path available and what it can deliver in terms of a multinational's goals and objectives. The BP corporate responsibility programme in Casanare, Colombia, is a systematic and strategic approach to extracting oil in the midst of violent conflict, and one of the most innovative available. It enables us to explore some of these questions.

This chapter has argued that a detailed case study of the interactions between oil and its socio-political environment can reveal much more about the relationship between oil and armed conflict than a focus on armed actors alone. With its relatively sophisticated institutional development and highly educated policy makers, Colombia illustrates that policy failure – or even policy collusion at the national level – can play a highly significant role in the escalation of violence around a valuable natural resource. The corollary is that oil and armed conflict are contingent variables. Each context can reveal important moments when policy choices might have averted the escalation of armed conflict to the point where it is almost impossible to reverse and in which oil provides the economic opportunity for the prolongation and intensification of that conflict.

Such a case study is also important for what it reveals about the learning capacity of multinational oil corporations. Increasingly sensitive to the threat of reputation loss, seriously affected by the incapacity of national and local governments to provide solutions to situations of complex conflict in the zones in which they are working, they are wary about taking on state-like roles but are increasingly having to confront their responsibilities as corporations; the corporations are having to learn fast. BP responded to the adverse international media attention of 1996–98 and to its mistakes on the ground, and has developed a nuanced, ethical as well as commercial approach to the oil-producing region of Colombia where it has worked since the end of the 1980s. BP is not the only oil company to do this. In Colombia, Hocol was already developing a new approach to security rooted in the community in the early 1990s; the Association of Oil Producers of Colombia has also actively sought to develop new approaches. But BP Amoco, with size and resources on its side, has been able to drive forward its approach so that today it claims to be a 'new model of corporate social responsibility, where private corporations work in voluntary partnership with civil society organisations and government authorities in a joint effort to manage social issues and to contribute to sustainable development' (BP 2003).

Nevertheless it is always dangerous to get too attached to models in complex and evolving social situations. This chapter is not putting forward the BP example as a 'model'. Rather it is drawing attention to the innovative learning process in the corporation, to the commitment of its Colombian team on the ground in Casanare, and to its willingness to risk looking 'beyond the perimeter fence'. The success of its new strategy remains fraught with daily problems and challenges and is also contingent. Among the contingencies is the willingness of the Colombian state to take seriously its responsibilities to the broader citizenry of its country, rather than the defence of an élite. It is likely that the paramilitaries of Casanare will seek one day to legitimise wealth accumulated through violence and extortion in order to join that élite.

Ethical corporate social responsibility requires an ethical, legitimate and law promoting national and local state to be truly effective.

NOTES

1. The case study is based on three field visits to Casanare. The first, in 1997, was by invitation of the UK's Inter-Agency Group involved in a dialogue with BP. I was a 'participant observer' in this dialogue process and in a workshop held in Aguazul in 1998 with all the actors in the region to discuss the impact of oil. I also subsequently and alongside the Inter-Agency Group brought findings from the field visit in Casanare to the attention of BP personnel in Colombia and London. For the second visit, in 2001, I was offered support by BP. I stayed in the BP base for security reasons but I organised my own programme and members of the company were not present when I interviewed people. During the third visit, in 2002, I stayed independently in Yopal. In the course of these three visits I sought to view the problem from several angles. It was not possible for me to travel into rural communities, but I met many people from these communities in Yopal. I have conducted over 80 individual interviews, and several group interviews. I am indebted to the help and support of many people in Casanare and Bogota for making this field research possible.
2. The emphasis in this chapter is on multinationals, particularly BP-Amoco, but Ecopetrol and the Colombian Oil Producers Association have also played a significant role in this shift of thinking.
3. Indra de Soysa (2001) argued for the importance of disentangling 'the complex relationship between the "honey pot" effect, Dutch disease, dysfunctional politics and conflict'.
4. A. Peñate, 'Arauca: Politics and Oil in a Colombian Province', unpublished M.Phil thesis, University of Oxford, St Anthony's College, 1991, p. 43. Its territory is 23,818 square kilometres, roughly the size of Wales
5. The inter-institutional commission that visited Arauca and Casanare to report on the human rights situation in 1995 commented: 'The new source of economic benefits and development of the departments' petroleum, has not yet brought beneficial results for the community. The most palpable case is that of Arauca, where the royalties for oil extraction and for the section of the Caño Limón–Coveñas pipeline passing through the department have been spent in public works which are not priorities for the communities. In some municipalities expensive and unnecessary sports centres have been built, and cycle tracks that have no relevance to the activity of the region, to mention some examples. But the investment in the improvement of infrastructure (communication routes) and in basic public services has been minimal, above all if one takes into account the atmosphere of administrative corruption that has traditionally surrounded the execution of public expenditure in the said departments' (see Procuraduria General de la Nacion, 1995).
6. Cusiana has reserves of around 1.5 billion barrels, and Cupiagua around 500,000 million. The smaller Volcanera-Florena Pauta bloc near to El Morro was found to be commercially viable at the end of 1997. The production facility of a further bloc in Niscota, near the municipality of Nunchia was under construction by 2002. These are the confirmed areas of interest to BP. Other companies are exploring a total of around 30 wells in the *piedemonte* as of

1999, and Hocol in a consortium of companies had signed an association contract to develop another bloc.

7. Prior to these discoveries, Casanare had been producing oil since 1983 in small but not insignificant quantities that represented about 4.3 per cent of national output. This oil was mostly located in the *llanos*, with 39 per cent in the municipality of Trinidad.

8. The human rights situation in Arauca has been well documented. See, for example, Amnesty International's report on Arauca, 'Laboratory of War', April 2004.

9. The Association of which BP was the operating company was required under a 1991 regulation (phased out by 2000) called the 'Special contribution for the Reestablishment of Public Order', known as the War Tax, to pay the Colombian Treasury on a per barrel basis. It also had an arrangement with the police, which began in 1992, to guard every BP rig. The police bore the brunt of guerrilla attacks on the oil installations. The Association also had a security agreement with the armed forces through the Ministry of Defence. This was formalised in 1995, when a three-year agreement was signed worth $54 million in cash and kind payments to the army (J. Pearce, Development, Conflict and Corporate Responsibility: The Case of Casanare, Colombia, unpublished confidential report, 1998).

10. The history of some of these groups goes back to the 1980s, when the drugs cartels allied with ranchers, businessmen and sectors of the armed forces and police to create death squads and private armies to eliminate guerrillas and social undesirables.

11. Between 1995 and 1997 the Autodefensas de Cordoba y Uraba (Cordoba and Urabá Self-Defence Groups) under Carlos Castaño led the process of build- ing a united movement which, on 18 April 1997, became the Autodefensas Unidas de Colombia (AUC).

12. The Colombian army has a long history of human rights abuse. It was deemed responsible in 1993 for 54 per cent of political killings in Colombia according to the US State department annual report on human rights in Colombia. Over the next few years its record apparently improved and by the mid 1990s only 4 per cent of killings were attributed to it and 60 per cent to paramilitary groups. Human Rights Watch and other organisations have traced the evidence of the way the army assisted operations of the paramilitary groups by, for instance, allowing them through army blockades (see Human Rights Watch 1996). Evidence of army–paramilitary collaboration was clear in Casanare in my field trip in 1998, and is recorded in my unpublished report, 'Development, Conflict and Corporate Responsibility: The Case of Casanare, Colombia'. The few who monitor the human rights situation in Casanare today claim that the violations continue.

13. Calculations of the distribution of the population in these zones differ widely from each other. The Departamento Administrativo Nacional de Estadística (DANE) and Instituto Geográfico Agustín Codazzi, Bogota, esti- mated (1999) that 40 per cent of the population live in the low-lying plains which cover 82 per cent of the territory, and 60 per cent in the rest.

14. Interview with historian Ricardo Villamarin, 1 May 2002.

15. A comment by Santiago Franco, advisor to the Governor of Casanare, in a meeting of BP's Group Gestor, 30 April 2002.

16. Pérez Angel suggests that the Indian population declined from 89,048 in 1825, to 27,700 in 1897 (1997:198). Jane Rausch cites other sources which

calculate the Indian population of 1835 at 6625, falling to 3000 in 1914, suggesting that statistics should be treated with caution. There does seem to be agreement that violent conflict between Indians, cattle ranchers and peasant settlers from Boyaca characterised this region after independence. By the late 1990s there were estimated to be only 4786 Indians in Casanare living in ten reservations (see Departamento Adminstrativo de Planeación 1998).

17. In 2002, Recetor remained in the hands of the ELN and Chameza was controlled by the FARC. 'The guerrillas control everything in the town,' a priest who worked there for four years told me, 'down to the peasant's personal life'. Interview, 28 April 2002.18. Interview Red de Solidaridad, Yopal, 4 April 2002.

19. The presence of oil in Casanare pre-dated the large-scale find of Cusiana and Cupiagua.

20. A study by Fedesarollo (2002) of the impact of oil on the Casanare economy found that neither African palm oil production nor ranching had declined due to oil, although plantain, potatoes and yucca had suffered a decline since 1994. The two former activities are in the hands of the large landowners, and their survival suggests that these powerful families did not look entirely to oil for their future.

21. The 1997 report on human rights in Casanare and BP by the Defensoria del Pueblo (People's Advocate's Office) noted 30 complaints by BP of guerrilla attacks in 1996, one of which caused the death of an engineer working for the Distral company. Other attacks included shooting at helicopters and during seismic tests. A senior security advisor for BP's operations in Casanare estimated in 1998 that there were only about 200 guerrillas targeting the BP oil installations (Interview, June 1998). By contrast the army presence in Casanare at the time was around 3000 troops. Sophisticated electronic surveillance equipment strengthened BP's security enormously, enabling guerrilla movements around the BP installations to be rapidly detected.

22. The fact that the ELN tried to intervene in these does not mean that they were not legitimate social protests in which people participated for reasons other than support for the ELN tactical vision. Confusing all social protest with guerrilla activities is a mistake often made by the Colombian armed forces and paramilitary groups, and one which has led to the killing of many social activists.

23. In the elections of 2002, the FARC threatened to leave Casanare without electricity for four years if the people voted for Uribe Velez, the candidate favoured by the paramilitary, and clearly the front runner on my arrival in Yopal shortly before the elections in April 2002.

24. Violence in Colombia generates its own vocabulary. In Casanare, the vocabulary around cattle theft is very rich. There is even a word for those thieves who had the task of altering the brand on the cattle: *cachilapero*. The private guards of the cattle ranchers were the *camporolantes*.

25. The Public Prosecutor (Fiscalía) reported in January 1998 on the human rights situation while investigating allegations against BP. He stated 'Certainly in this department there has been a rapid expansion of paramilitary groups or private justice groups. Since 1994, in other investigations in places other than Yopal, that are located on the main roads across the department, this Procurator General noticed some of these illegal groups. They are sustained by ranchers and landowners, who, considering the inability of the state both politically and militarily to respond to the guerrilla presence, find

in these unchecked associations a way to defend their interests. It is no secret that the self-styled "Self-Defence Groups of Cordoba and Urabá" have come into the region bringing with them all the barbarity and inhumanity of a conflict which has turned into a series of massacres and selective assassinations, using techniques that, far from being a normal armed response to a subversive group, have taken an insane and cowardly form, such as cutting off limbs of defenceless citizens' (Fiscalia 1998:30, my translation).

26. There were eleven confrontations in 2000; in April these took place between the AUC and the 28th Front of the FARC in Paz de Ariporo, resulting in the death of 30 AUC members and 18 guerrillas (Defensoria del Pueblo 2001). Sometimes the FARC operates alongside the ELN, on other occasions the two groups are in mortal conflict with each other.

27. Contradictory information exists on the paramilitaries. Most people talk of two groups, although the police commander, Teniente Coronel Alvarez Flores, suggested there are three. He identified the third as the Autodefensas Campesinas del Casanare, which dominates the *llanos* and belongs to the Bloque Oriental which includes Boyaca, Casanare, Cundinamarca and Meta (interview, 24 August 2001). The report of the Defensoria for the year 2000 suggests that in October that year the Frente Heroes de San Fernando, Bloque Centauros, made an appearance in Nunchía, Pore and Paz de Aripora, as did a mobile company covering the region of Boyaca, Casanare, Cundinamarca and Meta. It is not surprising that the police chief acknowledged that he simply lacked the resources to deal with the paramilitaries. 'I have no people to arrest HK,' he acknowledged. 'HK' is a much feared member of the Autodefensas Campesinos del Sur, who is reported to have been accidentally arrested by the army and mysteriously allowed to escape.

28. It should be emphasised that, even in the midst of this situation, there were those trying to build a different strategy. For instance, in the wake of major workers' unrest on the African palm plantations, some local professionals in the municipalities sought to prevent the violent polarisation that had accompanied agro-industrial sectors elsewhere in Colombia. An NGO, the Fundacion para el Desarrollo de Upia, was set up in 1987 in order to build dialogue between the municipality, social groups and the private sector; it attempted to establish a regional development approach, but could not persuade the departmental governor. It has survived with great difficulty and is now participating in BP's efforts to build partnerships for development in the region. Interview with Ricardo Villamarin, 26 April 2002.

29. A number of self-defence groups took advantage of the 1994 law which authorised rural security cooperatives to support the state security forces in preventive, defensive and intelligence functions. The Autodefensas were given legal recognition which enabled them to organise and act more openly. The human rights abuses that were committed by the cooperatives later led to their disbandment.

30. These details are based on interviews with local people who must remain anonymous.

31. The paramilitaries have engaged in some audacious acts of recruitment, such as the kidnapping of 200 young men from Villanueva in 2000. They have also created a network of informers. In 2001, all 500 taxi drivers of Casanare were ordered to Villanueva and told they were expected to work with the paramilitaries. They carry out 'social cleansing operations'; for example, in August 2001 they threw a bomb into a brothel in Yopal. They are

responsible for human rights atrocities against anyone suspected of guerrilla sympathies or who comes from guerrilla-influenced territories. They carry out kidnappings and extortion of local oil contractors and businesses.

32. The data is not available to make the correlation proposed by Collier and Hoeffler about the positive relationship between low foregone earnings and conflict, as this would involve knowing how many young men of what age and what schooling level joined armed groups in this period. However, the proposition is plausible.

33. There were 14 murders in Yopal in 1988 and 79 in 1998; Aguazul had only 8 in 1988. See Galindo León and Jáuregui (1998).

34. These are figures from the Defensoria report (2001). Figures from Medicina Legal quoted in the Corporación Excelencia report of 2001 (page 19) are similar: a total of 917 murders between 1997 and 2000 – a threefold increase, which moved Casanare to fourth place in the list of departments in the country with the most homicides; the rate increased from 74 to 105 per 100,000 people between 1997 and 1998.

35. Interview with Red de Solidaridad, Yopal, 2 May 2002.

36. *Las Asociaciones* (May 1996) 'Casanare 2000: Una vision del futuro'.

37. Interview, August 2001

38. Given the evidence of the flow of internal displacement from rural area to municipal centres and Yopal itself, the impact on the conflict of this demographic shift should not be underestimated.

39. Such as 'The Bonanza of Cusiana Begins. Municipalities and Departments will Receive US$3,500 million in Eleven Years', *El Tiempo*, June 1993.

40. The 'salario petrolero' or oil wage, together with various perks, was worth around 13,000 Colombian pesos in 1997 compared with the average agricultural worker's wage of between 8000 and 9000 pesos (DANE/IGAC 1999:309).

41. During a workshop in Aguazul organised by Oxfam Colombia and the Colombian NGO Censat, in which I participated on 12 June 1998, it was clear that the population had very high expectations and did not understand that employment prospects would decline when Cusiana became operational.

42. Interview with Defensora del Pueblo, 26 April 2002.

43. Interview with Gustavo Zarate, author of the study, 8 June 1998.

44. Production of the two local agricultural crops, *platano* and *yuca* have indeed declined significantly since 1994 (Gaviria et al 2002).

45. The Colombian Peasants Association, or ANUC, was initially a government-sponsored organisation which was set up in 1970. Nationally it grew into one of the country's most radical social movements, within which all the guerrilla organisations tried to build influence.

46. The community came together initially to protest about a problem with a nearby oil well. BP responded and the community, led by Edgar Ortíz, decided to organise to press for improvements in the village infrastructure. In this period, BP responded in a rather ad hoc fashion to such demands, but it encouraged the peasants to maintain their Association and seek proper social investment from the municipality. In 1997, the leaders requested an interview with the Commander of the 16th Brigade, mediated by the Defensor del Pueblo. This meeting took place on 16 March, and the words of the community recorded by the Defensor articulate the dilemma facing independent efforts to organise in Casanare's poor communities: 'In the meeting, the people explained to Lieutenant Colonel Gersain Sánchez Portilla that the

municipal administration's only response to their request for social investment was in some meetings to brand them as guerrillas and in others as
paramilitaries. According to them, this situation made their lives even more
difficult as the area was already classified as "red". They identified themselves as peasants, members therefore of the civil population who were not
party to the armed conflict, but they feared the consequences of this stigma-
tization and the misunderstandings that it could generate.' The fate of Asoccocharte is emblematic of the militarisation of Casanare and the closure of
spaces for civil action. During local elections, the guerrillas moved into
Union Charte and burnt the ballot boxes. This confirmed paramilitary and
army suspicions that the village was working with the guerrillas. Around
June 1997, paramilitaries entered the village and killed the driver of the local
truck and owner of the local shop. In May 1998, the paramilitaries returned.
From evidence carefully collected afterwards by the Defensor, it appears that
they came in the night, turning off the main Agauzul–Yopal road at the Rio
Charte bridge, and arrived at dawn in the village of Union Charate. They
arrested Edgar Ortiz, a companion, a local female police inspector and a
mentally disturbed man who had fatally mistaken the paramilitaries for the
FARC. These people were taken away around 10.30 in the morning, when
mysteriously the army checkpoint normally placed at the Union Charte
bridge had been removed. The four were never seen again. Interview with
Defensor del Pueblo, Yopal, 12 June 1998.

47. While I cannot quantify this involvement, the statement is based on numerous interviews with community organisations. Many of the women's leaders have not stopped their activities, although a number have lost leadership
positions in the Juntas, but they now occupy other, relatively safer spaces for
social action such as the environmental movement. On 24 November 2001,
some 50 women took part in an unprecedented march to the main square in
Yopal to commemorate the International Day of Non-Violence Towards
Women, during which they received much verbal abuse and hostility from
the men in the town. Interview with women leaders, Yopal, 1 May 2002.

48. To the best of my ability I have interviewed at length most of the actors
involved in the complaints against BP and put their arguments to BP, and I
have studied all the reports which have investigated BP's role in Casanare.
There are still unanswered questions about the role of BP security staff in the
1994–96 period. However, there is no evidence to suggest that BP was
involved in the murder of Arrigui or the later murder in 1998 of Carlos
Vargas, the President of Corporinoquia, which, as far as I could ascertain,
was more likely to be linked to private family matters and threats from
armed groups.

Vargas was the brother-in-law of the governor, whose wife (his sister) had
been kidnapped and later released by the ELN. He was a respected environmental campaigner who was elected to the head of the environmental
watchdog for the Orinoquia region, Corporinoquia. As head of Corporinoquia, Vargas was involved in imposing fines on BP for infringements of environmental regulations, but there was no evidence of bad relationships
between the two. It is extremely unlikely that BP would be prepared to
collude with his assassination for punishing these infringements. The corporation had much more serious conflicts with other local leaders who have
remained alive. Nor is it likely, after what happened following Arrigui's
murder, that BP would court further bad publicity. However, the lack of an

effective judiciary makes BP vulnerable to many accusations which can never be fully investigated. Lawyers brought into this situation, lacking deep local knowledge of the complex, often mafia-like nature of the violence, may sincerely mistrust the multinational, but the most serious problem in the department is the generalised climate of impunity.

49. Interview with the Defensor, who had visited the barracks and seen Soler Gomez.

50. The environmental impact of oil is a huge source of ongoing conflict in Casanare, in which genuine environmental concerns have become enmeshed in opportunistic agendas against BP. Oil does cause environmental problems which are a source of great concern for communities. But monitoring the environmental impact of an oil company is a skilled and difficult task. A number of serious NGOs have emerged to do this work, but in very difficult circumstances. Many feel that the company does not take their complaints seriously; the company in turn believes the complaints are due to lack of information, and has promoted environmental training. BP has a very sophisticated environmental programme and a very serious investment in this area, but problems inevitably arise, and in the situation of Casanare these can create resentment and hostility towards the company. Interviews with CENSAT, Mata de Monte, Aguaviva, Rodolfo Puente and Mauricio Pozos, August 2001 and April 2002.

51. Interviews with Fanny Nuñez and other ACDAINSO leaders in 1998, 2001, 2002.

52. The report concluded (page 6) 'Oil companies that deploy security forces to protect their installations and personnel bear responsibility for the actions those forces undertake. In Arauca and Casanare, the army has dedicated entire brigades (the XVIIIth in Arauca and the XVIth in Casanare) to protect-ing oil production. The companies cannot ignore the human rights violations committed by those units; indeed the companies' dependence on the army and police for their survival gives them a tremendous moral responsibility. In both departments, the army units – albeit to different degrees – have been allegedly involved in extrajudicial executions which have not been resolved.'

53. The report failed to find evidence to support or refute the allegations against BP, leaving a margin of doubt amongst those who still felt BP had been culpable directly or indirectly, or had used its power to influence the Fiscalia. Further investigation of the role of DSC in providing illegal training in lethal weapons to the police took place. It also exonerated DSC but was not made public.

54. BP has a 15 per cent share, along with Total, Ecopetrol and two Canadian companies, in the Oleoducto Central S.A. (OCENSA) pipeline which was completed in 1997 and runs 800 kilometres to the coast. DSC was responsi-ble for the security of the pipeline and set up an OCENSA security depart-ment headed by Roger Brown. In October 1998, the *Guardian* revealed that Brown had been sacked for his dealings with an Israeli security company, Security Shadow.

55. The secretary of the present Governor was kidnapped in 2001 and has still not been released. It is rumoured that the paramilitaries are holding her hostage.

56. The decrease in Arauca's production that year and in 2001 due to the pipeline bombing explains the sudden drop and reinforces the argument

that the pipeline became a focus of strategic military activity and extortion of payments from pipeline repair companies, and these activities became more important than the revenues it could generate locally. Arauca plunged into a deep fiscal crisis as a result of the sudden fall in oil revenues on which it had become highly dependent.

57. Interview with Red de Mujeres, Yopal, 1 May 2002.

58. The Colombian peso fluctuated between 2,300 and 2,900 pesos to the US dollar between 2001 and 2005. Roads account for 21.7 per cent of expenditure from royalties in the department as whole, compared to 4.7 per cent for agriculture and production, and 10.5 per cent for servicing the debt.

59. The institutions include the Procuraduría General, the Defensoría del Pueblo, the Fiscalía de la Nación, and the Contraloría. My own findings echo the conclusions of the study by the Corporación Excelencia en la Justicia (2001).

60. One fiscal had been shot in front of state investigators and legal personnel in a school in Yopal in 1994.

61. Interview with Ricardo Villamarin, 1 May 2002.

62. Interview, 29 April 2002.

63. Interview with Santiago Franco, advisor to the governor, 1 May 2002.

64. An illustration of how this works is a story of an Ecopetrol manager in a village. He was approached by the guerrillas who demanded that he hand over his vehicle. The manager objected, as it belonged to the company. Knowing that he would have to comply or lose his life, he responded that he would give it to the guerrillas as they had arms but not because they had authority. While this is a minor example that ended with the loss of a vehicle, the form of words contained a moral argument that left the company with a sense of dignity.

65. The first national forum met in Paipa, 1 and 2 February 2001. This information is based on extended interviews with Alejandro Martinez, President of the ACP, on 17 August 2002.

66. In the *llanos* (Meta, Casanare and Boyacá), the Nororiente (Arauca and Norte de Santander), Magdalena Medio (Antioquia, Sur de Bolivar, Santander, Sur del Cesar), Centro y Alto Magdalena (Huila, Cundinamarca y Tolima), Sur-Occidente (Caquetá, Putumayo, Valle and Narino) and the north (Caribe).

67. Interview with Ramiro Santa, Government and Community Affairs Team Leader, 26 April 2002. I was unable to independently verify Hocol's history in Huila, although I have checked the claims in other interviews where possible.

68. Interview with Ramiro Santa, 1 May 2002.

69. Interview, 26 February 2002.

70. John Browne in 'International Relations: The New Agenda for Business', the 1998 Elliot Lecture, St Anthony's College, Oxford, 4 June 1998. An interview on 11 March 2004 by Oliver Balch with John O'Reilly, senior advisor to BP on security matters in Colombia in 1997, with whom this author had much contact during that year, also illustrates the impact of the international attention on BP and the discussions that emerged. O'Reilly states that his original position had been: 'As long as it wasn't BP itself committing the offences and we were obeying the laws of the country, then that's as far as our responsibility goes.' However, 'experiencing first hand what it is to do business where the rule of law is arbitrary and social infrastructure is almost non-existent' persuaded O'Reilly of his argument's shortcomings: 'We're the

intruder. We're going to change their [the local community's] lives more than any government will do. Therefore, although there's a responsibility on both sides, the responsibility on us, the company, is greater because we're the new ones in the equation.' O'Reilly went on to use the lessons from Colombia in a new role as senior vice president for external affairs of BP Indonesia. See also http://www.ethicalcorp.com/content_print.asp?Content!D=1768, last accessed December 2005.

71. Stephen Fidler, *Financial Times*, 8 October 1996.

72. Interview with Mauricio Jimenez and Alfonso Cuellar, 16 February 2001.

73. Interview with the mayor of Nunchia, 25 August 2001. He suggested that this strategy was bearing fruit. The mayor was a man with 25 years of experience in public office, an individual looking for support to maintain a commitment to the common good of his community and used to living in an area of ELN influence with increasing paramilitary incursions. He was studying the impact of oil on the other communities of Casanare, and was supportive of BP's new approach of lowering expectations about the potential impact of oil, developing a system of local peace judges to mediate conflicts and training and preparing the leaders and the contract workers who would service BP. He was expecting that his municipality would gain some 700 jobs, but was aware that these jobs would not last beyond the construction of the CPF. In 2004 it was announced, however, that the Nunchia well was dry; the impact of this on local expectations and local conflict dynamics remains to be seen.

74. Interviews with Maria Cecilia Lopez and Jorge Guzman, August 2001 and April 2002. Observation of meeting of Grupo Gestor, Yopal, 30 April 2002.

75. Both events took place while I was in Casanare in May 2002. A helicopter with 13 civilians was shot at but managed to land safely, and a contract worker for the company who had been kidnapped by the ELN was executed.

76. Interview with Pedro Rosas, Ecopetrol Casanare, May 2002.

77. Interview with community activists from Aguazul, 24 August 2002.

78. *El Tiempo*, 'Denuncian que paramilitaries exigen cuotas burocráticas a alcaldes de Casanare', 26 April 2004.

79. *Semana*, 3 May 2004 (cited in Zandvliet and Reyes 2004). This report states that there were over 70 homicides in Yopal in the month of January alone, mostly linked to killings between rival paramilitary groups fighting for territorial control.

The field visit by Zandviliet and Reyes found that 'fear seemed to be a non-issue until we asked why people are not able to hold the government more accountable, knowing the amount of royalties that flow to the government and its designated purposes. Unanimously, people said they fear being critical of the local authorities and the possibility of being targeted, allegedly by illegal armed groups' (2004:11).

80. "The reality of war in Colombia is stark, and the department of Arauca has been particularly hard hit by the armed conflict which has ravaged the country for four decades. As is tragically the norm in modern conflicts the world over, it is the civilian population that invariably bears the brunt of the repression and violence inflicted on it by the warring parties – the security forces and their paramilitary allies, and the armed opposition groups. This is the case in the oil-rich north-eastern department of Arauca where economic interests, especially those associated with the control of Arauca's substantial oil resources (and the attempt by the guerrillas to sabotage them and gain

capital from extortion of the oil industry), have fuelled the conflict for more than 20 years. The number of civilians killed in the department makes for chilling reading. Although the figures differ according to which source is consulted, estimates suggest that in the municipality of Tame alone, which has a population of only some 55,000, at least 175 people were murdered in 2003, compared to 144 in 2002 and 86 in 2001.

Rather than shielding civilians from hostilities, recent government measures, which form part of its 'democratic security' strategy, have exacerbated the human rights crisis in Arauca. The creation of a network of civilian informants, some of them paid, and of an army of 'peasant soldiers' required to collaborate with the security forces has put civilians in danger of attacks by the guerrillas. The approval in Congress of a law that grants judicial police powers to the armed forces is likely to facilitate the already existing practice of launching often spurious criminal investigations against human rights defenders and other civilians. These tactics are designed to tarnish human rights defenders and social activists by accusing them of guerrilla activity, exposing them to heightened risk of violent attack by paramilitaries, regardless of whether or not investigations uncover evidence of criminal wrongdoing. With the military 'policing' themselves, very few, if any, are likely to be investigated for human rights violations.

Under the government of President Álvaro Uribe, human rights and social activists continue to be killed, 'disappeared', arbitrarily detained, threatened and harassed. Moreover, while expressing an interest in maintaining dialogue with NGOs, in practice government, security forces and other state officials are frequently and increasingly treating human rights defenders and social activists as subversives, labelling them as such in public statements and targeting them during intelligence and counter-insurgency operations. This has exposed many of them, including those in Arauca, to threats and attacks by army-backed paramilitaries. On 8 September 2003, President Uribe attacked human rights NGOs describing some of them (without specifying which ones) as 'political manoeuvrers ultimately in the service of terrorism who cowardly hide behind the human rights banner'." (Amnesty International 2004).

81. This is in contradiction to some traditional assumptions that private sector interests, particularly those of foreign companies, might best be protected by authoritarian, even repressive, national regimes.

82. Eric Hobsbawm has suggested that the redistributive function of the modern state is its most indispensable function, even today when globalisation has questioned so much about the state: 'It is to this day the main mechanism for social transfers, that is to say for collecting an appropriate fraction of the economy's total income, usually in the form of public revenue, and redistributing it among the population according to some criterion of public interest, common welfare and social needs' (1996:276).

83. Campaigns by Global Witness and Transparency International have been particularly effective in this regard.

84. By 'state-like', I mean undertaking tasks of promoting: development; conflict resolution; local dialogue between private sector, voluntary associations and municipal authorities; and new approaches to security – in other words, functions that might be expected to be promoted by a central (democratically elected) authority.

BIBLIOGRAPHY

Amnesty International (2004) *Laboratory of War: Repression and Violence in Arauca, Colombia* (London: Amnesty International).
Asociación Colombiana del Petroleo (2001) 'Viabilidad de las operaciones frente a factors de riesgo socio-político', transcript of a public forum held by the ACP in Paipa, 1 and 2 February 2001.
British Petroleum Corporate Affairs Management (2002) *BP in Casanare: Building the Future* (London: BP).
British Petroleum Exploration Company (2003) *Long-Term Regional Development in Casanare, Case Study, May 2003*: www.bpd-naturalresources.org/pop_up/casanare/full/html/right1.html, last accessed October 2005.
Castaño, C. (2001) *Mi Confesión* (Bogotá: Editorial Oveja Negra).
Celis, G.G. (1994) *Cusiana o La Bonanza al Revés* (Bogota: Promover Editores ltda).
Collier, P. and Hoeffler, A. (2001) *Greed and Grievance in Civil War* (Washington, D.C.: World Bank).
Contraloria Departmental de Colombia (2002) *Inversion Regalias Departamental de Casanare* (Yopal: CDC).
Corporación Excelencia en la Justicia (2001) *Estudio para identificar las necesidades de justicia y la viabilidad de un programma de justicia alternativa en el Departamento de Casanare, contrado por la BP Exploration Company (Colombia) Ltd, con la Corporación Excelencia en la Justicia* (Bogota: CEJ).
CRECE (1995) *Construcción de un Sistema de Cuentas Economicas y Sociales para Casanare Informe Final* (Manizales: CRECE).
DANE (Departamento Administrativo Nacional de Estadistica) (1986) *Colombia Estatistica, 86* (Bogota: DANE).
DANE/Instituto Geográfico Agustín Codazzi (1999) *Casanare: Características Geográficas* (Bogota: DANE).
Davy, A., Sandoval, F. and McPhail, K. (1998) *BPXC's Operations in Casanare, Colombia: Factoring Social Concerns into Development Decision-making* (Washington, D.C.: World Bank).
Defensoria del Pueblo (1998) *Informe sobre la explotación petrolera en el Casanare y Problemas Ambientales* (Casanare: Defensoria del Pueblo).
—— (2001) *Informe Relacionado con la situación de derechos humanos en el departamento del Casanare correspondiente al año 2000, Agenda Para Casanare-Siglo XX1* (Bogota: Defensoria del Pueblo).
Departamento Administrativo de Planeación (1998) *Gobernacion de Casanare, Plan de Desarrollo* (Yopal: DAP).
De Soysa, I. (2001) 'The Resource Curse: Are Civil Wars Driven by Rapacity or Paucity', in Berdal and Malone (eds) *Greed and Grievance: Economic Agendas in Civil Wars* (Boulder, Colo.: Lynne Rienner).
Dureau, F. and Florez, C. (2000) *Aguaitacaminamos: Las transformaciones de las ciudades de Yopal, Aguazul y Tauramena durante la explotación* (Bogota: Tercer Mundo).
Ecopetrol (2002) *Opportunities for Hydrocarbon Exploration and Production on Colombia* (Bogota: Ecopetrol).
Fiscalía General de la Nación (1998) *Unidad Nacional de Derechos Humanos, Fiscalia Regional Delegada* (Bogota: FDN).

Galindo León, P. and Jáuregui, M. (1998) *Casanare: Sueños y realidades* (Bogota: Inter-Agencies Groups).

Gaviria, A., Zapata, J.G. and González, A. (2002) *Petróleo y Región: El Caso de Casanare* (Bogota: Fedesarrollo).

Gitsham, M. (2003) *Corporate Social Responsibility in Practice: Action on the Ground by BP in Casanare, Colombia* (MA dissertation, unpublished).

Hobsbawm, E.J. (1996) 'The Future of the State', *Development and Change*, Vol. 27, No. 2.

Human Rights Watch (1996) *Colombia's Killer Networks: The military–paramilitary partnership and the United States* (New York and Washington: HRW).

—— (1998) *Colombia: Human Rights Concerns Raised by the Security Arrangements of Transnational Oil Companies* (New York: HRW)

Molana, A. (1995) *Del llano llano, Relatos y Testimonios* (Bogota: El Áncora).

Pérez Ángel, H.P. (1997) *La Hacienda Caribarbare: Estructura y Relaciones de Mercado, 1767–1810* (Villavicencio: Corpes Orinoquia).

Posada, A.R. (1997) 'Compra de Tierras por Narcotraficantes', in F. Thoumi (ed.) *Drogas Ilícitas en Colombia: Su impacto económico, politico y social* (Bogota: Editorial Ariel).

—— (1998) 'Regionalización de los conflictos agrarios y la violencia política en Colombia', in Anzola, L.S. (ed.) *Municipios y Regiones de Colombia: Una mirada desde la Sociedad Civil* (Bogota: Fundación Social).

Procuraduría General de la Nación, Fiscalía General de la Nación, Defensoría del Pueblo, Consejería Presidencial para los Derechos Humanos, Asociación Nacional de Usuarios Campesinos-UR, Fundación Comité de Solidaridad con los Presos Políticos (1995) *Informe de la Comisión Interinstitucional sobre la Situación de Derechos Humanos en los Departamentos de Casanare y Arauca* (Bogotá: Procuraduría General de la Nación).

Rausch, J. (1999) *La Frontera de los Llanos en la Historia de Colombia (1830–1930)* (Bogota: Banco de la Republica/El Áncora).

República de Colombia, Ministerio Público y Defensoria del Pueblo (1997) *Informe Derechos humanos en Casanare y BP* (draft, Bogota).

Yergin, D. (1991) *The Prize: The Epic Quest for Oil, Money and Power* (London: Simon and Schuster).

Zandvliet, L. and Reyes, D. (2004) *Looking at the Principles Behind the Practices: BP Operations in Casanare department, Colombia* (Cambridge, Mass.: Collaborative Learning Projects, Corporate Engagement Project).

Conclusion

Mary Kaldor and Yahia Said

As this book went to print, several of the conflicts examined in the case studies were showing signs of stabilisation. Peace efforts seem to be bearing fruit in Angola, Aceh and Nagorno Karabakh. Even Chechnya, which was closest to state collapse of all the case studies, was normalising. An increasing share of its oil industry is emerging from the shadows, thus denying Chechen rebels and rogue Russian officers both an incentive and a means to perpetuate the conflict. In Aceh progress was driven by events which have nothing to do with oil, namely the tsunami and the imperative to cooperate to ensure the delivery of humanitarian aid. Does this support the sceptics' view of the absence of a link between oil and conflict? Does it show that oil can have a mitigating impact on conflict, especially when prices are high?

The case studies in this volume reveal a complex relation between oil and conflict. The strategic importance of oil to the global economy, and the need for a relatively sophisticated state infrastructure to safeguard contracts and protect supplies, coupled with pressures from civil society, can induce cooperative behaviour and promote stability. The threat of disruption of oil supplies and the rents they generate which can result from state collapse creates an incentive for cooperation between all parties. The strategic importance of oil also means that oil conflicts are rarely forgotten.

At the same time the world's insatiable demand for oil is the main driver behind oil rents – the extraordinary profits generated from its sale give rise to a 'rent-seeking cycle'. This process has a transformative impact on both state and conflict. The dynamics of this cycle are determined by competition to capture oil rents at different levels. At the global level, geopolitics are shaped by Great Powers' pursuit of these rents. At the micro level, greed motivates individuals and groups to capture them. At the national level, petro-states represent the intersection of national, private and global rent seeking.

Jenny Pearce's story of the 'perimeter fence' applied to the case of the Casanare region in Colombia is a metaphor for all these levels. The 'old oil wars' of the nineteenth and early twentieth centuries were largely defined by geopolitics. Their goal was to secure oil which could be exploited behind perimeter fences defended either directly by the Great Powers or by their agents, local authoritarian regimes. Since then, rent seeking has spread to national and local levels, making it very difficult to defend perimeter fences. Indeed, the plethora of actors competing for a share in the rents, the persistent and 'state un-building' nature of 'new oil wars', as well as pressures from civil society, mean that the more traditional defensive security measures are adopted – the more 'old war' strategies are pursued – the more instability is generated.

A different, cooperative approach has to be adopted. In her chapter on Colombia, Jenny Pearce talks about the need to go 'beyond the perimeter fence' and to replace defensive strategies with strategies of engagement. BP's new security model in Casanare is an example of such strategy. It relies on cooperation with the local communities. However, this strategy can only work if it is adopted at all levels – global, national and local.

In this concluding chapter, we reiterate the key importance of finding ways to overcome the rent-seeking culture that is associated with oil dependence, and stress that success can only be achieved through cooperative as opposed to competitive and confrontational approaches. This is the basic principle that underlies any effort to design policies aimed at managing the destabilising effect of oil dependence. In what follows, we suggest some directions for policy at global, local and national levels.

GLOBAL AND REGIONAL LEVELS

Perhaps the most important conclusion of this book is that geopolitical competition, which is the key characteristic of 'old oil wars', is counterproductive if the aim is to secure the supply of oil. Growing demand by the emerging economies – China and India in particular – and concerns over dwindling reserves and 'peak oil' are prompting industrialised nations to pursue geopolitical strategies which result directly or indirectly in further supply disruptions, growing price volatility and state weakness in oil exporting nations, thus creating a vicious cycle.

Geopolitical concerns over the Baku–Tbilisi–Ceyhan pipeline have hardened Russia's position on Chechnya and the Transcaucasus and hampered the resolution of the region's conflicts. Support offered at various times by the United States, the Soviet Union, Russia and France to the various factions in Angola's civil war was also motivated by geopolitics. It only served to perpetuate that conflict. Three years after the invasion of Iraq, exports are stuck at 1.5 million bbl/d, well below the pre-war level of 2.5 million bbl/d, not to speak of Iraq's actual potential. It is not clear when the country will be stable enough to sell the oil that all parties are hoping for.

The alternative to this approach is for leading consumer countries to pursue cooperative strategies aimed at working together with exporters, multinationals and global civil society to resolve conflict, promote human rights and democracy, and prevent state failure. Such an approach should be based on the concept of a common human security rather than the zero sum frameworks of national interest and geopolitics. Since the end of the Cold War and the growth and changed nature of various international missions to conflict zones, elements of such a multilateral policy approach, involving a complex agenda of peacekeeping, institution building and reconstruction, are beginning to be developed even though this is often in contradiction to more traditional geopolitical approaches.

It is often the case that oil companies and consuming countries are primarily concerned with maintaining good relations with producer governments, even if this means support for authoritarian and failing states. It is often difficult to engage in conflict prevention or democracy-building efforts in a competitive situation when this might jeopardise future contracts. There has, for example, been markedly less international criticism of Azerbaijan during recent elections than there has of neighbouring Georgia; yet, in the long run, outside pressure for democracy-building efforts in Georgia may mean that it will be more stable than Azerbaijan. Likewise, the atrocities committed in Chechnya hardly affect international relations with Russia. One way round this dilemma is to adopt a multilateral approach and to deal with state, regional and global levels through partnerships. Oil companies and foreign governments do work with international institutions like the World Bank or UNDP on development issues. It would be important also to work with regional and global political institutions concerned with conflict and human rights, like OSCE or the Council of Europe in Europe, or the UN at a global level. A four-way partnership involving civil society, companies, governments and international institutions could offer a mechanism for strengthening civil society while not jeopardising state relations.

Examples of multilateral initiatives which strengthen this type of cooperative approach in relation to oil revenues are the Extractive Industry Transparency Initiative (EITI), the Voluntary Principles on Security and Human Rights, and the Kyoto Protocol. The EITI was an initiative of the British government, proposed by the NGO Global Witness and the campaign of the Open Society Institute 'Publish What You Pay'. It has been signed by some 20 countries, who have committed themselves to publish oil company payments and government revenues so as to reduce corruption and increase transparency and accountability.[1] The Voluntary Principles have been signed by the United States, the UK, Norway and the Netherlands as well as major oil companies and NGOs. They involve commitments to respect human rights in safeguarding oil installations.[2] In addition, international attention in efforts to solve certain conflicts, such as Sudan, can also be regarded as a more cooperative approach.

A more ambitious proposal, which would complement cooperative approaches to conflict prevention and democracy building, is for a new international energy regime which would reflect the interests of the full range of stakeholders – producers, consumers, governments, international agencies and NGOs. Existing organisations like OPEC or the IEA reflect a particular set of interests and a particular time in history. There is a need for a broader institutional forum to investigate such issues as the social, political and environmental cost of oil or the need to look at oil in terms of a transition, which could be as short as 30–50 years, to a post-oil era.

THE LOCAL LEVEL

Multinational oil companies have traditionally addressed issues of oil and conflict from the perspective of ensuring the security of staff and equipment, and reducing the political risk of long-term investments through close relations with host governments. Today there is a growing awareness that attempting to address these issues in a specific, localised or narrow way is not sufficient, and that a more global, holistic approach is needed. Defensive strategies and implicit support for authoritarian regimes have damaged company reputations and have contributed to conflict. As the chapters on Colombia, Nigeria and Indonesia show, BP's experience in Columbia, Shell's experience in the Niger Delta and ExxonMobil's experience in Aceh, for example, have led to a rethinking of traditional approaches.

Already, new approaches are being developed and, in particular, BP's strategy in Casanare, developed out of a negative learning experience, is often held up as a model of potential best practice at community level. Here we enumerate three elements of what might be needed for a more cooperative, community-based approach to security.

Dialogue

Involving stakeholders in an ongoing dialogue is an essential prerequisite for any local oil project, in order to get a better understanding of the character of the conflict at local levels. Evaluation of the political and social impact of conflict as well as understanding of the key actors in conflicts need to become an integral and ongoing part of every oil investment. Companies, local government and civil society, as well as state representatives and representatives of other institutions such as international organisations, need to meet for intensive discussions about such issues as the Baku–Ceyhan pipeline or the tsunami impact in Aceh.

Participation

A distinction can be drawn between social responsibility and participation. The former tends to focus on local philanthropy and is largely designed to improve public relations. As the Nigeria case study shows, this can easily result in an extension of the rent-seeking culture to local

NGOs and community organisations as they compete for the funds made available for social responsibility projects. Participation means involving local governments and civil society groups in decisions about what could be done to help the community and contribute to conflict prevention.

Human rights

Respect for human rights is crucial where security measures have to be taken. This applies to the military, the police and international peace-keepers, as well as security units employed by oil companies. The Voluntary Principles have become a significant guide for some international companies in their safeguarding of production facilities. More efforts should be made to ensure that these principles are being implemented. Sometimes, it is difficult to implement these principles where they are not respected by producer governments. This is why it would be important to incorporate the principles into multinational efforts to promote reform of the security sectors in producer countries. The possibilities of further regulating responsibilities and obligations regarding security and human rights in standard contracts could also be investigated.

THE NATIONAL LEVEL

An important theme of this book is that the problems of oil dependence are political as much as economic. Policy making is often confined to a narrow circle of oil and finance experts, who can be quite defensive. Often, the most efficient approaches for managing oil wealth are the ones likely to face most resistance from entrenched interests. Alternatively, policy making may be carried out by politicians behind closed doors, ignoring both expert advice and wider public opinion or exploiting populist appeals. Neither approach is right. Very often a policy that may seem prudent from a technical or economic perspective may not be viable, or may even be catastrophic, from a political or social perspective and vice versa. Thus, for example, proposals to eliminate fuel subsidies, as in Iraq, which makes sense from the point of view of economic and environmental efficiency, could greatly exacerbate instability. On the other hand, the direct distribution of oil rents to citizens, as is happening currently in Venezuela, may seem politically fair and popular; yet it may lead to a culture of dependence, undercutting more productive activities, and accelerating the 'Dutch disease'. The 'rent-seeking cycle' (see Introduction), which causes countries dependent on oil to grow more slowly and to be less democratic and more conflict prone than their peers, is exacerbated by one-sided policies. Conversely, a holistic approach is the best way to confront the challenges of oil dependence.

The main aim of policies adopted at a national level should be to counter the culture of rent seeking and prevent the dynamic which leads to the 'rent-seeking cycle'. Substantive rather than formal democracy is the main defence against such a dynamic and the abuse of oil wealth. By substantive democracy, we mean genuine political equality as opposed to formal procedures. Substantive democracy must involve democratic politics as well as democratic institutions – a democratic culture of social relations, underpinned by fair, transparent and accountable procedures (Goetz et al 2000). A system of checks and balances, both formal and informal, is necessary to allow civil society, business and government to monitor and hold each other to account. Security is also important so that citizens can make decisions on the basis of debate and discussion, not of fear. Too often, democratic reforms in oil-producing and post-authoritarian or post-conflict countries are reduced to 'majoritarian' elections. There is now a growing body of research that shows that holding elections in the absence of other institutional and cultural prerequisites for democracy, including security, can further destabilise these countries by, for example, promoting identity politics (Bastian and Luckham 2003).

The fundamental elements of substantive democracy that are especially important for oil-dependent countries if they are to escape the rent-seeking cycle are discussed below.

Open, rational and informed debate about oil policy

Debate can help produce and sustain consensus over optimal policies and mobilise constituencies to counter rent seeking. Debate should be based on a notion of public interest as opposed to sectarian or party interest. But, unfortunately, such a debate is itself greatly hampered by rent seeking. Ethnic, sectarian and regional groups and political parties try to stake a claim or monopolise decision making about oil under justifications of ideology or identity. Discussions about oil often mask and poison more important debates about federalism and governance in general. Moreover, the debate is often ill informed. Passions run high even when the differences are insignificant. Discussions over the future of the Iraqi oil industry exemplify all of the above. Despite expert advice in favour of consolidating the oil sector under a national oil company, sectarian politicians in control of the constitution-drafting process opted for a model which may cause the sector to fragment along regional lines. In Iraq there is great anxiety about the prospect of oil sector privatisation, although hardly any of Iraq's policy makers have advanced this option. There are also concerns that production-sharing agreements or other licensing methods can have the same impact in terms of loss of state control or revenues to the benefit of foreign partners.

Transparency

Timely and accurate information on all aspects of the oil economy is a precondition for effective public debate. As Terry Karl (2005) says, 'civil society is useless without information.' Transparency is especially important when the debate is being carried out in the absence of established democratic institutions and other elements of the system of checks and balances. Transparency and accountability should apply equally to private and public actors, domestic and international. It is important to promote various revenue transparency initiatives. First, information about payments to governments by international oil companies needs to be made publicly available. Oil companies need to keep to a minimum the amount of confidential information in production-sharing agreements and other contracts signed with host governments. It could also be important to standardise such contracts, in order to eliminate loopholes which can be used by corrupt governments to divert oil revenues, and to share information on contractual processes and structures. Elements of this are included in the UN Global Compact. Second, governments need to publish information about revenues and how they are spent. Third, there is a need for various international initiatives to promote transparency, such as the Extractive Industries Transparency Initiative.

Accountability

Whatever model of oil management is adopted (oil funds, nationalisation or regional distribution), the lines of accountability need to be crystal clear. There have to be formal procedures, whether judicial or parliamentary, through which policies can be evaluated, approved or challenged on an ongoing basis. Moreover, these procedures need to ensure domestic public accountability, involving all relevant stakeholders, and not just accountability to political leaders, oil companies and international institutions.

Involvement of civil society

The public debate must involve citizens who are not competing for office (or funds) and who are ready to debate this in the public as opposed to the private interest. Hence the oil debate should involve a myriad of groups and institutions such as women's groups, educational establishments, churches and mosques, student groups and other young peoples' organisations. Moreover, real efforts should be made to explain technical language and translate expert arguments into common sense arguments. Thus it is very important to encourage the formation of independent NGOs like Revenue Watch or Global

Witness, who can develop independent expertise and explain this to the public.

Meanwhile, practical elements of national policy based on the principles of substantive democracy might include those discussed below.

Organisation, ownership and governance of the oil industry

Regardless of the model chosen to manage the oil industry, a level playing field needs to be established that offers a fair deal to all actors. This is best provided for through a clear regulatory environment which should govern privatisation and foreign investment, and have effective mechanisms for enforcement and implementation. If a national oil company is in place, there should be a clear division between its commercial and regulatory roles. This is best achieved by establishing a separate body for standards and regulations. Norway is an example of this approach.

Managing oil revenues

Oil revenues and all related payments should run through the central government budget under parliamentary supervision. Transparency and integrity of the budgetary process are preconditions for successful oil revenue management. Proper budgeting requires that the Ministry of Finance and relevant parliamentary bodies should be provided with accurate, audited data on all oil and gas production, sales, revenues, taxes and other payments and expenses.

Various models are available for the allocation of oil revenues to subnational regions and for deciding the respective share of these revenues managed by the central and regional governments. Distribution on the basis of production, population or needs should be complemented by equalisation mechanisms. In Canada, oil-producing regions retain a significant share of oil revenues but there are mechanisms to equalise the impact on other regions. Oil-revenue allocations should be governed by the principles of equity, justice and development for all. As the experience of Columbia, Angola and Indonesia shows, oil allocations are no substitute for the hard work needed to deal with inter-community relations or the relations between the centre and regions.

Oil-dependent countries need to be able to follow a range of economic measures to offset the negative economic effects of oil dependence which contribute to conflict. Such measures need to be able to:

- stabilise income and expenditure, and smooth out fluctuations caused by oil price volatility

- save some of the oil wealth for future generations and create the basis for a sustainable economy in the future, and
- reduce or eliminate the negative impact of oil rents on non-oil traded-goods sectors in the economy, and prevent inefficient specialisation in oil and non-traded goods.

Oil funds are often cited as the most effective method to help address these issues. All too often, however, the funds become a vehicle for extra-budgetary spending, thus opening new avenues for corruption and abuse. Funds have to follow the highest standards of transparency and accountability and should be part of an integrated budgetary process. Iraq in the 1970s restricted the use of oil revenues for current expenditures, diverting the bulk to a special 'investment fund' that was not used for current government expenditure. The result was to move most government spending outside the budget.

One of the main roles of oil funds is political, as they illustrate to the public that oil revenues are not income but an asset that is being converted from the form of oil reserves to other forms through the export of oil. Sustainable spending thus can only be based on the return on investments made from the oil fund. The Norwegian oil fund is an example of this approach; it is integrated into the state budget and is the mirror image of the government's non-oil balance. The government borrows from the fund when the balance is in deficit and saves to the fund when it is in surplus. Alaska is another example of this approach. Here, part of the returns from investments made from the oil fund are distributed to the public.

Enabling environment

Special attention should be devoted to developing human resources in oil-producing countries in the public and private sector and within civil society. Training is needed not only in technical disciplines but in areas of transparency, accountability and advocacy.

There is a need to strengthen anti-corruption institutions and initiatives. Focus should be devoted to strengthening the independence of these institutions and initiatives from the government, leadership by example and preventive approaches. Transparency and disclosure are important for anti-corruption efforts. It is important to keep in mind, however, that a non-corrupt institution cannot survive for long in a corrupt environment. Azerbaijan, Chad and Cameroon are all examples of countries where robust safeguards were put in place to protect oil revenues from abuse. In these cases the international community including states, international organisations and civil society played an important role in both pressuring the governments to adopt these safeguards and in assisting them in their implementation. In all these countries, however, these safeguards were introduced in an environment rife with corruption and in the absence of a democratic culture. Unless the endemic corruption and authoritarianism are addressed in a holistic way the safeguards are likely to be short-lived. International cooperation is needed not only to provide technical know-how and experience but also to provide political support from international state and non-state actors to ensure transparency and accountability.

GREEN ZONE, RED ZONE

Iraq today is divided into a green zone and a red zone. The green zone is where the government and foreign embassies are housed. It is a suburb of Baghdad, heavily guarded, with fountains and palaces, palm trees and grass. It is there that Iraqi politicians and foreign diplomats, who are not allowed to leave the zone, busily plan the future of Iraq. The Iraqi ministries are partly housed in the green zone and partly in mini-green zones throughout the city: requisitioned buildings that are heavily guarded. The rest of Iraq is the red zone. It is full of activity – people, shops, meetings, kidnappers and suicide bombers. It is a mixture of debate and self-organisation, extremism and crime.

The green zone and the red zone can be used as a metaphor to describe the gulf that exists on a global scale between the global green zones, where the political élites live and occasionally meet in summits, and the global red zone – a heterogeneous, complex world characterised both by innovation, energy, debate and economic activity, and by what Fred Halliday calls 'global rancour', the frustration, humiliation and powerlessness experienced by millions of men and women, not only in the Middle East but all over the world.

Oil revenues have always accrued to those living in the green zone and oil installations have been traditionally protected in green zones. 'Old oil wars' are wars between states competing for control over green zones in different parts of the world – geopolitical competitions for the control of territory. Yet, despite ever heavier security measures, green zones are increasingly vulnerable not just to mortars, shells, snipers and suicide bombers but also to propaganda, information and damage to reputation. As already suggested, the more 'old war' strategies are pursued, the more instability is generated. Peace can only be achieved by involving the red zone and breaking down the division between green and red zones. This applies at all levels – international, national and local.

NOTES

1. See www.eitranparency.org, last accessed 20 July 2006.
2. See www.voluntaryprinciples.org, last accessed 20 July 2006.

BIBLIOGRAPHY

Bastian, S. and Luckham, R. (eds) (2003) *Can Democracy be Designed? The Politics of Institutional Choice in Conflict-torn Societies* (London : Zed Books).

Goetz, A., Luckham, R and Kaldor, M. (2000) *Democratic Institutions in Contexts of Inequality, Poverty and Conflict* (London: IDS).

Karl, T. (2005) *Managing Iraq's Oil Wealth* (London: LSE/IRW).

Notes on Contributors

Mary Kaldor is Professor of Global Governance at London School of Economics and Co-Director of the Centre for the Study of Global Governance, LSE. She previously worked at the Stockholm International Peace Research Institute (SIPRI), and the Science Policy Research Unit and the Sussex European Institute at the University of Sussex. She has written widely on security issues and on democracy and civil society. Her books include *Global Civil Society: An Answer to War* (Polity Press 2003) and *New and Old Wars: Organised Violence in a Global Era* (1999). Most recently she co-edited *A Human Security Doctrine for Europe: Project, Principles, Practicalities*, with Marlies Glasisu (Routledge 2005). Mary was a founder member of European Nuclear Disarmament (END), founder and Co-Chair on the Helsinki Citizens' Assembly, and is currently a governor of the Westminster Foundation for Democracy. She is convenor of the Study Group on European Security Capabilities established at the request of Javier Solana.

Terry Lynn Karl is Professor of Political Science at the Centre on Democracy, Development and the Rule of Law, and Gildred Professor of Latin American Studies, at Stanford University. She has published widely on comparative politics and international relations, with special emphasis on the politics of oil-exporting countries, transitions to democracy, problems of inequality, the global politics of human rights, and the resolution of civil wars. Her works on oil, human rights and democracy includes *The Paradox of Plenty: Oil Booms and Petro-States* (University of California Press, 1998), *The Bottom of the Barrel: Africa's Oil Boom and the Poor* (2004 with Ian Gary), and the forthcoming *Overcoming the Resource Curse* (with Joseph Stiglitz, Jeffrey Sachs et al). Karl has published extensively on comparative democratization, ending civil wars in Central America, and political economy. She has conducted field research throughout Latin America, West Africa and Eastern Europe.

Yahia Said is a Research Fellow at the Centre for the Study of Global Governance, LSE. His experience combines academic research with private sector work and activism. Prior to joining the LSE he worked as a corporate finance consultant with Ernst & Young in Russia. He also worked as a project coordinator with the Helsinki Citizens' Assembly in Prague. Yahia specialises in issues of economic transition and security in post-authoritarian and post-conflict societies. At LSE he coordinates the Magic Lantern Project that aims to build a network of civic initiatives from Iraq, Central Europe and the West, in order to support Iraqi civil society. His publications include 'The New Anti-Capitalist Movement: Money and Global Civil Society', co-authored with Meghnad Desai, in *Global Civil Society 2001* (Oxford University Press 2001), 'Oil and Activism' in *Global Civil Society 2004/5* (Sage 2005), and *Regime Change in Iraq*, co-authored with Mary Kaldor (CsGG, 2003).

Robin Luckham began his academic career in Nigeria in the 1960s and his first book on the Nigerian Military was published by Cambridge University Press in 1971. Since then he has held positions at universities in Ghana, the USA (Harvard), Australia (Peace Research Centre, Australian National University) and the UK, where he is a Research Associate at the Institute of Development Studies, University of Sussex, following retirement. His most recent books include *Can Democracy be Designed? The Politics of Institutional Choice in Conflict-torn Societies* and *Governing Insecurity: Democratic Control of Military and Security Establishments in Transitional Democracies*, both published by Zed Press in 2003. He chairs the international advisory group of the Global Facilitation Network on Security Sector Reform, and he continues to research and write on the interface between political violence, democracy, security and development.

Okechukwu (Okey) Ibeanu is Professor of Political Science and Dean, Faculty of the Social Sciences at the University of Nigeria, Nsukka. He is also the Special Rapporteur of the United Nations Human Rights Council on the adverse effects of illicit movement and dumping of toxic waste on human rights. Professor Ibeanu was previously programme officer of the MacArthur Foundation overseeing its human rights and Niger Delta programmes. A former Fellow of the United Nations University, Tokyo, he has also been a visiting scholar at Queen Elizabeth House, Oxford University and the Woodrow Wilson Center, Washington D.C. Professor Ibeanu sits on the boards of many research institutions including the Centre for Democracy and Development. He has published extensively on the Niger Delta and Nigerian politics in general including *Civil Society and Conflict Management in the Niger Delta* (2005). His latest book entitled *Oiling Violence* (2006) is on the proliferation of small arms and light weapons in the Niger Delta.

Philippe Le Billon is Assistant Professor at the University of British Columbia with the Department of Geography and the Liu Institute for Global Issues. Before joining UBC, he was a Research Associate with the Overseas Development Institute (ODI) and the International Institute for

Strategic Studies (IISS). His research interests include the political economy of war and reconstruction, geographies of violence, governance of extractive sectors, and corruption, and his research focus is on primary commodities and armed conflicts. His most recent books are *Geopolitics of Resource Wars: Resource Dependence, Governance and Violence* (Routledge 2005) and *Fuelling War: Natural Resources and Armed Conflicts* (Routledge 2005). He has also written several articles and policy papers, including 'From free oil to 'freedom oil': terrorism, war and US geopolitics in the Persian Gulf 'with F. El Khatib (*Geopolitics* 9(1), 2004).

Kirsten E. Schulze is Senior Lecturer in International History at the London School of Economics. Her current research interests are on the Aceh conflict, the Maluku conflict, Islamists groups, and security sector reform in Indonesia. Her past research has been on the Lebanese civil war, the Arab-Israeli conflict, and the Middle East peace process as well as the Northern Ireland peace process. She has written numerous articles on the Free Aceh Movement, the strategic dynamics of the Aceh conflict, counter-insurgency operations in Aceh, and the history of the Aceh conflict. She has also written reports on the tsunami aid in Aceh and the Aceh Monitoring Mission for the European Council. Her books include *The Free Aceh Movement (GAM): Anatomy of a Separatist Organization* (East-West Center, 2004), *The Jews of Lebanon: Between Conflict and Coexistence* (Sussex Academic Press, 2001), *The Arab-Israeli Conflict* (Longman, 1999), and *Israel's Covert Diplomacy in Lebanon* (Macmillan 1998).

Jenny Pearce is Professor of Latin American Politics and Director of the International Centre for Participation Studies in the Department of Peace Studies, University of Bradford. She is a specialist in issues of violence, conflict, social change and social agency in Latin America. More recently she has also worked on problems of participation and conflict in the north of England. Amongst her most recent publications are: (with Jude Howell) *Civil Society and Development: A Critical Exploration* (Lynne Rienner 2001); 'Policy Failure and Petroleum Predation: The Economics of Civil War Debate viewed from the War Zone' (*Government and Opposition* 40(2) 2005); 'Bringing Violence 'Back Home': Gender Socialisation and the Transmission of Violence Through Time and Space' (*Global Civil Society Yearbook 2006/7*, Sage 2007). She is currently convener of the research group on Participation, Violence and Citizenship at the Institute of Development Studies, University of Sussex.

Index